Circle Soccer Training

For purposes of better legibility, we have decided to use masculine (neutral) forms of address, and gender neutral "they" where applicable throughout this book. This of course also refers to women.

This book was carefully compiled. However, the information is supplied without liability. Therefore, neither the author nor the publisher can accept, or are liable, for potential detriments or damage resulting from the information presented in this book.

STEPHAN KERBER | FABIAN SEEGER

CIRCLE SOCCER TRAINING

100 GAMES AND DRILLS
TO IMPROVE GAME COMPETENCE

Meyer & Meyer Sport

British Library Cataloguing in Publication Data
A catalogue record for this book is available from the British Library

Originally published as: *Kreisfußball: 100 Trainingsformen zur Verbesserung der Spielkompetenz.*
© 2018 by Meyer & Meyer Verlag

Circle Soccer Training
Maidenhead: Meyer & Meyer Sport (UK) Ltd., 2019
ISBN: 978-1-78255-169-0

All rights reserved, especially the right to copy and distribute, including translation rights.
No part of this work may be produced—including by photocopy,
microfilm or any other means—processed, stored electronically,
copied or distributed in any form whatsoever without the written permission of the publisher.

© 2019 by Meyer & Meyer Sport (UK) Ltd.
Aachen, Auckland, Beirut, Cairo, Cape Town, Dubai, Hägendorf, Hong Kong,
Indianapolis, Manila, New Delhi, Singapore, Sydney, Tehran, Vienna

Member of the World Sports Publishers' Association (WSPA), www.w-s-p-a.org
Printed by Print Consult GmbH, Munich, Germany

ISBN: 978-1-78255-169-0
Email: info@m-m-sports.com
www.thesportspublisher.com

CONTENTS

FOREWORD 10

1 1 INTRODUCTION 12
    1.1 Basics 12
    1.2 Concept 16
    1.3 Principles 25
    1.4 Elements 28
    1.5 Player conduct 32
    1.6 Trainer conduct 33
    1.7 Instructions 34
        1.7.1 General instructions 35
        1.7.2 Technical instructions 36
        1.7.3 Tactical instructions 37
        1.7.4 Motoric instructions 39
    1.8 Readability 40
    1.9 Naming 40
    1.10 Practical help 41
    1.11 Legend 55

2 GETTING STARTED 56
    2.1 Running with focus on motor skills and profile 57
        2.1.1 Archer – circuit 1 (arch run) 57
        2.1.2 Chronograph – circuit 2 (tempo run) 58
        2.1.3 Compass – circuit 3 (tempo run) 59
        2.1.4 Icebreaker – running duel 1 (tempo run) 60
        2.1.5 Crossing the line – running duel 2 (tempo dribbling) 61
    2.2 Catching with focus on agility and dexterity 62
        2.2.1 Earth's core – catching game 1 (handball) 62
        2.2.2 Geocenter – catching game 2 (dribbling) 63
        2.2.3 Ringed planet – catching game 3 (dribbling) 64
        2.2.4 Nucleus – catching game 4 (dribbling) 65
        2.2.5 Orbit – catching game 5 (obstacle) 66
    2.3 Technical forms with focus on ball handling, coordination and two-footedness ... 67
        2.3.1 Asteroid – squad competition 1 (passing) 67
        2.3.2 Meteor – squad competition 2 (taking the ball) 68
        2.3.3 Ferris wheel – free passing 1 (colored goals) 69

	2.3.4	Ringside seat – free passing 2 (colored goals)	70
	2.3.5	Ring of fire – free passing 3 (commands)	71
	2.3.6	Ring parable – technical circle 1 (ball control)	72
	2.3.7	Racing cycles – technical circle 2 (combinations)	73
	2.3.8	Milky Way – technical circle 3 (goalkeeper)	74
	2.3.9	Cosmos – technical circle 2.0 (footwork)	75
	2.3.10	Dimension – technical circle 2.1 (position play)	76
	2.3.11	Ecliptic – technical circle 2.2 (free running)	77
	2.3.12	Roulette – technical circle 2.3 (running)	78
	2.3.13	Gravitation – indoor circle 1 (ball control)	79
	2.3.14	Hyperion – indoor circle 2 (ball handling)	80
2.4	Small matches with focus on individual tactical behavior		81
	2.4.1	Explosion – chaos 1 vs. 1	81
	2.4.2	One-way road – frontal 1 vs. 1	82
	2.4.3	Passing lane – side 1 vs. 1 I	83
	2.4.4	Eye of the needle – side 1 vs. 1 II	84
	2.4.5	Hemisphere – complex 1 vs. 1	85
	2.4.6	Eagle eye – variable 1 vs. 1	86
	2.4.7	Rotunda – technical start 1 vs. 1	87
	2.4.8	Octagon – double 1 vs. 1	88
2.5	2.5 Big matches with focus on group tactical behavior		89
	2.5.1	Universe – 2 vs. 2 – technical start	89
	2.5.2	Helicopter – 4 vs. 2 – numerical advantage	90
	2.5.3	Fan – 3 vs. 3 – running start	91
	2.5.4	Earth's rotation – 4 vs. 1 – center play	92
	2.5.5	Sunray – 4 vs. 2 – center play	93
	2.5.6	Sector coupling – 5 vs. 3 – center play	94
	2.5.7	Hodgepodge – 4 vs. 4 – variable center play	95
	2.5.8	Mosaic – 4 vs. 4 – complex center play	96
3	3 MAIN COMPONENT		98
3.1	3.1 Reading aid for understanding the central circle playing forms		98
3.2	3.2 Central circle playing forms with focus on playability and swiftness		100
	3.2.1	Reflection	100
	3.2.2	Crosshairs	102
	3.2.3	Disk	104
	3.2.4	Half-moon	106
	3.2.5	Panorama	108

3.2.6	Hurricane	110
3.2.7	Propeller	112
3.2.8	Sun wheel	114
3.2.9	Pentagon	116
3.2.10	Pentagram	118
3.2.11	Target	120
3.2.12	Dartboard	122
3.2.13	Galaxy	124
3.2.14	Virus	126
3.2.15	Wheel of fortune	128
3.2.16	Roundtable	130
3.2.17	Maze	132
3.2.18	Turntable	134
3.2.19	Labyrinth	136
3.2.20	Cell nucleus	138
3.2.21	Carousel	140
3.2.22	Molecule	142
3.2.23	Soap bubble	144
3.2.24	Orbit	146
3.2.25	Water lily	148
3.2.26	Shamrock	150
3.2.27	Fortress	152
3.2.28	Colosseum	154
3.2.29	Roundabout	156
3.2.30	Chessboard	158
3.2.31	Planetarium	160
3.2.32	Pulsar	162
3.2.33	Stonehenge	164
3.2.34	Pyramid	166
3.2.35	Lotus flower	168
3.2.36	Atlas	170
3.2.37	Revolver	172
3.2.38	Tornado	174
3.2.39	Elevator	176
3.2.40	Quattro	178
3.2.41	Bull's-eye	180
3.2.42	Triangle	182
3.2.43	Diamond	184
3.2.44	Pantheon	186

	3.2.45	Triad	188
	3.2.46	Hexagon	190
	3.2.47	Perspective	192
	3.2.48	Sky disk	194
	3.2.49	Sundial	196
	3.2.50	Rhombus	198

4 CONTINUATION 200
4.1 Conceptual continuation 200
- 4.1.1 Rolling a five – adaptation (technique forms) 202
- 4.1.2 Home port – preparation (handball play) 203
- 4.1.3 Ying and Yang – subsequent handling (goal) 204
- 4.1.4 Crop circles – continued play (alternative actions) 205
- 4.1.5 Mandarin – continued play (aiming) 206
- 4.1.6 Cheeseburger – sphere of action (multidimensionality) 207
- 4.1.7 Hamburger – sphere of action (complexity) 208
- 4.1.8 Constellations – asymmetry (playability) 209
- 4.1.9 Butterfly – asymmetry (play comprehension) 210
- 4.1.10 Pac-Man© – shaping (creativity) 211

5 OUTLOOK 212

APPENDIX 214

Bibliography 214

Image credits 214

CONTENTS

FOREWORD

Markus Hirte

The demands of the players in soccer have been growing constantly over the past decades, and this trend will only continue. The tempo of play is getting faster, the actions quicker. Cognitive skills will be of special significance in facilitating this development, along with physical and technical requirements. These cognitive skills include perceiving, analyzing, deciding, and acting. Quick and suitable decisions that consider the individual's technical and conditional circumstances are a prerequisite for optimal solutions in complex playing situations.

The methodical approach for making action during the game faster and more effective is recognizing spheres of play and action and using them for the idea of the game. This book describes this approach with numerous forms of play, while also considering the development of technical requirements with introductory varieties of techniques. The necessary creative solutions for passing, playing on and playing through new spaces help to create enthusiasm for the game, and thus a variety and intensity of movements.

The authors were motivated to create something new and enticing for the players. They wanted to help to advance skills as a major approach to further training. They have been working on this concept for many years and have had very positive experiences with constantly confronting players with new playing ideas in various spaces, thereby improving their perception and coherently accelerating their actions and decision-making.

I hope you have fun and learn a lot as you read this book. It will provide a lot of motivation to train.

Markus Hirte
Athletic director
Talent promotion
Deutscher Fußball-Bund e.V.

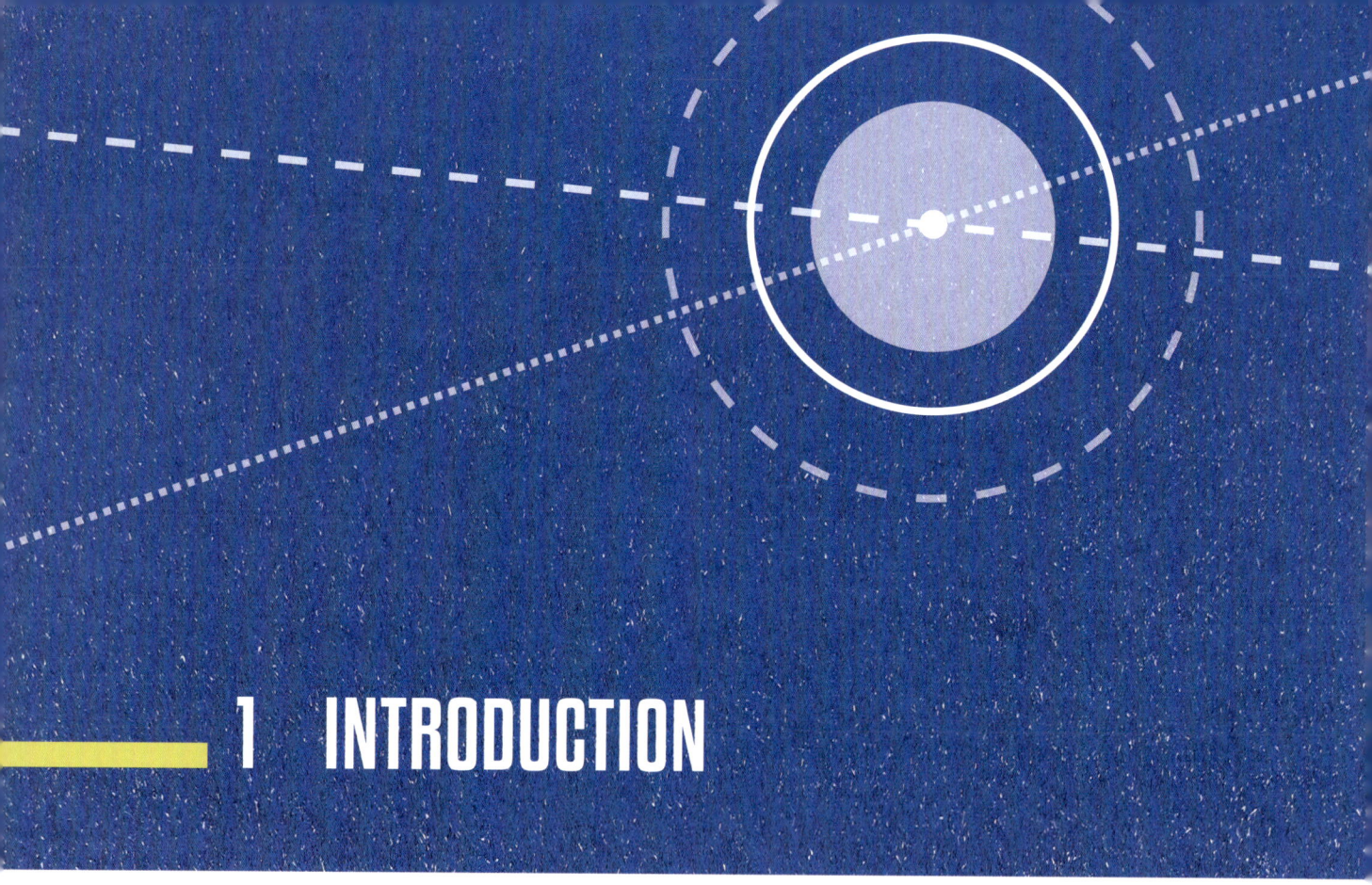

1 INTRODUCTION

1.1 BASICS

The primary focus of this book is playing forms in circular fields. The overarching objective is the accentuation of all aspects of modern soccer through the variable playing of shapes, spaces, zones, and target fields, in conjunction with special playing and challenge/provocation rules. Numerous variants were developed during the creation and conception of these playing forms. With a sensitized view of circular shapes, the widest variety of topics served as inspiration. A closer look around you will allow you to discover innumerable circles, round patterns, or arched surfaces. Even looking at soccer you will find circles with the soccer ball itself, the circle in the middle of the field, and then the eleven-meter mark.

STAR IMAGE
TRAINING PLANS SPORT SPINNING TOPS
CHURCH WINDOWS ARCHITECTURE NATURE
TURNTABLE
SQAURE OF THE CIRCLE
ASTRONOMY CENTER POINT SYMBOLOGY
BOWLING BALL GEOMETRY FLOWER OF LIFE
HISTORY SOAP BUBBLE

INTRODUCTION

These circles contain forward movement, dynamics, footing, stability and strength. Starting with these potentials, the circle was self-evident as a playing surface, and used as the framework for improving playing competence. Something that is round can indirectly influence the playing structure of new players. This initial thought was reinforced during the work process by practical experiences, allowing players to participate in special games.

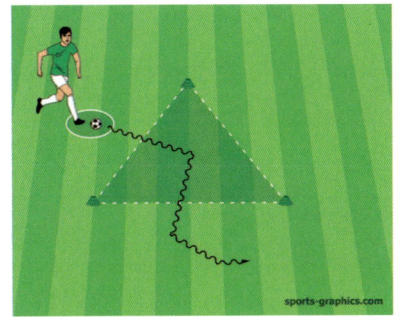 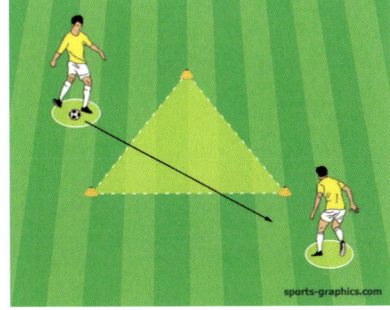 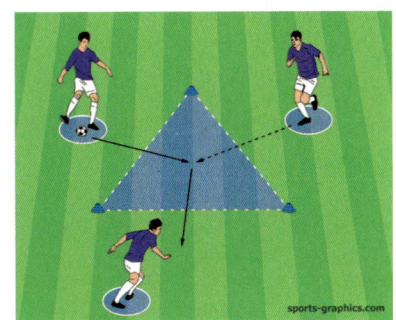

Fig. 1: Dribbling *Fig. 2: Passing* *Fig. 3: Playing with a third person*

The idea of playing triangles came around three years ago. Points could be scored and objectives achieved by making directional changes and feints while dribbling through a triangle (Fig. 1), either with a diagonal pass over two lines of a triangle to a teammate (Fig. 2), with a timed pass into a triangle to a teammate and subsequent control, or a pass to another side of the triangle (Fig. 3). The arrangement of multiple triangles in the playing field resulted in very complex playing forms with various tasks, depending on the focus. This interconnection played a significant role in soccer and remains a trend. Squares were added, followed by circles.

Considerations of geometric shapes aim to create constantly changing playing situations and are to be worked into usual training sessions in order to make the players want to run and have fun. This is confirmed by the implementation of numerous training units using these shapes, shown in the age groups between E-youth and A-youth. In fact, it is clear through the players' unleashed motivation and the joy in their faces that they have the absolute call for movement and willingness to run. They want to try something new, and it seems as though these playing forms are just what talented soccer players need and seek to have fun as they play.

With regard to the objective, the players form a network, linking with one another through passes, showing off great combinations and scoring points together that way. The players are always ready to get moving, switch gears without complaint, and are constantly pursuing because otherwise there will be no opportunity to win. The circular playing forms create an ongoing learning process with simultaneous intensity and action.

What makes these playing forms special is that alternative actions are always being considered because there are always new solutions to be found. The circle forms therefore counteracts monotony and loss of excitement. The primary objectives also include learning in a variety of game contexts and constant perception of changing game situations. The focus lies on playable training forms that first motivate the players to find original solutions, and which (albeit secondarily) lead them toward a defined movement or action pattern.

The triangles, squares, and circles offer the players challenging objectives within the entire playing area. As these arrangements are merely for playing and passing over, they indirectly serve as obstacles or opponents. They thus simulate an opposing formation and allow for the transition to the big game. Triangles (Fig. 4) or squares (Fig. 5) may be used, and combinations (Fig. 6) worked towards, in order to get players used to the round formations and corresponding circular fields.

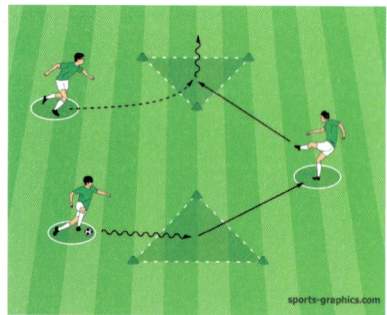

Fig. 4: Triangles

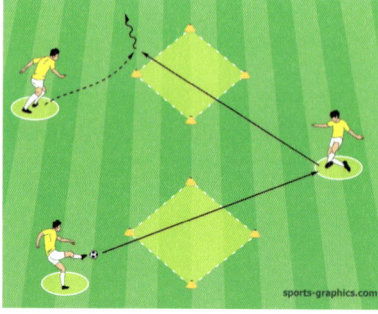

Fig. 5: Squares

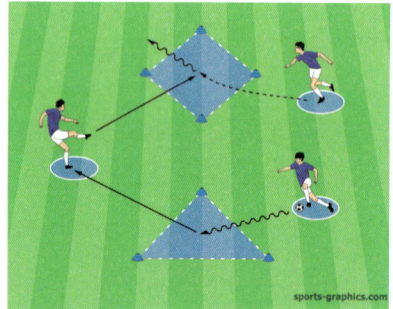

Fig. 6: Combinations

With the shapes, fields and zones shown here, multifaceted training in playing forms aims to increase player quality at all levels, allowing players to play the game because of the game. Playing through the formations creates the necessary pressure for precision, the forcefulness needed for passing, and the ability to distance players from one another. Different playing situations are always linked to the various passing directions. The usage of both feet also holds room for experience and learning opportunities for each individual player.

While dribbling, the players in possession should still push forward despite pressure from opponents. It is important to stay focused on the objective and avoid playing backwards and losing speed. The game with various shapes requires agility, creating the willingness to push forward and promoting fun, creativity, and joy when playing.

Along with the influence on tactical playing behavior, the training with circle forms also offers room to improve certain techniques. During the technical training, the circular playing forms are separated from the isolated one-dimensional content in favor of comprehensive training during ongoing game situations. Along with the technical-tactical components, the influence on general competitive conduct and attitudes of individual players or entire teams can also be present. These components are implemented as worthwhile goals for development in the various circular playing forms.

Ideally the technical-tactical skills in the playing situation are combined with coaching assistance and commands. Many coaches want the players to communicate with each other, to call, scream and unwind. Practical training and playing often paint another picture. In the circular playing forms, there is an atmosphere in which the players mutually coach each other and offer verbal assistance almost automatically. A reflective manner of coaching for the implementation of the circular playing forms is not only required in this context.

The playing forms and control of playing rules offer opportunities to coach technical-tactical mistakes, but this is only necessary to a very small degree because the speed of the next action already demands one's full attention. That is why the situational accompaniment of these forms by the coach is oriented toward objective-based actions, and less toward focusing on mistakes. The playing forms impart experience and knowledge of the game, and thus require the coach to be more independent. Following the rules for achieving the team's objective is the unmistakable task of the coach and the team.

The knowledge that many training forms are contained within a rectangular framework induces highly specific behavior, which then goes on to fuel the engine of development for the variable and innovative conception of the circular forms. There was the sense that the overstrained vertical game concept led to one-dimensional conduct by the players. This was because it was overwhelmingly utilized and had many consequences, such as boredom or the functional reduction in training. Training without passion, emotion and enthusiasm is a nonsensical waste of time.

Through a motivating concept with attractive provocation rules and scoring, the circular forms try to trigger game-like actions and offer differentiated training and uniform improvement for the individual players within complex game situations. These training forms are based on resources and potential, and thus leave the realm of cut-and-dry patterns and schematics. The potential overstrain or powerlessness in complex playing situations yields the bold finding of solutions through optimal reactive speed.

1.2 CONCEPT

›› The circular shape provides a complex playing and action framework

The basic idea of the selected playing forms in a circular layout aims to improve cognitive skills that are primarily achieved via the complex framework. It is important to first visually capture the newly designed circles, to orient oneself in them as quickly as possible, to be able to quickly follow the directions of play, and to play through the entire space with both feet with technical and tactical efficiency.

This framework offers chances and opportunities to recognize shapes and spaces, causing the players to take a close look at the playing field. All shapes are designed in a way where the ultimate goal is either a final follow-up in the form of a pass or a goal at the end of the play. The central circle forms must always be supplemented with miniature, small, or large goals. Goal shots are always accentuated and improved alongside the situational playing conduct in this manner. Goal quality and one-on-one dribbling skills are considered the most necessary skills for purposes of the circle forms.

›› The playing rules provoke the desired player conduct

The rules in the circle forms allow for the incorporation of specific trends from the big game and the provocation of certain playing actions. The rules for the circle forms are highly demanding for the players and also heavily reduce the need for coaching, requiring rather short instructions. Objectives are bound or tasks are assigned such that either playing actions must be performed outside of the circle before subsequent rules allow for a point inside the circle, or the game begins with actions inside the circle before the focus is placed on goals or teammates outside.

The rules can also have an impact on the passing or dribbling techniques. Once two passes have been played inside the circle, a player can dribble the ball out. This may be expanded, e.g. the player with the ball must make contact with the ball three times and the opponent has the opportunity to pursue, or various dribbling styles are required under pressure from opponents.

Whereas common playing forms often strive for possession rules that place greater focus on contact quotas or passing, the objectives of the circle forms deliberately place less emphasis on passing and actions. This creates the quick opportunity for the team with the ball to achieve sub-objectives.

As a result of this, intensity increases. The conduct of the offending and defending teams are brought to a high level when it comes to action and movement speed. This also corresponds to the modern trend of quickly taking advantage of an imperfectly formed opponent for playing in the attack zone. Furthermore, this creates no opportunity for the players to be passive with needless passing. In the circle forms, every player is required to give their all.

The configuration of the playing rules offers a lot of room and potential for alternations, variations, and linking individual objectives. This potentially endless framework helps the circle forms evolve. Simple plays are thereby made more complex and are extremely positively received by the players up to the point that the players are waiting for new expansions and variations from the coach.

Of course it is also possible to implement the rules in such a way that deliberately short or additional passes are made, rhythm changes are induced, or an opponent is lured over. Rules also sometimes replace long-winded explanations. The players want to play games that are always given new life and are profitable.

›› The playing time regulates intensity, density and quality

Alongside the playing rules, the playing time is also an important factor that must be considered. Most circle forms are ideal for a three-on-three, three-on-three-plus-one, four-on-four, or four-on-four-plus-one playing scenario and should be played with a format that allows for intervals of 3 x 3 minutes.

With regard to the cognitive challenge with corresponding intensity, short playing phases with brief breaks are advised, similar to the big game itself and time-outs. The short break provides the coach with the perfect opportunity to discuss a scene that was just played out. It is also possible to let situations play out in slow motion, or draw attention to an element that has not yet been played.

The playing time can be controlled by the number of balls. In order to score points, the teams playing against each other can receive five balls in alternation. Once the right to the ball changes, there is a chance to take a break. The coach must keep an eye on the clock while closely monitoring the intensity of the playing situations, seeing the density and quality of actions within them. Here, too, the playing time can be shortened or lengthened.

Experience in the application of circle forms has shown that good control must be possible in periods of strain, depending on age and playing level, so that the short-term and highly intensive moments of pressure form the bridge into the game itself. The highly intensive phases with only brief breaks in the plays are becoming an ever more important aspect of sprint-dominated soccer and the competitiveness of individual players and entire teams. This can have a positive learning effect on the size and layout of the playing areas and consistently selected number ratios of the teams, in that the moments and opportunities for switching off and losing concentration are minimized.

›› The circle forms influence motor skills, movement and running behavior

The circular playing areas and field elements create playing situations that have an impact on actions, movement and motor skills. The manner of running, running toward, running through, and running over lines, zones, and spaces helps to enhance agility and, above all else, various turning movements with and without the ball. Lateral motion is one primary training focus where quick, diagonal backward turns are addressed. These are especially advantageous when stronger shifting movements are used in situations against the ball.

By using the circles as playing areas, many situations can arise in exercise sequences, technique-oriented competitions, and actual games in which the curves of the circles are run along in a special, arched manner. This is a major benefit over the usual rectangular or square playing areas, as the curved runs are applied in modern professional soccer for running against chains and to the opponents' backs. There is also a motoric variation of the rather line-based and straight running behavior often observed in rectangular and square playing areas. These runs are easier for the opponent to read and anticipate, and are thus hardly a challenge. Curved runs can be effectively applied in the wing and center.

›› The objectives identify the center as a critical action space

The circle forms can be played through such that the border of the circle is used directly as the outer edge. This shape facilitates free-running in a curve along the edge. Furthermore, by limiting the action space there is a focus on the rules, which first require the completion of playing tasks inside the circle. Exiting from the center of the circle over the outer line after a stipulated number of passes can be followed by shots to the miniature, small or large goals.

In the following game without the usual outer line, the events of the game may distance themselves far from the circle and its outlying goals in the attempt to score goals. Even in situations that are drifting away from the center and from the objective, there are potentials and tasks to the extent that the players are now expressly required to return to the center of the action. For the player in possession, this induces objective-oriented effort with the ball, requiring their teammates to link up with them and provide team support. Some of these situations can also lead to short breaks for all players in intensive playing phases.

These playing phases may be hard to bear from the usual perspective, as there is no direct sprinting or power. The trainer often calls for speed in these situations. The incorporation of a new ball to a position far from the current playing situation to conclude the break can also be avoided in the challenging circle forms. The new playing situation created by the incoming ball has no real basis in the game. It is only used as a means of honing adaptability.

The circle forms prefer more authentic momentum and the necessity to play toward the target area. There is significant added value for the individual player in the acquisition of greater playing skills, in that the indirectly applied curved runs help to expand their own motor skills. This applies just as much to the defenders who are acting against the ball. The result is a fundamental automatism of all circle forms. The training objective of the team in possession is the other side's learning objective.

The organization and structure of the circle forms thus focus on the circle as a shape, neglecting other marking cones as field markings outside of the circles. One could also speak in an overblown fashion of playing forms without border markings, thereby getting on the nerves of every organized and whistle-happy coach. Experience with the circle shapes clearly shows that the players are led to central objectives by the concept in order to hunt for points, and thus quickly play toward the target areas. The marking of other border lines as the limits of the field is therefore less important. If a team in possession drifts too far away from the objective, this results in shared amusement.

›› Possession aims to threaten, dominate and master the central circle space

The outer areas far from the circle or the edges of the circle may also be interesting for playing through or over. The primary interest, however, lies in central orientation and the inside of the circle. Taking over and claiming the central circle playing space and the resulting points are equally as important as achieving a variety of possible continuations in various directions.

Taking a look at professional soccer, the scope of ball contact numbers in the central playing space in the opponent's side is often low. Arguments to explain this often try to claim that this zone is well covered by the opponent's defensive midfielders, and so the game tends to play through half-spaces or wings. With this basic assumption, less attention is drawn to the center or the threat of the vertical depth. In light of this risk factor, the pull to the side occurs too early.

The glance over the shoulder and subsequent loophole trained by the center-oriented circle forms results in more options that challenge the defense and facilitate various attacks for the offending team. This consequently contributes to increased playing and movement speed, as shown by the high density of action and playing intensity in the training units. The circle forms generally improve the quality of actions and movement speed, and the sprint-based continuation of the game up to the final action can be increased by the playing rules.

›› The circle involves all players in intensive actions

In the traditional four-on-four playing forms, it is possible to observe behavior that causes the players to leave intensive actions to their teammates, or to retreat from the challenging momentum of the game through targeted passing. What sounds like intent is an all too human behavior in order to not blindly run into an overwhelming situation. In the circle forms, it is apparent that the players are often forced to concentrate, to stay in intense situations and remain involved. It helps to envision a living game console.

In order to add further weight to this, let's take a look at the so-called standard playing forms. These have provided coaches and players with well-known flows and images without being more closely examined in regards to how sufficiently intensive these are for many players, if they offer sufficient diversity of actions, if they facilitate action density for each interval, and if they offer efficient playing situations that must constantly be resolved.

In this regard, it is important to evaluate the action radii of individual players. Just because the standard playing forms require a certain base conditioning does not necessarily mean that this will even approach the quality of countries like Spain or Portugal. An approximation, differentiation, or dominance can be achieved through high-quality vertical playing in conjunction with optimal passing quality. This playing style comes with endless, or professional, offense concepts in order to be able to implement the quick standard in the attack zone or final third near the goal. Many teams falter in this area, to the benefit of the stable defense of the opposing team.

» Playing through small zones fosters precision and creativity

An important aspect of the circle forms is playing through small spaces into which the players sprint, run back and forth, turn in or turn out. These actions and movements require an idea which, using the offense with and without the ball as an example, helps against opposing inner defenders. In this context, the spread-out game in the circles across interfaces, gaps or edges creates an additional learning method that promotes passing techniques and conduct that eliminate any benefits for the opponent when carried over into the game.

This training concept thus creates the necessity for some passes to be hidden without the passing player having discussed it with the recipient beforehand. The passes are sent off early or shortly after dribbling, and thus require high precision with both feet. Soccer players often prefer to master tight spaces with both feet.

This concept thus entails a certain flow and unleashes potential that ultimately is attributed to the players so that they may implement these forms and master them. With the ability to maintain possession of the ball and play through the tightest of spaces in a variety of ways or achieve objectives through quality techniques, the circle forms foster high-quality, skilled and fun usage of both feet.

» The offense's playing solutions require an adequate response from the defense

The circle forms promote offensive solutions. The goal is to find target fields, play through them as per the current objectives, and score under pressure. The team in possession tries to challenge the opponent, to move them and force them to wear themselves out. For the team without the ball, it is necessary to work well together and immediately react to the possessing player's actions. This places emphasis on action and activity, and applies equally to the offense and defense. If a continuation by the stealing team after taking the ball is not halted immediately, the disadvantage can only turn into an advantage with difficulty, and the situation can only be evened out with extreme effort.

The time pressure for the defense's reception of the opponent's action is a very worthwhile side-effect of the circle forms, and is not at the expense of the offense's formation. One major characteristic of the playing concept for the circle forms is the hunt for multiple points through multiple objectives at the same time. This intensifies the requirements of the defensive players. Quick consideration and decision-making by the offense also helps the defense make prudent decisions. The consequences of decisions quickly become apparent in the points scored, and the results of the game are closely related to the dedication and teamwork applied.

›› The playing context allows for constant learning

The concept of the circle forms links the learning of playing situations to conditional factors. It has long been known that this creates a distinctive memory factor. The circle forms follow the principle that the players are constantly learning during the game. Rarely are the players at the same spot for just a few moments, or even in the same zone or position. Every type of player with a corresponding profile type should be motivated to run. Permanent involvement and participation in the game requires running. The circle forms teach the players running intensity.

This training allows the players to be willing to work and run intensively in all directions. A quote by stopper Mats Hummels, who helped initiate many defensive and offensive maneuvers by the German team during the 2014 World Cup in Brazil and who was happy to have so many actions with the ball, fits here. This is an expression of his teammate's trust in his technical and footwork capacity.

The circle forms strive to link playing with running. With regard to the stopper's position, it should by no means be believed that all they do is run alongside the others and help with one attack after another. Rather, even for defenders it is necessary to have flexibility and running skills.

›› Scoring promotes technique and speed of execution

The concept of the circle forms strives for multi-layered provocation rules and scoring systems. These rules can effectively influence the players' actions. The configuration of the rules can also specifically aim to influence individual technical actions which are then trained in a playing action as opposed to static exercise formations. For example, if a line of the circle must be dribbled over in order to score a point, then the playing conduct is geared toward targeted dribbling. Optimal ball control and the critical first contact required for it become the primary focus of the flow of the ball.

When objectives are combined for points, e.g. dribbling must be followed by a pass followed by a stipulated number of passes in a certain sector, multiple techniques are required and trained. This also requires all players to keep an eye on what is happening.

In the real game it often happens that a player who is dribbling and has no opportunity to pass is left with additional, power-sapping contacts because their teammates have shut down. Players who are thinking along with the player in possession are especially critical for scoring points. It is important that the possessing player's intentions are recognized and that their own behavior is adjusted in terms of synchronized running and the creation of passing opportunities. In modern professional soccer in particular, passing options to teammates help with the usage of passing feints, namely to get out of critical one-on-one situations.

›› Combination of objectives opens up a variety of possible solutions

Scoring points and goals in the circle forms are considerably different from the traditional scoring systems. Points here are often based on steps that add up to a point. Objective A must be completed before objective B can even begin, followed by objective C which requires a certain action in order to ultimately score a point.

In this context, the two-plus-one rule was developed as a special point for the circle forms. In the two-plus-one situation, the team with the ball has a certain strategic freedom as to which step is completed first. It is thus possible for a point to be scored by dribbling through a corridor (objective A), followed by a pass over a circle line (objective B) and a pass into a target field (objective C).

Depending on the situation, it is also possible to select when the first objective commences and whether dribbling through the corridor will precede the pass over the line or not, thus making it the first step. These options let the players work together spatially and temporally.

›› The point system allocates responsibility and allows for success

In the circle forms, the point system creates a number of opportunities to score points, meaning that every player can contribute. Each player is afforded a certain responsibility, the ability to trust themselves, and the chance to share in the success. Even if a player is only involved in one of three necessary steps, they directly help secure the points. This may mean that they were included in the passes because of their skills, in the action for their bold dribbling, or their running along with the play, thereby indirectly gaining assurance.

The trainer may also emotionally help in the steering of these processes. The circle forms require the coach's attention and memory.

» Striving for objectives and bonus actions develops a winning mentality and hunger for success

On another level entirely, the players score points through their hunger to win. Like young dogs, they want to help score points through their own actions for purposes of the tasks assigned to them. The role of the point seeker and point earner should by no means be dismissed as a mundane accompaniment on the margins. Rather, this role fosters determination, a drive for success, and a winning mentality.

The scenarios that arise in the circle forms draw the players to engage in impressive, determined and offensive conduct toward the objective, and are just as critical as the disposition of all passiveness. The multi-tiered point system also includes bonus actions and bonus balls.

After fulfilling a rule of play and achieving an objective, the game may continue with the addition of a bonus ball. The bonus action is then equivalent to a pass with a normal soccer ball by the trainer. This bonus ball must be carried over to the next objective within a certain amount of time or after a certain number of ball contacts. The idea of the bonus action must also be implemented with other balls (e.g. tennis ball, handball or softball). These balls can be used to eliminate opponents or take shots at the goals. This hones adaptability skills and speed of execution.

» Linking final follow-up actions facilitates diverse conclusions

Along with the game elements, the final action in the form of the goal is of primary importance. The objectives in the circle forms also consider the opening or closure of goals, depending on the respective rules. Aside from the cognitive aspects of the concept itself, goal shots are intended to occur both qualitatively and quantitatively.

In standard forms, it is normal to have two goals. In the circle forms, the objective is to play toward the next challenge while keeping an eye on the conclusion. The configuration of the circle forms aims to provoke forceful and precise shots, as well as goals from a wide range of angles.

» Technical training in the circle structure helps introduce and prepare the playing forms

The main circle forms entail a short period for coordination and practice. The marked playing area is played with technical exercises and competitions. This type of warm-up allows the talented rookie players to play through the successive scenarios of the circle forms. The follow-up behavior is much clearer and more precise. The players are better and more capable of remembering the rules through the layout of the field.

Another benefit lies in training incentives with colored marking cones. This aids in the consideration of technical elements that arise in the following sequences. Technical processes, such as dribbling with frequent feints, various types of ball control, or precise passes are highly polished. The symmetry or asymmetry of the field structure can also influence the players. The circle forms thus offer an alternative to traditional techniques and tasks.

» The game concept offers multi-layered and multidimensional design options

Ultimately, some crucial aspects of the game's layout must be emphasized. Individual and group training can be conducted with and without the ball. Players' skills are improved with game-like actions in motivational training structures. Number ratios from three-on-three, three-on-three-plus-one, four-on-four, four-on-four-plus-one, and greater sizes offer very good opportunities to address coordinated interactions and objective-based teamwork.

The offensive actions in the circle forms are shaped by quick decision-making, mutual coordination, positioning at strategically critical target points, and situational playing and running through various zones. The defensive actions against the ball concern all shifting and tightening processes, and involve the redirecting of passing routes, doubling up against the opponent, and ball-oriented pushback.

The group tactics can also be linked with individual training objectives and can specify special tasks for individual players so that other aspects such as two-footedness or feint frequency are addressed as well. Ultimately the differentiation of individual objectives, the formulation of certain rules, or the setup for points help define the areas on which the training will focus, control the desired player conduct, work out the various playing elements, and regulate the fundamental level of complexity.

1.3 PRINCIPLES

›› Using areas of action

The principles primarily concern the recognition and usage of the critical areas of action. Through this, the game players learn how to perceive and assess their position, as well as learning determination and orientation in spaces, and how to adapt as quickly as possible to the objective at hand. Because there are different objectives within the playing area in the form of lines or other geometric shapes, players are compelled to pay attention to their own position on the field.

Contrary to static exercise formats, training with constantly changing situations already emphasizes alertness and concentration. The principles in the circle forms make the shape itself the main focus. The shapes define the content. This means that the circle forms foster an understanding of grid-shaped fields via playing through, running through, and pulling out of spaces and zones. It helps the players to structure and perceive the normal large playing field as a sort of chessboard.

›› Playing through shapes

Other principles are closely linked with the individual shapes and combinations of multiple, and sometimes different shapes. Tunnels, corridors, tubes, sectors or arches are important shapes, some of which are repeatedly associated with special actions. Technical actions such as bold, quick dribbling and high-quality initial ball contact are usually required when entering tunnels, passing through tubes, or going over the smallest curved lines. Pass combinations and tactical group sequences are especially emphasized in the outer areas, individual circle sectors, or marginal spaces. The different geometric shapes are thus closely associated with the individual actions or behaviors of multiple players.

›› Threatening the center

A frequently recurring principle is the permanent threat to the center by the player with the ball. The selection of the circle as the playing area is justified by this principle. The threat to the center should occur from nearly every starting position inside and outside of the circle. As a reaction, the opposing team (namely the defense), can act all the more tightly closed and compact. This in turn would initiate the intensive offense that is desired.

In traditional training forms, central objectives are all too rare. Even in the event that penetration into the central area is prevented by a compact defense, this results in other opportunities and solutions. The opening of tightened and closed spaces poses another great, rewarding challenge for the players for threatening the center and not turning away from its nucleus too early. The center ultimately constitutes a very sensitive location, and is equivalent to a major nerve center that facilitates all directions and continuations once it has been overtaken.

›› Bold entry

One major principle of the playing forms lies in the connection of technical ball actions with inner zones that are to be played through. A preceding objective initially lies in the completion of a technical ball action outside of the circle in order to then get the opportunity to score a point inside the circle. This means that the completion of an objective within the circle is first facilitated by precise technical execution.

A successful technical action allows the player to enter the center of the circle, and is linked with scoring. This principle aids in the formulation of objectives by which a point is scored, e.g. dribbling into the circle after two complete passes outside of the circle, or a pass through the center into the circle after ball control involving a backward turn. With regard to the actual game, the opponents are so challenged by technical and strategic offensive preparations in this manner that the actual, critical target area opens up.

›› Purposeful exit

Another principle of the circle forms lies in achieving objectives inside the circle, with the subsequent possibility of scoring a point in the outside. The emphasis here rests on profitable follow-up and final actions after achieving individual objectives. After the middle of the circle has been dribbled or passed through, or a combination thereof, certain target areas in the peripheral spaces or final shots to the small, large or mini-goals in the outer area are in play. The transferability for the big game lies in the deliberate play toward the center in order to threaten the space that is dangerous for the opponent, to play through it, and escape the opponent via targeted follow-up actions and take advantage of gaps that open up.

›› Claiming the center

Entering and exiting are comprehensible terms for players when the rules and principles are being explained. The principles of entering and exiting into circle fields aim to take over the center. This relates to the basic idea in the big game of dominating tight spaces, in particular the center. The combination of objectives in the inner and outer areas is configured such that it is possible to score points in both zones.

Another connection to the real game lies in the fact that there is not just one possible solution, but rather always at least two. Promising decisions help the team in possession dominate the game by claiming the center. Entry into the circle to score points is highly stimulating to the players, even in situations with greater intensity and high opponent pressure. Exiting with acquired points is just as interesting, and as important as a swift retreat to escape opponent pressure and score.

» Playing over levels

Playing over as many opponents as quickly as possible with offensive ball control or deep passes is one of the challenges of professional soccer. Playing over levels is an elementary prerequisite for preparing for goal opportunities in the real game. This element is reflected in the circle forms in that there are objectives that induce the playing over of lines or zones through dribbling or passing. The passing distances can differ depending on the shape and emphasis. Long passing distances are required when the individual objectives involve large zones or partial segments of the entire circle. On the other hand, the passing distance decreases when the players are required to play past multiple small circles.

Here, too, the real game serves as a means of orientation for the rules or desired actions. Once an opposing wall closes up certain areas, tightens zones, and blocks deep passes, it is fundamental that the opponents' compact positioning must be broken up through forceful, sharp passes and the playing speed toward distant targets is maintained. Playing over thus means passing beyond a circle or a shape, and is linked with the objective of not giving the opponents the chance to outnumber the respective player.

» Making decisions

A wide variety of shapes such as lines, arches, peripheral areas, sectors, half-circles, corridors, tubes, central zones and outer areas, when combined with the various playing and provocation rules, open up a broad range of actions. The individual playing situations constantly compel the players to jointly make appropriate decisions and opt for expedient conduct. The constant decision-making in complex playing situations touches on elementary partial aspects of speed of execution, and is a recurring principle in all circle forms with multiple solutions. The learning situation in ongoing playing scenarios is a dynamic opportunity for experience and action that cognitively and permanently compels the players to assess the decisions that they have made and are implementing.

» Making it fun

Certain elements are set up by the principles, and different behaviors are brought about. First and foremost, they should make the players want to play through the spaces. This entails the desire for something new, a wonderful mindset that makes the players want to play new games for the sake of the game, to devote themselves to it and enjoy doing so, to have fun. The living circle forms are far from monotonous, endless loops. You can hear this in the sounds of the game.

With all respect for the required level of training and the module used, there is a significant difference between mundane and boring passing sequences, and the relatively intense and joyous circle forms.

1.4 ELEMENTS

In differentiating between the concept and principles, the following elements help to describe the central and recurring aspects and components of the circle form. The elements highlight the fundamental effects on individual players or groups, as well as the possibilities of influencing the fundamental attitude of entire teams.

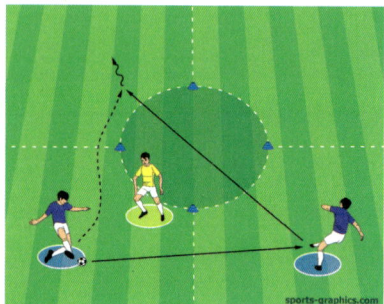
Fig. 7: Double pass

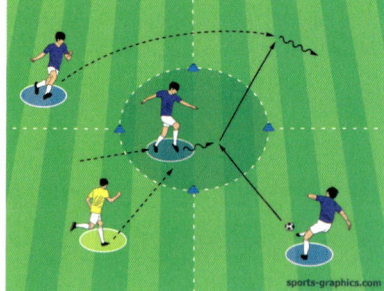
Fig. 8 Running back

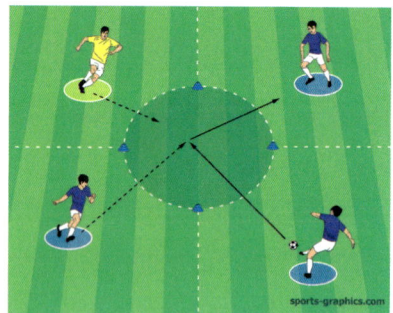
Fig. 9: Playing with a third

In order to achieve objectives in the circle forms, the players in possession exhibit the classic group-tactical processes through their actions, such as double passes (Fig. 7), running back (Fig. 8), playing with a third (Fig. 9), zig-zag combinations, or vertical and transverse passes. The joint hunt for points becomes more comprehensive and trains players to look for partners and teammates, to anticipate the possessing player's intentions, and to keep an eye on upcoming actions by players with and without the ball.

A successful observation process in the current situation is then followed by a quick, joint, and initiative decision. At this point there is another difference from the usual training forms in which there is often a lack of initiative runs, and there is usually no room for it at all.

The defensive playing actions are primarily focused on defending the target areas. The joint actions in the game against the ball are shaped by mutually strengthening support and mobility. This is why defensive tactics are common, self-evident and with no need for long hesitations or instructions. These include aggressive doubling (Fig. 10), tightening the center (Fig. 11), or pushing back at opportune pressing moments (Fig. 12) to take the ball.

As long as a team offers no joint defense, the team in possession will score easy points, not let the ball be taken from them, and not have to worry about possession and points by the defense. An intensive defense is thus automatically hidden in the circle forms.

INTRODUCTION 29

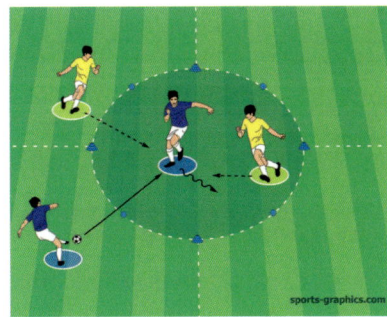
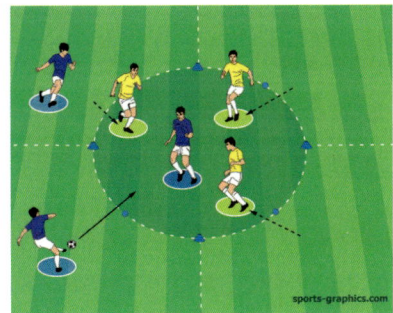

Fig. 10: Doubling   *Fig. 11: Tightening*   *Fig. 12: Pushing back*

For purposes of tactical behaviors, certain positions can be used without the ball depending on the objective. Running and positioning without the ball are significant in actual competitive situations. In these scenarios it is crucial for the players in possession to have good opportunities to continue the game so that attacks can be continued without skipping a beat and opportunities to score can be made. Optimal positioning of the player with the ball in relation to the passing player and the direction of play is thus critical.

This idea is considered in some circle forms. In conjunction with the objectives in some forms, critical and significant positional points can be identified. These are located on and near the ends of lines or edges of other shapes like diamonds, squares, or triangles. At these points, there are optimal opportunities to continue the play or directly score points after receipt of the ball and targeted control.

This creates an awareness among the players that they are always thinking together, identifying critical spaces and constantly assessing and optimizing their own positions in the field. The players must hone their view of specific zones and areas of action where critical actions are being performed, points are being scored, or goals are being threatened. The action requirements for open positions facing the field or the opposing goal become all the more significant. This indirect introduction to orientation with regard to significance trains the players to have a well-timed view of optimal positioning and greater efficiency in their actions.

The formations used within the circle forms contain lines, divisions, zones and fields. These in turn offer the players a variety of learning opportunities for being able to understand the offense and defense zones of the entire game. On this basis, strategies for taking the ball and threatening the goal via target spaces can be developed. In playing fields without any lines outside of the field border, this behavior is left to chance and is largely based on combating the individual player. The circle forms should facilitate spatial as well as individual orientation. The players must orient themselves consistently in the playing field with its different zones, and face potential one-on-one situations in these spaces.

An important and recurring element of the circle forms is the bonus ball. The bonus ball comes directly after a successfully completed action and may be in the form of a small, hand-sized ball thrown into the field, for example. The bonus ball would thus trigger an intensive continuation appropriate for the game, and implement an additional action with a clear motoric objective.

These small balls are not to be considered merely playful ideas, nor only used for a greater change of gears. Rather, they are used to give the panting and eager players a new objective, demanding new willingness to run and sprint. The players run up to any playing situations that open up at some point and want to carry this all the way to the goal with speed and quality. This has an impact on the entire team's attitude and creates a ravenous joy for the game.

Along with the bonus ball, the trainer ball is also important. This is the pile of balls next to the trainer. The trainer always has the opportunity to bring entirely new balls into play in order to respond to a ball that has entered a goal, resolve completely disjointed situations, or cause a desired change of gears.

Fig. 13: Small zones

The playing elements also include adhering to distances among the players in the current playing situation. The playing spaces are sometimes quite tight. It would be the wrong approach if the playing flow created in this manner mainly involved plays facing the ball, counteracting good cooperation with optimal distances for passing options. Nuanced spatial behavior results from the different objectives in the circle forms. On the one hand, the players must heavily tighten up around certain areas, linking together closely and forming a grid in certain zones. On the other hand, the players also run to each other in large, open areas in order to create passing or dribbling options.

These alternations are implemented into the circle forms almost like an automatism. The shaping through a wide variety of marking elements keeps the smallest zones and tight spaces open, where intensive techniques can be required. As an individual playing element, the finest technical execution and optimal foot control are demanded in these zones. The players are required to exhibit adaptability and two-footedness during the flow of the game with spatial, opponent and time pressure (Fig. 13).

The recurring elements in the circle forms are encountered just as often in the big game itself. Bold, open and targeted dribbling is required in the often critical one-on-one situations or speed runs through gaps and interim spaces in modern soccer. Well-placed markings and lines within the field create a tunnel in the circle forms. These narrow, about 6m long areas must be used optimally in the context. If lateral defending is prohibited for the defense and they may only play forward, these narrow spaces can facilitate speed dribbling and getting past oncoming opponents (Fig. 14).

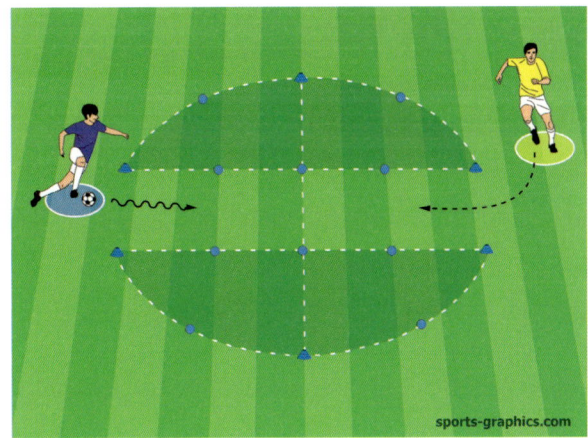

Fig. 14: Tunnel dribbling

If there is too much pressure from opponents, the forms and playing rules may create exit opportunities for the player in possession. Securing the ball under unstoppable pressure from opponents is the first priority even in the upper leagues. In a constantly tightening playing situation, risky playing and keeping the ball too long upon losing passing points in other areas means losing the ball and risking a counter from the opponent.

Exiting is discussed in these situations when it comes to the circle forms. This is not like exiting from a burning vehicle, but rather the idea that a new space must follow a space that has just been played through. Each action by the player in possession constitutes a prompt to the opponent, and thus immediate acceptance of the ball while running.

The elements created in the circle forms stem from the interplay between the circular playing fields, the different playing and challenge rules, the different objectives and subsequent flow. They concern defensive and offensive actions alike, as well as individual actions and flows in which multiple players are involved. The elements of the circle forms can be found in modern professional soccer to varying degrees, and promote the broad education of the modern player.

1.5 PLAYER CONDUCT

The players are equipped with additional curiosity and a desire to play new games and forms. There is also great interest in new playing fields, attractive tasks and conducts relevant to the game. The sense that a new playing form also promotes personal growth serves as additional motivation. One major incentive is the joy that is contagious among the players, the hunger to keep the ball moving with great combinations, and the emotional conclusion by scoring a goal.

Along with the fundamental competitive attitude, other conduct must be observed during these games. It must always be ensured that possessing players keep their eyes off the ball without the coach having to instruct them. This is often presented by the organizational framework and specific playing rules. In game situations in tight spots, explosive and dynamic discontinuations can often be seen, especially on the rim of the circle.

Coaching among the players is also highly encouraged. Verbal coordination and instructions are required to complete current objectives and jointly play toward zones, fields, lines or goals. It is important to observe the opponents' and teammates' behavior and anticipate ideas. The audible and timely calling of effective instructions is difficult for many players and is often self-evident in the circle forms even without coaching by the trainer. These effective instructions can later become the self-evident calling of tactical details when the impulse is present.

The experiences and movement patterns of desired runs, intensive free-running, clear offsetting, and running forward and backward without the ball serve as a good measurement for the great significance of the circle forms. If these forms were simple, monotonous, boring and predictable in their momentum, this would result in a backslide and no intensive contribution.

If an objective within the circle is achieved and this moment is crowned with a team action outside of the circle, the players will adjust to the playing rules with their behavior, quickly go back outside and then run back again in order to score the point. This entails greater offering and free-running. The players are always on the move so that they can score in the offense or prevent scoring in the defense.

The eye and visuals are important factors for the qualitative description and assessment of the circle forms. Players are trained in precise perception by the field markings of cones and pads in different shapes and colors. Some players are uncertain in critical moments or can rarely clearly say where they are aiming when shooting toward the goal. In this context, the circle forms strengthen players' vision and draw their attention to gaps, a center, distances, ranges, or the colors of individual marking cones.

With this additional skill, the players can have a more comprehensive view of the game. The fear of potential physical contact and losing the ball can be replaced by inner calm when opponents are approaching, and a close look at the situation is possible in these pressure situations. Players' eyes and glances should be observed during the moment. They will develop a visual and cognitive feel for the game in succession.

The opportunity to achieve objectives and score points becomes more difficult when they keep their eyes on the ball and continue to do so while in possession. The circle forms strongly affect decision-making and thus impact the players' reaction speeds. The players weigh passing, dribbling or free-running more effectively and therefore make quick and effective decisions. In conjunction with technical aspects like fake-outs or feints, the players exhibit more diverse behaviors in tight moments. Powerlessness in constricted spaces is replaced by nuanced competence.

As illustrated, the circle forms have various impacts on the players' technical and tactical behavior. With a cohesive focus, influence on the fundamental attitude and behavior of the players can be seen as the circles all have different objectives that require quality playing to be achieved. The orientation toward success has a captivating impact on the substance of the game, and lets individual players and entire teams develop a winning mentality.

1.6 TRAINER CONDUCT

The introduction and implementation of the circle forms in practice requires an acclimation and orientation phase, for the players as well as the trainer. The trainer should approach this phase with calmness and patience. Many trainers have developed an analytical perspective throughout years of experience, and it immediately responds to players' mistakes and calls for improvement. In the initial orientation phase and introductory training units, the coaches should react reasonably, and in cases of doubt not even say anything, or speak up.

The trainer can be seen by their players as a good, alert, competent coach when the players are allowed to play in peace and the coach exhibits positive, objective behavior during interruptions. The circle forms function as a control tool for coaches and offer the chance to ensure the flow of the game so that technical and tactical actions can be addressed afterwards.

Many players will become more accepting this way, instead of feeling halted or inhibited by the trainer's first call for a time out after a short playing period. It is better for the players to gain trust, process the playing form (shape, rules, objective) in peace, try it out for themselves, perhaps make their first small mistakes and use these as a learning tool.

We perceive coaching in the circle forms as more of an atmosphere-building leadership role that respects the individual players and, above all, supports them emotionally. The introductory explanations in trainer practice are primarily the description of the game rules. Long-winded phrasing and elucidations of the many possibilities have been left out. A long verbal description phase generally causes the players to not be able to remember everything, and the desired transfer into the next sequence is infeasible.

That is why coaching in the circle forms focuses on instructions. The instructions accompany the players within the form and provide assistance with short terms and a distinctive choice of words. In practice, the specific wording continues to slightly change. Practical experience has shown that certain words put too much pressure on the players while other words break down blocks and facilitate liberated playing. This means that when using the instructions, the coach must always deliberately choose their phrasing, omit disruptive words from their vocabulary, and create positive words and empowering formulations.

1.7　INSTRUCTIONS

The instructions should provide the players with motivating assistance to keep the game moving. They are deliberately kept open to actions and solutions so that they do not restrict or inhibit the game. Instead the instructions are automatically internalized as a form of activation, much like learning new words in a language.

The general instructions are based on fundamental conduct and include team-based defensive and offensive actions simultaneously, touching on players' attitudes, willingness, and conduct. The technical instructions aim to improve certain techniques or make them more effective. These instructions are geared toward players who are bringing their repertoire of techniques to the current game situation and stand out from the immediate play. The tactical instructions are based on the interplay among the team and groups of players. Specific instructions are intended to sensitize players to team conduct and optimize tactical cooperation.

Coaching of the circle forms is also marked by motoric instructions. These aids aim to have a targeted impact on body movements, physical feints, or positioning. The motoric instructions listed here will be familiar to a seasoned coach and can be used as direct instructions for specific playing situations. From a broader perspective, the various terms, different key words and specific instructions are a complex and difficult topic when it comes to everybody needing to speak the same language, or if the same actions are to be associated with individual coaching terms.

For the circle forms, the verbal side is not overly dominant, so the player should not rely solely on coaching to improve their playing. Instead, they should also improve their form through the form, so to speak. One of the primary goals of the circle forms is to create a team, develop a team mindset, and achieve optimal conditioning for relevant game situations. Herein lies the methodical result of rounding out players' development through the circle forms.

1.7.1 General instructions

›› Well done!

This instruction is an important way to strengthen and reinforce good plays and desired player conduct. Usage of this instruction allows for both substantial tasks as well as the praise that is critical for enjoyment while playing. It can make players happy even in challenging situations.

›› **Beautiful! Great! Bravo! Super! Awesome!**

›› Master the form!

This instruction gives the players the clear indication to want to win the game, to master it and decide the match. This indirectly places focus on results and activates the hunger for success. The imaginary pointer finger guides the players toward an effective and objective-based playing style.

›› **Focus on the objective! Win the match! Score points! Match the form!**

›› Check the playing area!

This instruction prompts the players to check their individual position by looking around and over their shoulders, and honing their orientation skills. However, long-term training with complex circle forms helps to achieve fundamental improvement of perception, meaning that this instruction will rarely have to be applied. The game phases are so cognitively challenging that a small, helpful instruction is all it takes to recall the playing area.

›› **Check your position! Use your position! Position yourself!**

›› Observe while running!

This instruction prompts the players to actively run instead of maintaining a passive position, so that they may readily enter defensive or offensive situations. If the player has the ball, then this instruction is used to tell them to keep the ball in motion and offer passing options.

›› **Keep the ball moving! Move the ball! Run for points!**

›› Look to the center!

This instruction gives the players a task, namely to look towards the center from outside of the circle in order to identify any weak spots and gaps. By constantly focusing and threatening the center, this instruction aims to produce passes, dribbling and runs to the opposing center.

›› **Look to the center! Find the center! Play through the center!**

›› **Form a grid!**

This instruction means to run close together and reduce distances. With regard to the playing situation and achieving of certain objectives, this instruction is equivalent to creating nearby passing points for the player in possession so that they may pass to teammates running alongside them, and outnumber and outplay the opponents. This instruction also touches on the tactical behavior of positioning the possessing team closer together in order to lure the opponent and use newly open spaces.

›› **Move up! Push back! Keep yourself open! Keep threatening the center!**

›› **Threaten the space!**

This instruction unmistakably strives for energetic playing that threatens an opposing interim space through dribbling or passing. It helps lead the players on possession on paths that facilitate points or advantages, prompting the active and effective pursuit of objectives.

›› **Focus on the interim space! Use the space! Use the gap!**

›› **Find the shape!**

This instruction is clear but leaves room for options and possible solutions. This instruction does not compel the players to follow one specific path, but rather gives them leeway in how they play and act. Even when the opponents follow this instruction, it is difficult to predict the opposing team's resulting behavior.

›› **Look for the fields! Focus on the objective! Play through the zone!**

1.7.2   Technical instructions

›› **Dribble up!**

This instruction is geared toward conduct in possession, which prompts a player to quickly dribble to an opponent in order to outplay them one-on-one. This instruction is supposed to stir up competitiveness so that players try to take chances and advantages for their own team.

›› **Open dribbling! Complete the run!**

›› **Long and short passes!**

This instruction tells the players to use different types of passes so that they are much more unpredictable for their opponent. The instruction simultaneously affects the opponents' area of alertness, and also has a positive effect on the level of play.

›› **Change pass forcefulness! Make hidden passes! Pass with both feet!**

›› Pass with your body low!

This instruction draws the focus to the quality of passing, and applies to circle forms that are based on the objectives as well as teamwork and combinations. This instruction implies that individual passes are performed with greater force, thus creating sharper passes.

›› **Pass and run away! Forceful passes! Passes with a message!**

›› First contact far from the opponent!

This instruction aims to get the player to continue the game quickly without being bound while dribbling or in a face-off. It creates more intensity and demands for players with and pursuing the ball, as ball control entails more effort for the defender.

Control away from the opponent! Hunt with the first contact!

›› No easy ball loss!

This instruction, with emphasis on "easy," means that mistakes are made and allowed in complex circle forms and intense situations. It also highlights that simple mistakes counteract the objective of the game, and loss of the ball also means more work for the player's own teammates.

›› **Secure possession! Stay on the ball! Protect your possession!**

1.7.3 Tactical instructions

›› Run and rescue!

This instruction gives the player an energetic signal and prompts them to act in a way that equalizes any disadvantage. This call does not request hesitant behavior, but rather should encourage sacrificial conduct with commitment, sprinting, and physical involvement for one's own teammates.

›› **Suicide run! Run! Rescue! Offer help!**

›› Screen off the center!

This instruction is supposed to give an indication to the defensive players acting against the ball and invoke a closure of the center of the circle. It's important to prevent the opponents from scoring and not allow for any passing or dribbling options. Ideally the ball orientation heavily reduces the passing and action angle to the center.

›› **Don't let anyone into the circle! Work together against the ball!**

›› Keep binding the opponent!

This instruction tries to lead a player from space-oriented behavior to team-oriented behavior, so that simple ball acceptances and turning motions are prevented through stubbornness and physical contact. With this signal, the players acting against the ball are moved to open themselves up to the opponents while running so that they can inhibit potential objectives on time and remove them.

›› Look for opponent contact! Mark an opponent!

›› Time your running!

This instruction should help a player awaiting the ball to facilitate optimal continuation of the game with situationally appropriate running. The players must check their running speed and adjust it accordingly in order to prevent passes to the center or certain zones, or stop an idle phase after receipt of the ball.

›› Run in the circle! Pull into the circle! Start at the right moment!

›› Defend early!

This instruction is a strong indication to the defense to abandon an anticipatory and passive stance toward an early attack, similar to forechecking so that the opponent cannot approach their objectives without resistance. This instruction is supposed to create an agile, willing and sprint-ready attitude that does not lead to rash actions, but rather bold stealing of the ball, followed by opportunities and room for counter-actions.

›› Start again! Push forward! Run to the player with the ball! Push to the center!

›› Where are you standing?

In the short term, this instruction ensures quick orientation and can be swiftly implemented with a simple look to the side so as to receive a tactical follow-up to a teammate's actions with the ball. This instruction serves as a reminder of independent orientation in the area with the goal of better positioning.

›› Inside or out? Where are you? Middle of the space or outside?

›› Lurk on the edges!

This instruction can refer to one or more circles, and pertains to a curved and timed run on the corresponding circles. With regard to this run, this instruction strives for the players to start inward toward the middle of the circle or position themselves on the outside for a ball action.

›› Run in the curve! Pull in! Move to the side! Curved run!

1.7.4 Motoric instructions

›› Use visual feints!

This instruction aims to consider the playful nature of the game and the fun of faking opponents out, and requires players in possession to achieve benefits for an optimal continuation of the game via various feints. Shaking one's body for a clear training objective allows the players with the ball to escape opponent pressure and stay unpredictable.

›› **Use passing feints! Use closing feints! Indicate the dribbling!**

›› Combine running with deceiving!

This instruction tries to impact the repertoire of feinting and fake-out movements not solely related to ball control, and to make the player's agility stand out. It's about developing bodily awareness and to understand the usage of the body as the best feint there is.

›› **Make passing options possible with bodily feints! Trick with your body!**

›› Run on your front foot!

This instruction aims to influence individual running behavior and tells the players that an agile running style on the front foot facilitates optimal turning movements and explosive escape behavior. As a reminder of light-footed movements, this instruction tries to make the player think of optimal foot usage during the current playing situation.

›› **Stay mobile! Quick feet! Be light on your feet!**

›› Stand open to the direction of play!

This instruction concerns a player's position relative to the playing field and other players, and requires them to take an optimal position. A playing position through which the player has an optimal view of the playing field and which considers the critical spaces and zones is desired.

›› **Look into the field! Open position! Keep your perspective!**

1.8 READABILITY

This book is divided into the introduction, main body, and continuation. The introduction and its 40 introductory training forms aim to get players used to the circular shapes and fields. It primarily deals with perception of the playing field as a circle and becoming acquainted with and differentiating the center and outer areas, and different playing areas.

The introduction begins with small games, running and catching games. The methodical sequence of acclamation continues through process-oriented techniques and one-on-one or two-on-two forms, and ends with game and competition forms with small and mid-sized teams. The introduction thus presents information that serves to prepare players for the circular forms with greater numbers.

The main body contains the central circular forms. These 50 different forms embody the playing concept introduced here. Each circle form is distinguished by a unique shape and equally unique field. A specific game idea is presented for each form. This idea includes the various objectives. The images are used to sketch out the different elements of the game and are followed by coaching suggestions.

The continuation develops advanced ideas. In this section, 10 expansions are presented that can offer follow-up actions or additional solutions. These options can be applied to all central circle forms of the main body.

1.9 NAMING

The training forms presented each have their own name. The names stem from a simple explanation of the shape being used. These names help to recognize the shape and understand the image. More creative names are also possible. In these cases, the names are used to stir interest, rouse the imagination and incite enthusiasm. The names of the individual training forms can be used in the implementation with players on the field so that the terminology can tell a story, points can be emphasized, or motivation can be stirred.

1.10 PRACTICAL HELP

With help from some practical tips, constructing the circles on the training grounds is simple and quick. It is easiest when you lay out the shapes nearest to the center first, and then lay the outer markings. For some designs, it is sensible to first set a marking cone as an orientation point right in the center, which can then be removed after the design is complete (Fig. 15/1). A ball can also be used for this purpose.

Fig. 15: Marking the center

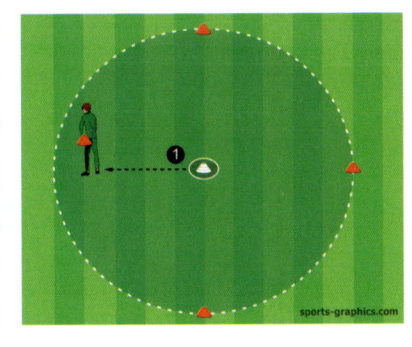

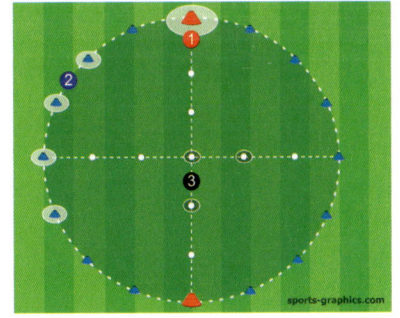

Fig. 16: Marking variants

Depending on the design, it is wise to use large, small and colored marking cones in conjunction with marking wedges, pads, slalom poles or coordination tires. The usage of these different marking elements should be based on the objectives and the resulting conduct with the ball. By this logic, large and easily visible marking cones are more suitable for zones far from the center (Fig. 16/1). Small marking cones are better for marking lines and circles that are played through when running or for combinations (Fig. 16/2).

The usage of flat marking wedges or pads is recommended when the area to be marked is frequently played through with the ball and there is a lot of dribbling or face-offs (Fig. 16/3). In essence, it is possible to lay out the different designs with a variety of marking cones. Depending on the shape and objective, it is possible to use circles that are laid out with a total of six markings (Fig. 17), eight markings (Fig. 18), or ten markings (Fig. 19).

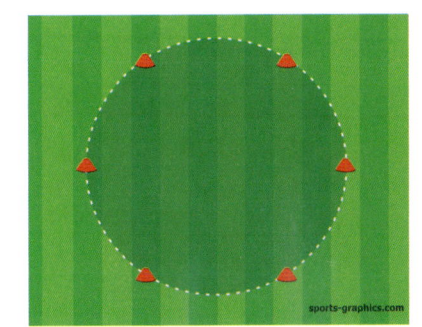

Fig. 17: Six markings

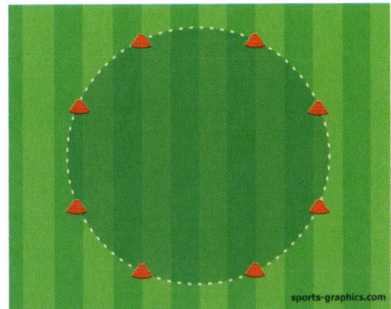

Fig. 18: Eight markings

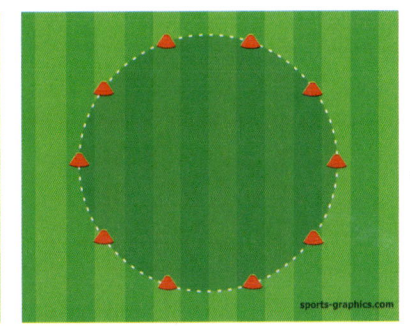

Fig. 19: Ten markings

For the sake of illustration and organization, some practice examples are shown on the following pages. This should highlight that small deviations and imprecise placement are not a problem. Impressions on fields of various sizes are also shown.

42 CIRCLE SOCCER TRAINING

Exemplary field structure

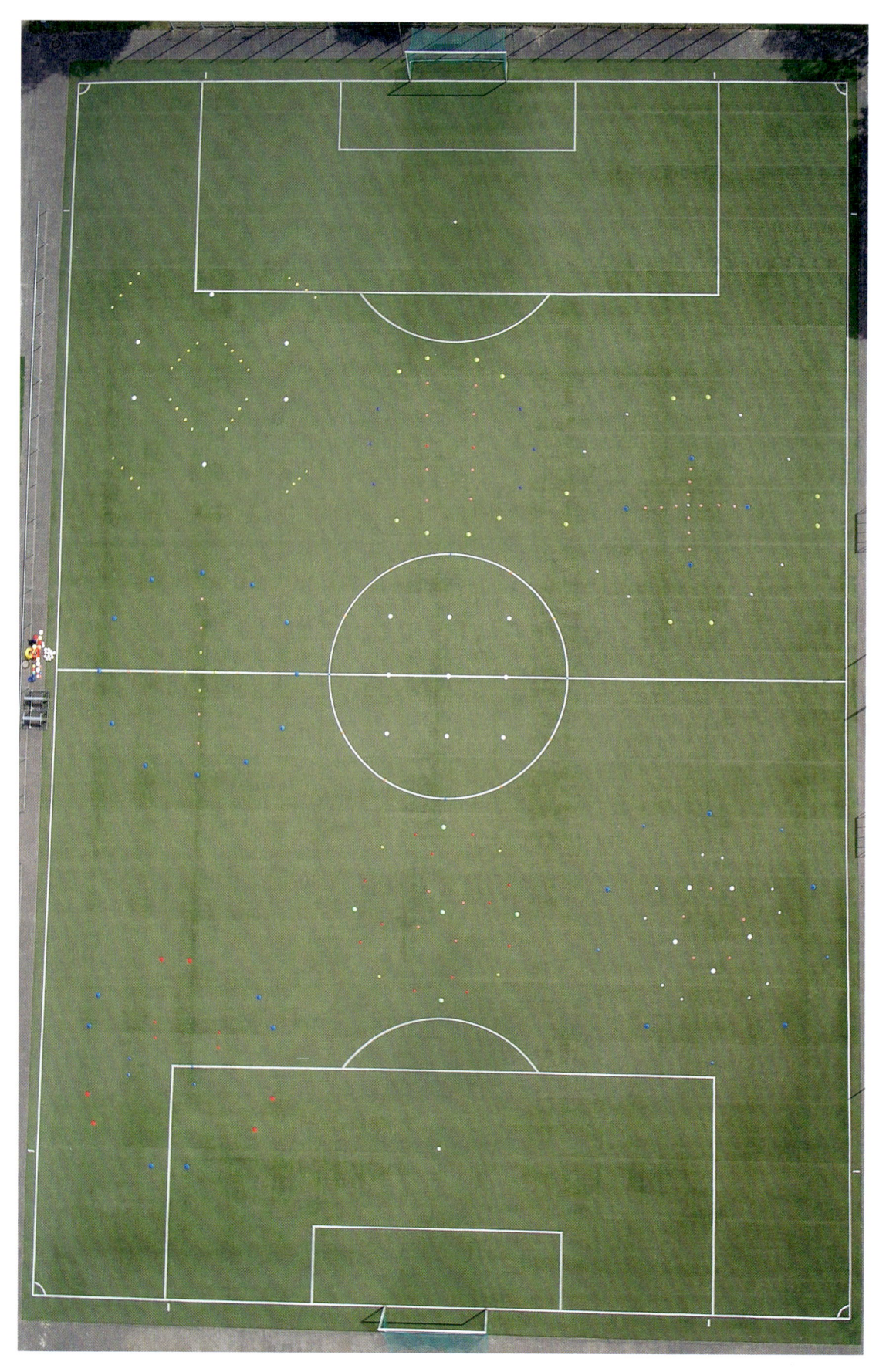

Fig. 20: Eight circular fields

INTRODUCTION 43

Exemplary field structure with zone markings

Fig. 21: Eight circular fields with zone markings

44　CIRCLE SOCCER TRAINING

Practice examples (aerial view)

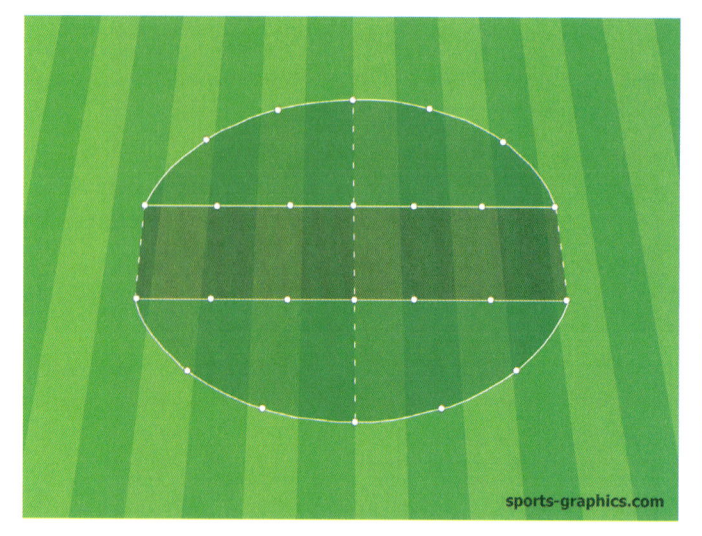

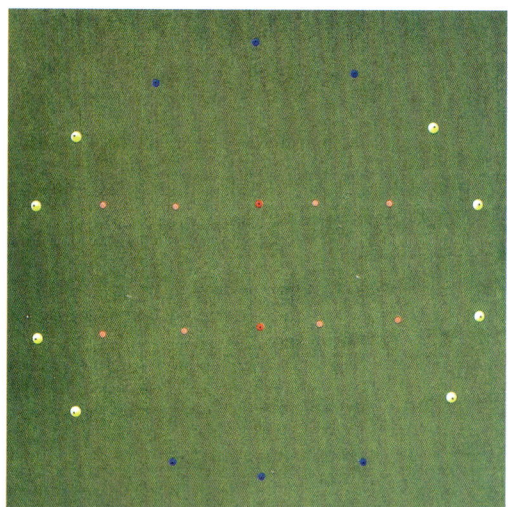

Fig. 22: Half-moon (pattern)

Fig. 23: Half-moon (practice)

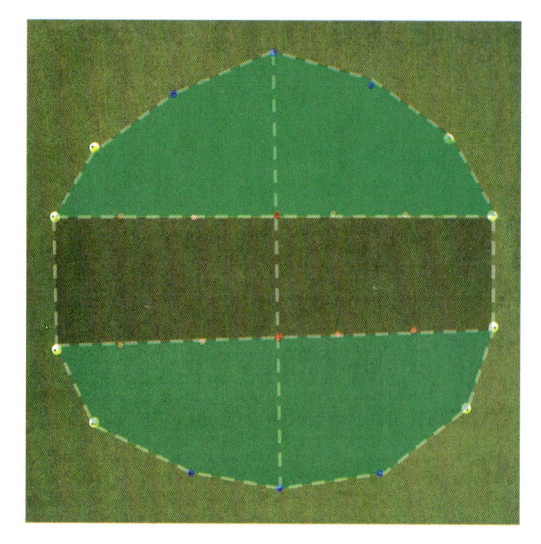

Fig. 24: Half-moon (comparison)

Materials: 8 large marking cones – 8 small marking cones – 8 marking wedges

Notes/sketches:

INTRODUCTION **45**

Practice examples (aerial view)

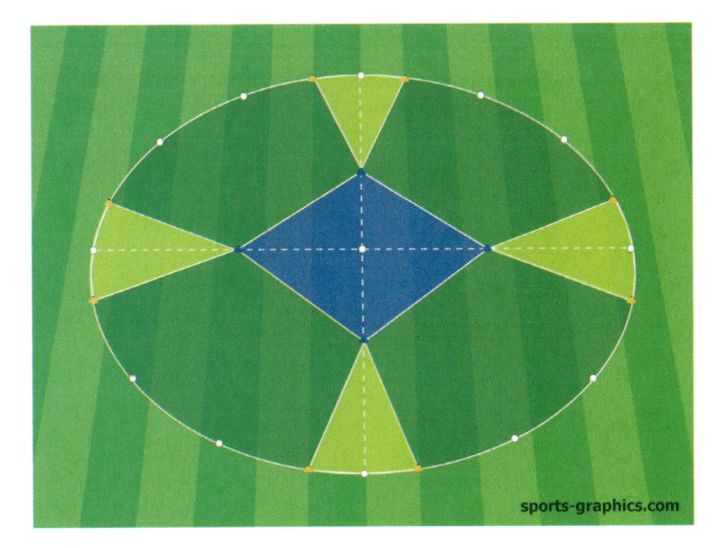

Fig. 25: Carousel (pattern)

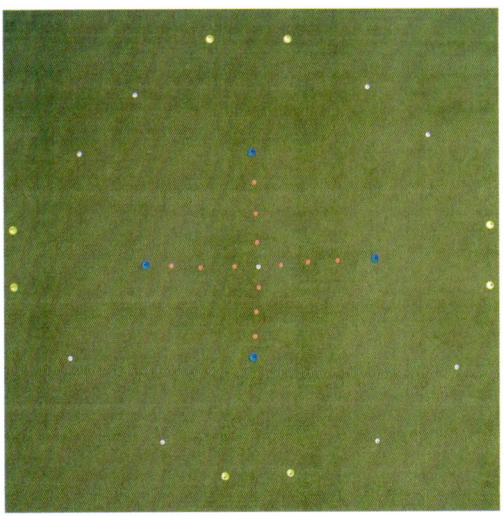

Fig. 26: Carousel (practice)

Fig. 27: Carousel (comparison)

Materials: 12 large marking cones – 9 small marking cones – 12 marking wedges

Notes/sketches:

46   CIRCLE SOCCER TRAINING

Practice examples (aerial view)

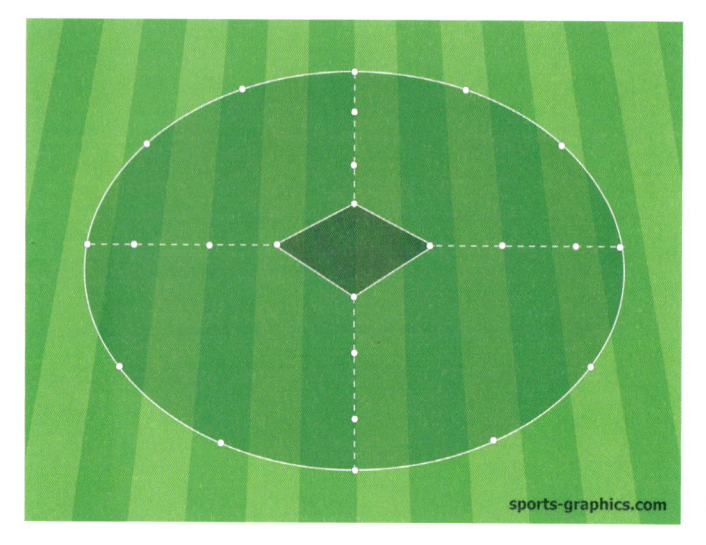

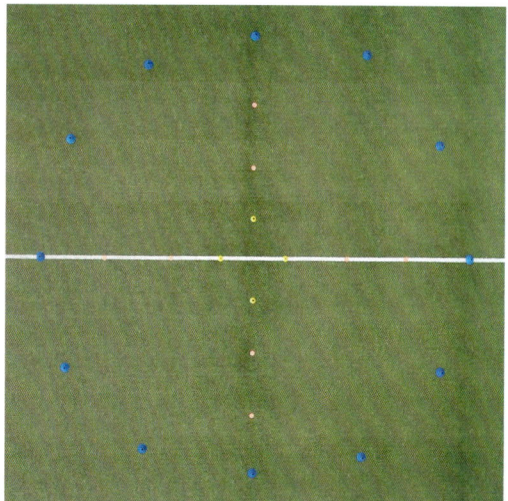

Fig. 28: Disk (pattern)

Fig. 29: Disk (practice)

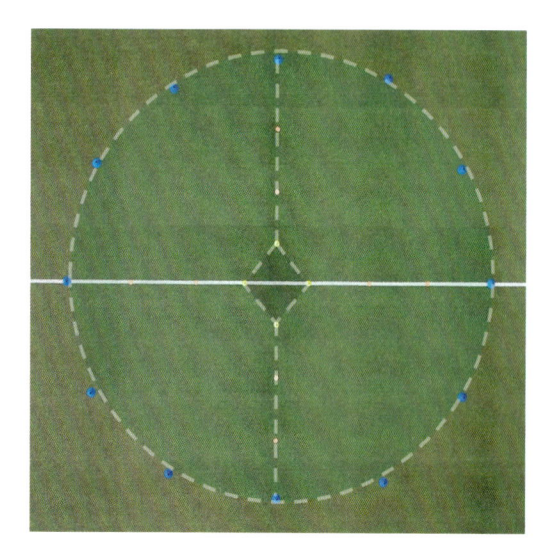

Fig. 30: Disk (comparison)

Materials: 12 large marking cones – 4 small marking cones – 8 marking wedges

Notes/sketches:

INTRODUCTION 47

Practice examples (aerial view)

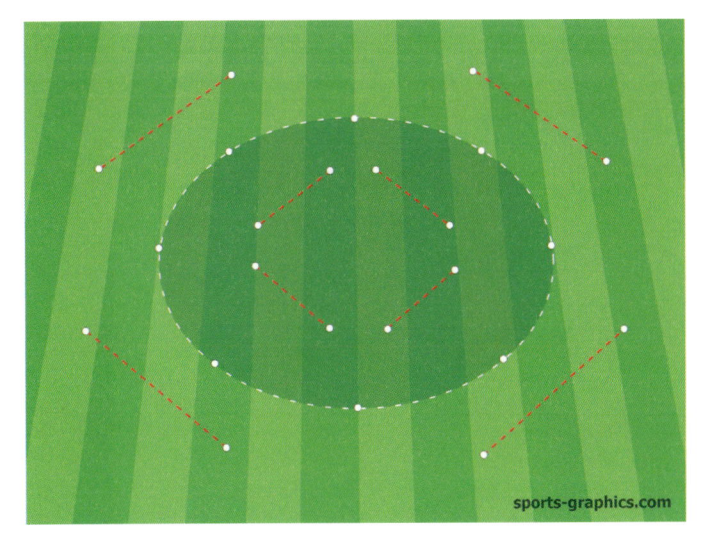

Fig. 31: Colosseum (pattern)

Fig. 32: Colosseum (practice)

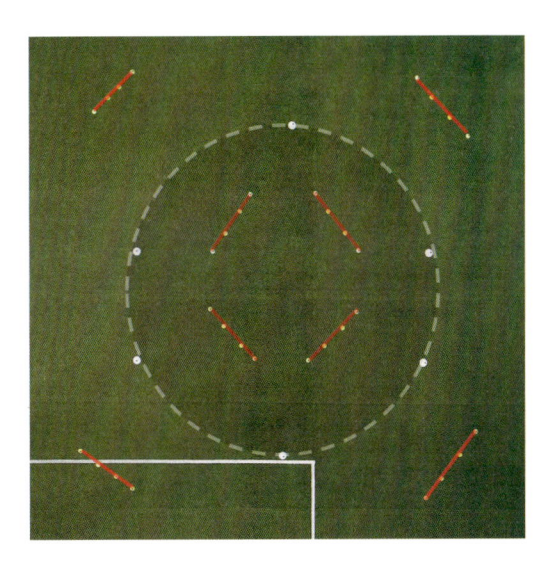

Fig. 33: Colosseum (comparison)

Materials: 6 large marking cones — 16 small marking cones — 16 marking wedges

Notes/sketches:

48 CIRCLE SOCCER TRAINING

Practice examples (aerial perspective)

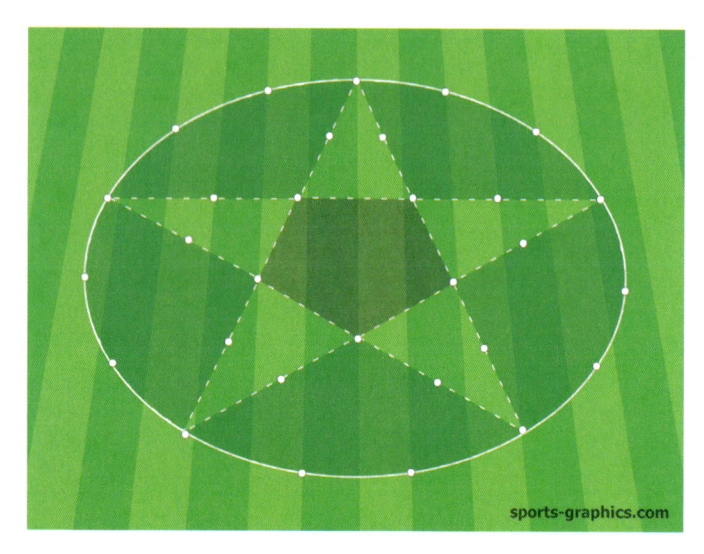

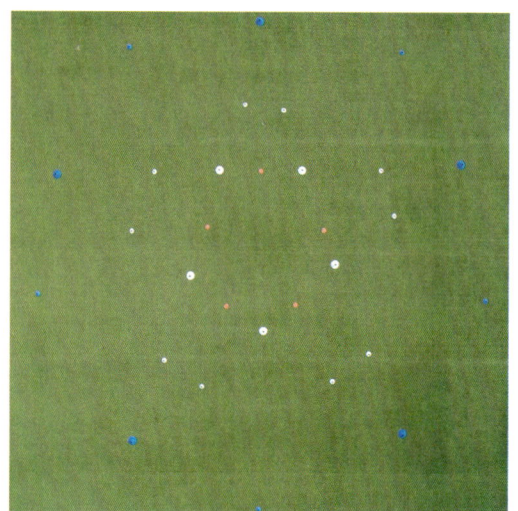

Fig. 34: Pentagram (pattern)

Fig. 35: Pentagram (practice)

Fig. 36: Pentagram (comparison)

Materials: 10 large marking cones – 15 small marking cones – 3 marking wedges

Notes/sketches:

INTRODUCTION 49

Practice examples (aerial perspective)

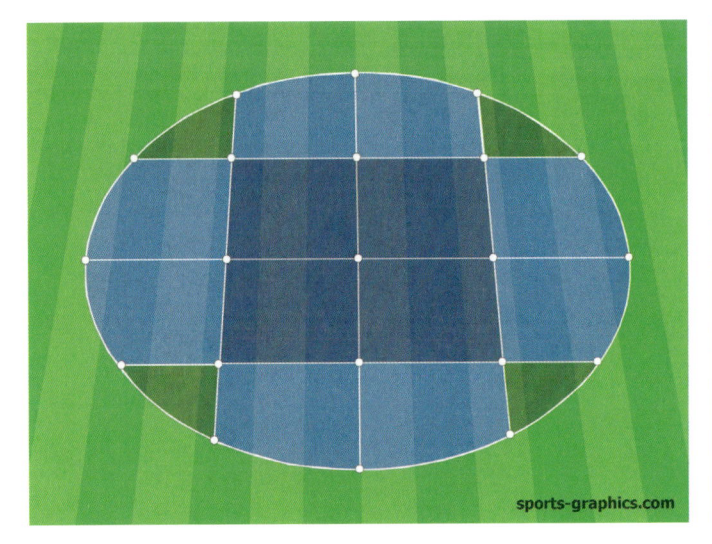

Fig. 37: Chessboard (pattern)

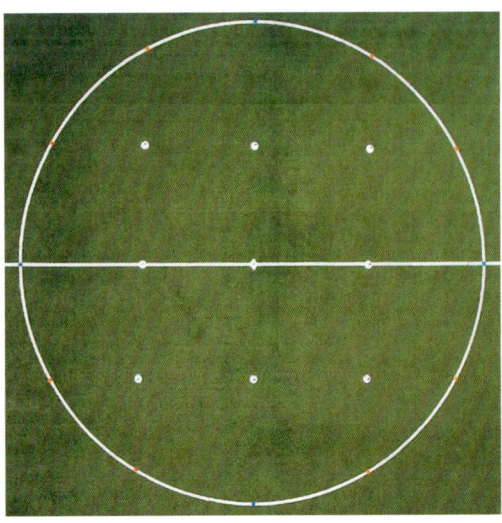

Fig. 38: Chessboard (practice)

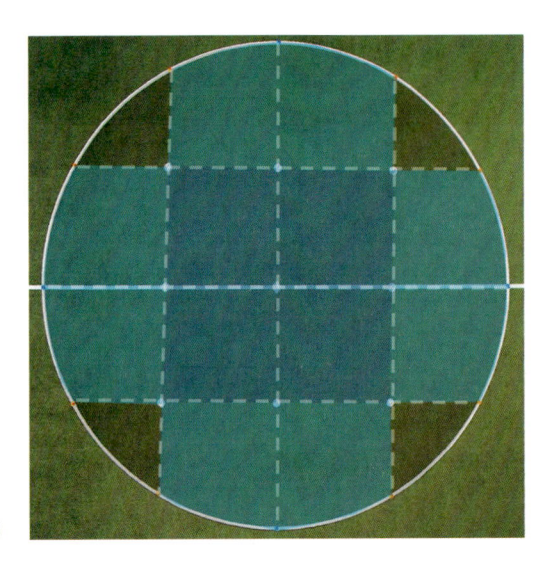

Fig. 39: Chessboard (comparison)

Materials: 9 large marking cones – 12 small marking cones

Notes/sketches:

50 CIRCLE SOCCER TRAINING

Practice examples (aerial perspective)

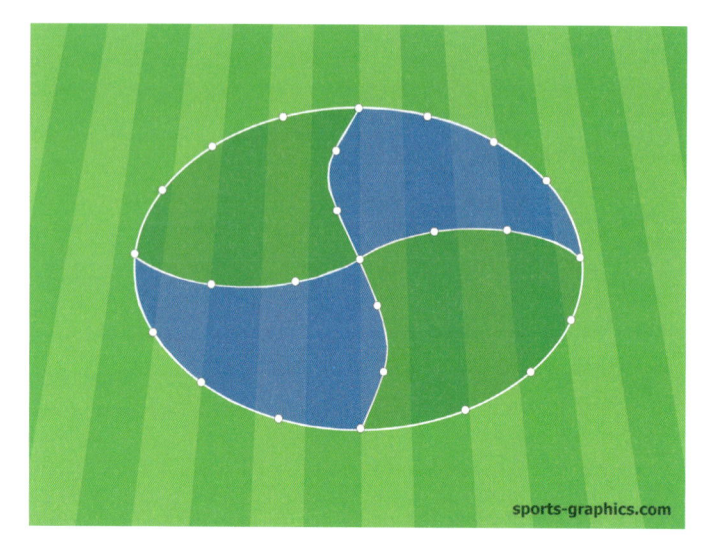

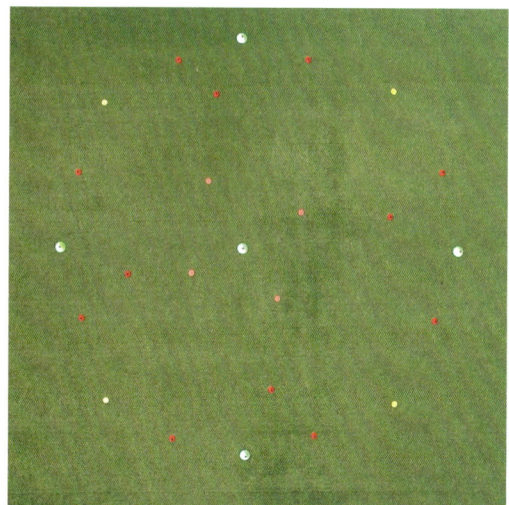

Fig. 40: Hurricane (pattern)

Fig. 41: Hurricane (practice)

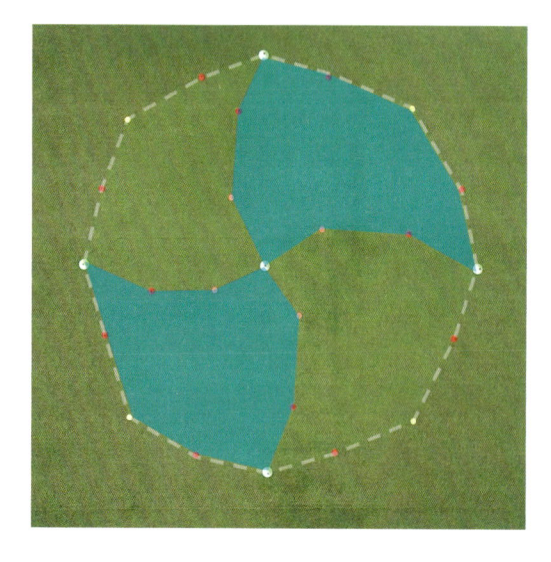

Fig. 42: Hurricane (comparison)

Materials: 5 large marking cones – 12 small marking cones – 8 marking wedges

Notes/sketches:

INTRODUCTION 51

Practice examples (aerial perspective)

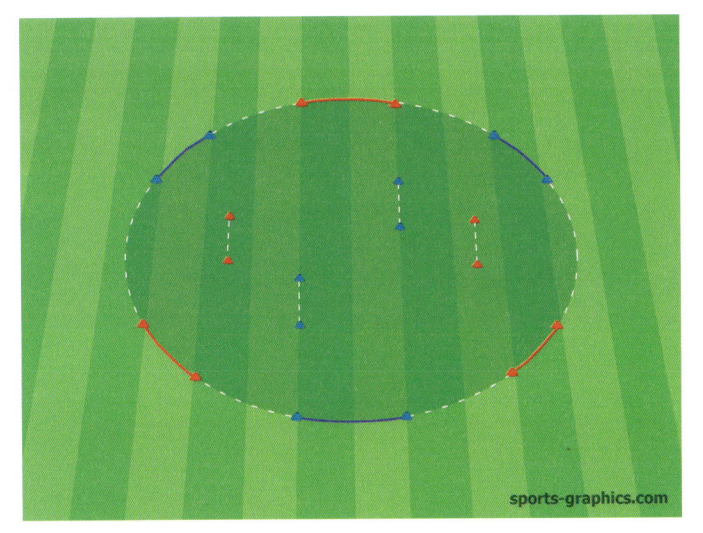

Fig. 43: Nucleus (pattern)

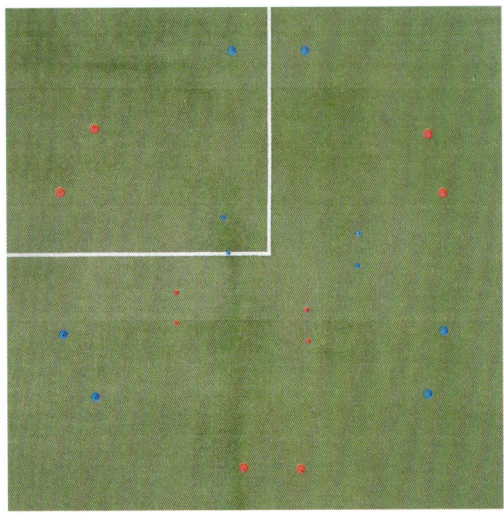

Fig. 44: Nucleus (practice)

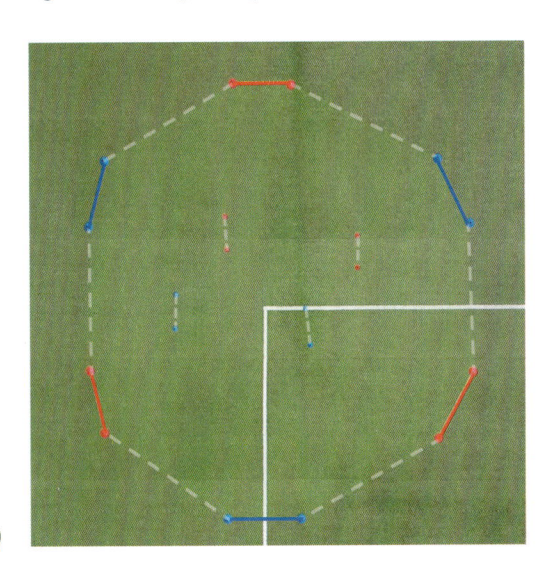

Fig. 45: Nucleus (comparison)

Materials: 12 large marking cones – 8 small marking cones

Notes/sketches:

Practice examples (side view)

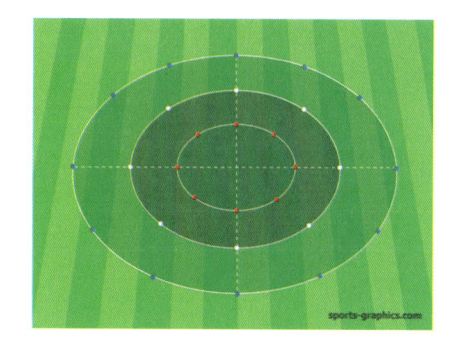

Fig. 46: Dartboard (pattern)

Fig. 47: Dartboard (practice)

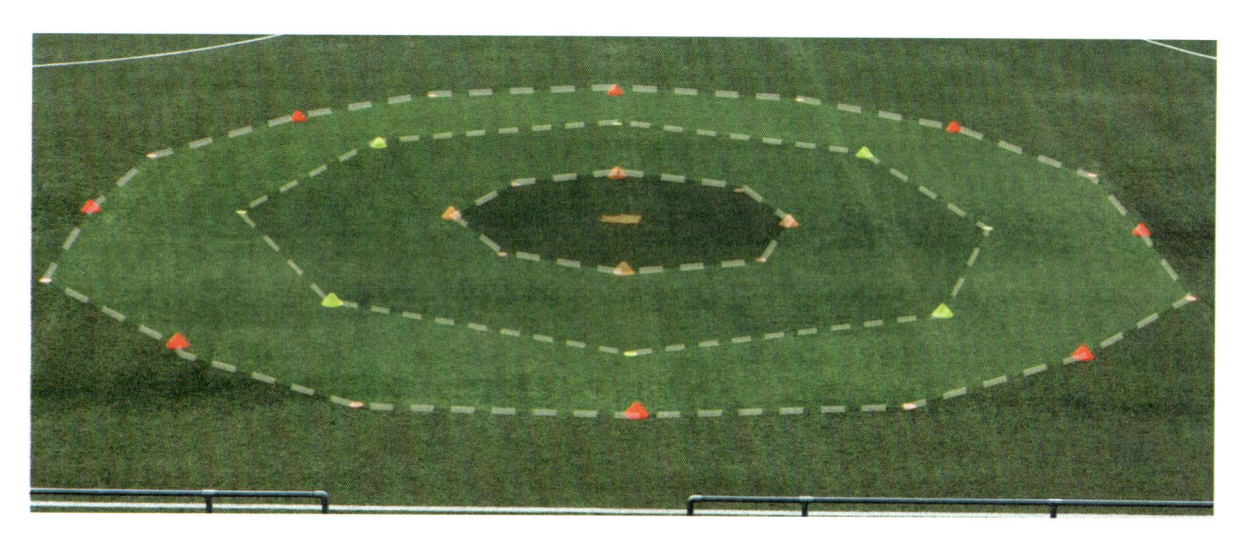

Fig. 48: Dartboard (comparison)

Materials: 16 large marking cones – 16 marking wedges – 1 marking jersey

Notes/sketches:

INTRODUCTION **53**

Practice examples (side view)

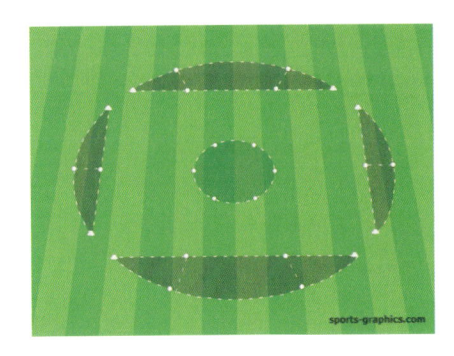

Fig. 49: Quattro (pattern)

Fig. 50: Quattro (practice)

Fig. 51: Quattro (comparison)

Materials: 30 large marking cones — 20 marking wedges

Notes/sketches:

54 CIRCLE SOCCER TRAINING

Practice examples (side view)

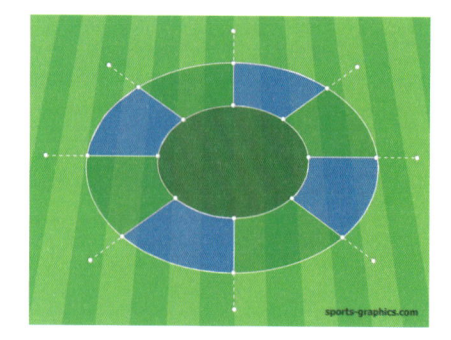

Fig. 52: Sun wheel (pattern)

Fig. 53: Sun wheel (practice)

Fig. 54: Sun wheel (comparison)

Materials: 8 large marking cones – 8 small marking cones

Practical help conclusions

The pictures should provide a fundamental overview of the actual structures, and attempt to illustrate that small deviations from the optimal layout are not very significant. The deviations should be ignored, and minor mistakes in the field structure do not affect the playing concept of the circle game patterns. This applies according to the materials used. It is not absolutely required that the pattern matches the exact number of large marking cones, small marking cones, or jerseys. Rather, there is enough leeway for creativity and the trainer's own unique touch in the structure.

INTRODUCTION

1.11 LEGEND

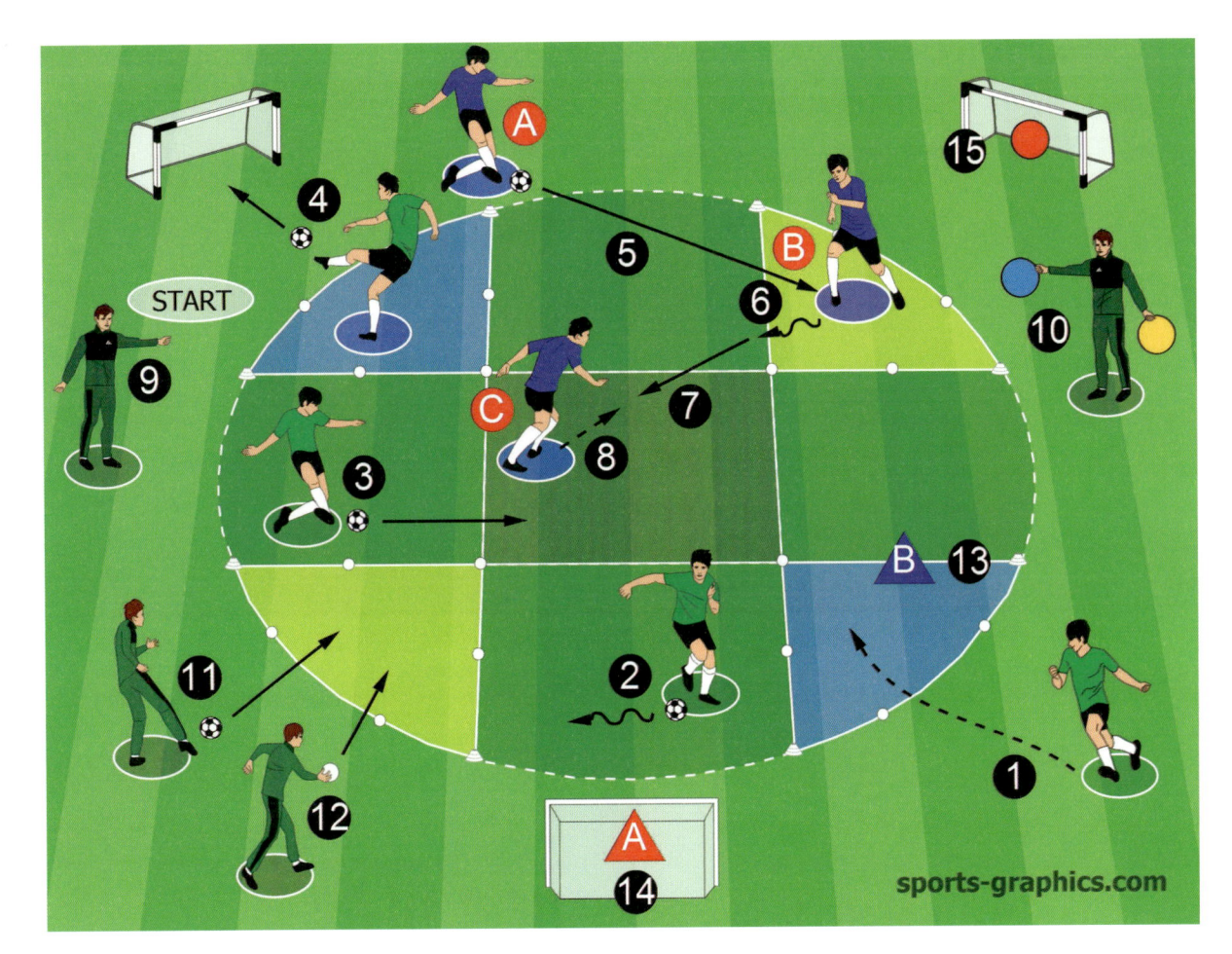

Fig. 55: Legend

① Path (dotted line)

② Dribbling (squiggly line)

③ Passing path (straight line)

④ Goal kick (straight line)

⑤ Player A passes to Player B

⑥ Player B completes the pass

⑦ Player B passes to Player C

⑧ Player C receives the pass

⑨ Acoustic trainer signal (speech bubble)

⑩ Visual trainer signal (color symbol)

⑪ Trainer foot pass

⑫ Trainer hand pass

⑬ Zone marking "letter"

⑭ Goal marking "letter"

⑮ Goal marking "color"

2 GETTING STARTED

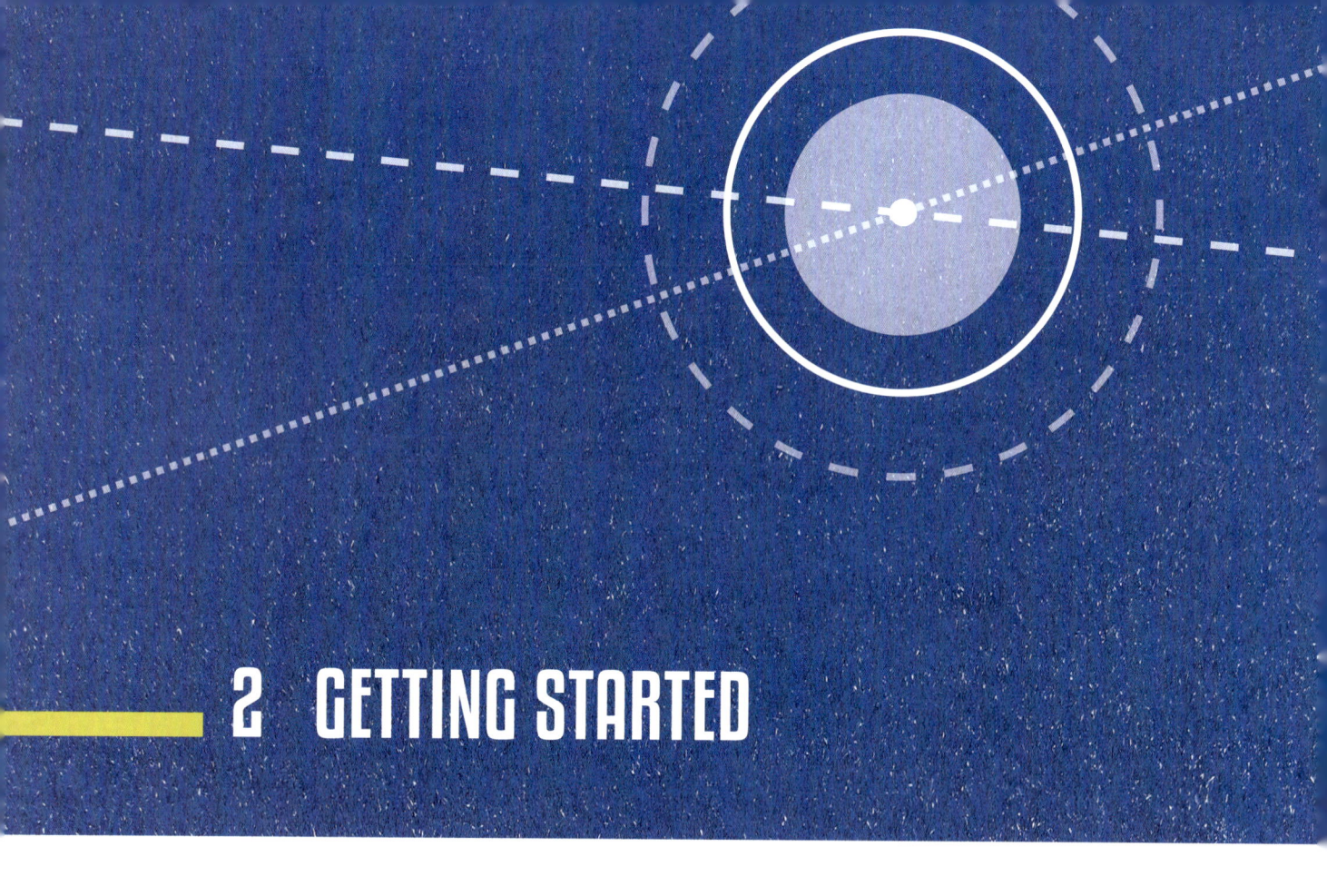

ORIENTATE 5VS3 CHAOS PLAY
SLALOM INDIVIDUALITY TEMPO RUN
TECHNICAL CIRCLE AGILITY ANTICIPATE
2VS2 RUNNING DUEL START TECHNIQUE
REACT DUALITY DRIBBLING RUN IMAGE
GROUP ACTIVITY
AGILITY ARCS 4VS2
1VS1 SMAL GAMES DECISIONS
RUNNING START STAGING COMPETITION
COMMANDS

2.1 RUNNING WITH FOCUS ON MOTOR SKILLS AND PROFILE

2.1.1 Archer – circuit 1 (arch run)

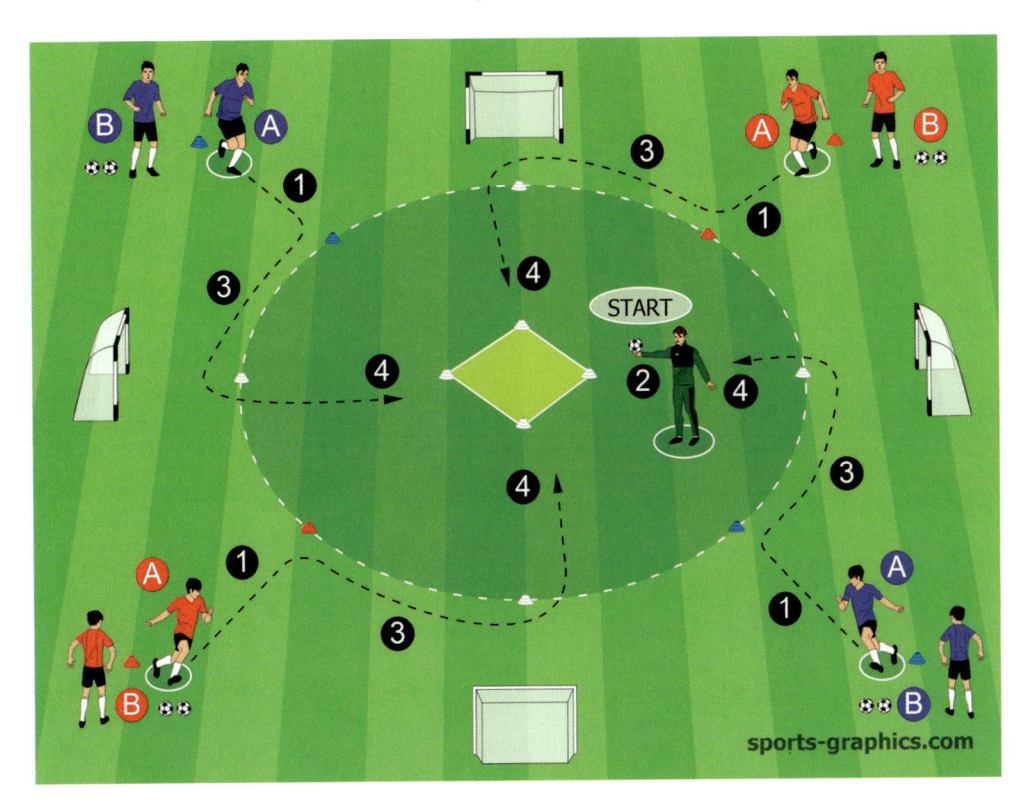

Execution, principles and elements

After the trainer gives the acoustic start signal, one player from each team runs from their own starting point toward the circle (see 1). While they run, the trainer drops the ball with only one hand (right hand here) (see 2), bounce (once here), and catches the ball again. Depending on the hand being used (right hand here), the players run around the circle in an arch (see 3). The bouncing of the ball (once here) determines how many marking cones must be run past before the players are allowed to run to the center of the circle (see 4). The training form prompts curved runs in the central circle edge, acknowledges awareness of the colored circle limit (see 3 and 4), and lets the players respond to a visual trainer signal. The run is then forced to the center and rewarded with a point assessment.

Provocation rules, point system and variants

The circle runs can be organized as one-on-one or team competition. The fastest player receives one point. The run up to the edge (see 1) can be variably organized with different elements of the running ABCs (sidesteps, high knee skips, etc.) or various starting positions (sitting, lying, etc.). The turn toward the center (3 and 4) can be specified with turning patterns (left/right). The requirements and content can increase and vary through ball execution (dribbling, feints, etc.) and shooting opportunities at the mini-goals.

2.1.2 Chronograph – circuit 2 (tempo run)

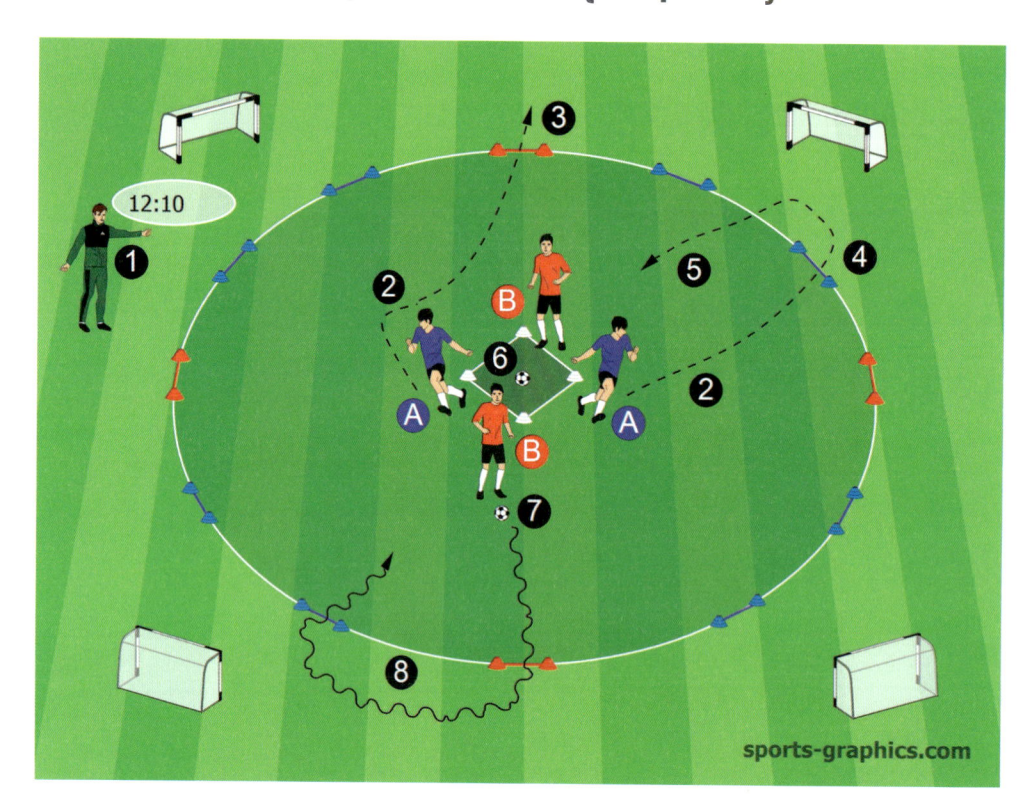

Execution, principles and elements

The edge of the circle, with different cone goals symbolizes the face of a clock. Two players from both sides act as a team and form the large and small hands of the clock. The pairs (A and B) position themselves at the center of the circle. The trainer then calls out a time (1). The players orient themselves (2) and run as quickly as possible to the goals corresponding to the hour (3) and minute (4), and back to the central diamond (5). The training form prompts awareness of the colored arc, orientation, processing of information, and transfer performance. The reaction and processing of the trainer signal is trained parallel to coordination with the teammate.

Provocation rules, point system and variants

The players can act under pressure from opponents and time because the trainer signal applies to both pairs simultaneously. The training form can thus be organized as a team competition with the earning of points for the faster team, or acquisition of the ball (6) for a subsequent two-on-two playing situation to the mini-goals. The requirements and content can vary through dribbling and feinting with the ball (7) as well as color signals (e.g. RED-BLUE) (8). The players' starting position may be diverse (sitting, lying, etc.) and variable. The complexity can be increased by having Team A respond to a daytime hour and Team B to a nighttime hour, with the respective other team operating as fielders.

GETTING STARTED **59**

2.1.3 Compass — circuit 3 (tempo run)

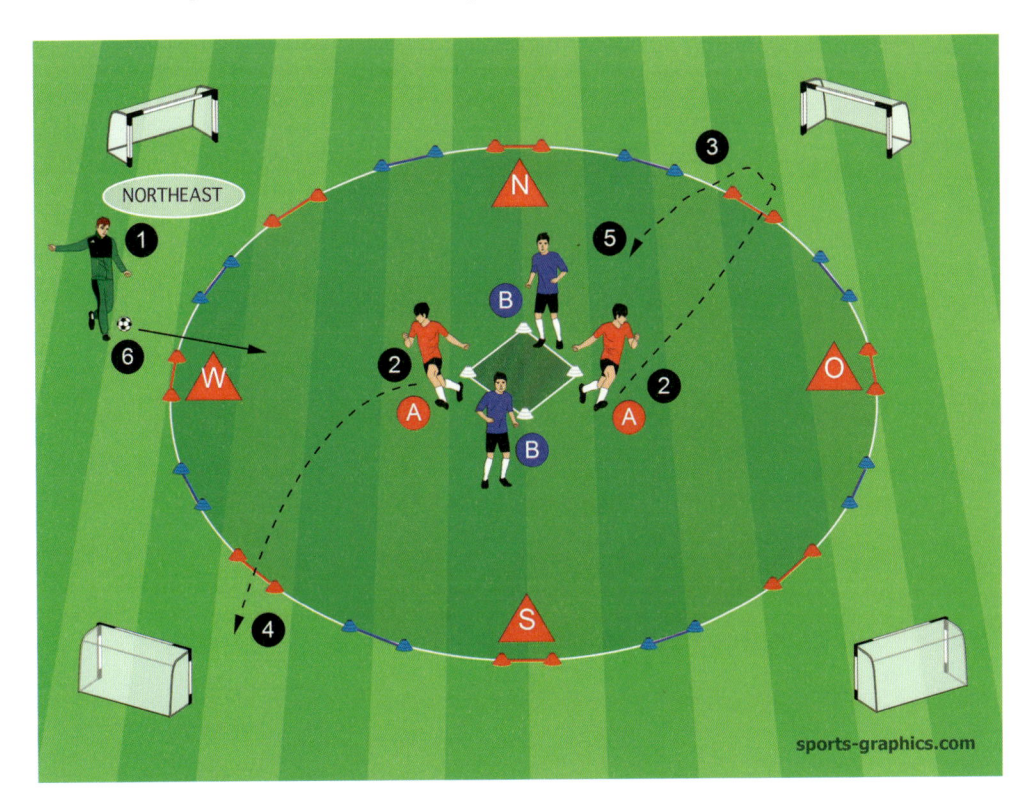

Execution, principles and elements

With different cone goals, the edge of the circle represents the directions of a compass. Two players from each team form a pair and play against the other pair. The pairs (A and B) position themselves at the center of the circle. The trainer calls out a direction (1). The players react (2) and one player runs in the direction that was called (3) while the other runs in the opposite direction (4). The players then run back to the central diamond (5).

Provocation rules, point system and variants

The runs can be organized as a team competition or one-on-one. One-on-one is possible by having both players racing toward the specified direction and corresponding cone goal, or by determining beforehand who will run in the specified direction and the opposite direction. For a team competition, both pairs act simultaneously and must reach the cone goals or the center faster than the opposing pair. The requirements and content may increase and vary through ball execution (dribbling, feint, etc.). After the runs, the trainer may pass (6) for a one-on-one or two-on-two situation toward the mini-goals.

2.1.4 Icebreaker – running duel 1 (tempo run)

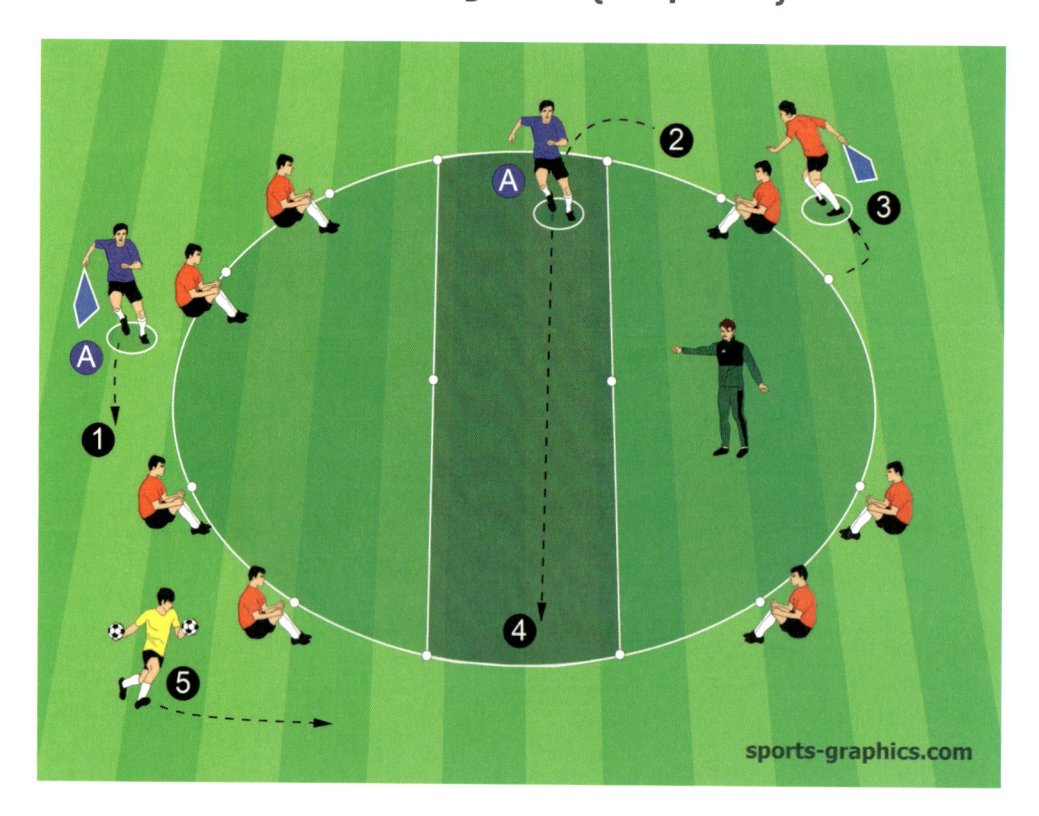

Execution, principles and elements

The players spread themselves around the circle in a sitting position, facing inward. Two runners hold a jersey (A) and run around the circle and the sitting players (1). Player As pick an opponent, placing the jersey over their back and thus turning them into a catcher. Player As then run away (2). The new catcher picks up the jersey and follows (3) in order to touch Player A with their hand before Player A has run through the middle corridor (4). The players practice running along a circle with subsequent tempo running to the center, and turning motions toward the middle. Holding onto a decision and unconditionally executing an action can also be emphasized. When the runner (Player A) passes over the target line during the tunnel sprint without having been touched by the opponent, the roles change.

Provocation rules, point system and variants

The requirements and content may increase and vary through ball execution (dribbling, feints, etc.). The players' starting position may vary (sitting, lying, etc.). Both Player As may run in opposite directions, resulting in resistance plays and more complex moments of awareness. Player As may also start with two balls in their hand (5) in order to drop one and continue dribbling with the other. This results in a dribbling contest.

GETTING STARTED **61**

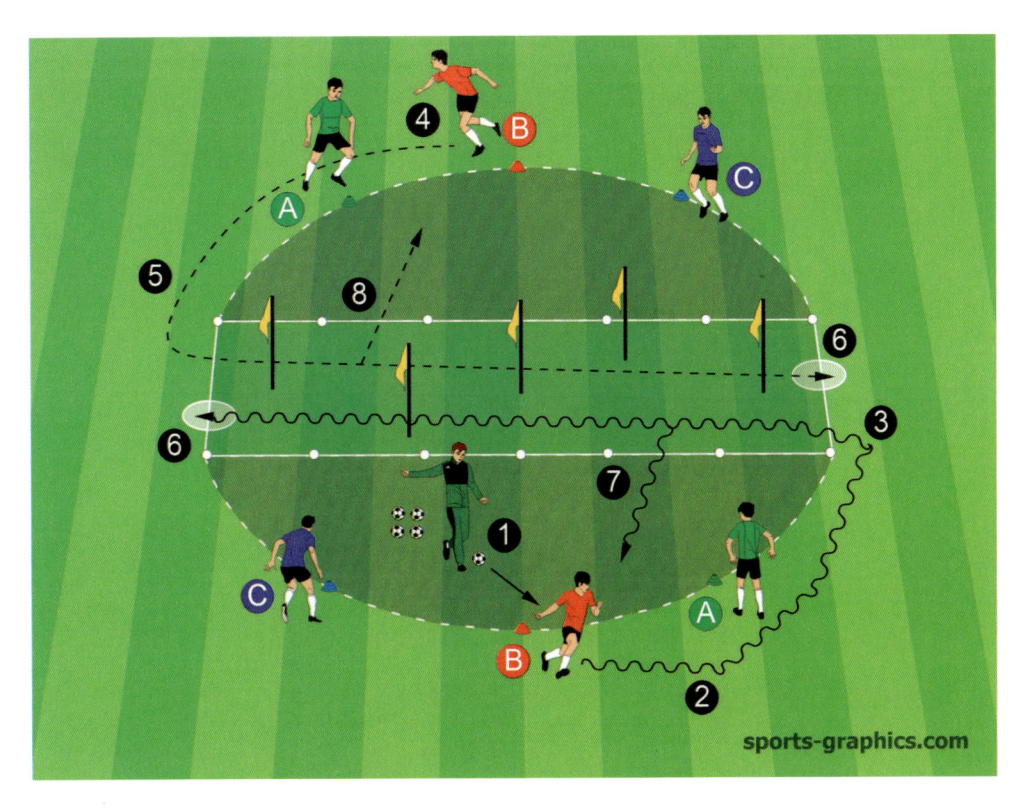

2.1.5 Crossing the line – running duel 2 (tempo dribbling)

Execution, principles and elements

The players form pairs (Pairs A, B and C) and spread out around the circle at their starting positions. The trainer passes to one of the players (1). The player with the ball (Player B here) takes the ball (2) and dribbles through the central corridor as quickly as possible (3). The partner reacts to the received pass (4) and runs opposite into the corridor (5). The first player to pass over the target line on the opposite side (6) wins. The focus here lies on making a decision (2) and subsequently adhering to it, and spirited execution of that decision through movement. The player with the ball also runs toward the center and threatens the opponent's danger zone. During the race, the players position themselves along the arc and the entrance and exit of the corridor.

Provocation rules, point system and variants

The requirements for the player with the ball may be increased by defining specific dribbling forms or feints. The training form may also be organized as a catching game. The hunting player reacts, steers toward the same entrance, and tries to tag the player with the ball before exiting. The players' starting position may vary (sitting, lying, etc.). Furthermore, the player with the ball may be able to exit via the half-circle (7), to which the opponent must respond (8). Additional running tasks may be required at the central slalom poles in order to run slalom races.

62 CIRCLE SOCCER TRAINING

2.2 CATCHING WITH FOCUS ON AGILITY AND DEXTERITY

2.2.1 Earth's core – catching game 1 (handball)

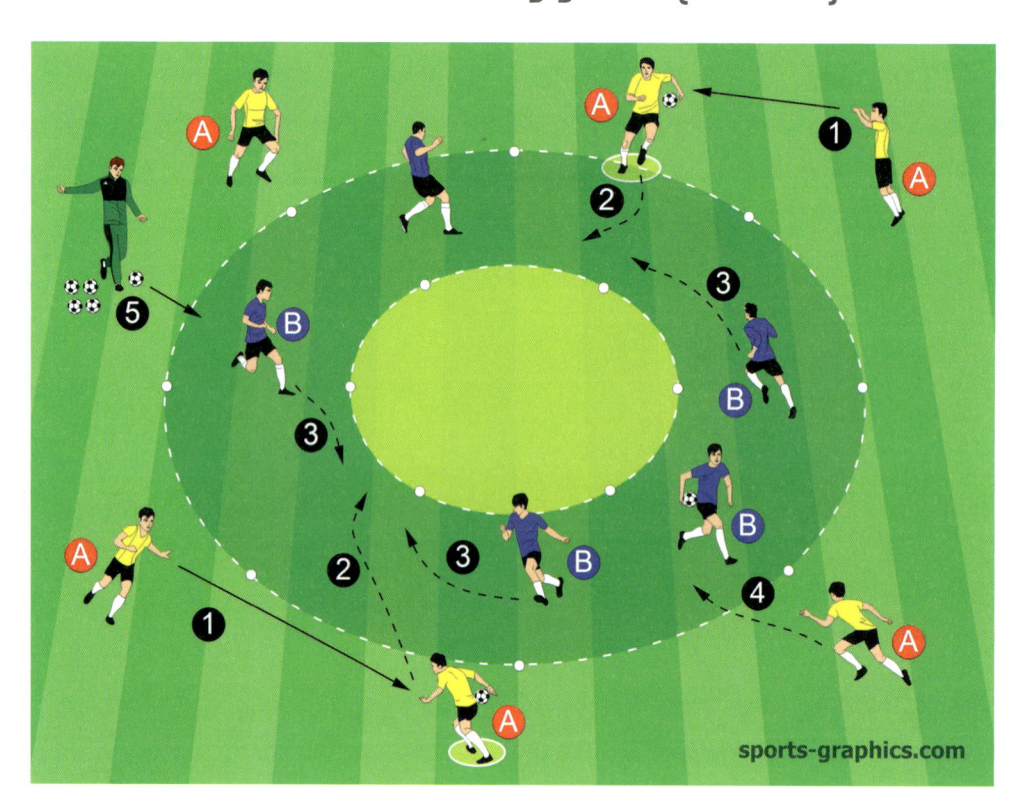

Execution, principles and elements

Player As pass the ball to each other by hand outside of the circle (1) and try to use gaps to penetrate to the center of the circle with a run and the ball in their hands (2), without being tagged by the opposing players (Player Bs). The players with the ball should provoke, recognize, and boldly use gaps in the opponents' defensive wall. A run toward the center (2) that has already begun can be interrupted by a return pass. The focus lies on courageous and unconditional orientation toward the center. However, an action can be disrupted and reorientation is also possible.

Provocation rules, point system and variants

The requirements can be increased in that the players with the ball bounce it while running (2), execute running tasks (e.g. turns), or must keep dribbling the ball. In a second step, the players with the ball can be forced to run back to the outer edge after reaching the center without being tagged. The intensity can be amplified by a point competition with a time limit, with points being won when a player reaches the center without being tagged by an opponent (Team A), or a player with the ball can be tagged (Team B). Alternatively, the players in the center can each be holding a ball and trying to knock out the incoming players with this ball (4). The trainer can also commence a five-on-five playing situation with a pass (5).

2.2.2 Geocenter – catching game 2 (dribbling)

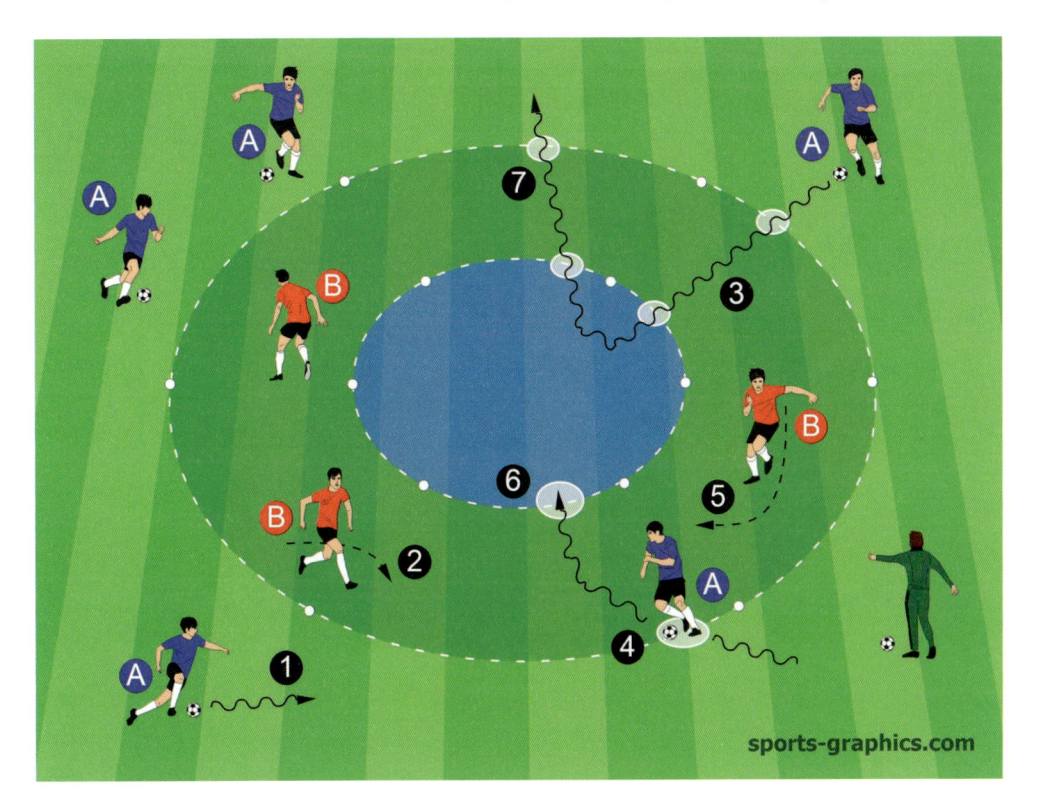

Execution, principles and elements

Player As possess the ball outside of the circle and are dribbling (1). Player Bs defend the center and move around as a wall (2). Player As try to detect gaps and use them through dribbling (3) to reach the center of the circle without being tagged by an opponent. After the circle has been entered (4), Player B's can become active (5) and tag the players who have the ball. The focus lies on the bold and unconditional orientation toward the center. Even after an unsuccessful attempt, the players remain in possession of the ball and may start a new offensive a short time later.

Provocation rules, point system and variants

The defending players receive a point when they tag one of the opponents who has the ball. The offensive players receive a point when they reach the center without being tagged (6). Double points can be awarded when the players reach the center and then return to the outer edge without being tagged (7). The requirements can be increased by having the player with the ball perform a specific feint while running (3).

2.2.3 Ringed planet – catching game 3 (dribbling)

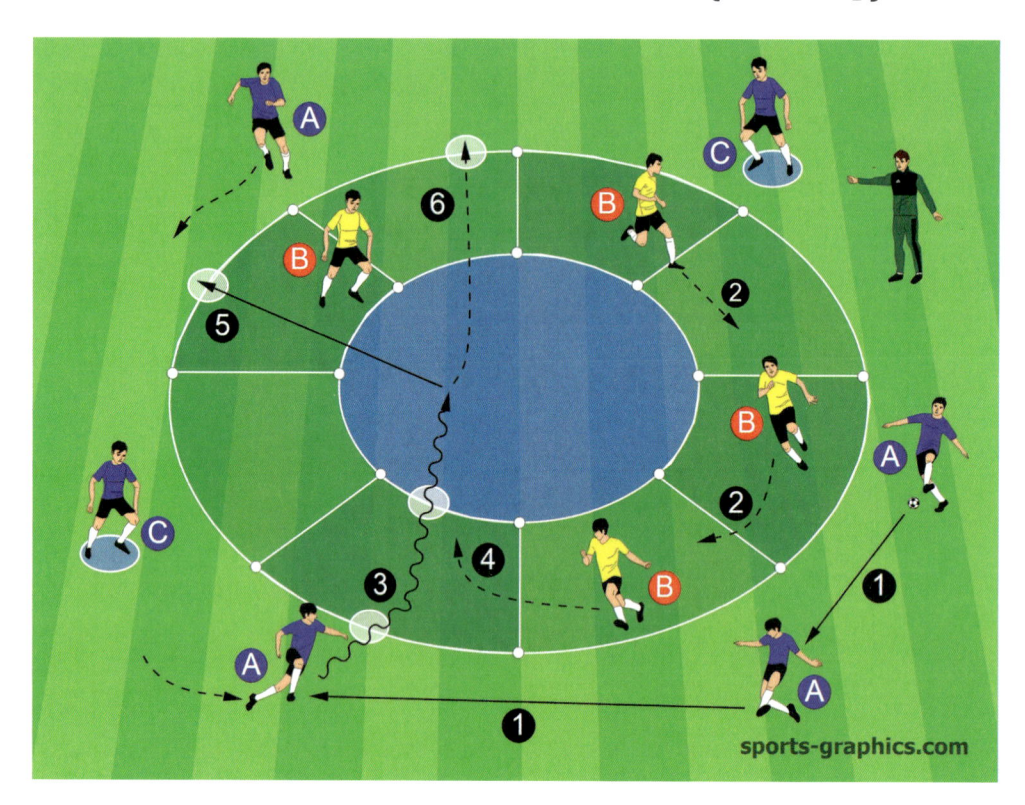

Execution, principles and elements

Player As circulate a ball among themselves (1). Player Bs move like a wall to defend the center (2). Player As try to dribble into the center of the circle with a player in possession of the ball (3) without being tagged by an opponent (4). After successfully reaching the center, the player with the ball must deliver a pass outside of the circle (5) in order to run to position (6) and thereby score a point. The focus lies on courageous and unconditional orientation toward the center. After reaching the center, a follow-up action (5 and 6) is required. The actions toward the center should be prepared according to the situation (1), and sustainably and boldly implemented after the decision has been made (3, 5 and 6).

Provocation rules, point system and variants

In order to increase concentration and precision, the players with the ball can have a ball contact quota while passing (1) and dribbling (3). A certain feint (stepover, fake pass, fake shot, etc.) may be required before the pass in the central zone (5). The number ratio should be configured such that the outside players can be in the majority (Player Cs).

2.2.4 Nucleus – catching game 4 (dribbling)

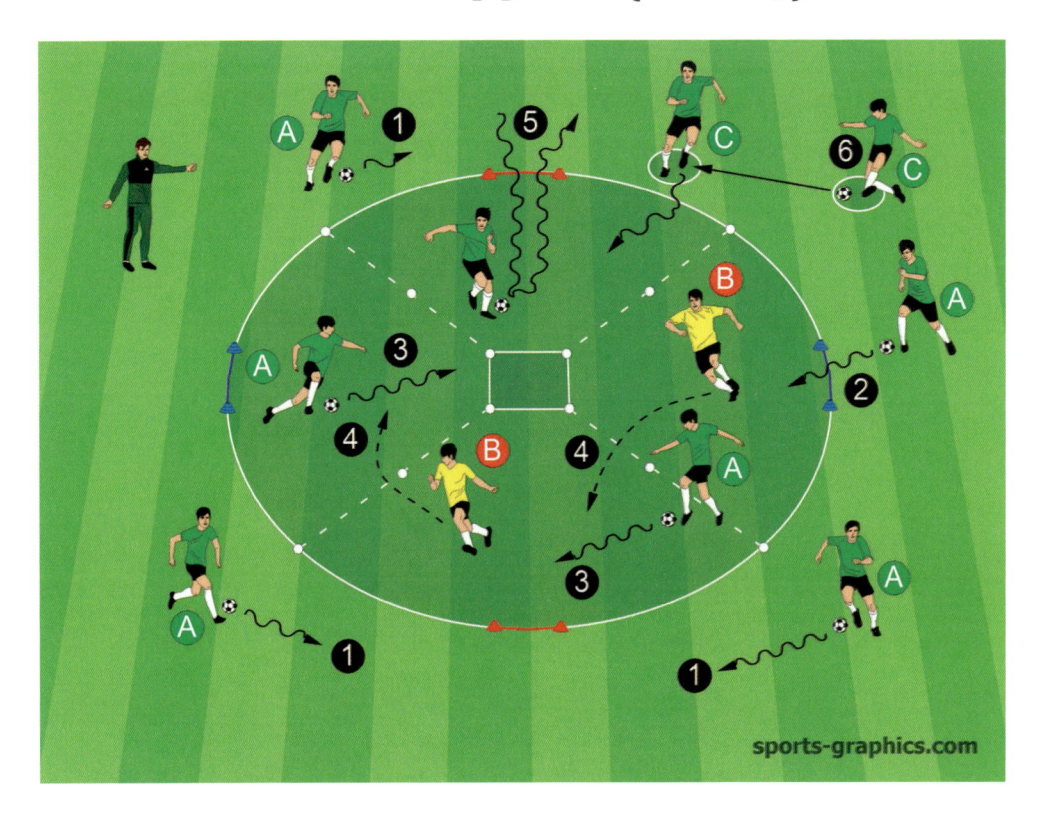

Execution, principles and elements

Player As each have their own ball and dribble around the outside of the circle (1). Player As try to get into the circle (2) through the central field if possible, and back to the outside (3) without being tagged by a Player B (4). The players may only enter the circle through one of the four cone goals (2) and must dribble through another cone goal when exiting to earn a point. The players practice their orientation toward cone goals on the arc and colorful entries and exits.

Provocation rules, point system and variants

The player earns one point when they exit through a different-colored cone goal. Double points are earned when the player exits through the same-colored cone goal, and triple points when they are able to dribble through the central field when doing so. The central field can be declared a safe zone where the catchers cannot act. The training form becomes more difficult when the players with the ball have to perform one feint for each circle sector, or must fulfil dribbling tasks (left, right, alternating, etc.). Cut movements with entry and exit through the same cone goal can also be combined (5). It is also possible for two players to function as a team (Player Cs) (6).

2.2.5 Orbit – catching game 5 (obstacle)

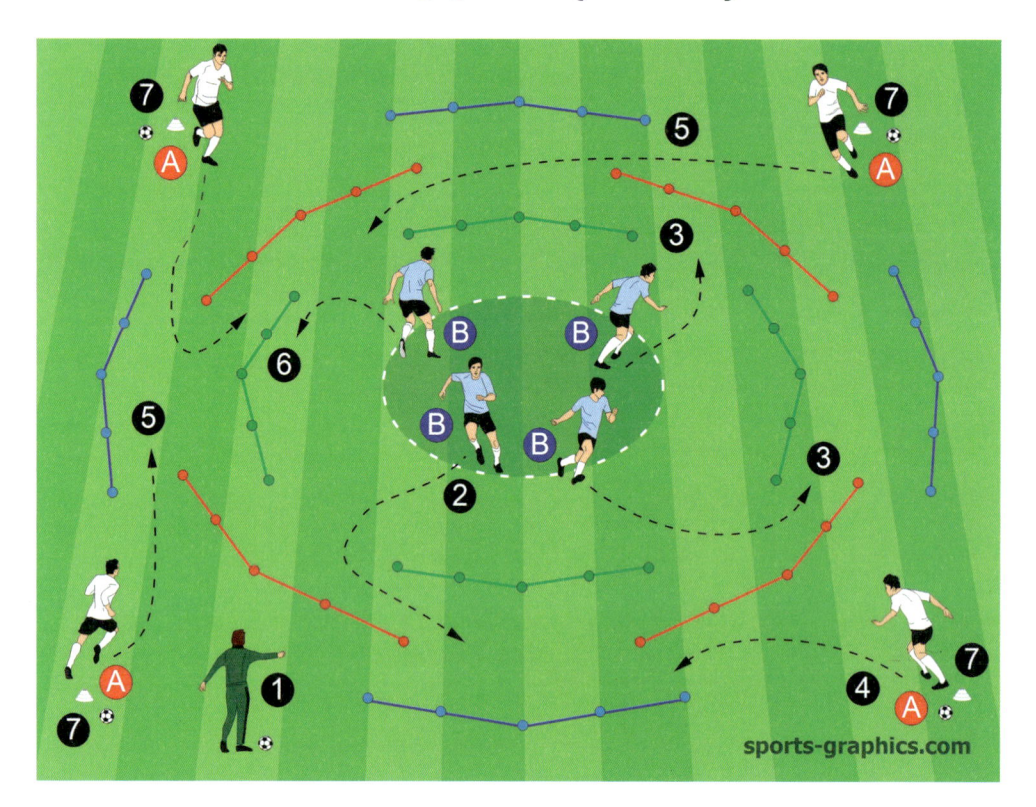

Execution, principles and elements

The field consists of an inner, central circle and multiple circular and arching lines, color-coded with multiple marking cones. Outside of the field are four starting positions. Player As position themselves at the outside starting position, and Player Bs do so in the central circle. After the trainer gives the signal (1), Player Bs (2) react and start to leave the circle without being tagged by an opponent. Player Bs may not run over the lines (3), but instead must use the interim spaces with curved runs. Player As also react to the trainer's signal (4), but are also unable to run across the lines (5), and rather must try to catch Player Bs and tag them. Player Bs respond to the catchers' running paths and may use the lines strategically (6).

Provocation rules, point system and variants

The catching game can be played with a ball, thus making it more difficult. Player As each pass a ball into the center (7) and Player Bs must get out of the circle while dribbling with their feet without being tagged. Points can vary, e.g. a catcher receives more points the closer they are to the center when they tag an opponent.

2.3 TECHNICAL FORMS WITH FOCUS ON BALL HANDLING, COORDINATION AND TWO-FOOTEDNESS

2.3.1 Asteroid — squad competition 1 (passing)

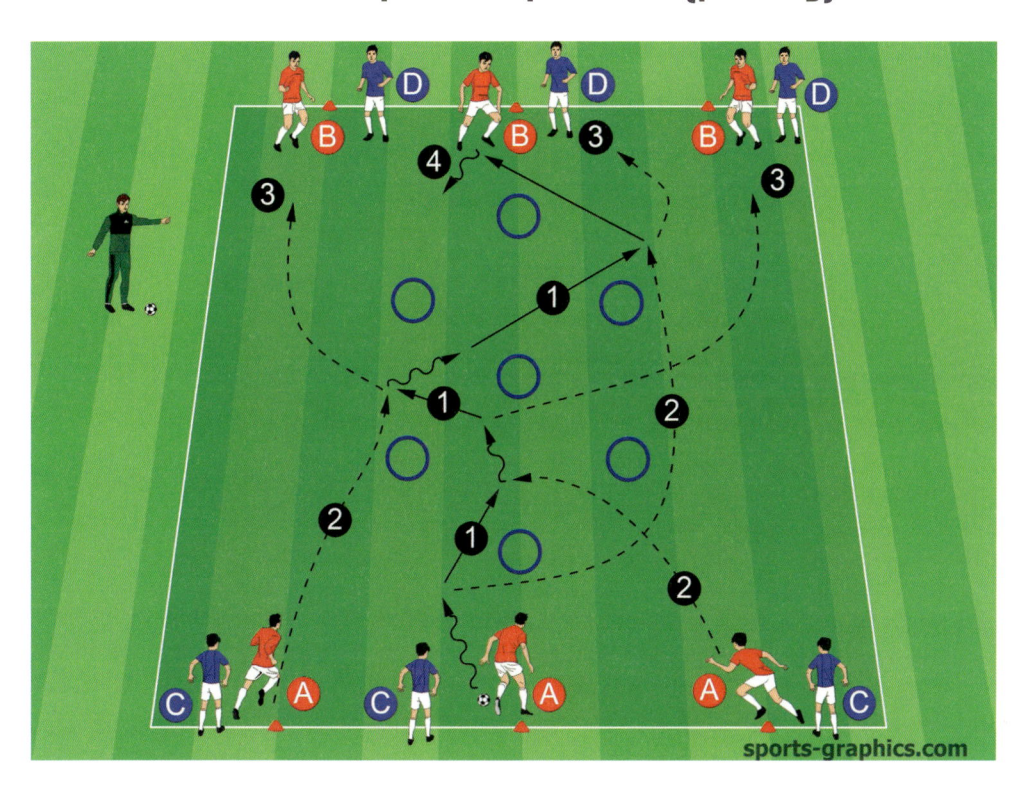

Execution, principles and elements

The players work in teams of three. Team A starts out in possession of the ball in three starting positions, and then heads toward the center. In the center, there are multiple coordination tires. The player with the ball passes it deep to one of the coordination tires (1), in the path of a teammate. The teammates move freely, with paths deep into the field, and may only start running after the pass has been made. The ball must always have been passed to the tires in front of the recipient (1 and 2). The reacting team takes the waiting position on the opposite end (3), after a subsequent pass to the new group, and Team B starts a new play-through (4).

Provocation rules, point system and variants

Circular fields with marking cones may be used instead of the coordination tires. This creates more wiggle room for the players, with just as many more variations. For example, the players can be required to have stepped into the coordination tires while running (2), or take the ball directly into one of the marked fields. Two teams may also start simultaneously, so that the team playing on the other side of the field functions as an obstacle, providing more complex incentive. Passes by hand may also be allowed. It must be ensured that the players always select different running paths.

2.3.2 Meteor – squad competition 2 (taking the ball)

Execution, principles and elements

The players work in teams of three. Team A starts out with possession of the ball and starts toward the center from three starting positions. There are multiple half-circles and arcs in the center placed with marking cones. The players combine pass and running paths to reach the other side, performing certain tasks as they do this. The players run around the arcs and receive a pass in order to dribble through the arcs (1). They then dribble through the arcs with a feint (2), or alternatively play around the arcs in a zig-zag or bypassing the third player (3). They then pass the ball through the last arc (4) to the next group, and take on the opposing positions (5). The goal (6) is precise positioning and running with clearly defined objectives and target zones.

Provocation rules, point system and variants

The arcs can be played through with specific passing techniques or linked with feints, and can be configured in a variety of ways. The return (Team B) can be organized with deep passes through the arcs. Neutral players can also be used and integrated into the pass combinations (7).

2.3.3 Ferris wheel – free passing 1 (colored goals)

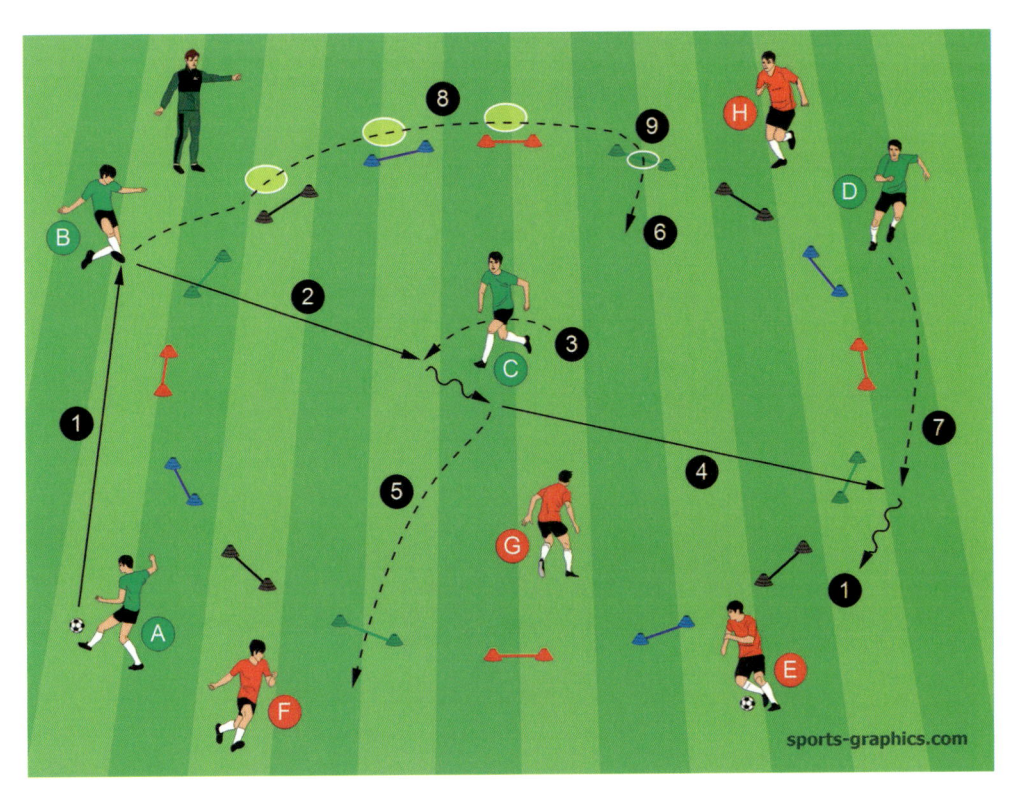

Execution, principles and elements

The players have one ball per team. One player from each time (here Player Gs and C) is in the middle of the circle. The other players are outside of the circle and circulate a ball with free passes (1). The players may pass to the players in the middle. Then the player who made the pass switches places with the player in the center. The play to the center is coupled with a follow-up action. The follow-up action should be similar to a match, namely in the form of concise processing, controlled dribbling, or a finishing outward pass. The running paths should be precise and along the edge of the circle (8), and combined with piercing cut movements (9).

Provocation rules, point system and variants

The players can be instructed to perform certain pass and running paths as per the colored or neutral cone goals, configured with the color of the teams' jerseys. After a pass from outside through a like-colored cone goal (2), the opposing center player (3) can pass the ball back outside (4) through a like-colored cone goal as a follow-up action. The players can change positions through the cone goals that have not been played (5 and 6) before the next player becomes active (7).

2.3.4 Ringside seat – free passing 2 (colored goals)

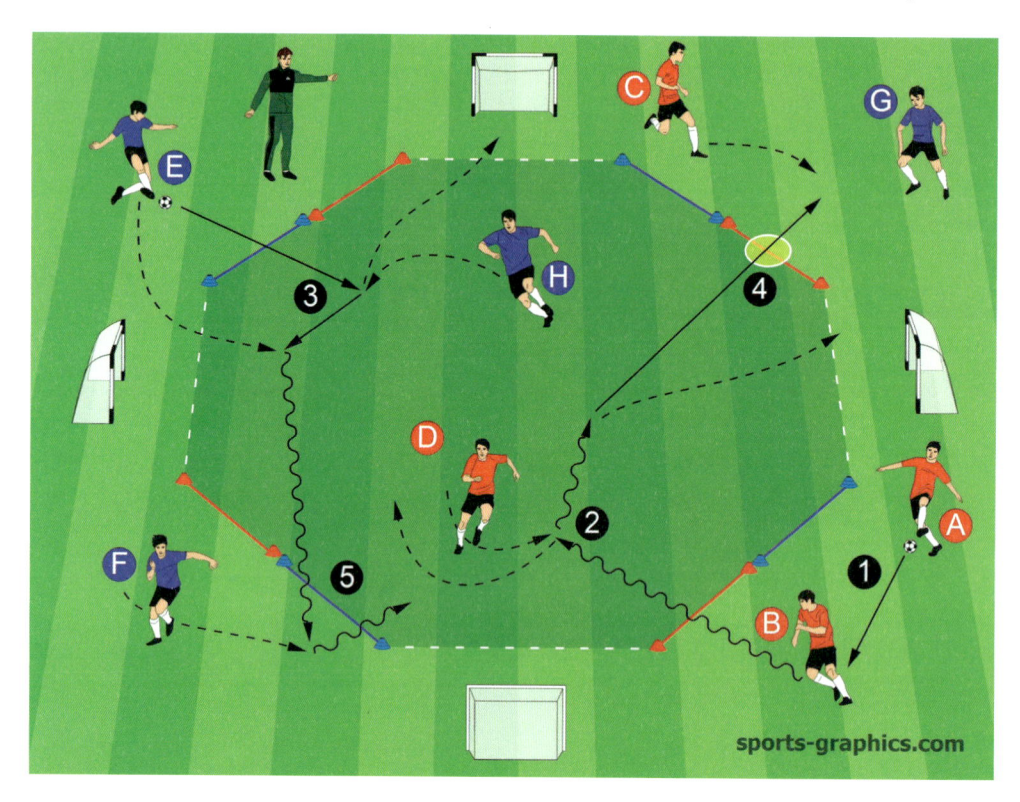

Execution, principles and elements

The teams each pass a ball freely among themselves. One player is always in the circle and the others are outside of it. The players can enter the circle through the colored and neutral cone goals, exit again, and change positions. The players first let the ball stay outside (1). Passing and positioning rules can be set for pass combos and position alternations. The players prepare to pass to the center. This pass to the center always means a follow-up action with passing and running in order to leave the center again in different directions.

Provocation rules, point system and variants

The outside players can induce a position switch, e.g. via simple dribbling into the circle (2) or a double pass with a run around a cone (3). After receiving the ball, the central players can, for example, pass through a cone goal (4) or simply dribble (5). The pass combinations and position changes can vary in configuration, be continued, or be performed openly without rules. Concentration and precision can be increased by dribbling and passing technique rules (left, right, etc.) and by limiting ball contact. Achievement of individual objectives can be followed by a game for the mini-goals (4 and 5).

GETTING STARTED 71

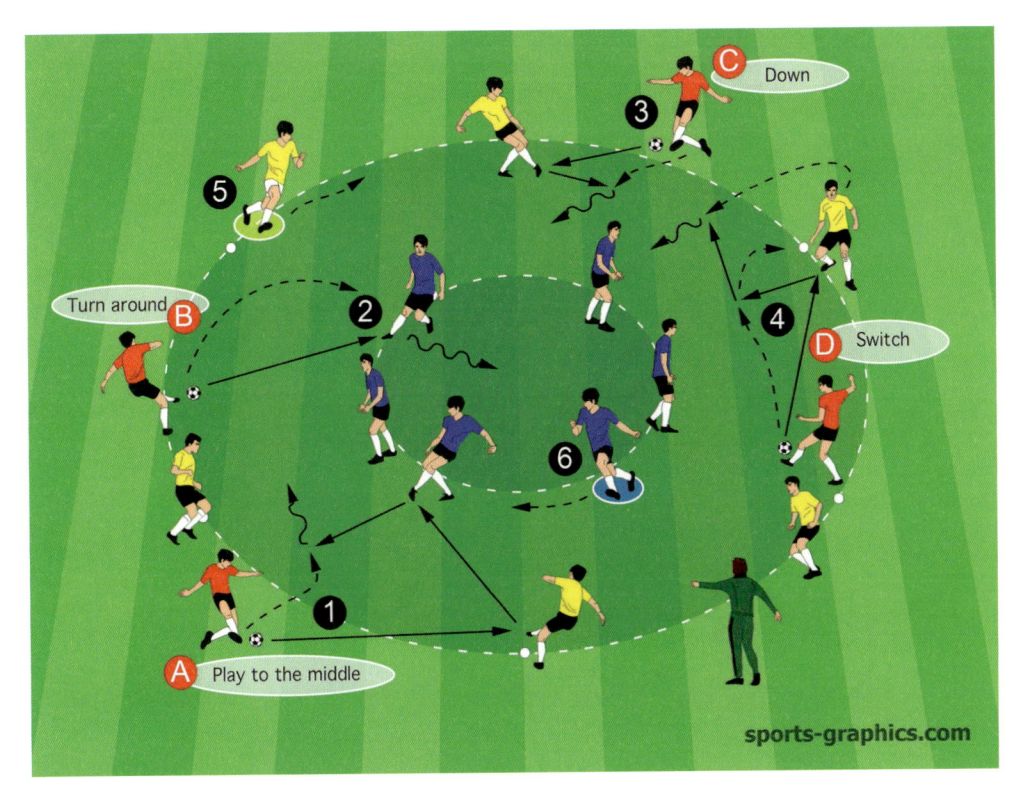

2.3.5 Ring of fire – free passing 3 (commands)

Execution, principles and elements

The players spread out in fixed positions along the inner ring (blue players) and outer ring (yellow players). Some players (red players) have possession of a ball and can pass to all players without a ball on either ring. With every pass, the passing player gives a command that specifies the subsequent action, or induces a stipulated position change. The focus lies on the various levels of the circle, from an outer area with lots of room to a denser center. The commands may vary in competitiveness for the outer (more room) and inner ring (more time).

Provocation rules, point system and variants

The commands, flows, and position changes may vary, be continued, or be performed openly without rules. The command "play to the middle" creates a combination of outer and inner ring (1). The command "turn around" means the recipient turns around, dribbles away, and the passing player takes their spot (2). The command "down" means a backward pass (3). The command "switch" induces a double double-pass with subsequent position change (4). The players with the ball decide freely which command they associate with the current pass. The flows become more dynamic when the players awaiting the ball are constantly in motion and are open along the rims of the circles (5 and 6).

2.3.6 Ring parable – technical circle 1 (ball control)

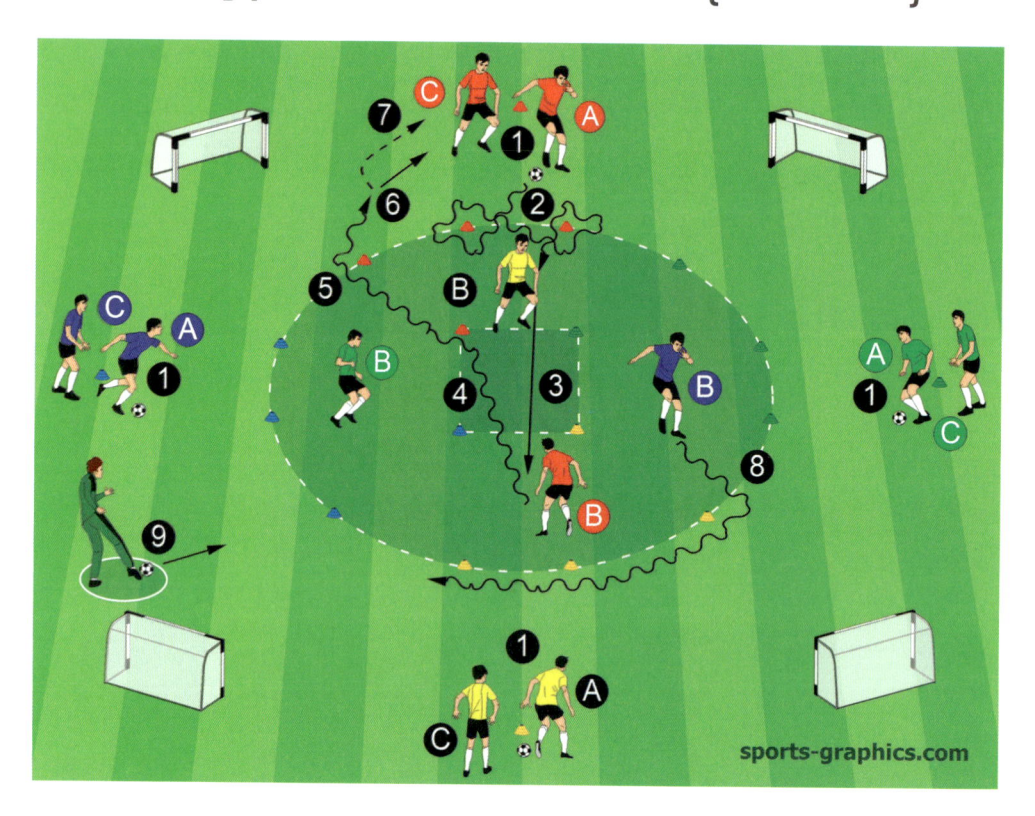

Execution, principles and elements

The teams compete against each other and try to perform a series of passes and dribbles in the quickest succession possible. The teams start with multiple players from a starting position (1). Another player positions themselves within the circle on the opposite side. The first player starts and performs a stipulated technique at their own two marking cones on the arc (2), and then passes the ball to their partner through the central field (3). The teammate dribbles into the central field and performs a feint at each of their own two cones (4 and 5) in order to then pass the ball to the next player on their team (6), and head to the next position (7). The first passing player (here Player A) takes the central position (here Player B). The other teams' flows are obstacles that must be cautiously played around so that the players' own respective flow is not interrupted.

Provocation rules, point system and variants

By defining the pass technique (left, right, half-height, etc.), the dribbling form (left, right, alternating, etc.), the running paths (running ABCs), feint requirements (body fake-out, stepover, fake pass, fake shot, etc.), or ball contact limits for Player Bs (4 to 6), the precision and concentration may vary and increase. The edge of the circle may also be used for precise running or dribbling paths (8). The technique flows may be organized as a competition, with one team as the winner and thus in possession of the ball for a subsequent game of six-on-six, or double three-on-three (9).

2.3.7 Racing cycles – technical circle 2 (combinations)

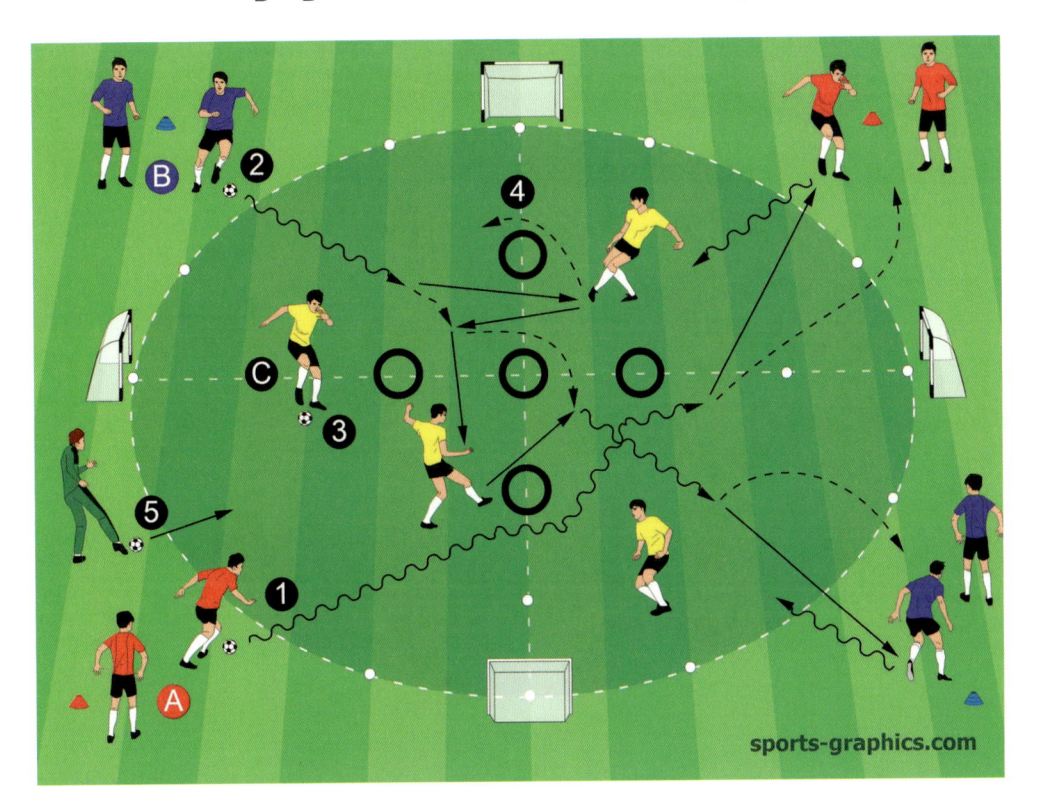

Execution, principles and elements

Group A and Group B switch between their starting positions outside of the circle. Group C is active within the circle. Multiple coordination tires are located within the circle field. The circle is divided into four sectors. All three groups work at the same time. The players in Group A dribble into the circle, perform a feint at two freely selectable coordination tires, pass the ball to the partner waiting opposite them, and take their position (1). The players in Group B dribble into the circle, perform a double pass with two players from Group C, and then perform a pass and position switch (2). The players in Group C combine their own ball in the inner field, functioning as obstacles for Groups A and B, and must focus on their own ball while also always switching over to passes from Group B as required (3). As a follow-up action, the Player C's must run around a tire after each pass in a curved run (4). A ball from the trainer can spontaneously induce a four-on-four-plus-four situation to the mini-goals (5).

Provocation rules, point system and variants

The double pass between Players B and C must be played around a coordination tire as an imaginary opponent. The position switch of Groups A and B is performed with a double double-pass. The players from Group C leave the previously played sector after completing an action, thereby always changing position. Group C may be required to play each pass through an interim space between two coordination tires.

2.3.8 Milky Way – technical circle 3 (goalkeeper)

Execution, principles and elements

The playing field is marked by three starting positions. Multiple players position themselves at each starting position, and one ball is placed at each end. Multiple coordination tires are located in the center. The first player from the group starts toward the center, performs a stipulated task and passes the ball to a player at another starting position, to then take their position. The players can choose between various flows according to the situation. The players can perform a double pass with the goalkeeper around a coordination tire (1), dribble through the coordination tires while including a goalkeeper (2), or pass to a goalkeeper, run through two coordination tires, and process the return pass (3).

Provocation rules, point system and variants

The goalkeepers or neutral players in the center can be given throwing rules with the left or right hand, or passing techniques with the left or right leg, processing and redirecting the passes accordingly with their foot. The rules for the players may vary widely.

2.3.9 Cosmos – technical circle 2.0 (footwork)

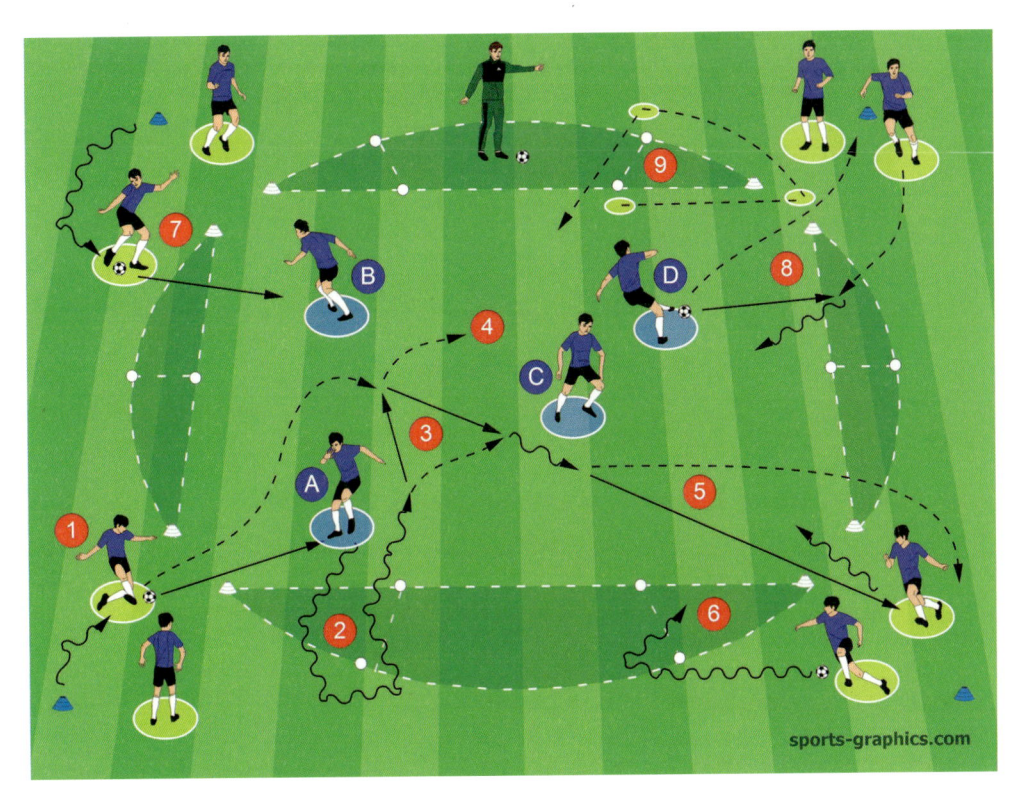

Execution, principles and elements

The playing field is marked by four starting positions. Multiple players position themselves at each starting position, and one ball is placed at each end. There are four other players in the center, one for each starting position (Players A, B, C and D). Multiple sections are marked off in the circle. The player with the ball dribbles from their starting position toward the center, and passes it to the player assigned to their team via an interim space in the center (1). The player in the center receives and dribbles over four lines of the outer section as quickly as possible (2). A double pass with the previously passing player is performed (3). The passing player is then the new player in the center, and the player previously active in the center (here Player A) passes to a player at a different outer position and switches to their starting position (5).

Provocation rules, point system and variants

While dribbling, the player with the ball can be assigned various feints or foot switches (2). The lead-up to a new action can vary from dribbling (6) to a pass through a field (7). The position switch can be made more precise with a targeted pass (8). Certain runs (free running, drop-off) can be required at the arc segments (9).

2.3.10 Dimension – technical circle 2.1 (position play)

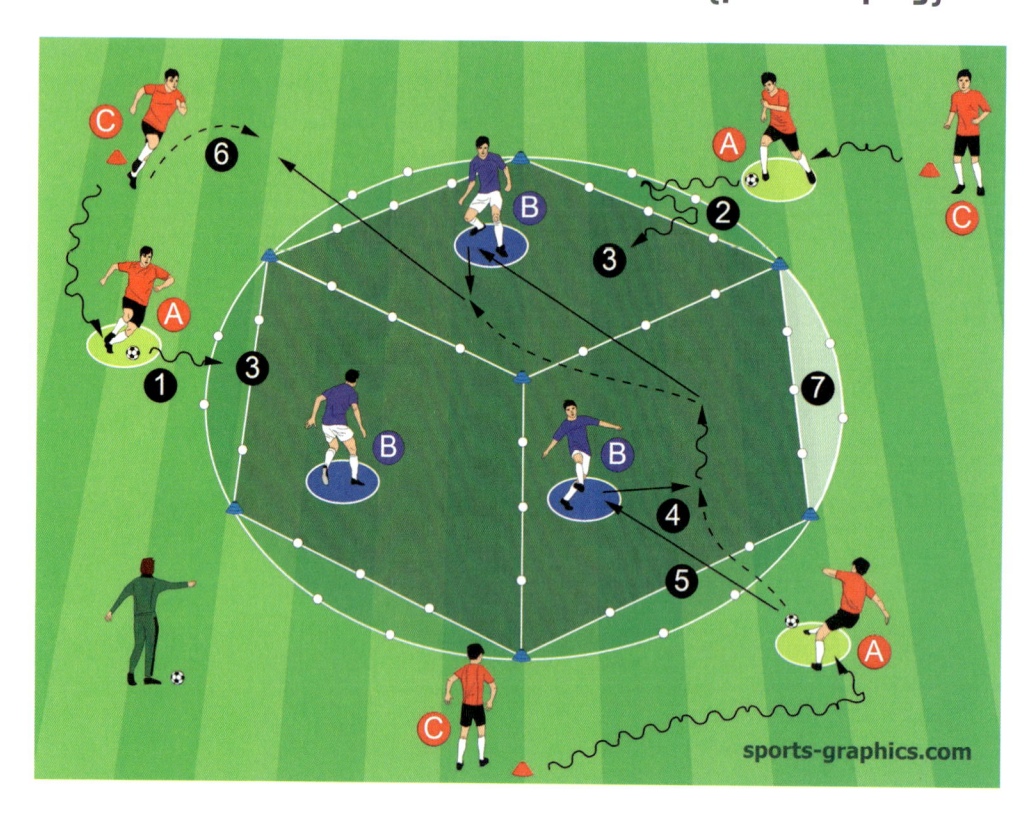

Execution, principles and elements

At the center of the playing field is a circle which is divided into sections by three rectangles. Outside of this circle are three starting positions, at each of which are one player with a ball and one waiting player without a ball (Players A and C). One central passing player is positioned in the three large sections within the circle (Player B). The three Player As dribble up with the ball into the small, arched field first (1) where they then perform a feint or stipulated technique (2) before dribbling further into the center (3). The Player As must then pass to either of the Player Bs (4). After processing the return pass, Player As pass to one of their outside players and then take their position. As an alternative to the specification of a technique (2), the small, arched field can also be bridged with a long pass (5). After every ball action, Player Bs move to a different sector. The player who has received the pass must step aside from the starting cone before receiving the pass (6) and then start a new action.

Provocation rules, point system and variants

The dribbling task in the small, arched field can be differentiated and made more precise. For example, topping movements and changes of direction can be defined with the lines, or various feints can be used. The edge areas can be specially used for technique objectives (7).

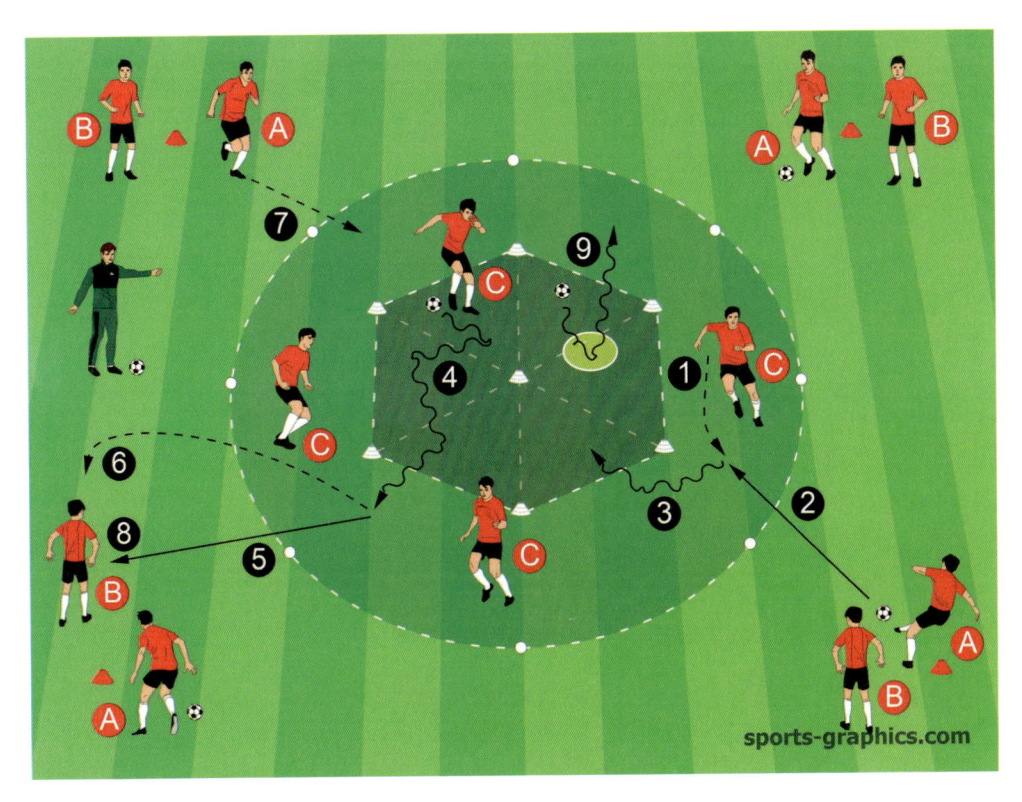

2.3.11 Ecliptic – technical circle 2.2 (free running)

Execution, principles and elements

At the center of the playing field is a circle, marked on the inside with multiple triangular sections. Outside of the circle are four starting positions. At each starting position is one player with a ball (Player A) and one waiting player (Player B). Four players without a ball are located in the interim space within the circle (Player C). The Player Cs call for a pass from one of the outside players (1), receive a forceful low pass (2), and receive it in the center (3). Player Cs also perform a stipulated technique (e.g. various feints) in one or more sectors (4). They then direct a pass to either of their outside players (5) from the interim space, to then take the vacant position outside (6). The previous passer (2) runs up to the vacant position in the center (7) and starts a new action on their own (1). The player who receives the pass stays outside and waits for the next player who calls for the ball from the center (8).

Provocation rules, point system and variants

The technique tasks (4), the types of ball processing (3), and passing can be configured in a variety of ways. The inner lines allow for technical tasks that allow for cutting movements and changes of direction.

2.3.12 Roulette – technical circle 2.3 (running)

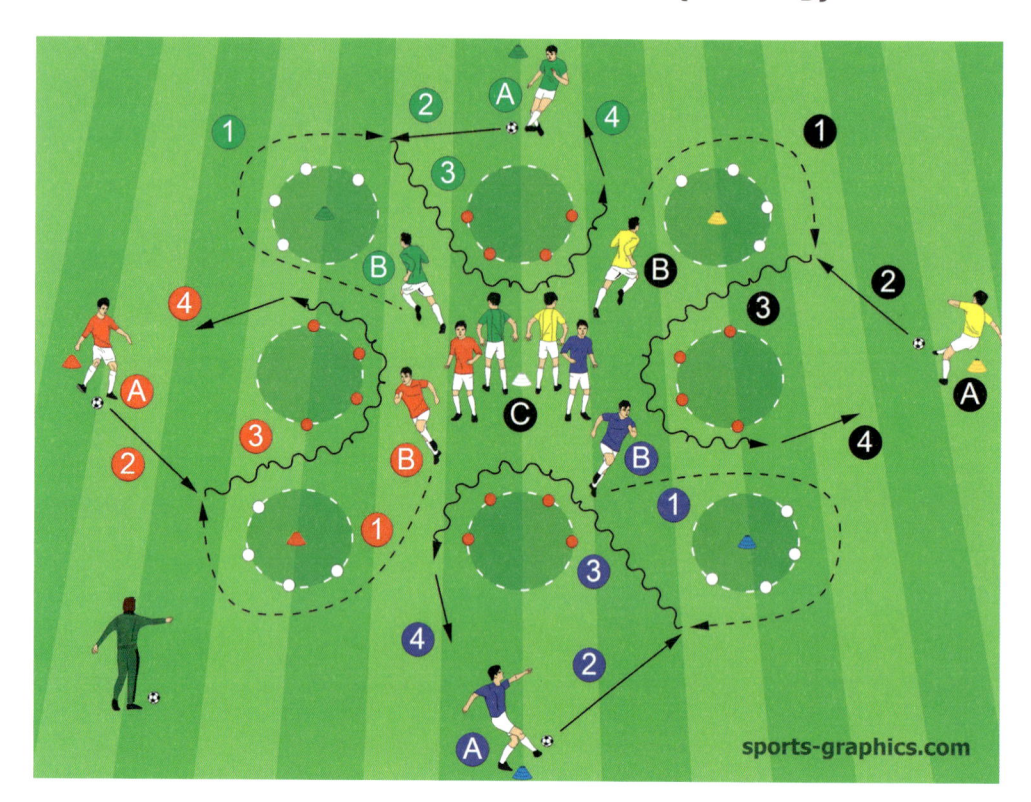

Execution, principles and elements

Located in the center of the playing field are multiple half-circles in a rectangular formation, open on the inside and outside. The players work with the arches marked with marking cones while running and dribbling. One player with a ball (Player A) is located at each of the four outer positions. In the center are two players from each group (Players B and C). Upon the signal from the trainer, the first four players (Player B's) run toward the circle in their own color marked with a cone (1), run around it in an arc, receive a pass from the outside player (2), process the pass, and dribble around the next half-circle over the center (3). The players then play the ball back to the outside player and return to the central starting position (4). The outside players first remain outside as passers for a short period of time and after a few circuits, switch positions.

Provocation rules, point system and variants

The trainer can define different signals that must be answered. Number 1 can mean the player's own cone, number 2 can mean the cone to the left of the player's own cone, number 3 can mean the one to the right, or number 4 can mean the one diagonal to it. The cone that is called out must be run around as a warmup motion (1).

GETTING STARTED 79

2.3.13 Gravitation – indoor circle 1 (ball control)

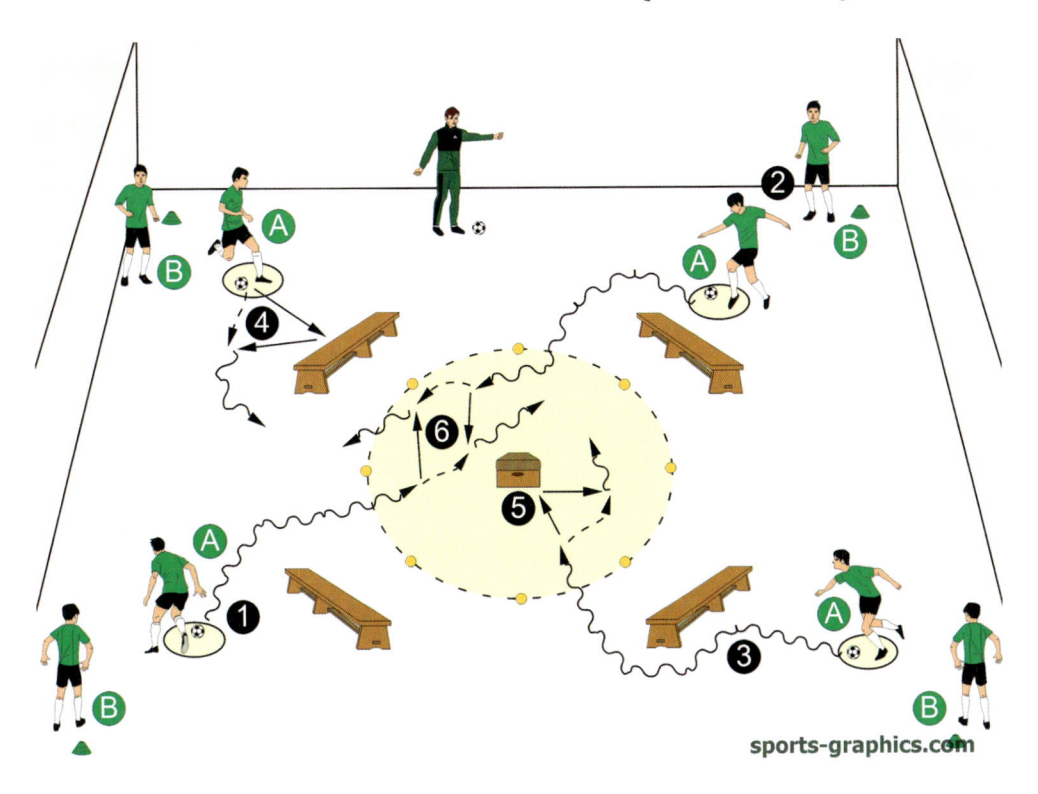

Execution, principles and elements

Marked in the center of the field is a circle which contains a box. Outside of the circle are four benches that have been tipped over, and four starting positions. At each starting position is one player with a ball (Player A) and other waiting players (Player B). The four Player As dribble up simultaneously (1), play through the central circle, and then pass to the player opposite and take their position. The receiving player processes the pass and starts a new action (2). Before entering into the circle, the benches can be used as imaginary opponents for feints (3) or as a ricochet wall for passing (4). In the central circle, the players can be required to perform various feints, to use the box as another ricochet wall (5), or switch balls with another player in possession of a ball (6).

Provocation rules, point system and variants

The rules may vary and be freely selectable or firmly defined. Foot usage during dribbling, feinting, or passing can be stipulated. The players may also freely select the outside players to pass to.

2.3.14 Hyperion – indoor circle 2 (ball handling)

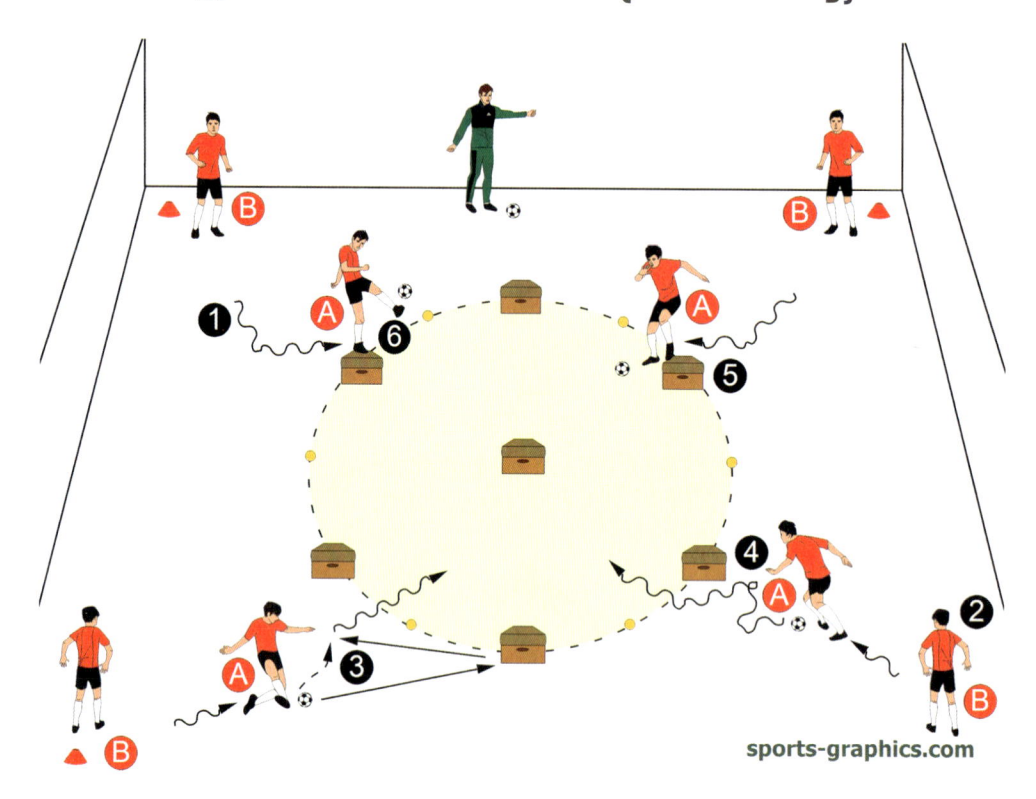

Execution, principles and elements

In the center of the playing field is a circle and a midpoint, marked with boxes. Four starting positions are marked outside of the circle. At each starting position is one player with a ball (Player A) and other waiting players (Player B). The four Player As dribble up at the same time (1), play through the central circle, and then pass to the opposite player and take their position. The receiving player processes the pass and starts a new action (2). The boxes can be used and played in a variety of ways depending on the specified rules. For example, the players must perform a double pass with a box (3), a feint in front of the box (4), touch the box with one foot while dribbling (5), or juggle over the box (6).

Provocation rules, point system and variants

The rules may vary, and be freely selectable or firmly defined. Foot usage while dribbling, juggling, or executing the feints may be stipulated. Competitions are also conceivable, in which 28 box sides or the various sizes of the box sides have certain meaning.

2.4 SMALL MATCHES WITH FOCUS ON INDIVIDUAL TACTICAL BEHAVIOR

2.4.1 Explosion – chaos 1 vs. 1

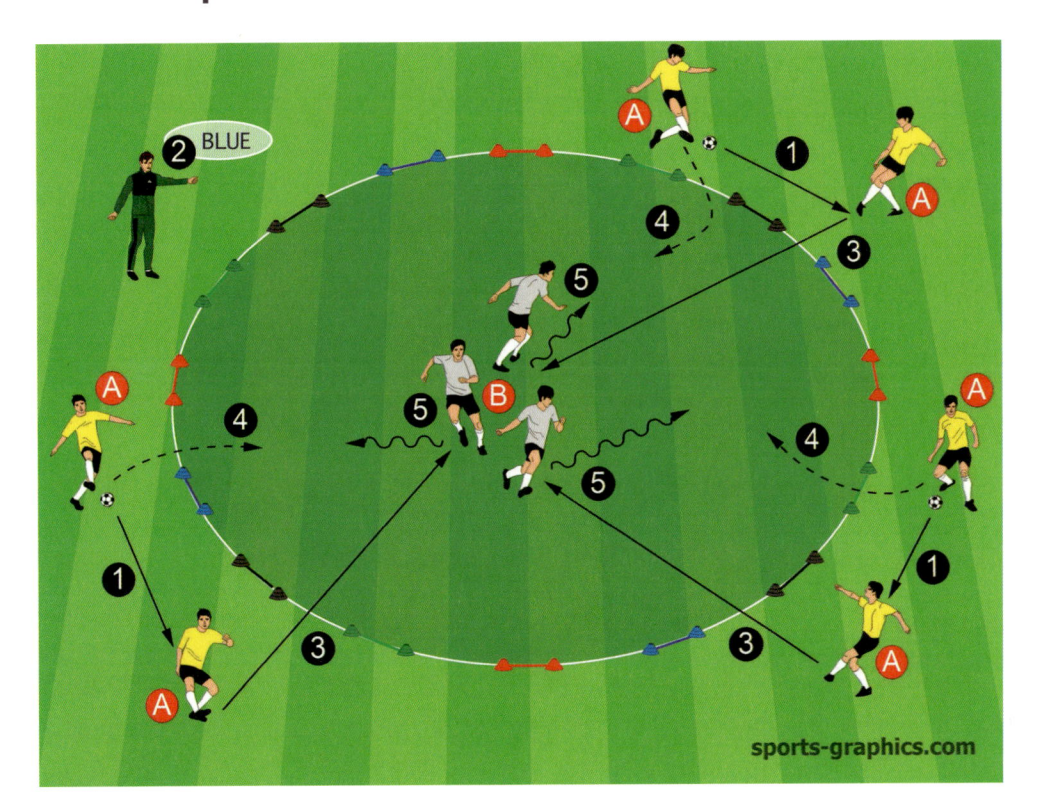

Execution, principles and elements

Player As freely pass three balls among each other outside of the field (1). The trainer issues a signal and calls out a color (2). The color that has been called corresponds to exactly four cone goals around the circle (here the blue ones). The players with the balls pass all three into the center (3). Player As who did not have the ball at the time of the signal run to the center (4), defend the goals that were called, and try to steal a ball. Player Bs, who had positioned themselves in the center, each process a ball and try to dribble through one of the goals that were called (5) to score a point. The focus lies on quick perception of the colored goals on the circle, and entails quick perception and the ability to make swift decisions.

Provocation rules, point system and variants

The training form can also be simplified or intensified by a variety of ratios for the attackers or defenders. The requirements for the attackers can be increased, e.g. when certain feints must be performed after receipt of the ball (5) or the opponents (Player As) only have to tag a player who has the ball with their hand. The attackers may also be required to perform certain dribbling forms (left, right, alternating, etc.).

2.4.2 One-way road – frontal 1 vs. 1

Execution, principles and elements

Player A passes the ball to Player B (1), and then immediately acts as the defender (2). Player B processes the pass and goes on the offense (3). Player B tries to dribble out of the circle over one of the lines A or B. Player A tries to prevent this after successfully stealing the ball, and dribbles over line C. The round one-on-one arena forces the game into the center through the middle. The threat of the possession and occupation of the center in the defense aims to present game-like behaviors.

Provocation rules, point system and variants

The intensity can be increased if Player B receives double points for not leaving the central corridor, and Player A receives double points for being able to steal the ball in the opposing side of the circle. A time limit can also start with the first ball contact by Player B or upon Player A stealing the ball, forcing the player in possession to find a quick solution to the one-on-one situation. The intensity of the pass (powerful, half-height, etc.) by Player A (1) also increases the attacker's precision. After reaching dribble lines A, B or C, it is possible to take a shot at the mini-goals.

2.4.3 Passing lane — side 1 vs. 1 I

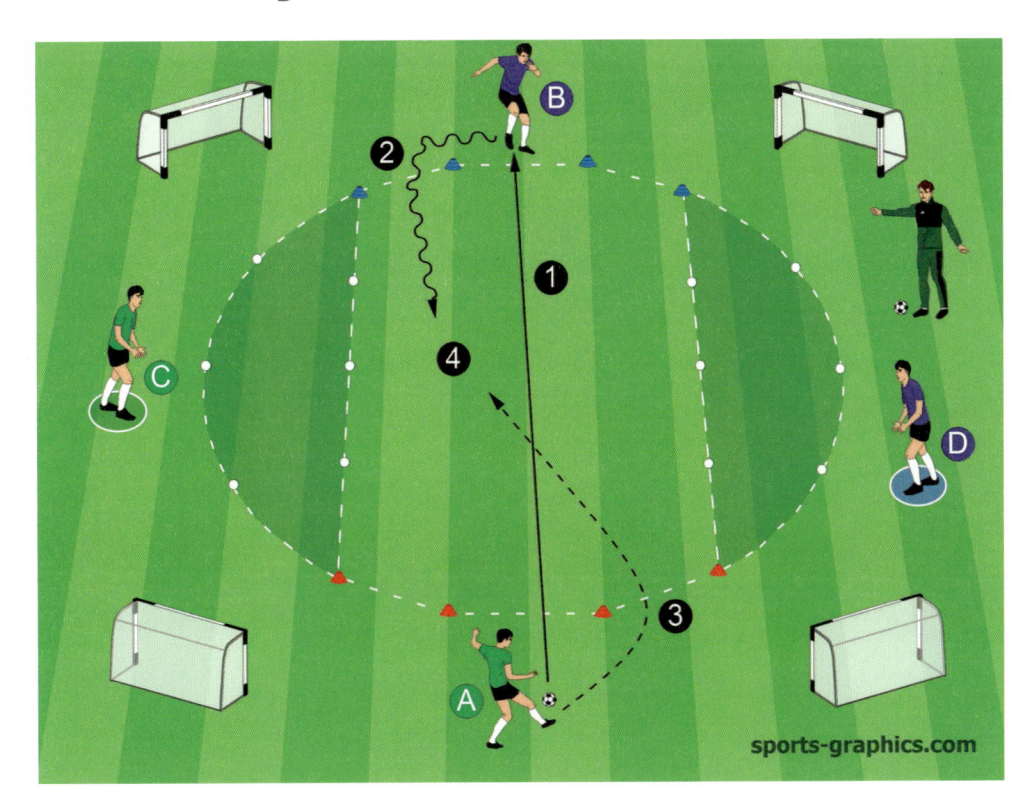

Execution, principles and elements

Player A passes the ball to Player B (1). Player B processes it to any side they choose (2), dribbles around a marking cone, back into the circle, and then acts as the attacker. Player A reacts and runs around the diagonally positioned marking cones (3) to then act as the defender in the circle (4). Player B tries to reach the opposite side, and Player A tries to force the attacker into one of the two edge areas or to retake the ball and counter. The round one-on-one arena forces the game into the center through the middle. The threat of the possession and occupation of the center in the defense aims to present game-like behaviors.

Provocation rules, point system and variants

The intensity can increase when a time limit is set upon Player B's first contact with the ball, or if dribbling and feints are required during the one-on-one (4). The intensity of the pass (powerful, half-height, etc.) by Player A (1) also increases the attacker's precision. The attacker can be given an advantage if the defender has to run around the farthest marking cone (3).

2.4.4 Eye of the needle – side 1 vs. 1 II

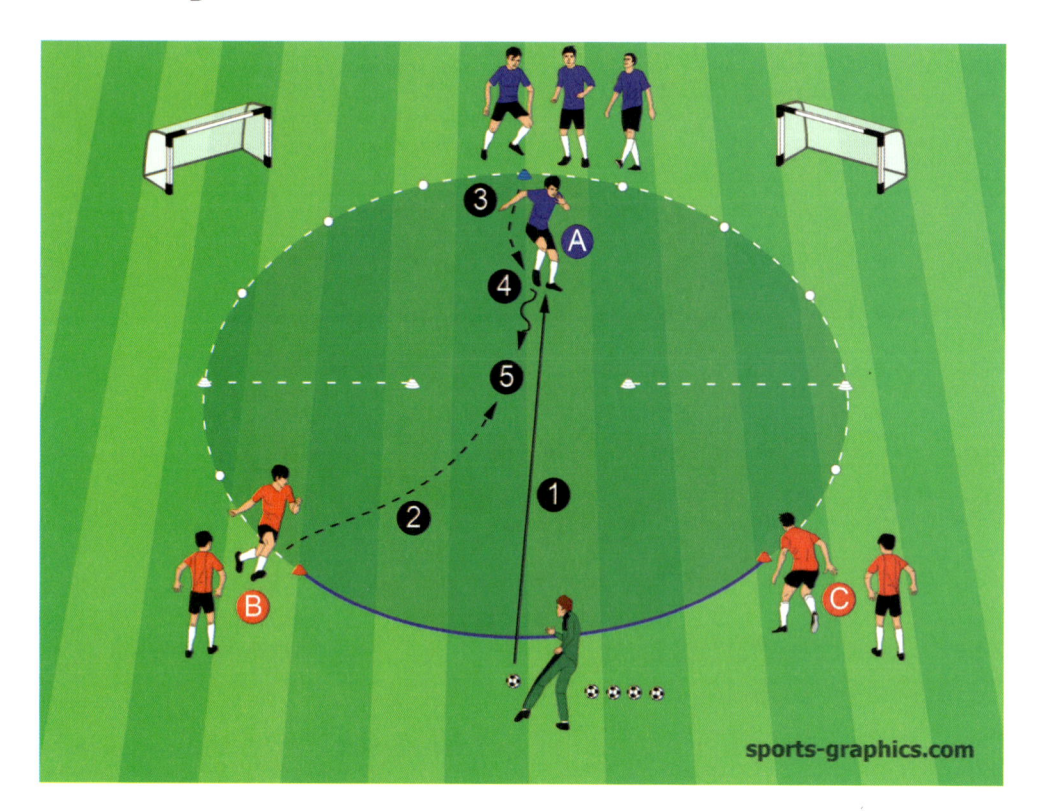

Execution, principles and elements

The trainer passes the ball to Player A (1). Two defenders (Players B and C) are located to the left and right of the trainer. Depending on which foot the trainer uses to pass the ball (here left), the player to the right or left (here B) positions themselves as the defender in the circle (2). Player A runs up to the trainer's ball (3), receives the pass (4), and tries to get past the opponent one-on-one (5). Player A tries to dribble over the opposite line of the circle between starting positions B and C to earn a point. Player B tries to prevent a point and counter through the central eye of the needle (5) after taking the ball, and reach the opponent's half of the circle or take the ball there. The round one-on-one arena and central eye of the needle forces the game to the center through the middle. The threat of the possession and occupation of the center in the defense aims to present game-like behaviors.

Provocation rules, point system and variants

The attacker receives double points when they dribble through the eye of the needle. Double points can also be awarded if the defender takes the ball in the opponent's half of the circle, to incite pressing and offensive defending. After achieving the offensive and defensive goals, shots can be taken at the mini-goals.

2.4.5 Hemisphere – complex 1 vs. 1

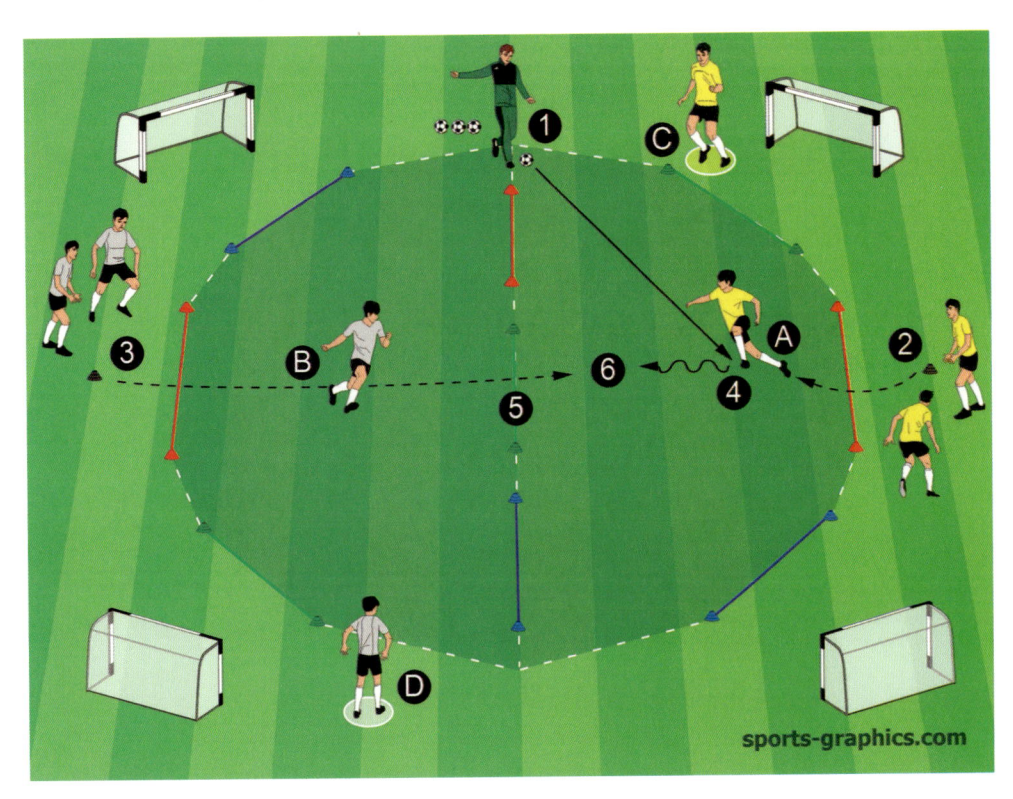

Execution, principles and elements

The trainer passes the ball to Player A (1). Player A receives the trainer's ball (2) and Player B starts out as a defender in the circle (3). Player A processes the pass (4). The defender tries to defend the front as quickly as possible to put the attacker in the opposing side of the circle (5). The attacker tries to get past the defender in a one-on-one and dribble through one of the three cone goals on the midline (6). The attacker tries to make the defender move through sideways dribbling, and get past them with good timing. After the center has been successfully played, a targeted follow-up action is required without skipping a beat.

Provocation rules, point system and variants

The attacker scores one point when they dribble through a cone goal on the midline, and double when they then dribble through the like-colored cone goal on the edge. The defender scores one point when they take the ball in their own half of the circle and dribble it through a goal on the midline, and double when they take the ball from the opposing side and dribble it through a cone goal on the rim. After achieving the playing goals in a one-on-one, the ball that has already been used, or a trainer's pass, can be used for a two-on-two situation with players C and D. It would then be possible to play with four mini-goals instead of the two previously used.

2.4.6 Eagle eye – variable 1 vs. 1

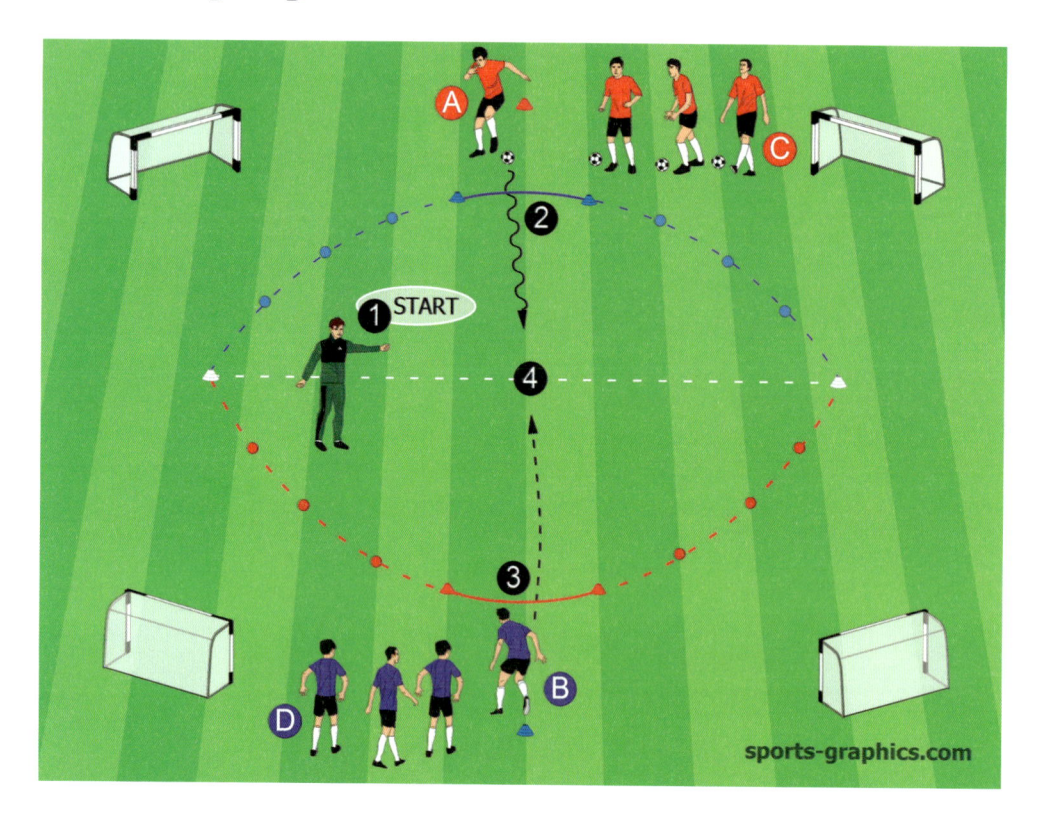

Execution, principles and elements

The trainer gives a starting signal (1). Player A then dribbles up to the center as an attacker (2), and Player B does so without a ball as the defender (3). The players try to score a point one-on-one by dribbling over the opponent's line (4). The entry goals (2 and 3) are worth double points and let the players hurry toward the center after a completed one-on-one situation. First it is necessary to draw the defender away with sideways dribbling and feints out of the center and away from their ideal line.

Provocation rules, point system and variants

The attacker can be given the option to turn back around after reaching the midline and to dribble across their own line. The defender is required to defend courageously and offensively, and meet with the attacker early (3). The attacker should try to quickly run forward without delay in order to have multiple options after crossing the midline. After achieving the objectives in a one-on-one, the players can shoot to the four mini-goals.

2.4.7 Rotunda – technical start 1 vs. 1

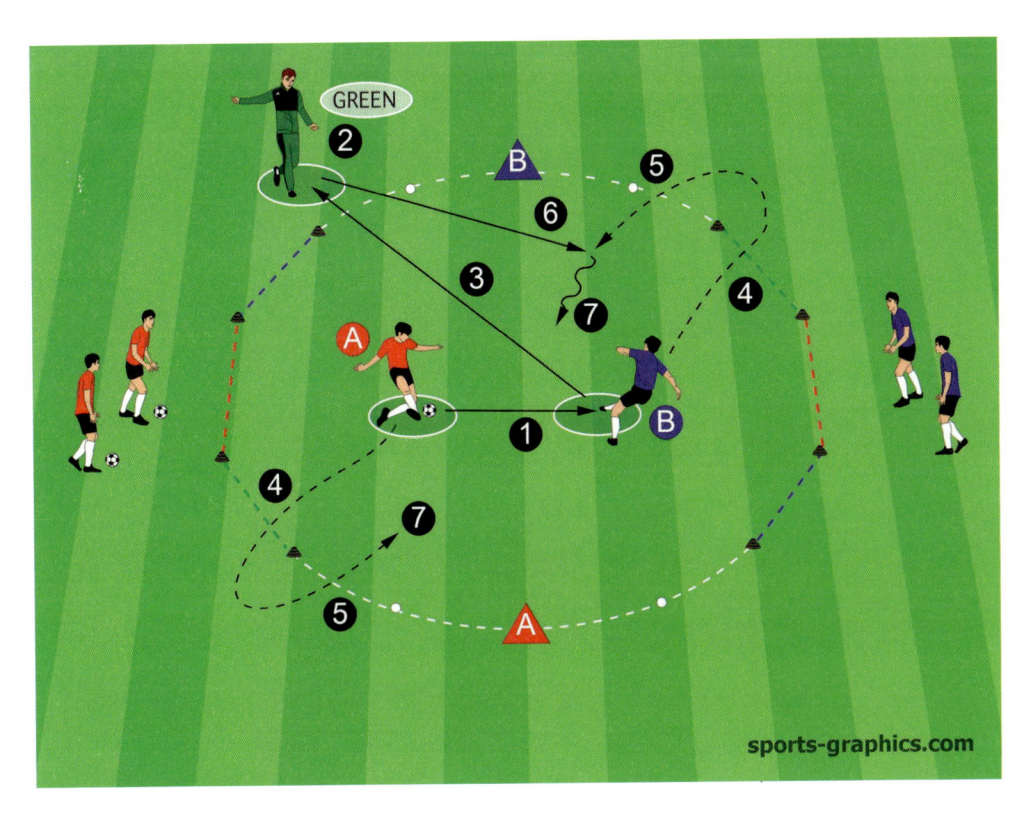

Execution, principles and elements

Players A and B freely pass a ball in open play (1). The circle is demarcated with different colored cone goals on the outer rim (blue, red, and green). There are two more cone goals on the sides (A and B). The trainer calls out one of the three cone colors (here green) as a starting signal (2). The player with the ball (here Player B) passes the ball to the trainer (3) and both players run out of the circle through the goal that was called (4) and then back into the center (5). The trainer brings the ball back into play (6). The player with the ball plays against a defender one-on-one (7). After fanning out, the quick return and orientation to the center is a sure way to success.

Provocation rules, point system and variants

The points can be awarded variably. The player with the ball could score by dribbling through one of the cone goals that was called, through one of the cone goals that was not called, through the opponent's like-colored cone goal, through the opponent's cone goal of a different color, or by dribbling over lines A and/or B. If there are multiple options for the player with the ball, the defender need only tag the player in possession with their hand to end the one-on-one situation.

2.4.8 Octagon – double 1 vs. 1

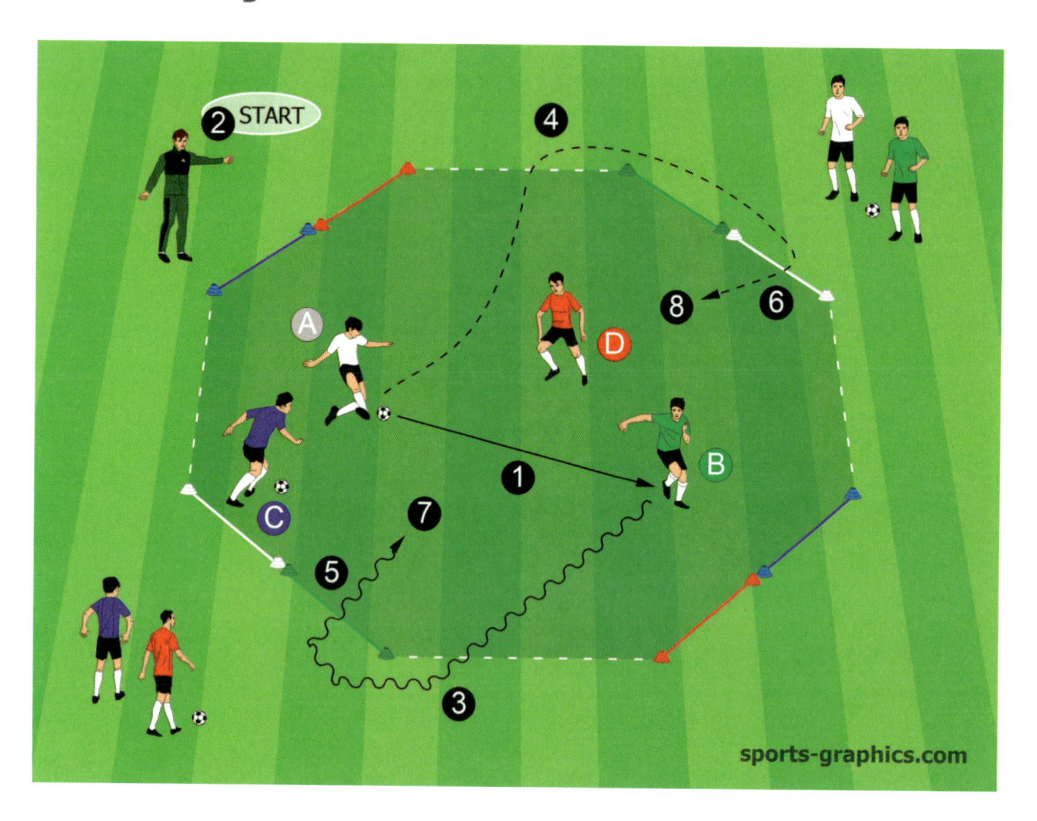

Execution, principles and elements

Players A and B form a pair, and Players C and D form a pair. Every player is assigned two cone goals the same color as their jersey. The pairs each freely pass a ball to each other (1). The trainer gives an acoustic starting signal and thus begins the lead up to the one-on-one situation. The player with the ball dribbles out from the circle (3) and the player without a ball reacts and runs out of the circle on the other side (4). The players dribble and run through one of their own goals back into the field (5 and 6). The attacker (here Player B) tries to score a goal by dribbling through the opponent's goal (7). The defender (here Player A) tries to counter through the attacker's goal (8) after taking the ball. The two one-on-one situations occur at the same time, in the same circle. This creates a chaotic situation with other players as obstacles.

Provocation rules, point system and variants

The attacking player can be given the chance to score a goal through the arches to the left and right of the cone goals to be played through. The four waiting players can function as neutral passers along the four neutral arches.

2.5 BIG MATCHES WITH FOCUS ON GROUP TACTICAL BEHAVIOR

2.5.1 Universe – 2 vs. 2 – technical start

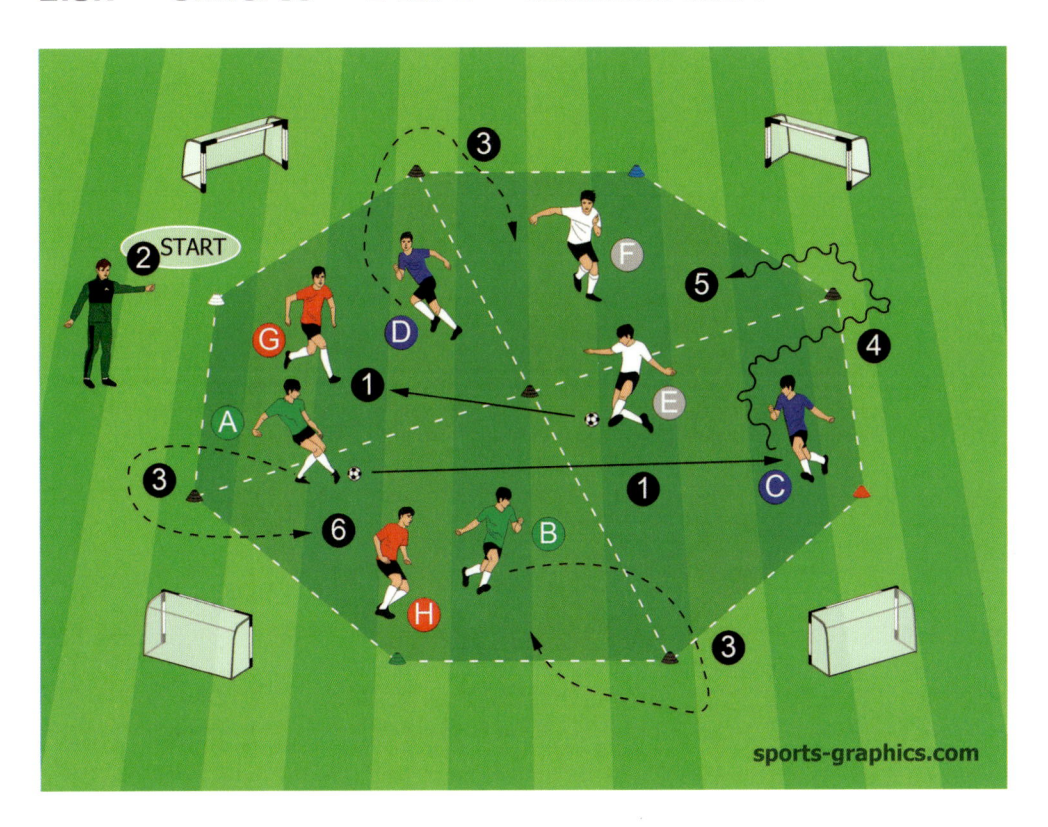

Execution, principles and elements

The players form four pairs (Players A/B, C/D, E/F, G/H). Each pair is assigned a colored marking cone on the outside. Pair A/B always plays against pair C/D, and E/F always against G/H. First the pairs each pass a ball to one another freely (1). After the trainer gives the signal (2), the four players run around the cones to the left and right of their own marking cone (3). The player with the ball begins dribbling (4). The team with the ball (here the blue team) is in possession and tries to dribble out of the field on the other side of the octagon and over one of the two lines to the left and right next to the opposing marking cone (here the green marking cone), in order to score a point (5). The opposing team (here the green time) tries to counter after taking the ball (6). Both two-on-two situations occur at the same time in the same circle, creating a chaotic situation with players as obstacles.

Provocation rules, point system and variants

Neutral players (e.g. a goalkeeper or other fielders) can create different ratios, or change the situations to two-on-two-plus-one or two-on-two-plus-two. The complexity increases when neutral players are allowed to interfere in both two-on-two situations.

2.5.2 Helicopter – 4 vs. 2 – numerical advantage

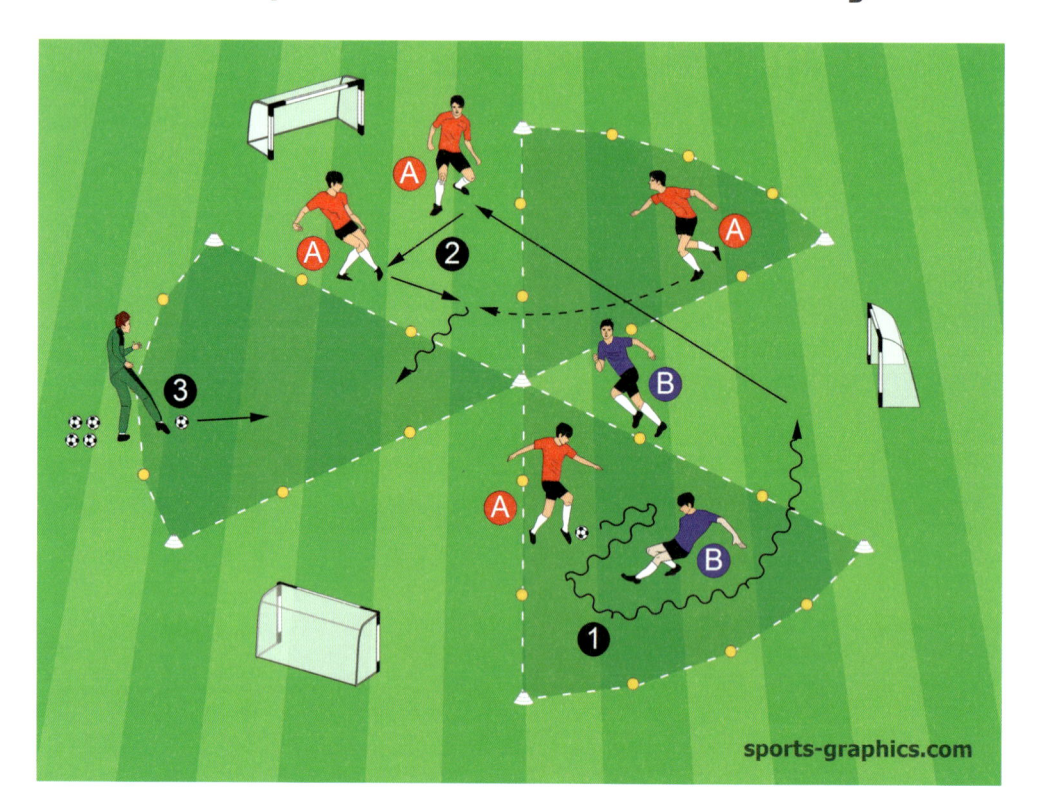

Execution, principles and elements

At the center of the playing field are three circle sectors, marked off by marking cones. Together with the interim spaces, there are six sections. Two teams play against each other. The team with the ball is in the majority (here four versus two) and tries to keep the ball to themselves for as long as possible without the opposing team being able to take it. The team with the ball can also score points when a player is able to make contact with the ball five times while dribbling in one of the three circle sectors and then leave the sector with the ball at their foot (1). The team with the ball can also score points when three players make a combination of passes in an interim space (2). The players in the minority are regularly switched out.

Provocation rules, point system and variants

The change of roles can be performed with one player from the minority team after each touch of the ball. The trainer can bring a new ball into play for this, and switch two other players into the minority team (3). The requirements for the majority team can be made more difficult by determining a maximum limit for ball contacts. After achieving the playing objectives or after the minority team has taken the ball, the mini-goals can be brought into play right away.

2.5.3 Fan – 3 vs. 3 – running start

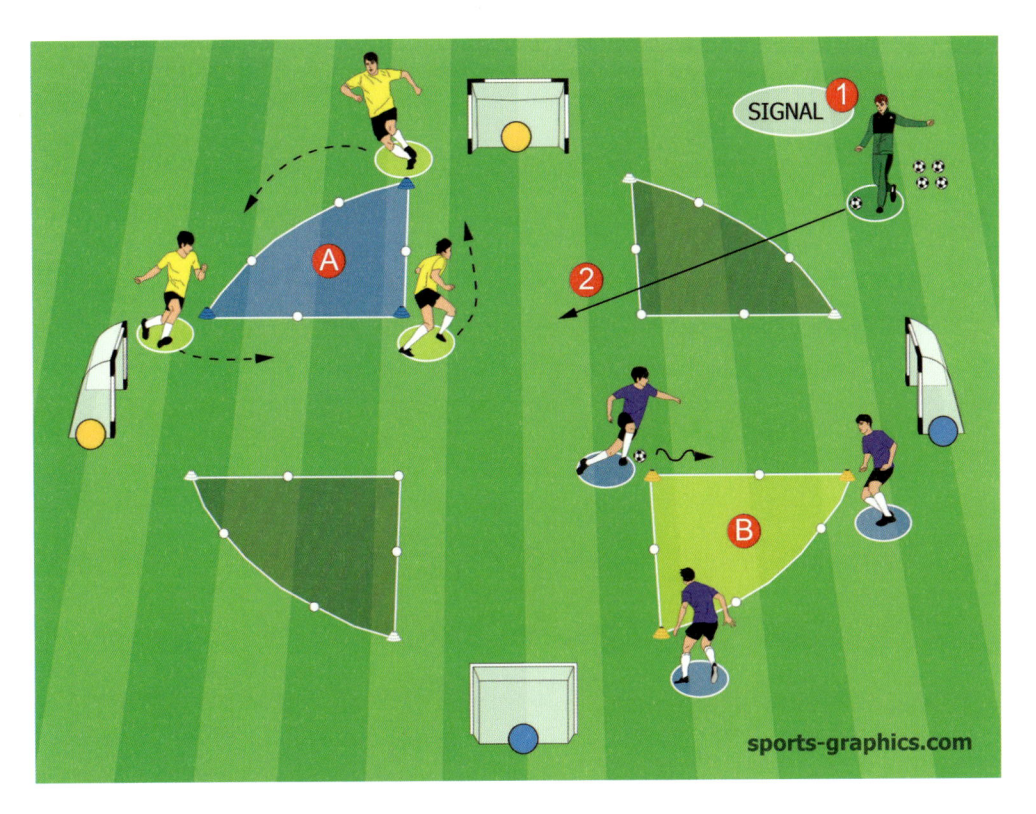

Execution, principles and elements

The field consists of four circle sectors. The four fields are each marked by the team colors and a neutral color. Before the three-on-three playing sequence begins, the teams must complete a competitive running warm-up to determine who will take possession of the ball. The teams position themselves on the opposing side. Every player is standing at a starting position. The trainer gives the starting signal (1) and starts the competition, as well as the sequence of a specified running task. The running task always ends when each player is back at their starting cone. The team that first arrives completely at their starting positions will then get a ball from the trainer (2). The sequence begins right after the end of the running task and with the pass from the trainer. The players now try to reach one of the fields by dribbling or with a pass, thereby scoring a point.

Provocation rules, point system and variants

Various running tasks can be assigned and associated with a signal. For example, the players can run clockwise around the starting sector, or counterclockwise, or run through another sector and return. The trainer must specify certain signals for these (1). The arcs can be assigned tasks from the running ABCs (e.g. backward running, hopping on one leg, etc.) (Team A). The running warm-up can be performed with the ball and may involve technical movements or passing combinations (Team B). The coloring of the different sectors and goals can also be associated with the objectives.

2.5.4 Earth's rotation – 4 vs. 1 – center play

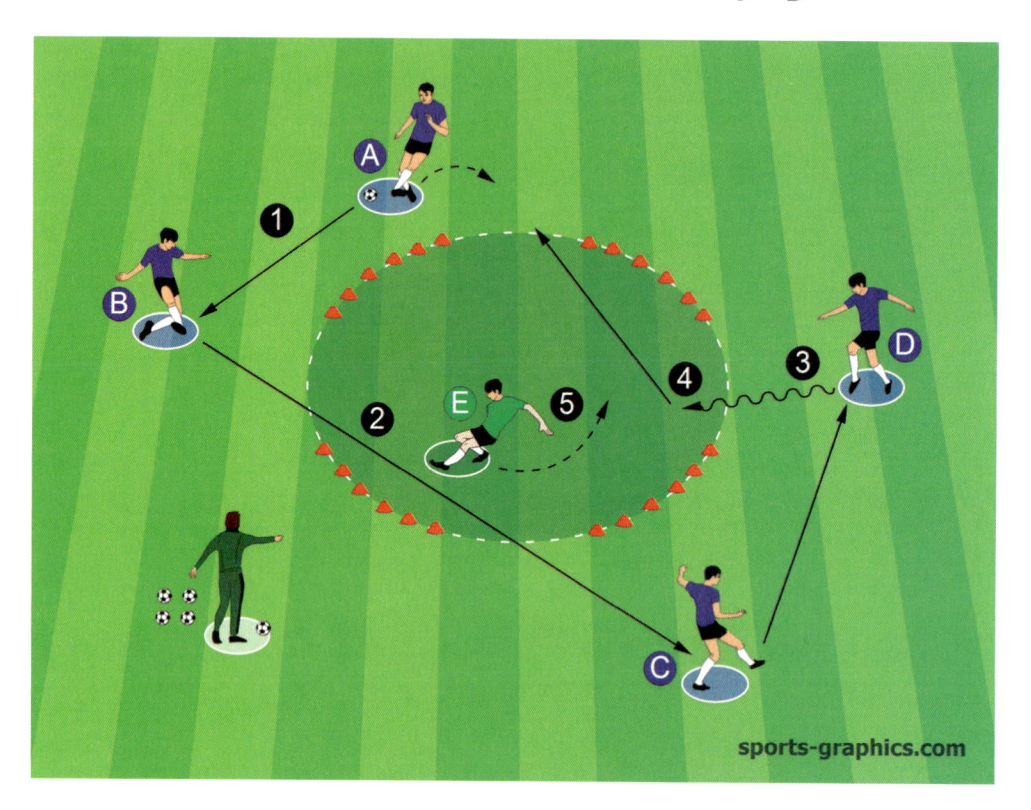

Execution, principles and elements

The players compete four-on-one. One player in the center of the circle may not leave it, and tries to touch the ball. Once they succeed, they may switch with the player who made the faulty pass. The majority team (here blue players) lets the ball circulate outside of the circle (1) and tries to make a pass through the circle (2). The red rows of cones may not be played over. In order to play a pass through the circle, the players may also dribble the ball into the circle (3) and make a pass out of the circle (4). The player in the center may only move within the circle (5). The focus lies on diagonal passes through the center, and always forces the players with the ball to threaten the center and boldly take advantage of gaps with dribbling and passes.

Provocation rules, point system and variants

Concentration and precision increase when the outside players are given a maximum ball contact limit, or may only make direct passes (2) through the circle. The playing situation can vary in ratio, e.g. four-on-two or five-on-two.

2.5.5 Sunray — 4 vs. 2 — center play

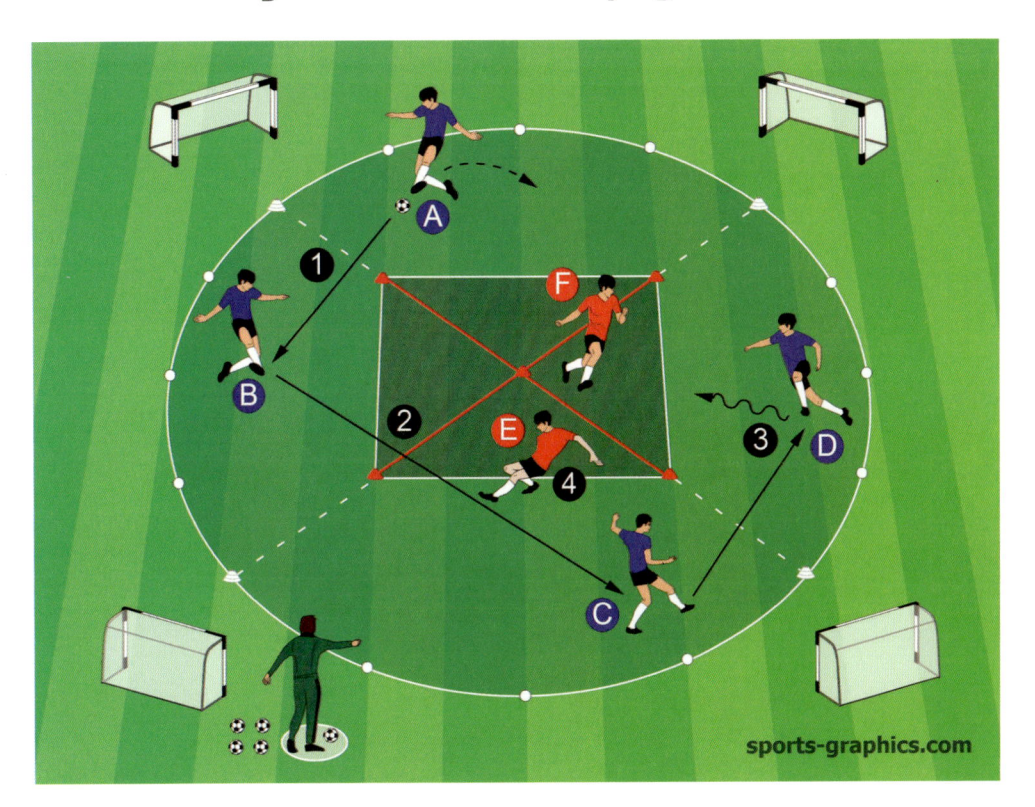

Execution, principles and elements

The players compete four-on-two. The players from the majority team (here blue players) are divided among the four zones and may not leave them. The two players in the center try to touch the ball. Once they are successful, they may switch places outside. The majority team (here blue players) lets the ball circulate outside the square (1) and tries to make a pass through the central square, thus playing through one of the four red marking lines (2). In order to make a pass through the square, the players with the ball may threaten the center while dribbling and push forward into the square (3). The focus lies on diagonal passes through the center, and always forces the players with the ball to threaten the center and boldly take advantage of gaps with dribbling and passing.

Provocation rules, point system and variants

Concentration and precision are increased when the players with the ball are given a maximum ball contact limit or may only make direct passes (2) through the central square. The playing situation may have various ratios (e.g. four-on-one or eight-on-four). After a specified number of passes over the lines (2) or after the ball has been taken, shots can be taken at the mini-goals.

2.5.6 Sector coupling – 5 vs. 3 – center play

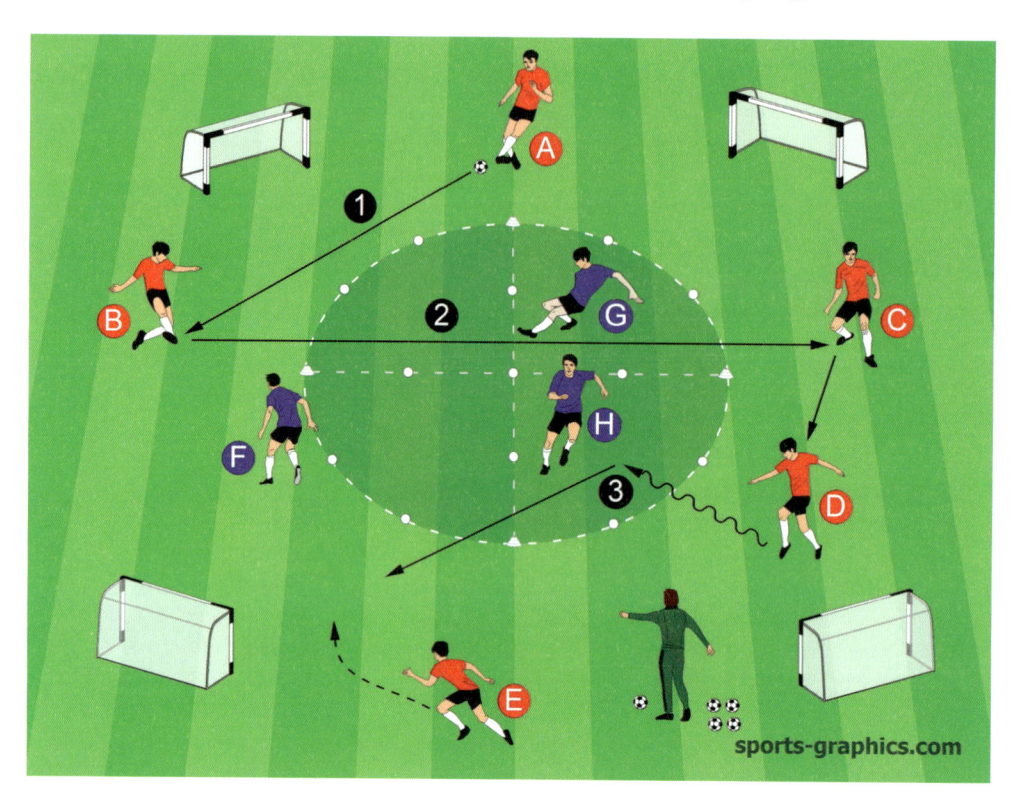

Execution, principles and elements

The players compete five-on-three. The players from the majority team (here red players) play outside of the circle and may only access it with the ball at their feet. The three players in the center of the circle try to touch the ball. Once they are successful, they may change positions outside. The majority team (here red players) lets the ball circulate outside of the circle (1) and tries to make a pass through a circle sector over the midlines (2). In order to be able to complete this pass, the player with the ball must threaten the circle with dribbling and dribble into it (3). The focus lies on diagonal and straight passes through the center, and always requires the players with the ball to threaten the center and boldly take advantage of gaps with dribbling and passing.

Provocation rules, point system and variants

Concentration and precision are increased when the players with the ball are given a maximum ball contact limit or may only make direct passes (2) through the central square. The playing situation may change to various ratios, e.g. six-on-four or seven-on-five.

GETTING STARTED **95**

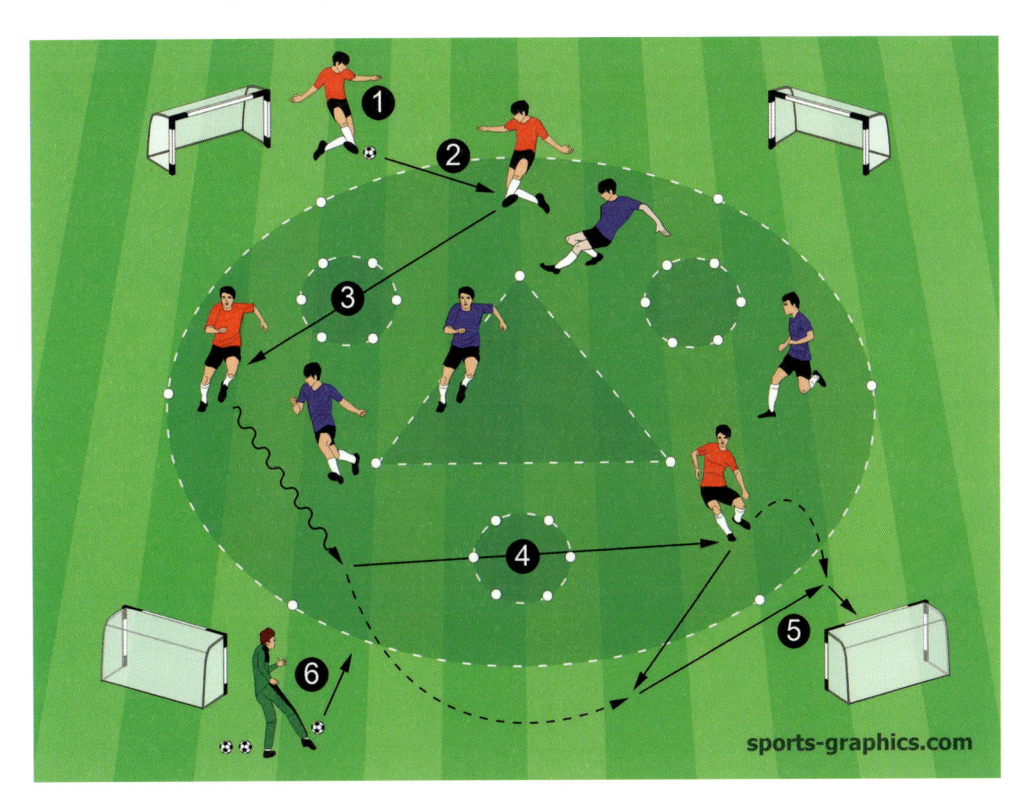

2.5.7 Hodgepodge – 4 vs. 4 – variable center play

Execution, principles and elements

A large, central circle is framed by four mini-goals. One triangular and three circular sectors are marked within the circle. The teams try to make a goal in one of the mini-goals. In order to be able to shoot toward a mini-goal, the team with the ball must first have played through the central circles or the triangle. The playing of the sectors within the large circle can be prepared through passes on the outside (1). After the triangle and circles have been played through after a specified pass sequence (3 and 4), the team in possession may strike at a mini-goal and complete the play (5). The specified pass sequence may involve two circles having to be played in succession (3 and 4), or the triangle and a circle. For the defense this means that the offense's not yet achieving playing objectives must be detected and prevented when possible.

Provocation rules, point system and variants

The fields within the circle may also be dribbled through (3 and 4). The pressure on the team with the ball and overall perseverance can be intensified if the ball can no longer leave the large circle after a pass into it (2), instead resulting in a change of possession. The play to the center can be accelerated and made more frequent if the team with the ball is allowed to make a maximum of four preparatory passes outside of the circle (1). The trainer can change gears with new balls (6).

2.5.8 Mosaic – 4 vs. 4 – complex center play

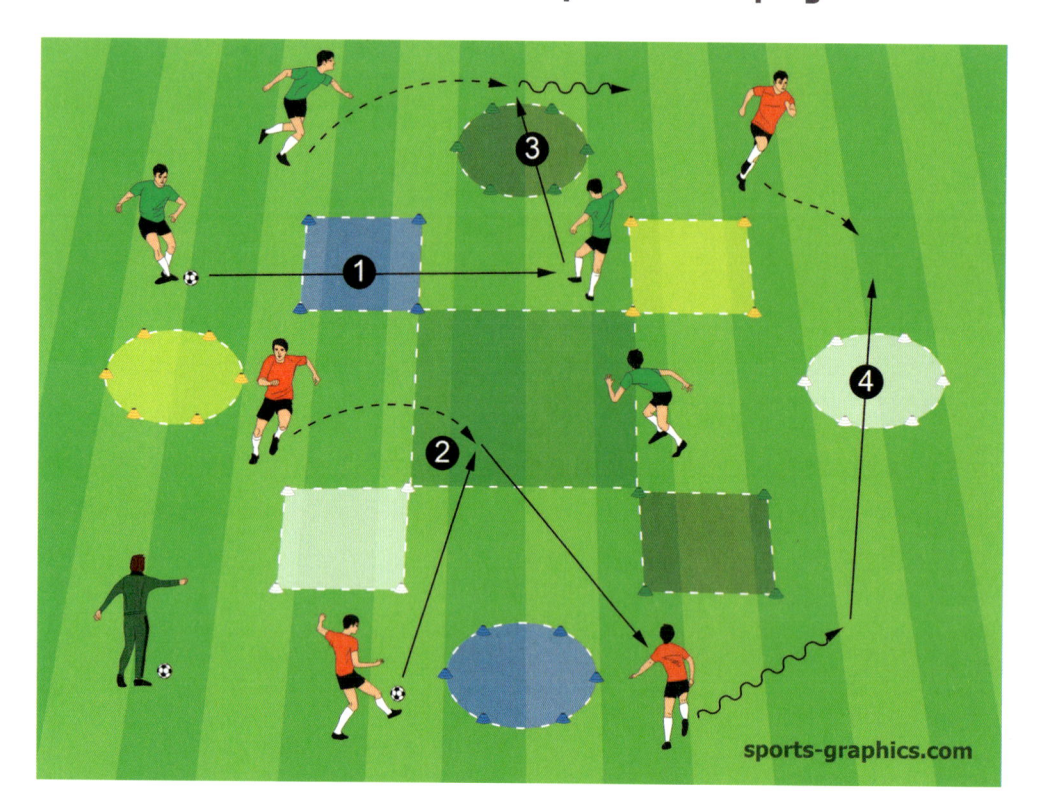

Execution, principles and elements

The teams play four-on-four. The team with the ball tries to play a circular field (3 or 4) after a rectangular or square field (1 or 2), thus scoring a point. The fields can be played by a pass over two lines (1), a pass out of the field (2), a pass through the field (3 and 4), or dribbling, depending on whichever is specified. The focus lies on the alternation between the center and outer area through differentiation of geometric field shapes.

Provocation rules, point system and variants

The playing form may be intensified when two rectangular/square fields must be played through before a point is scored through playing on a circular field. The fields may also be marked with different colored marking cones so that points can be based on playing through a specific color combination, and the players are required to act quickly. The central field can also be used so that a player with the ball has to meet a certain ball contact quota in it while dribbling, thus exposing them to greater pressure from opponents.

Notes/sketches:

3 MAIN COMPONENT

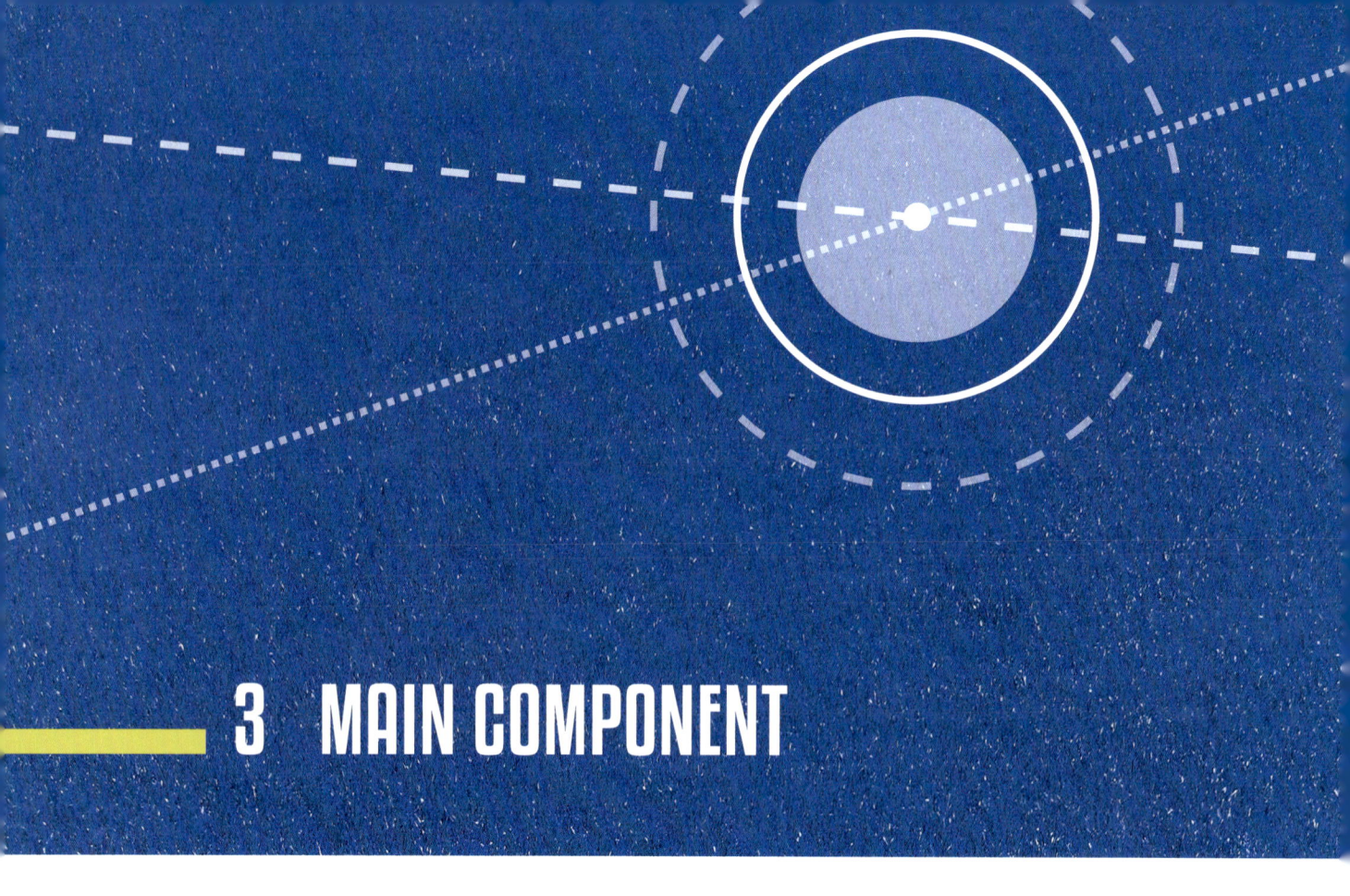

3.1 READING AID FOR UNDERSTANDING THE CENTRAL CIRCLE PLAYING FORMS

The central playing forms are shown on each double-page. There are two images for each playing form. The layout of the double-pages is consistent. The descriptions and explanations of the central circle playing forms thus always follow the same overview.

On the left side under the image are the explanations of the playing principle as well as additional aspects of the concept under the "Provocation rules, point system and variants" header. On the right side are the playing elements and conduct, as well as information on coaching points and instructions.

The playing principle, based on the graphic, describes the fundamental field and playing concept and provides an initial overview of the objectives. The provocation rules, point system and variants section describes other rules, additional objectives, possible point systems, and conceivable variants. Playing elements and conduct describe the pertinent conduct of the players as desirable technical-tactical elements. Coaching points and instructions then provide some specific instructions.

The central playing forms, along with the multifaceted playing concept, variable objectives and resulting conduct, are very complex and extensive. The respective graphics aim to depict many of the ideas. This is also why the circle playing forms differ from the depiction of usual playing forms. The image on the left side depicts individual playing objectives based on the text. It aims to illustrate how the fundamental playing idea presents itself within the field, and which technical-tactical processes can result in points.

3.2.8 Sun wheel

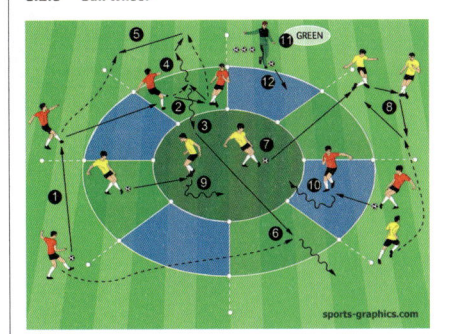

Playing principle

The field consists of a central circle and multiple arched circle segments (green and blue fields). The players have the opportunity to build up their game through secure passes into the outer zones (1) and score points through various zones.

Provocation rules, point system and variants

The playing form undergoes a differentiation when each team is assigned the blue or green zones, or the trainer determines the field to be played with each beginning pass (11). By specifying direct passes for the combinations for scoring (2 and 8), precision can be trained under pressure. One point is scored when two passes are played in one circle segment (2) and then the segment is exited by inward (3) or outward (4) dribbling. In order to earn double points, the team with the ball must connect one pass in the adjacent area (5) or in the opposite segment (6). One point is scored when an outer area is played through with three passes (8) after a pass from the center (7), or when a player successfully turns in the center (9) and the game is continued in the direction of play. This can also be implemented toward the center (10). Adaptability is trained with each new trainer ball (12).

3.2.8 Sun wheel (Continuation)

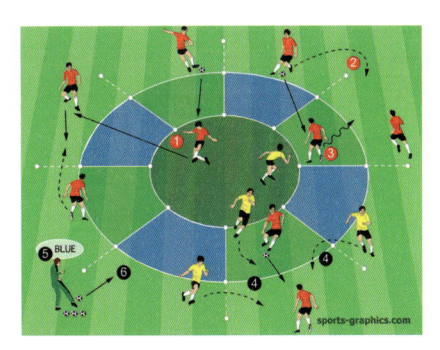

Playing elements and conduct

The playing form involves constantly making tactical decisions. The players are always required to implement tactically correct and promising solutions in order to take advantage of any possibilities and quickly score points (1). Offering and free-running behavior while indicating running paths (2) is just as important as permanent support through coaching and helpful commands. In the central area in particular, constant looks over the shoulder and peripheral vision (3) are necessary to be able to make the right decisions under pressure from opponents. In the defensive wall, joint tightening and pushing back into the outer field areas to prevent the opponent from scoring are elementary (4). New trainer balls and various trainer commands are constantly facing the players with changing situations, requiring them to stay alert so that they can react and adapt (5 and 6).

Coaching points and instructions

* Tighten up! Push back!
* Help yourselves! Give orders!
* Look over your shoulders!

The image is not exactly supposed to show two teams competing against each other. Rather, the various processes are shown in an exemplary manner, sometimes next to one another and presented as an excerpt without showing the real playing situation in its entirety. The number of players also varies. Ratios of three-on-three, three-on-three-plus-one, four-on-four, four-on-four-plus-one, or similar sizes are ideal for circle playing forms.

In order to illustrate the different playing ideas and objectives, more offensive actions in possession of the ball are shown than defensive actions. Multiple balls are also often shown so that the various objectives can be described.

This also applies to the image on the right side. Because of the many objectives, there can be an endless number of different modes of conduct and play elements. The image here also tries to sketch a number of the most important elements. Various elements are presented next to each other at the same time. They serve as examples which the trainer can use as a model to strive for.

The text descriptions and images make it clear that the circle playing forms vary widely. The images should provide ideas, and are not intended to be complete. Rather, the intent is to illustrate the underlying concept of the specific circle form and emphasize the pertinent play elements.

3.2 CENTRAL CIRCLE PLAYING FORMS WITH FOCUS ON PLAYABILITY AND SWIFTNESS

3.2.1 Reflection

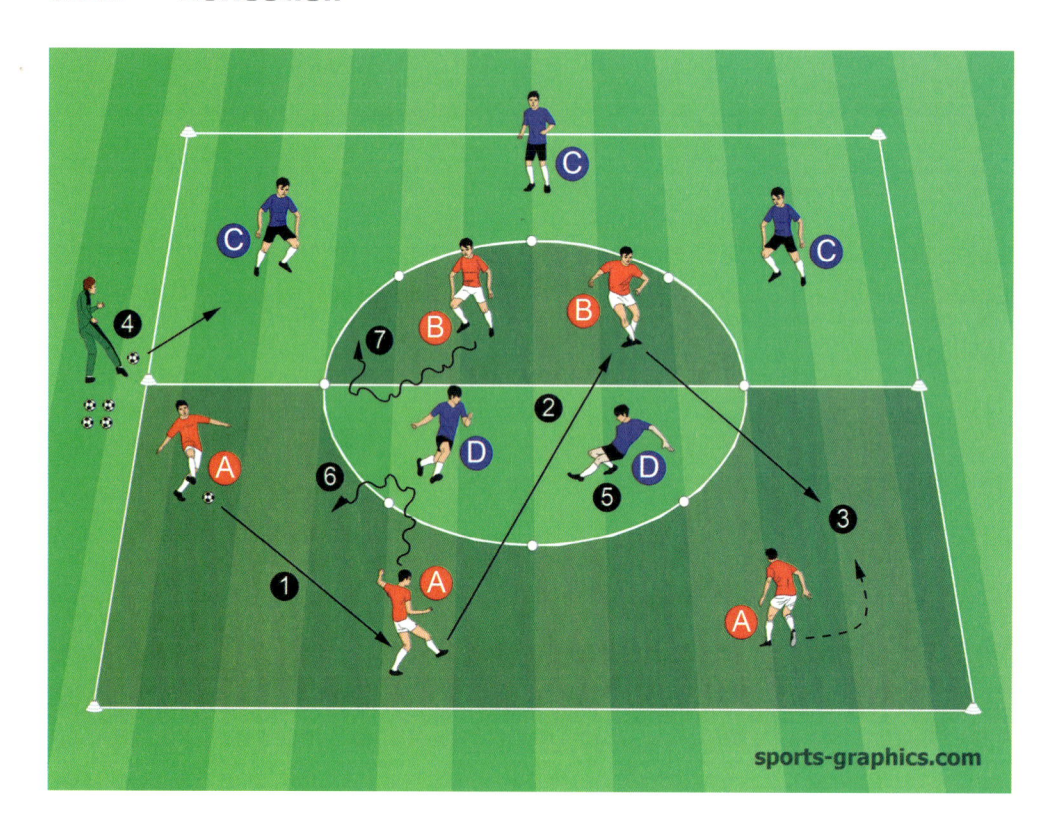

Playing principle

In a five-on-five playing form, three players are in each of the outer areas (Players A/C) and two are in each of the inside fields (Players B/D). The team with the ball tries to open gaps in the opposing wall (1) and make a pass to the two teammates in the other side (2). A point is earned when a play was continued by creating a passing point for a return pass (3). The trainer has the opportunity to set a time limit and bring a new ball into play after it has been exceeded (4). After the ball has been taken or a pass has been intercepted, the roles change right away and the game continues without interruption (5).

Provocation rules, point system and variants

The time limit can also be set for a maximum number of passes (1) up to a deep pass (2). The center can also be threatened by more points for dribbling through the opposing field (6). With each new trainer ball (4), the team giving the ball can be forced to change positions. The players would then automatically switch into the respective other field. For simplification and a warm-up, each team can make free passes with their own ball. This gets rid of opponent pressure, and the other team merely functions as an obstacle.

3.2.1 Reflection (Continued)

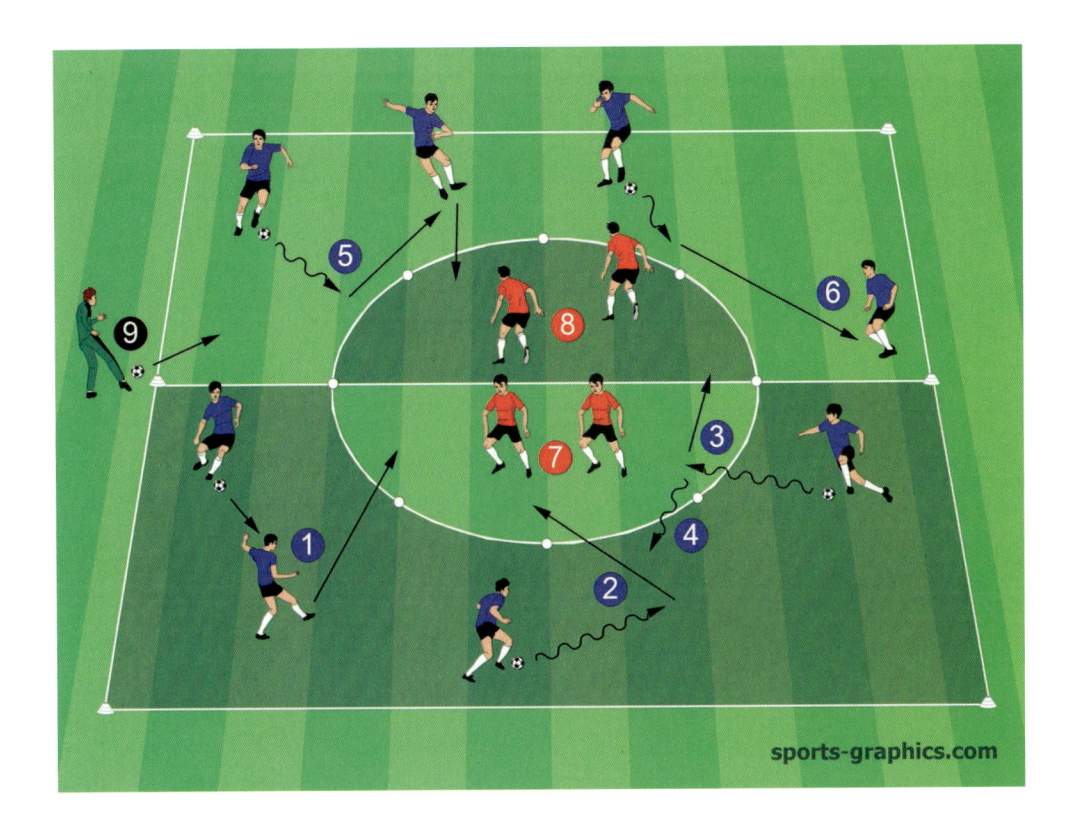

Playing elements and conduct

The central objective for realizing deep passes through the opposing area's defense forces direct, bold passes to the players' own central teammates (1) and gives the recipient a time advantage for the necessary return pass. Hidden passes against the opponents' shifting (2) are also promising. The center is also threatened by dribbling with a subsequent pass (3) or topping (4). In a specified and joint game with multiple players, dribbling, threatening and tearing holes with moves off to the side are combined (5). Optimal division of space and long-distance passes are a sensible way to prepare for the game (6) and to pull the opposing wall apart. The two defensive players must move together and in synchronicity (7), and stagger and cover themselves in width and depth (8). The trainer balls help switch the players' cognitive gears (9).

Coaching points and instructions

★ Threaten the center!
★ Look to the center!
★ Use the gaps!

3.2.2 Crosshairs

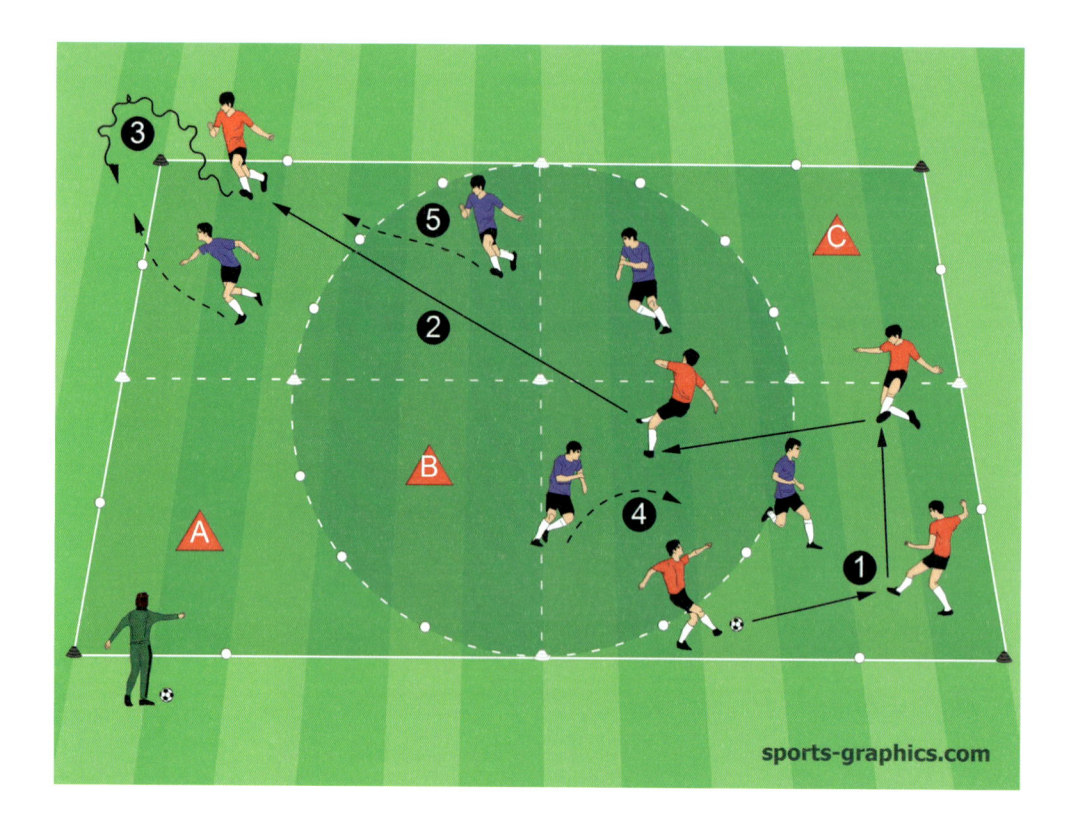

Playing principle

The field consists of an inner circle with four sectors and four more outside corner fields. The teams compete five-on-five and can score points by playing through the fields while following certain rules. Along with focusing on the central circle field, there is another playing principle in the alternation between the central play (2 and 4) and the chance to play through the outer positions or outer areas (1, 3 and 5).

Provocation rules, point system and variants

The team with the ball receives one point when two successive passes are made in one of the corner fields (e.g. field A), a diagonal pass is made from a central sector (e.g. field B) into the furthest corner field (field C) (2), or a player dribbles around an outer marking cone (3). The defending team is required to strengthen the center (4) and react to break-out actions by pushing back (5). The points can be awarded and differentiated based on play in the center or in the outer areas, e.g. if three passes in the central circle or two passes through outside border lines are considered one point.

3.2.2 Crosshairs (Continued)

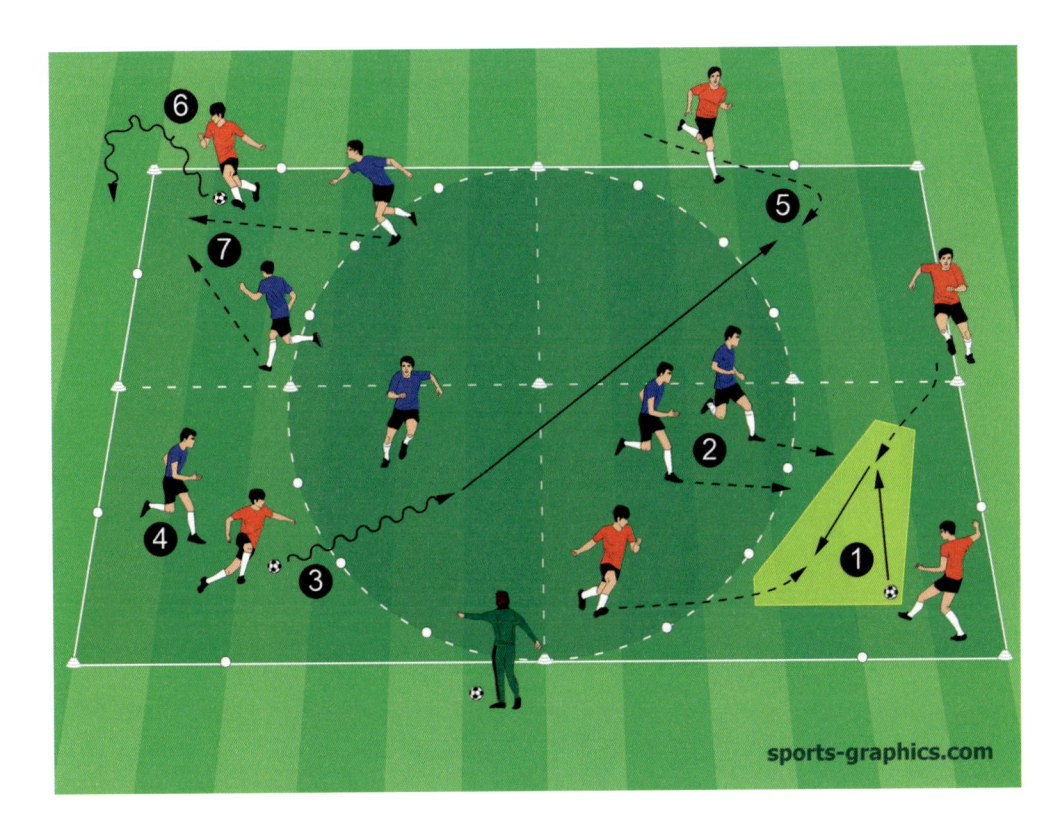

Playing elements and conduct

In the center are the offensive and defensive playing objectives associated with points. The defensive and offensive teams must conduct themselves in accordance with these objectives and outnumber the other in the various field zones (1). The defensive players are always required to make a decision based on the objectives and must keep the center or play to outside areas depending on the situation (2). The players with the ball are required to put pressure on the center (3) while ensuring a deep look without losing the precision and quality of their technical execution. The defensive players must recognize their opponents' play actions and deliberately counteract them (4). There should always be opportunities for deep passes in order to offer chances to step out and achieve objectives (5). The individual actions in the outer field area include swift actions with high opponent pressure (6). In these moments in particular, the defensive team has the opportunity to double (7) and take the ball.

Coaching points and instructions

★ Create a number advantage! Form triangles!
★ Dribble away! Bank!
★ Deep look into the center!

3.2.3 Disk

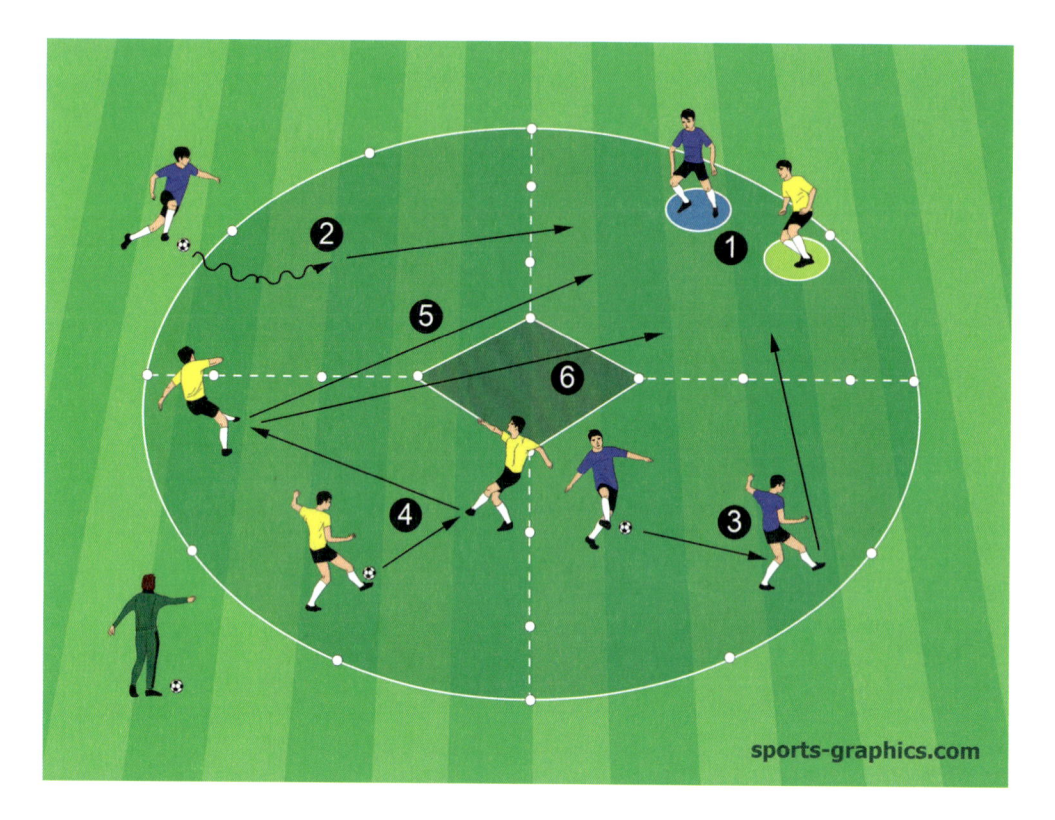

Playing principle

The circle field is divided into four sectors in the center by a diamond. The two teams play against each other and the team with the ball tries to fulfil certain objectives by playing through the various fields and earn points that way. The objectives are based on playing high, outplaying and deep distance passes.

Provocation rules, point system and variants

The teams earn points when a teammate positioned deep into the field (1) is passed to from an adjacent or furthest sector. The pass from an adjacent sector is possible after dribbling into the circle from outside (2) or after a pass within the sector (3). A pass from a far sector is only possible after three passes within the sector (4). The pass from a far sector can occur next to the central diamond (5) or through the field (6). The central diamond and demarcation lines of the individual sectors can be used for additional points. In order to force individual actions, points can be awarded if the diamond is dribbled through or a player dribbles over a demarcation line. Group tactical conduct is induced when other lines of demarcation have to be played in order.

3.2.3 Disk (Continued)

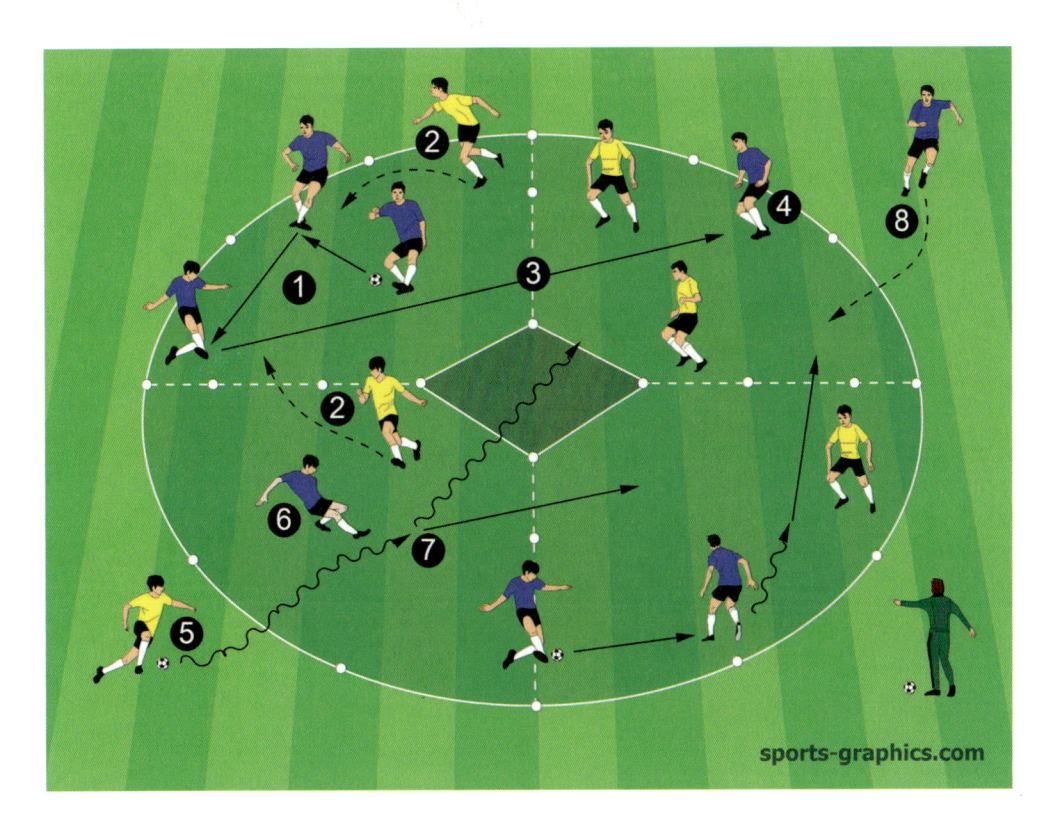

Playing elements and conduct
The team with the ball binds opponents (2) by creating outnumbering situations in critical zones (1), thus laying the optimal foundation for achieving the objectives. The objectives force the alternation between short and long, opening passes (1 and 3). This requires a chance to make deep passes and take advantage of gaps (4). Focus on the center is required (5). Players in possession and defensive players are also under constant pressure to make decisions because of the many objectives (2). Conduct is always based on points, and is thus objective-based (8).

Coaching points and instructions
- Create majority! Use majority!
- Create chances to make deep passes!
- Use gaps!

3.2.4 Half-moon

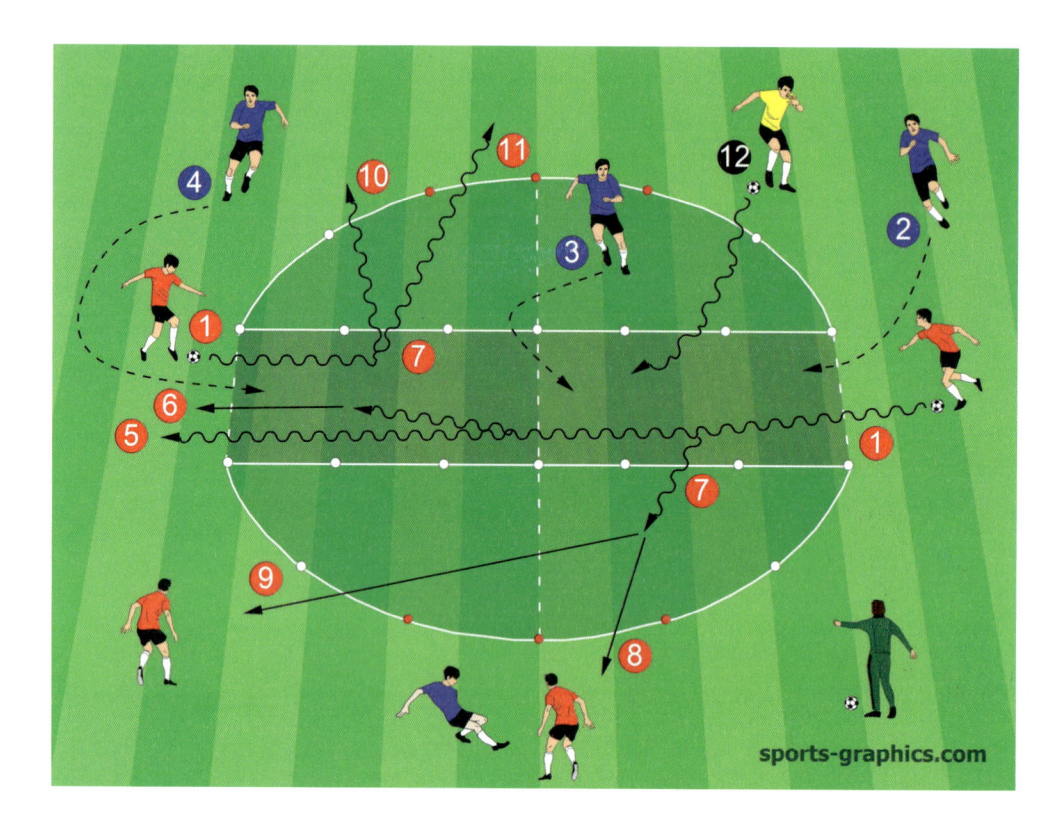

Playing principle

The central circle field is marked by a midline and a central tube or tunnel. The tunnel may only be played or run over with the ball. Two teams play each other with the goal of dribbling into the central tunnel from outside (1) and then scoring a point with various optional actions. One player from the defending team may enter the corridor behind the player with the ball (2), before the player with the ball over the midline (3), or before the player with the ball through the opposite entrance (4) in order to prevent the player with the ball from achieving their objectives. For simplicity's sake, it is advisable to also allow for alternative modes of entry (12).

Provocation rules, point system and variants

Successfully dribbling through the entire tunnel (5) and dribbling with subsequent pass through the entire tunnel (6) result in points. If there is too much pressure from opponents, the players with the ball may always run out (7) to avoid losing the ball. After running out, it is still possible to score a point via a short pass out of the circle sector (8), a long pass out of the circle sector (9), short dribbling out of the circle sector (1), or long dribbling out of the circle sector through the central cone goals (red marking cones) (11). Points may also be awarded for individual techniques (e.g. feint in a circle sector (7) after running out). Loss of the ball may also be met with a team penalty to make it more difficult.

3.2.4 Half-moon (Continued)

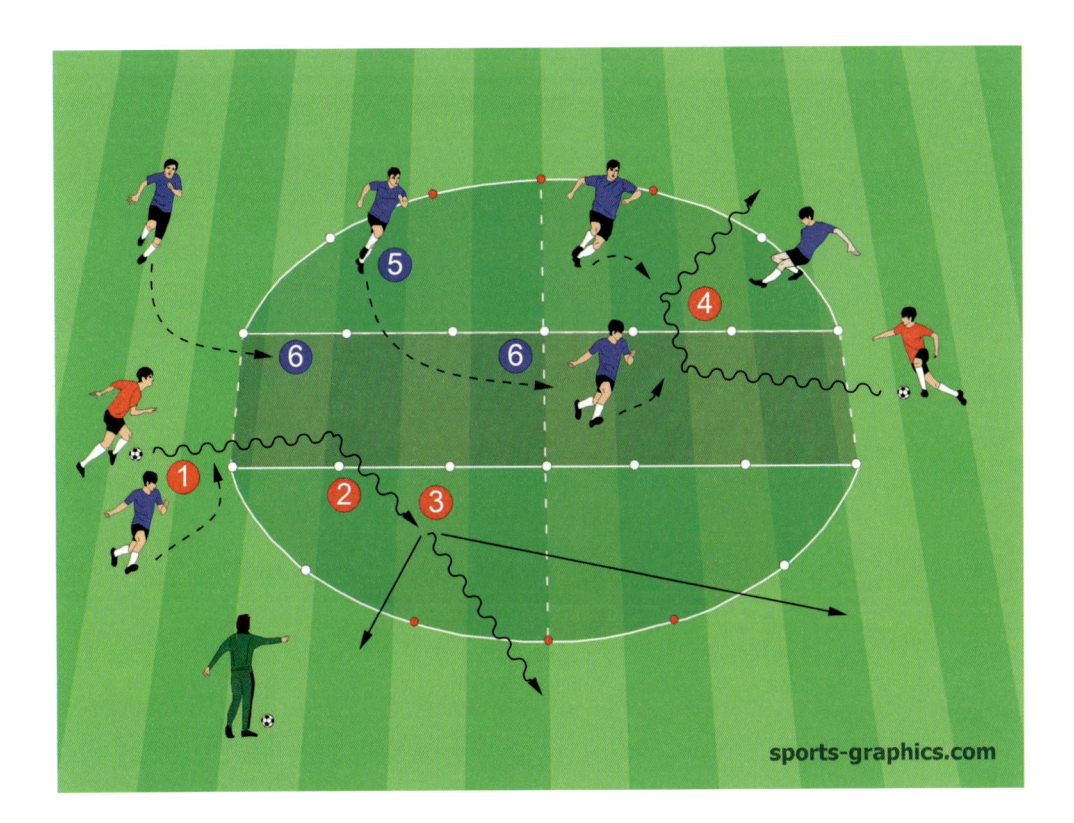

Playing elements and conduct

The offensive players with the ball are required to complete bold dribbling with high opponent pressure and resistance (1). It is always possible to break away or run out (2) and use this option deliberately if there is too great a risk of losing the ball, so that it can be kept. Running out entails more hierarchical objectives, in that after running out, points can be earned with various actions (3). Essentially these are technically honed executions under high opponent pressure in one-on-one situations. The defensive players are constantly required to detect and occupy strategically valuable positions (5). Entering and activating the individual defender to prevent points by the player with the ball also require sensible coordination and accordingly coordinated decisions (6).

Coaching points and instructions

- ★ Be bold! Complete your run!
- ★ Secure the ball! Get out from the side!
- ★ Pursue and chase!

3.2.5 Panorama

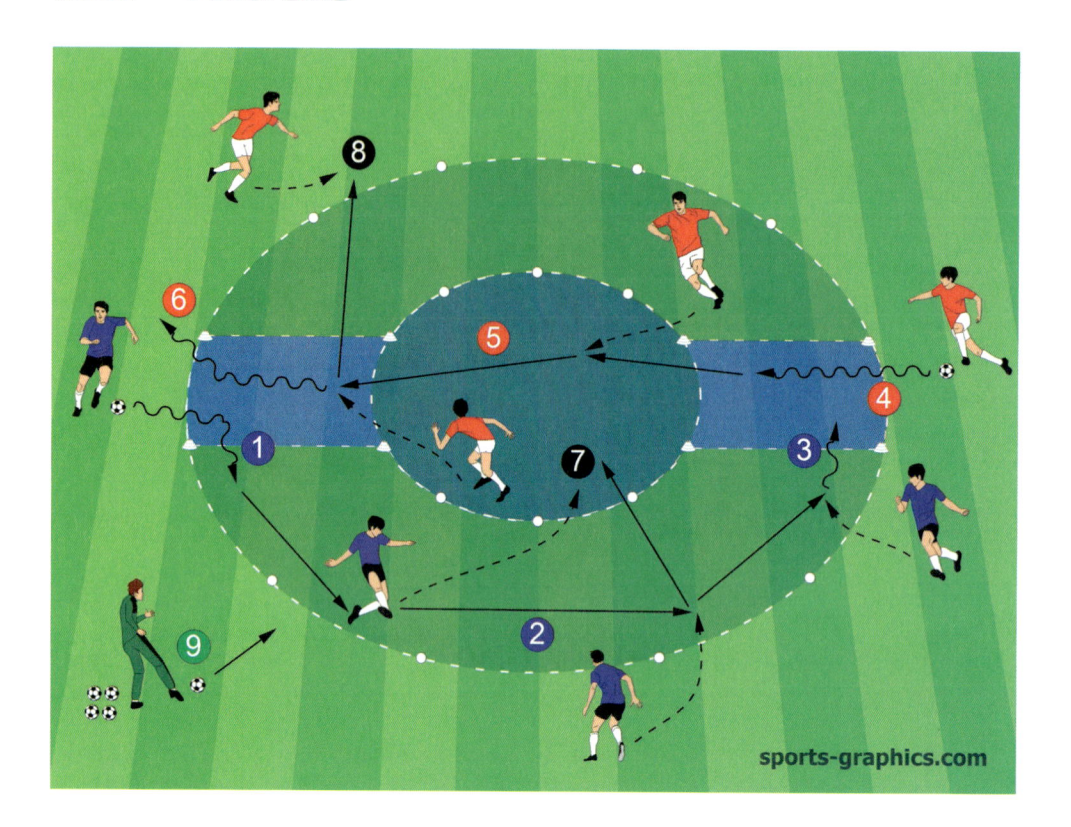

Playing principle

The playing field is marked by a central circle with two corridors. This creates two peripheral areas (green half-rings). These half-rings form critical zones for scoring points.

Provocation rules, point system and variants

The team with the ball tries to enter one of the two half-rings by dribbling or passing through a corridor (1) and playing through it by dribbling or passing (2) to get to the opposite corridor (3). It is also possible to play through the center (5 and 6) after entering (4). While approaching either of these objectives, it is always possible to exit inward (7) or outward (8) to secure the ball. The central circle can be used as a safe area. A pass from a half-circle into the field with subsequent forwarding into the opposite half-circle could be awarded with a point. Other objectives may be specified in the form of multiple passes (e.g. two or three in a row) in a certain zone (central circle, edges or outer zones).

3.2.5 Panorama (Continued)

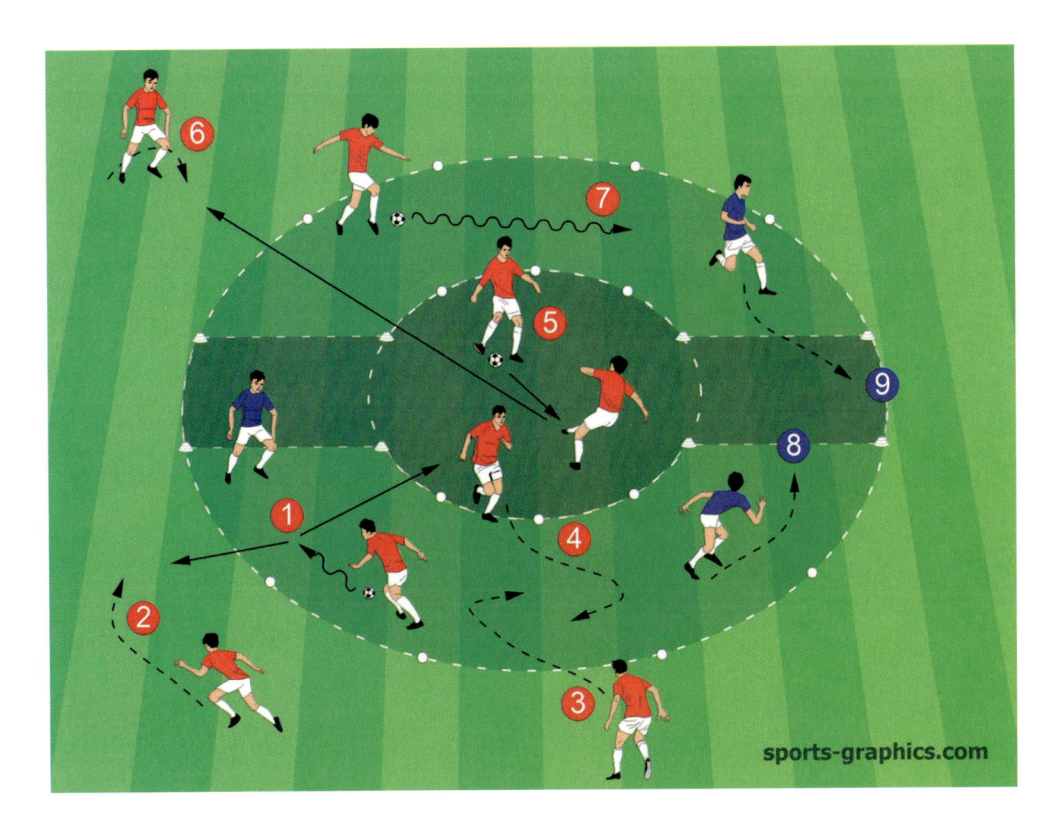

Playing elements and conduct

The various tactical options as per the various objectives always require sensible and appropriate decisions from the players with the ball (1). Offering and free-running conduct is required to a certain degree (2) in order to offer the player with the ball a chance to break away when there is pressure from opponents. Offering conduct is thus associated with open positions in (3) and outside of the center (4). Other focal points during the phases of possession lie in the alternation between short and long passes (5), the necessary creation of deep passing points (6), and the usage of open spaces through bold, swift and long tempo dribbling (7). In the defensive wall against the ball it is important that the tactical and critical zones are appropriately divided, occupied, and run toward (8 and 9).

Coaching points and instructions

- Dribble or pass? Make a decision!
- Make yourself open!
- Use the gaps!

3.2.6 Hurricane

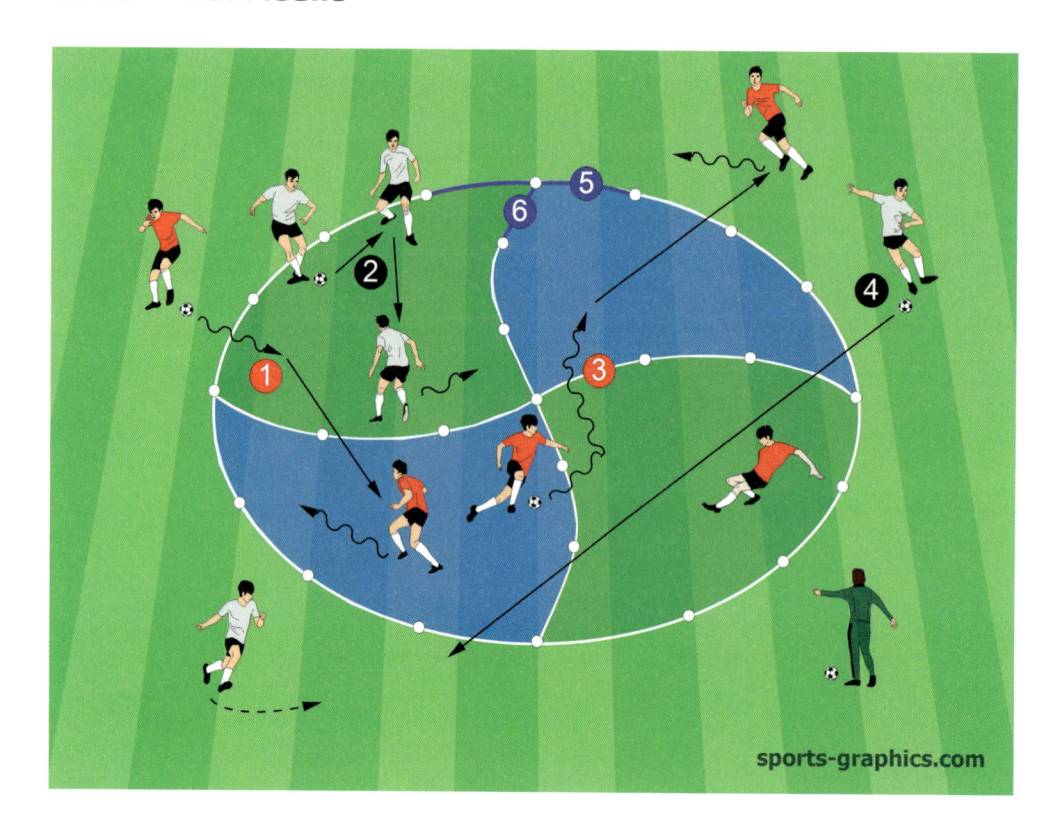

Playing principle

The central circle field is divided into four sectors with curved lines coming from the center. Various objectives are derived from these four sectors and their connecting lines, and the team with the ball tries to achieve them.

Provocation rules, point system and variants

The team with the ball scores a point when a player with the ball dribbles into the circle from outside and makes a pass to a teammate in a neighboring sector (1), when two passes are completed with three players in one sector (2), when dribbling over two lines within the circle is combined with a pass out of the circle (3), or when a pass is made through the circle over two lines (4). The objectives may be differentiated and made more difficult if the pass over two lines (4) must be made between two opponents, or if a pass to another player positioned in the circle must follow the dribbling over two lines within the circle (3). The end points of the connecting lines (5 and 6) may also be used as cone goals, through which multiple points can be scored. All playing zones can have their own technical follow-up actions. Double points could be achieved through a dribbling combination (5 and 6).

3.2.6 Hurricane (Continued)

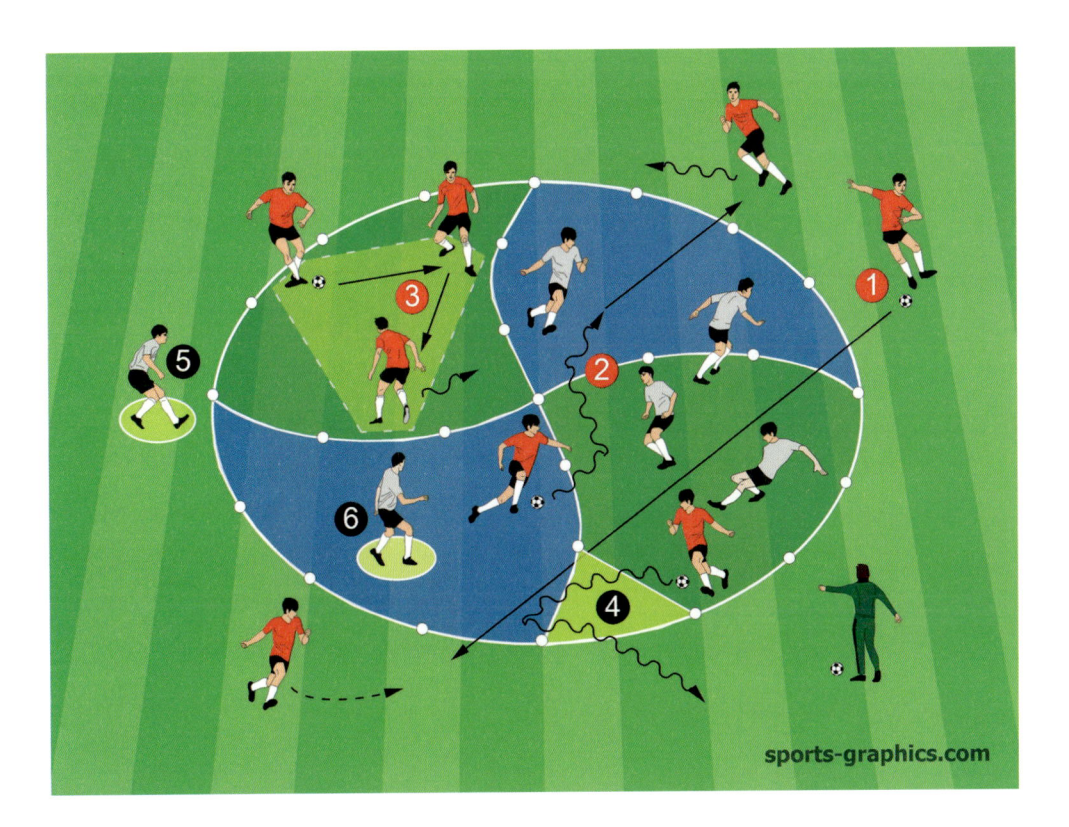

Playing elements and conduct

The center, which must be heavily occupied, is moved, pulled apart, and utilized by the team with the ball (1). The technical individual actions in close spaces should be performed with both feet (2) and boldly controlled with opening passes. The crowding and creation of outnumbering situations is especially required in the spaces of the four circle sectors by zone (3). The chance to define small zones via the end points of the connecting lines (4) provides room for precise tempo dribbling with changes of direction under pressure from opponents. The taking of tactically appropriate offensive and defensive positions is important in every phase (5 and 6).

Coaching points and instructions

- ★ Run on the dominant foot!
- ★ Move quickly with the ball!
- ★ Align yourself with the objective!

3.2.7 Propeller

Playing principle

The circle field consists of a center and wide corridors (zone A) and narrow corridors (zone B). Two teams compete against each other, trying to take the ball and achieve objectives with specified points.

Provocation rules, point system and variants

Individual dribbling through a narrow corridor (1) is awarded one point, and dribbling through a wide corridor (2) is awarded double points. Passing from one small corridor to the next one (3) is also awarded one point, as well as a return pass (4) or playing through a third person (5) with inclusion of the central circle field. Two passes in the center in succession (6) are awarded double points because of the narrowness of the space. The individual and group-oriented objectives can apply simultaneously or independently of one another. Depending on the focus area, the desired conduct should be awarded multiple points, but still be prepared with secure passes. The center can also be used in order to provoke long passes through the inner circle or individual dribbling.

3.2.7 Propeller (Continued)

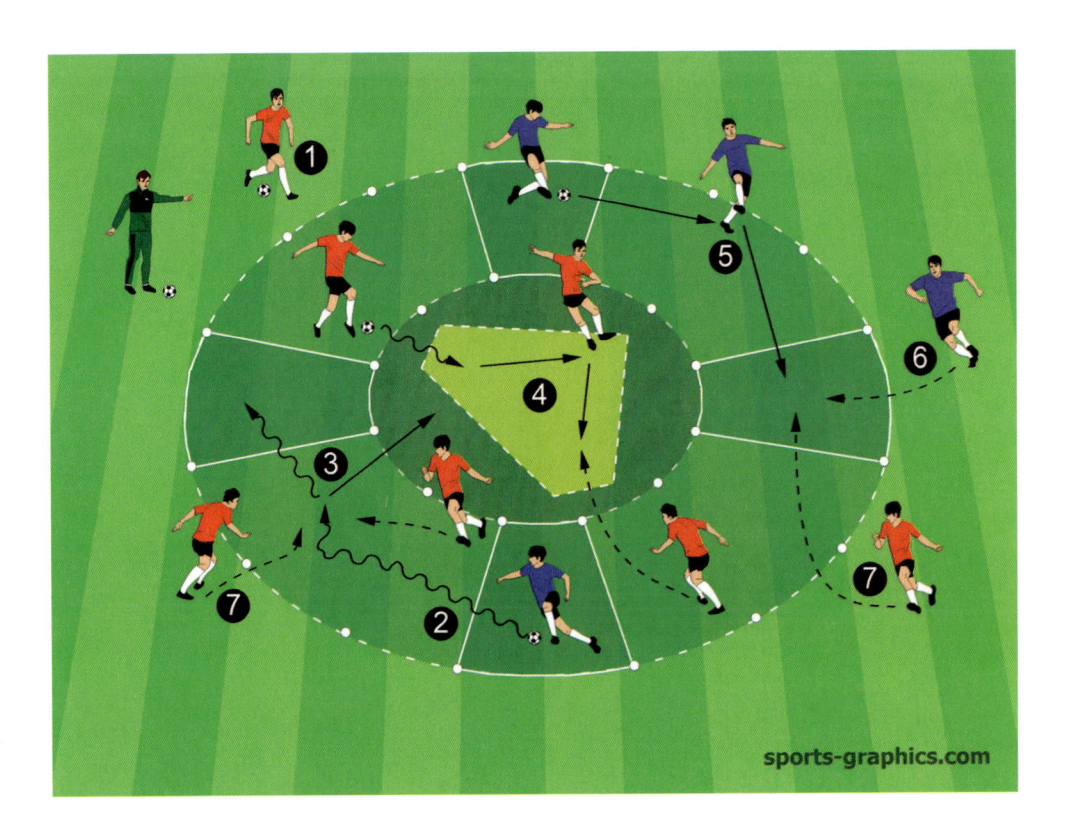

Playing elements and conduct

The players with the ball are required to constantly focus on the center and keep an eye on the players positioned there (1). The individual playing objectives must be achieved with bold dribbling, and often only after overcoming an opponent (2). The players should always remember alternative objectives and make smart decisions concerning the realization of the current objective or with regard to exiting and securing the ball or changing the objective (3). As a critical zone, the center should be occupied by a majority when possible (4). The passing techniques are performed with precision and swiftness (5) in order to achieve a currently desired objective. Coordinated and objective free-running conduct is necessary (6). When defending, it is crucial that tactically decisive zones are recognized and occupied to prevent the opponents from scoring points (7).

Coaching points and instructions

★ Technical precision!
★ Focus on the objective!
★ Strengthen the center!

3.2.8 Sun wheel

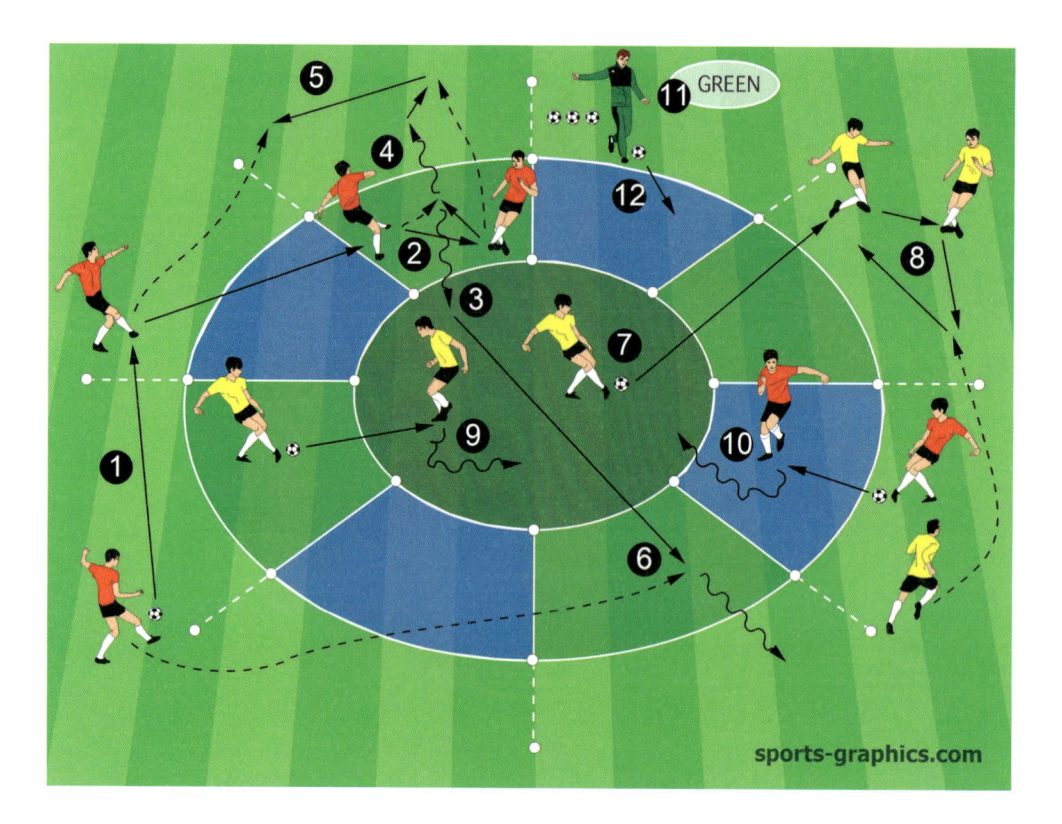

Playing principle

The field consists of a central circle and multiple arched circle segments (green and blue fields). The players have the opportunity to build up their game through secure passes into the outer zones (1) and score points through various zones.

Provocation rules, point system and variants

The playing form undergoes a differentiation when each team is assigned the blue or green zones, or the trainer determines the field to be played with each beginning pass (11). By specifying direct passes for the combinations for scoring (2 and 8), precision can be trained under pressure. One point is scored when two passes are played in one circle segment (2) and then the segment is exited by inward (3) or outward (4) dribbling. In order to earn double points, the team with the ball must connect one pass in the adjacent area (5) or in the opposite segment (6). One point is scored when an outer area is played through with three passes (8) after a pass from the center (7), or when a player successfully turns in the center (9) and the game is continued in the direction of play. This can also be implemented toward the center (10). Adaptability is trained with each new trainer ball (12).

3.2.8 Sun wheel (Continued)

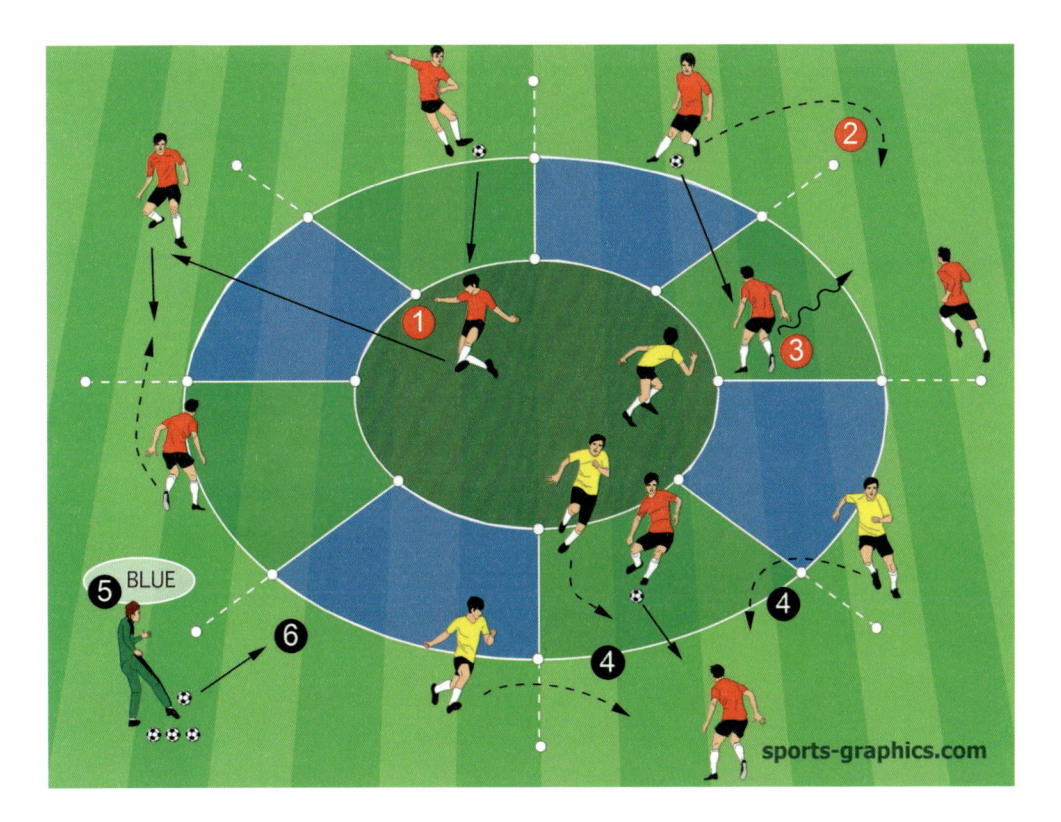

Playing elements and conduct

The playing form involves constantly making tactical decisions. The players are always required to implement tactically correct and promising solutions in order to take advantage of any possibilities and quickly score points (1). Offering and free-running behavior while indicating running paths (2) is just as important as permanent support through coaching and helpful commands. In the central area in particular, constant looks over the shoulder and peripheral vision (3) are necessary to be able to make the right decisions under pressure from opponents. In the defensive wall, joint tightening and pushing back into the outer field areas to prevent the opponent from scoring are elementary (4). New trainer balls and various trainer commands are constantly facing the players with changing situations, requiring them to stay alert so that they can react and adapt (5 and 6).

Coaching points and instructions

★ Tighten up! Push back!
★ Help yourselves! Give orders!
★ Look over your shoulders!

3.2.9 Pentagon

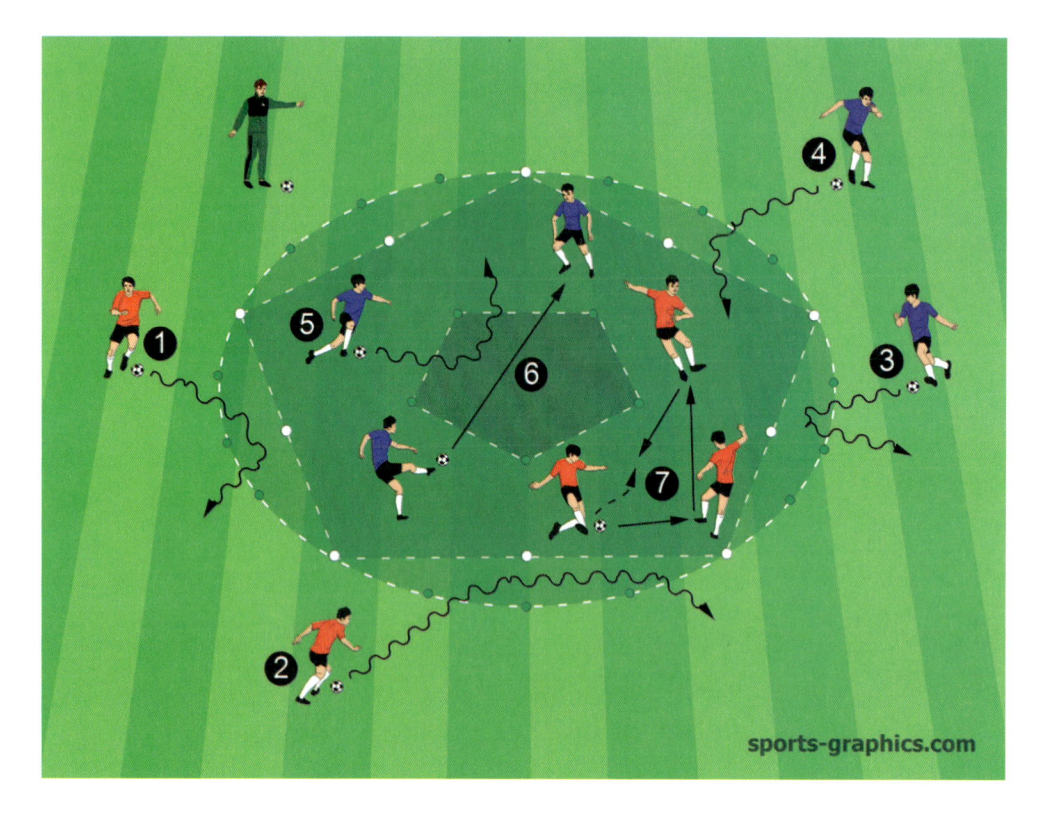

Playing principle

The playing field consists of an inner center, a ring field, and two smaller fields on the edges. The team with the ball can score points through individual or group-based actions.

Provocation rules, point system and variants

Points can be awarded for individual actions when a player dribbles from outside into a peripheral area, dribbles around one (1) or two (2) marking cones, and then leaves the field again. A feint in one of the peripheral areas can also be awarded a point when the game is continuing outward (3) or inward (4). Individual dribbling through the central field (5) can receive double points. The center can also be played through with a pass (6). A pass combination with at least three passes can receive a point in the ring (7). The individual dribbling actions can be intensified by including a follow-up action in the form of a pass. The value of individual or group-tactical actions may vary depending on the training theme.

3.2.9 Pentagon (Continued)

Playing elements and conduct

The players with the ball are constantly under pressure to make decisions concerning the objective and opponents' current position (1). The individual technical actions require high precision, including under high opponent pressure in tight spots (2). The defensive players in the peripheral area are constantly required to shorten distances, run up to players in possession, and push back (3). The center should be threatened when in possession (4). The defense must also protect and strengthen this area (5). The creation of majority situations in strategically valuable zones (6) is just as promising as preparatory passes in the outer areas (7). The usage of gaps (8) forces opponents into a tight spot and induces depth staggering and coverage of the defensive team (9).

Coaching points and instructions

★ Push back! Tighten up! Stagger!
★ Precise technical execution!
★ Synchronize!

3.2.10 Pentagram

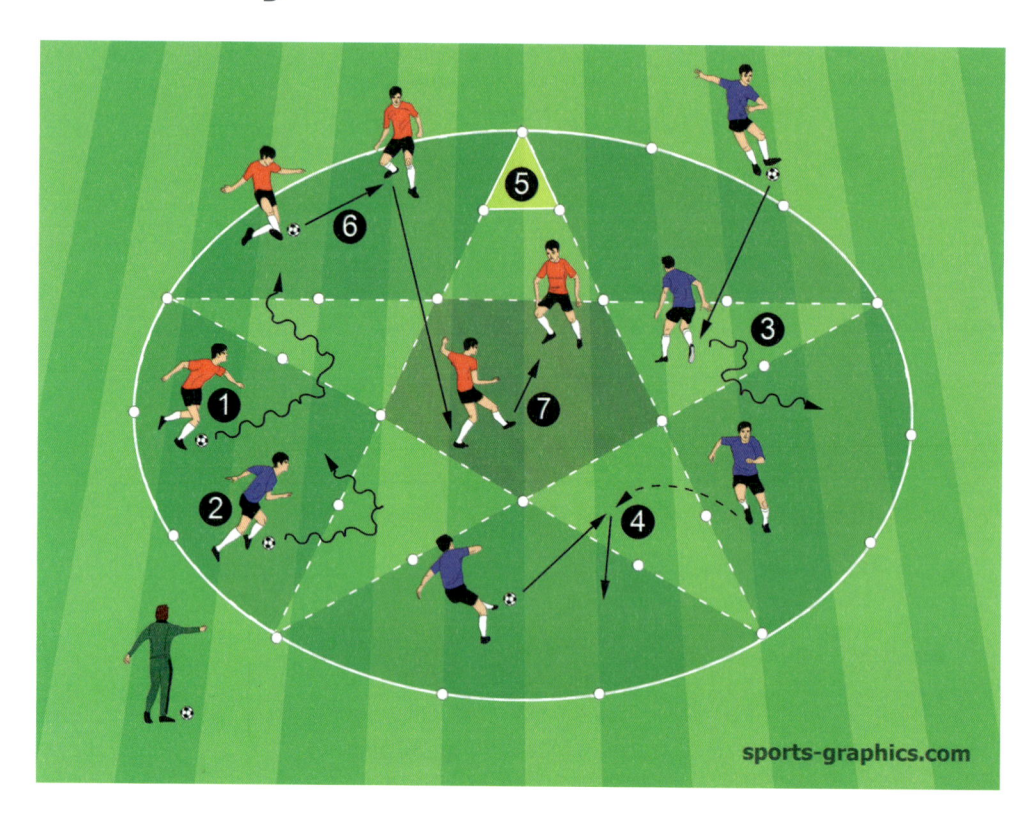

Playing principle

The playing field consists of a star and peripheral areas. The team with the ball can score points by following certain rules in the star points, peripheral areas, or in the center.

Provocation rules, point system and variants

An individual technical action results in a point when the player with the ball dribbles through a point of the star and performs a feint (1), changes feet in a point of the star (2), turns around after receiving a pass (3), or makes a timed approach to a pass and passes back to the passing player or another player (4). Double points are awarded if these individual technical actions are performed in the small end areas of the points (5). In the peripheral areas (6) or the center (7), a certain number of passes can be given a point. Certain feints or techniques may be required for the individual technical actions (1). The number of passes in the peripheral areas and in the center may vary. Individual actions with the ball may also be required in the peripheral areas or in the center.

3.2.10 Pentagram (Continued)

Playing elements and conduct

The various objectives for technical individual actions must be implemented precisely and under constant pressure from opponents (1). The variety and frequency of these actions require the defending players to be responsible for being competitive and prevent points from being scored (2). In order to be successful while defending, individual positioning is important and interventions are all the more important (3). The offensive players learn to time approaches from certain areas (4) in order to keep the defenders at bay and gain free space through running. The creation of majority situations in critical areas (5) is just as promising as individual positioning in open positions and within close range of strategically valuable playing zones (6).

Coaching points and instructions

★ Timed running! Open playing position!
★ Check your area!
★ Improve your playing position!

3.2.11 Target

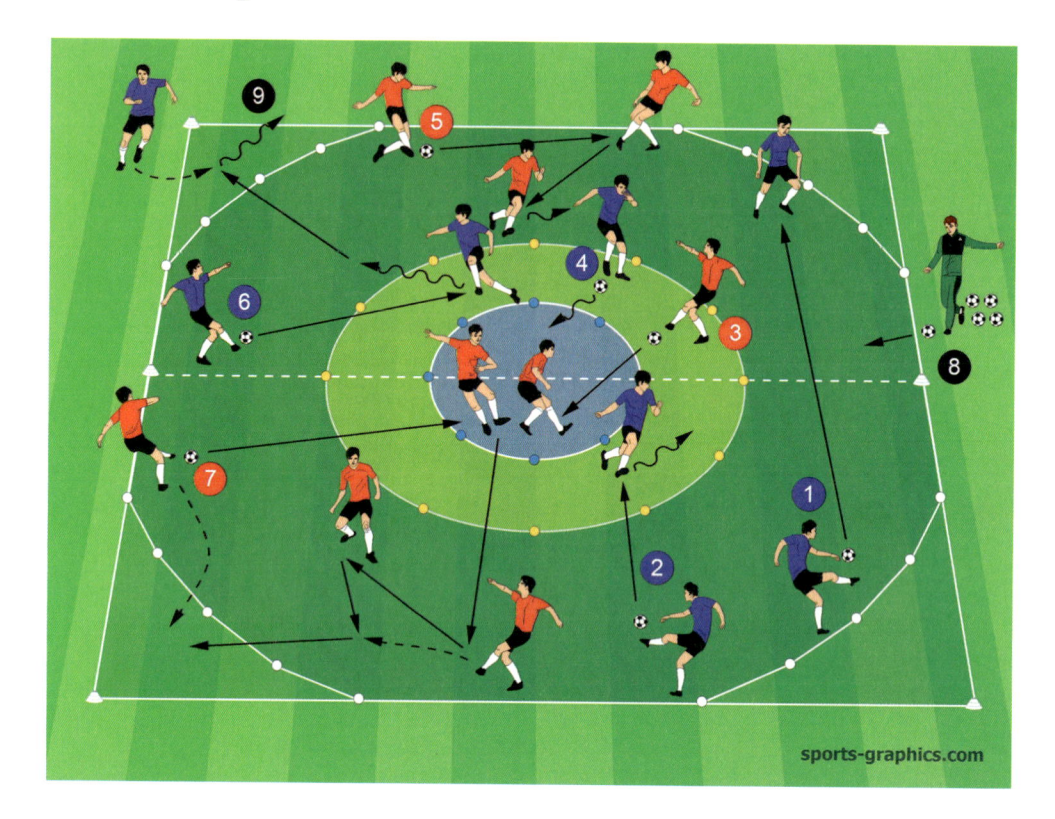

Playing principle

The playing form consists of rings around the center, each with different rules. The players can select and pursue different objectives. This increases the technical, tactical and coordination requirements.

Provocation rules, point system and variants

The team in possession scores when they play over the yellow wedge (1), the yellow wedge is passed to (2), the blue center is passed to (3), or the blue center is dribbled to (4). A specified number of passes within the outer green ring can also be awarded with a point (5). Various combinations are also given points. This results in one point when the yellow ring is played through with a corner field (6), or the center, ring and corner are played in succession in one half (7). Every trainer ball requires adaptability and reorientation (8), and after a corner has been successfully played through, mini or large goals can be used to create opportunities to finish the play (9). There are a myriad of combination opportunities for the various zones. After the wedge has been played, the center or a corner may have to be played, or two corner fields could be associated with the playing of the center. The various fields (GREEN, YELLOW and BLUE) may also have their own ball contact quotas.

3.2.11 Target (Continued)

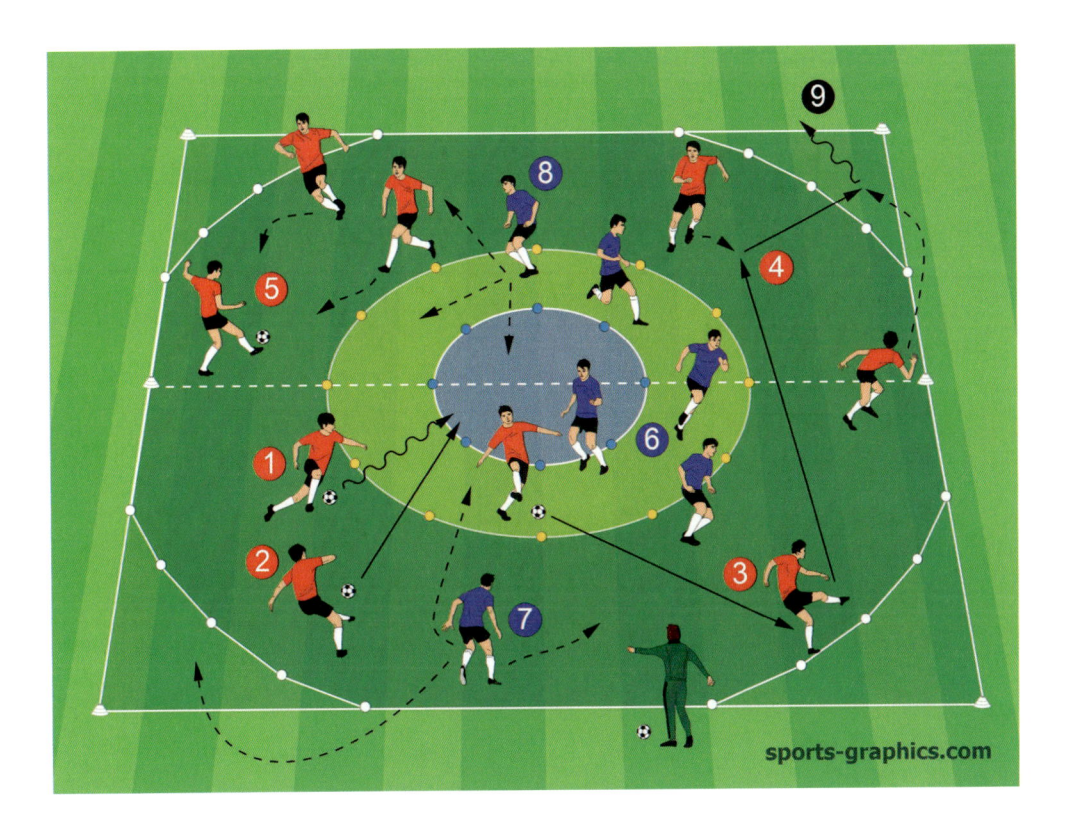

Playing elements and conduct

For the offense, it is critical for a constant pull toward the center, the use of gaps, and threatening the central zones by dribbling (1) or passing (2). Playing with long, forceful passes (3) is also possible if there is a more ideal destination for the pass (4). In essence, the creation of majority situations near the ball (5) is promising for achieving the desired objective. For the defense, it is critical that the central zones are monitored and the defensive wall works together while remaining compact and staggered (6). Strategically valuable and crucial positions should be recognized (7 and 8). Shooting at the goal after each objective by exiting through the corners may act as motivation for a rewarding follow-up (9).

Coaching points and instructions

★ Bind the opponents!
★ Make purposeful combinations!
★ Play through the center!

3.2.12 Dartboard

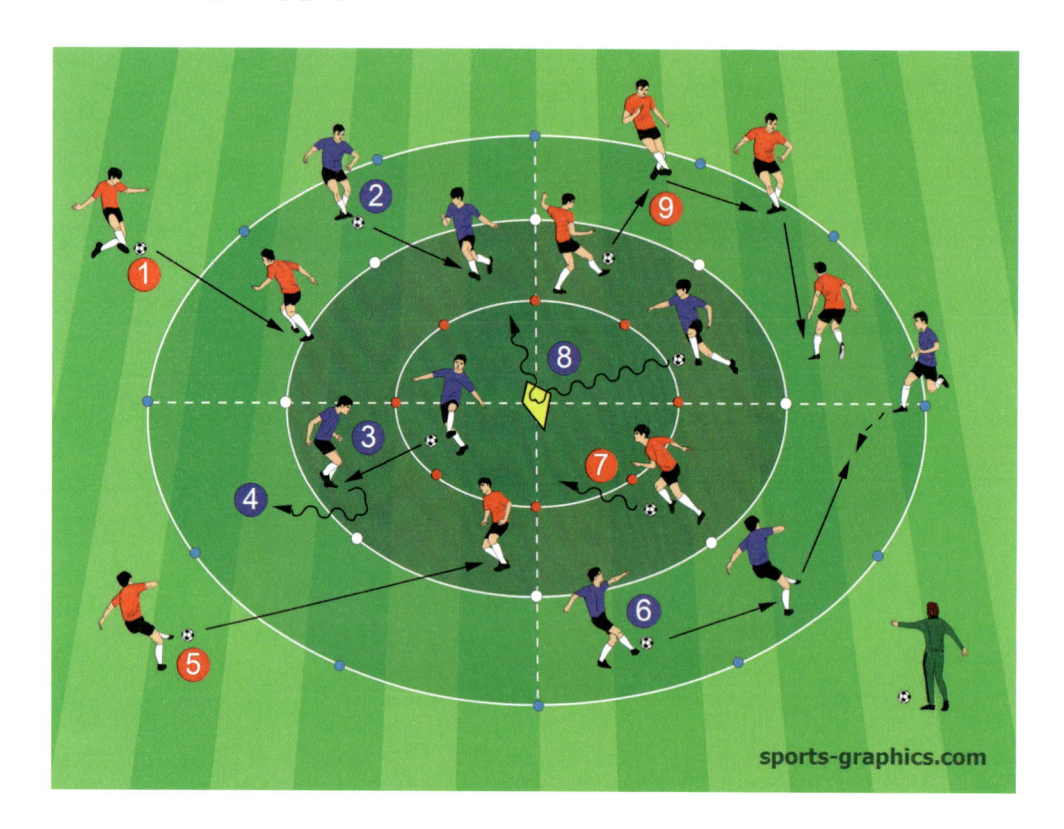

Playing principle

The playing field is like a dartboard, with a center and multiple rings. In the center of the field is a jersey which functions as the bull's-eye. The team with the ball score points with individual or group actions. The rings, connecting lines, or bull's-eye may be crucial to this end.

Provocation rules, point system and variants

The team with the ball scores a point with one pass over a line (1, 2 and 3). The value of these passes may depend on the proximity to the center, or the direction of play. After a pass, the recipient can score a point by taking the ball with the outside of the boot into another field over a line (4). An inward take of the ball will result in more points than outwards. This also applies to passing. Passes over inner lines (2 and 3) are more difficult than a pass over the outermost line (1). Double points are also possible if two lines ae played over with a pass (5), or two passes are realized in a ring (6). Individual dribbling into the central circle is also highly rewarded (7). Special points can be awarded if a player with the ball even touches the jersey in the center (8). Furthermore, combinations of (for example) a pass over a line and two passes in a ring are conceivable objectives (9).

3.2.12 Dartboard (Continued)

Playing elements and conduct

It is possible to secure the ball and make preparatory passes outside of the circle (1). An elevated view and constant orientation toward objectives is promising (2). With increasing proximity to the center, determination and courage become all the more necessary, especially when dribbling and focusing on the bull's-eye (3). It is required to have the ability to quickly make decisions with regard to the lines or ring fields to be played through, and with regard to the various objectives of different values. Situation-specific decisions must be made quickly and consistently played through, even with pressure from opponents (4). In the central playing area peripheral vision, frequent glances over the shoulder, and appropriate ball control are especially significant (5). Furthermore, good division of space in and by the rings is also promising (6).

Coaching points and instructions

★ Take the ball from the opponent!
★ Focus on the center!
★ Determined dribbling!

3.2.13 Galaxy

Playing principle

The playing field offers numerous fields, zones and interim spaces that can be played while dribbling or in groups. Special focus is placed on the narrow interim spaces between the blue and green zones.

Provocation rules, point system and variants

A pass or dribbling into the interim spaces next to and behind the blue triangles gets one point (1). Completely playing around a triangle can receive double points (2). Playing through the fields offers room for combinations. Points can be awarded when a combination of a blue triangle and a circle segment (3), or a pass is made from a circle segment to another circle segment (4). Inclusion of or playing through the center (5) is more valuable. The complexity can be increased, with points only being awarded for pass combinations with three different components from triangle, interim space, circle segment, and center or certain ball contact quotas. A detailed entry (6) or exit (7) into other fields or interim spaces may also be used to intensify the playing rules.

MAIN COMPONENT **125**

3.2.13 Galaxy (Continued)

Playing elements and conduct

The field structure includes trendy, new and unusual shapes. The players' attention is directed toward details and specific spaces because of this innovative zone distribution. The player with the ball focuses on constantly recognizing and reading the current situation with the ball at their feet (1) and automatically recognizing the most promising destination fields with an elevated view. The various round and sharp shapes make it possible to apply different running paths and running forms (2), and to change foot usage (3). Bold passing (4) and free-running (5) from tactically critical zones are trained and ultimately used to achieve security and self-assurance in playing forms (6). Depending on usage, the emphasized entry and exit opportunities train detailed and precise techniques between individual marking cones.

Coaching points and instructions

★ Use both feet!
★ Open position!
★ Master the forms!

3.2.14 Virus

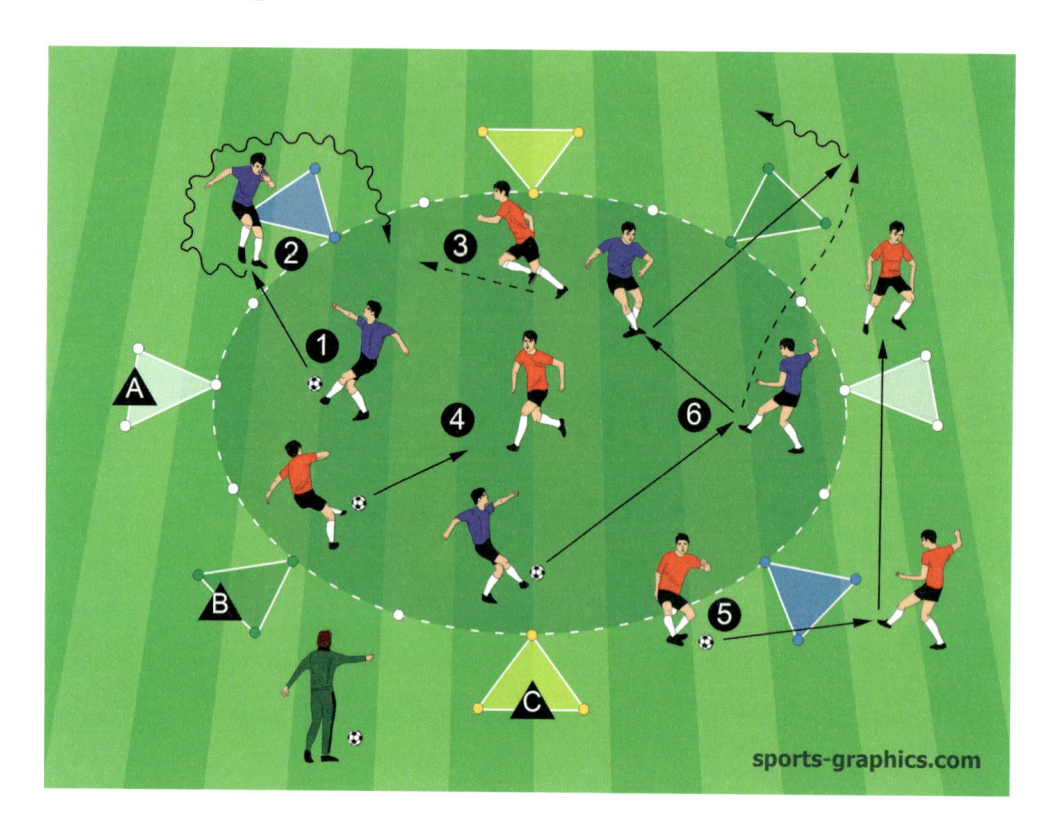

Playing principle

The playing field consists of a large circular field, with multiple triangular zones in various colors attached to it. As per the stipulated point system, the central circle and outer triangles can be played through independently or in combination.

Provocation rules, point system and variants

The team with the ball can achieve a point when a player is passed to from the circle (1), plays around a circle, and returns to the central circle without losing the ball (2). Valuable and open positions (2) in the offense, and pushing back and actively defending (3) in the defense are promising. The points can consider the central circle field and the triangles, with points being awarded when a certain number of passes are made inside (4), multiple triangular fields are played through in succession (5), or the circle and triangles are played through in combination (6). The color of the triangles may also be used as a tool. For example, certain sequences may have to be played through (A, B and C).

3.2.14 Virus (Continued)

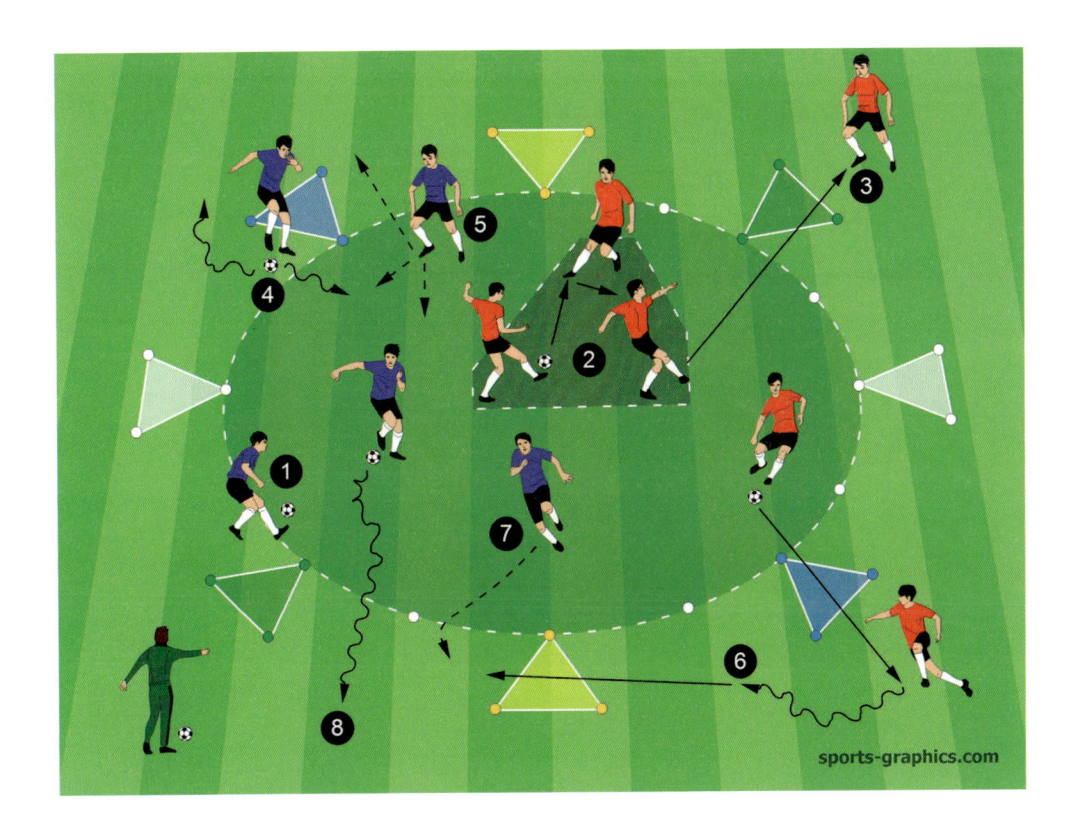

Playing elements and conduct

The form forces the players to constantly make decisions and adapt between the center and outer field area accordingly (1). This change is expressed in tightened playing situations in the center with multiple players in one small zone (2) and deep free-running in the outer tracts (3). The intense positioning of the play and individual players in offense (4) and defense (5) is decisive. The players are constantly required to choose between various optional actions, with consideration of the direction of different objectives (6). The teammates must create passing options with smart free-running behavior (7). After achieving individual objectives, final breakaways to activated mini or large goals in the outer area behind the triangles are possible (8).

Coaching points and instructions

★ Tighten up the center!
★ Check your position!
★ How can you score?

3.2.15 Wheel of fortune

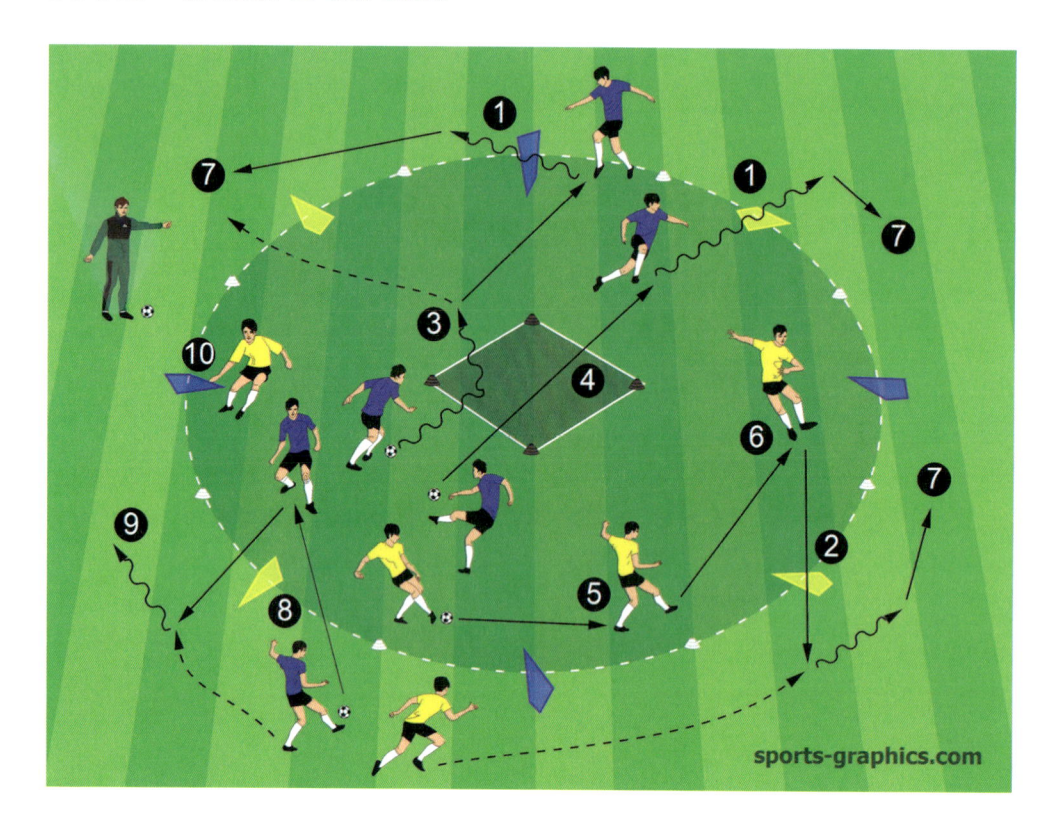

Playing principle

In the middle of a circle marked with jerseys is a diamond. Both teams can score by playing through the jerseys by dribbling (1) or passing over them (2). The play for the jerseys must be prepared by playing through the circle of the diamond. The jerseys may only be played through when a player with the ball has dribbled through the central diamond (3), made a pass over two lines of the diamond (4), or two complete passes have been made within the circle (5 and 6). This form becomes more complicated if the points are only awarded when a pass has been made following a play through the jerseys (7).

Provocation rules, point system and variants

The rules for playing through the diamond or the circle may vary and be associated with certain follow-up actions. For example, dribbling through the diamond (3) may have to be followed by a pass over a jersey (2), or a pass through the diamond (4) may have to be followed by dribbling over a jersey (1), dribbling (3) may be required before playing to the blue jerseys (1), a pass (4) may be required to play to the yellow jerseys (1 and 2), or the teams may only play through the jerseys matching their respective team color (5, 6 and 2). Playing through the central diamond may also require the specification of certain offensive means, such as a double pass, a third-person pass, or ball control out of the diamond. The jerseys may also function as imaginary opponents and be played around (8). A play to the goals may also be possible after achieving the objectives (9), or there may be a competition with the goal of depositing the jerseys in the central diamond as quickly as possible (10).

3.2.15 Wheel of fortune (Continued)

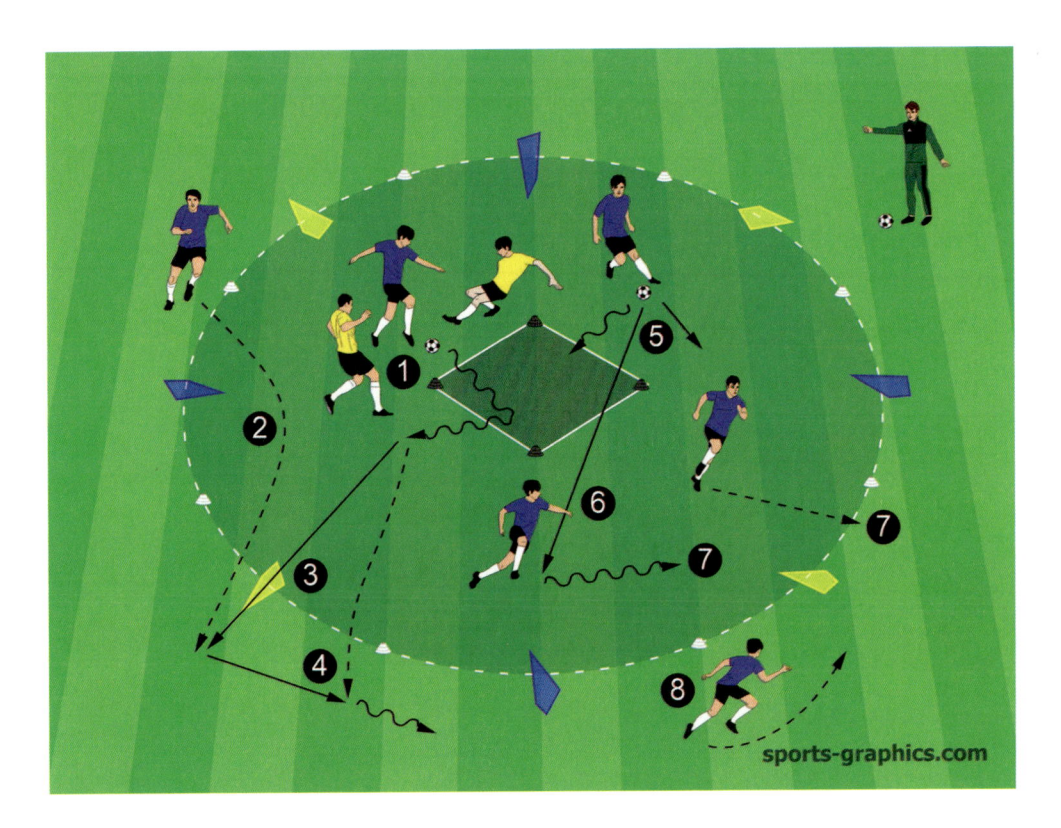

Playing elements and conduct

The variety of options and potentially unusual arrangement with jerseys requires calmness with the ball, especially in the center and with pressure from opponents (1). In order to achieve some objectives, deep runs behind the chain and curved/cut runs are promising (2). The play for the jerseys requires precise passing (3) and creates a follow-up behavior (and final behavior for the mini-goals later on) after escaping the center (4). The various options and possible objectives require adequate and appropriate decisions (5). The players are always required to recognize interim spaces, to approach gaps (6), to accelerate the speed of dribbling and play when necessary, maintain the game on the outside (7), and collectively adapt in coordination (8). Furthermore, there are various pressure situations for players with the ball, especially with the center, in which directions must be changed as quickly as possible with the ball at their feet (1). Dribbling with the ball while running and starting to run without the ball are understood as runs behind an imaginary defense chain, within the last third, and as a final resource after the game in the center (2).

Coaching points and instructions

- Pass into the gaps!
- Quick turns with the ball!
- Sprints! Tempo! Action!

3.2.16 Roundtable

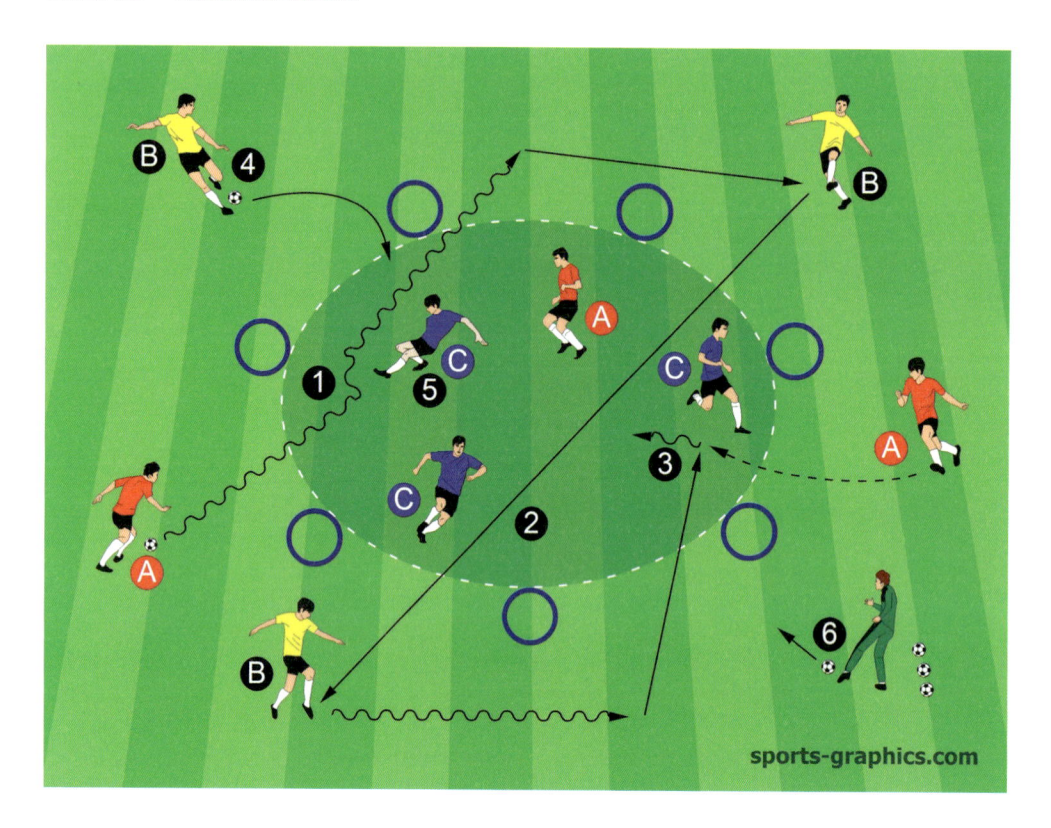

Playing principle

The playing field consists of a circle laid with coordination tires. The team with the ball must play through this circle. The game is set up with a majority/minority ration of three-plus-three-on-three. Two teams are in possession. After a missed pass or loss of the ball, the play continues uninterrupted and the team giving the ball changes into the minority. All players can move around freely. The team with the ball scores when a player dribbles through the circle and passes at least two coordination tires (1), when a pass goes past at least two coordination tires (2), or when a player runs into the circle and processes or forwards a pass (3). The trainer has the opportunity to play new balls, thus forcing the players to adapt, while using a color signal to determine which team will become the minority (6).

Provocation rules, point system and variants

The training form can be simplified when two teams make free passes for a competition, or made more difficult when the game is held with neutral players (e.g. four-on-four-plus-two) or in even numbers. The objectives can be differentiated, e.g. when a lob into the center is followed by receipt of the ball (4), dribbling into the circle is combined with an outward pass, or if the recipient of a pass to the center makes a direct return pass or passes to a third player. Failed center-based dribbling actions can become more significant with a special task (5).

3.2.16 Roundtable (Continued)

Playing elements and conduct

The offensive conduct chiefly involves interesting running aspects expressed in the periphery in the form of curved runs, running feints, and running fake-outs (1). Penetrating tempo runs (2) and downstream connecting runs (3) are also to be observed if no pass has been made. Focus is placed on running through and getting out of critical spaces accordingly. The center play can be prepared with long passes into the outer areas over the opponents (4), and involves deceptive and binding dribbling (5). The focus when passing should rest on forceful passes to keep the game going (6), and inside the circle intensive actions must be endured and overcome under opponent and time pressure (7). The players with the ball can train their technical skills while utilizing and testing their personal repertoire. A look over the shoulder is especially important in the center (8).

Coaching points and instructions

★ Where are the gaps?
★ Search for the gap! Find the gap!
★ Push forward! Cut through! Attack!

132 CIRCLE SOCCER TRAINING

3.2.17   Maze

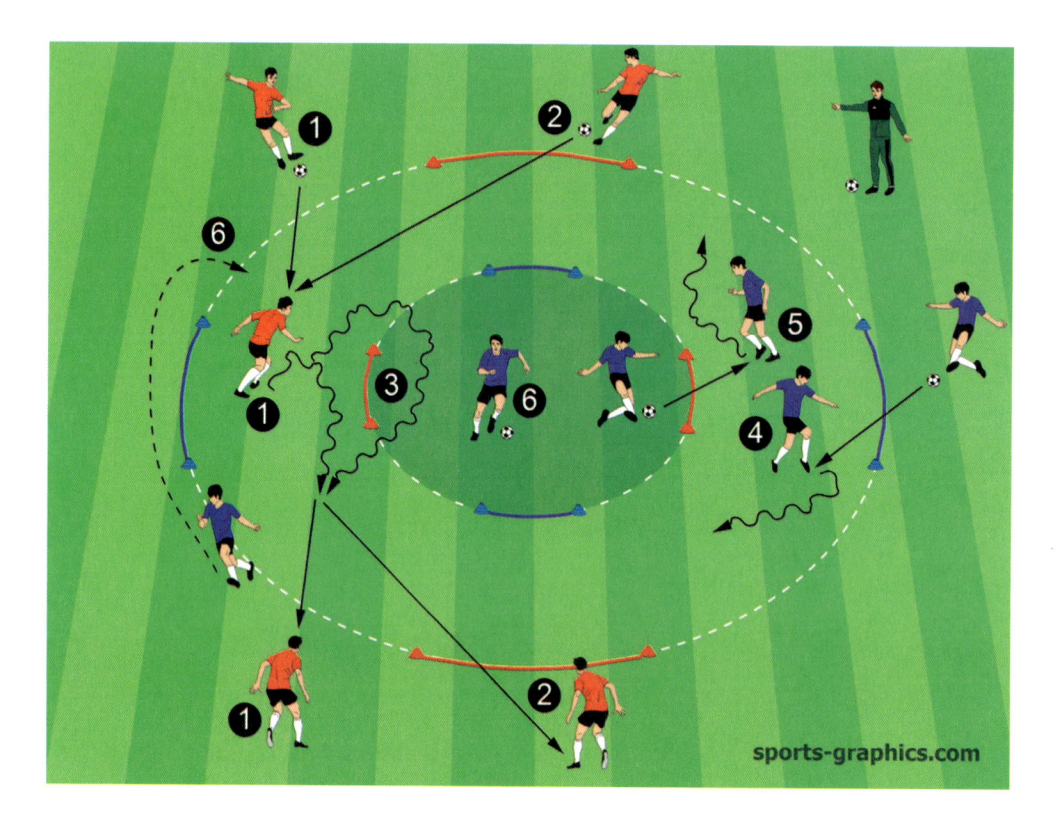

Playing principle
The playing field consists of an inner and an outer circle. Multiple cone goals of different colors are marked along both arcs. The point system, provocation rules and objectives may be based on the cone goals, inner circle field, or the outer ring including the outer area.

Provocation rules, point system and variants
The team with the ball can score if they complete a combination of entering the circle and exiting the circle on the opposite side (1). The requirements can be increased such that the team is assigned their matching cone goal (2) or if the center must be played through during this combination (3). The small marking goals close to the center or the large ones far from the center can also be used, with individual requirements. The blue cone goals can require ball control with the right foot (4) and the red ones can require ball control or technical action with the left foot (5). The teams score if this technical action occurs after a pass through one of the goals. A special point in the form of a running task can be awarded if one of the players in the team in possession is able to run to a large cone goal (6) while the entire running path for the team in possession is in the inner circle (6).

3.2.16 Roundtable (Continued)

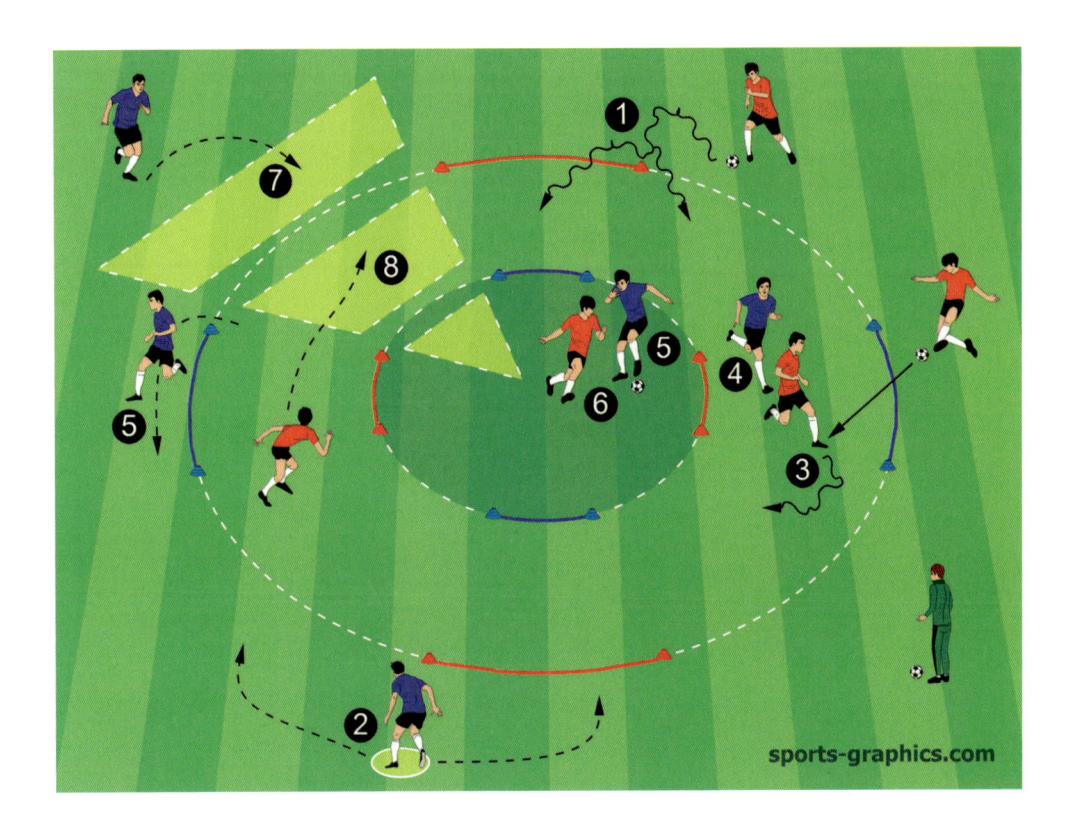

Playing elements and conduct

The various objectives in combination with the various colors constantly force the players to make decisions and require them to make the right decision that promises success for an objective (1). The positioning of an individual player at strategically valuable playing positions is elementary (2). The playing form automatically generates shoulder glances and the reaction to visual signals (3), as well as the execution of technical actions with opponent pressure (4). There are also behaviors that are independent from one another yet coordinated (5). In the center in particular, follow-through and robustness are required (6). The teams learn to recognize their teammates' strengths and weaknesses, and profitably apply them based on playing zones and objectives. Concerning the structure of various rings, and thus the respective levels, it is possible to form spaces between opposing chains and play defensively or offensively through the levels (7 and 8).

Coaching points and instructions

- Find the right gap!
- Recognize levels! Occupy levels!
- Run through levels! Free them up!

3.2.18 Turntable

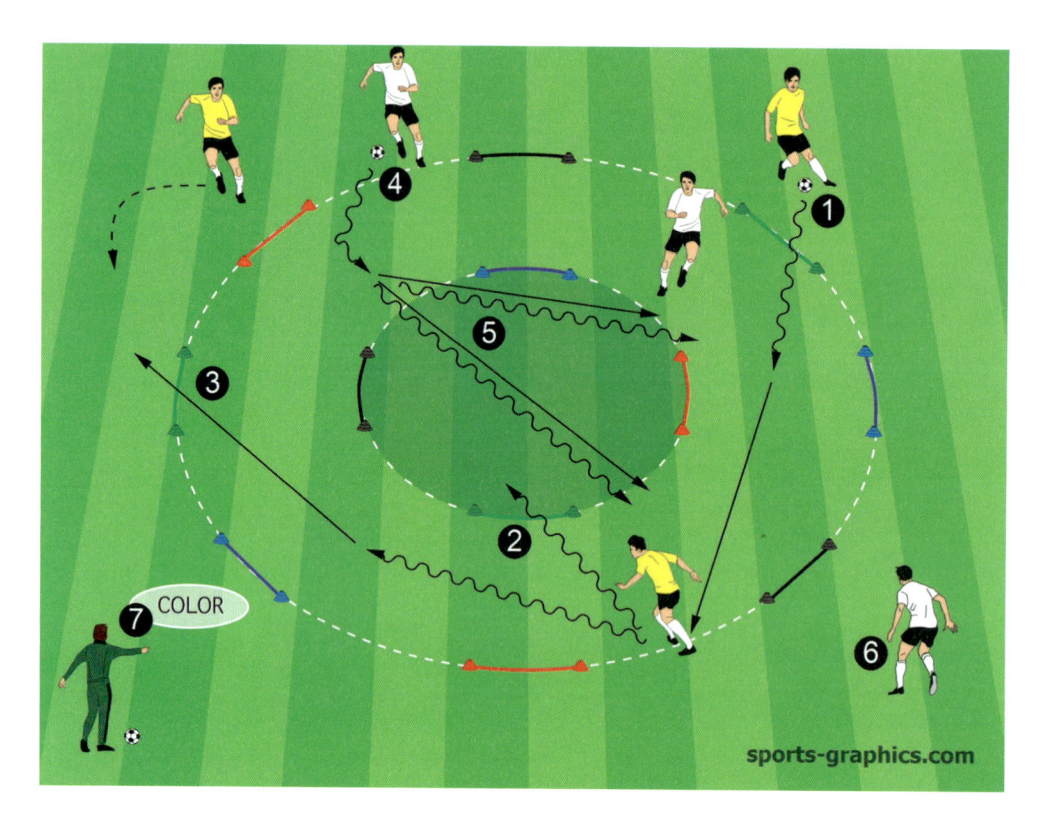

Playing principle

The playing field consists of an inner and outer circle. Cone goals of different colors are located on both arcs. The point system, provocation rules and objectives are primarily based on the colored cone goals and their interim spaces. The team with the ball scores when two or three like-colored cone goals (1, 2 and 3) are played through in combination. The circle must be entered from the outside (1) and exited (3) without losing the ball. A neutral cone goal can also be used for the entrance from outside (4). In order to score a point, this must be followed by a pass or dribbling through the central circle (5). This may also be completed by a deep pass out of the circle to a player on the outside (6), or the trainer may give color signals to stipulate the objective (7). Only a play with the cone goals that were called will then receive a point.

Provocation rules, point system and variants

The colored goals may be used in a variety of ways. For example, it is possible for color sequences to be specified with the respective cone goals played through in order. It is also possible that after entry through any given cone goal, only the colors to the left and right of the played goal may then be played through, resulting in a point. Passes through the outer goals with dribbling through the inner goals may also be combined.

3.2.18 Turntable (Continued)

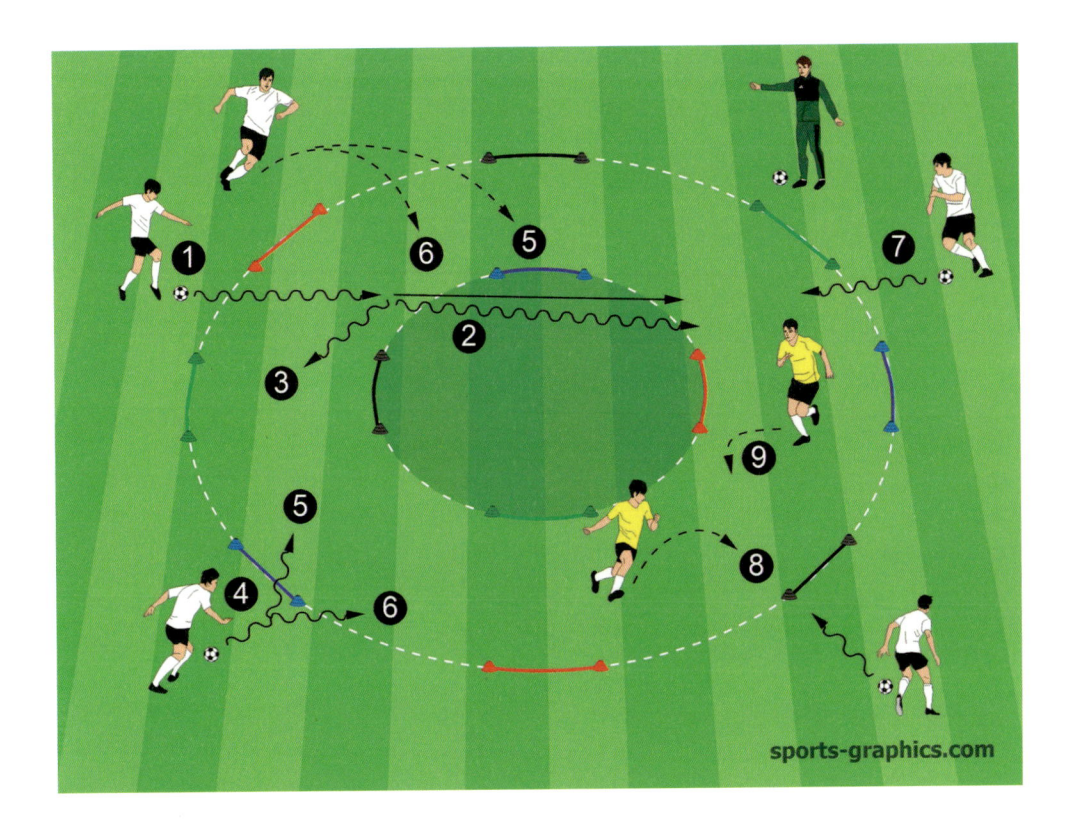

Playing elements and conduct

In the offense, tactical and smart decisions (1) are required. These decisions must also be implemented under opponent pressure (2) without losing the opportunities to exit for ball control (3). It is thus advisable to threaten strategically decisive zones and positions and act in a variety of ways that bind the opponents in these spaces (4). The search for optimal continuations while making quick decisions is elementary (5 and 6). The constant threatening, targeting, and dribbling toward the central playing field area is a primary and recurring element (7). In the defense, smart positioning and facing critical spaces and zones are required (8). The defensive wall should act jointly and in synchronicity when possible (9).

Coaching points and instructions

- Look to the center! Threaten the center!
- Threaten the gaps! Run through the ring!
- Recognize the colors!

3.2.19 Labyrinth

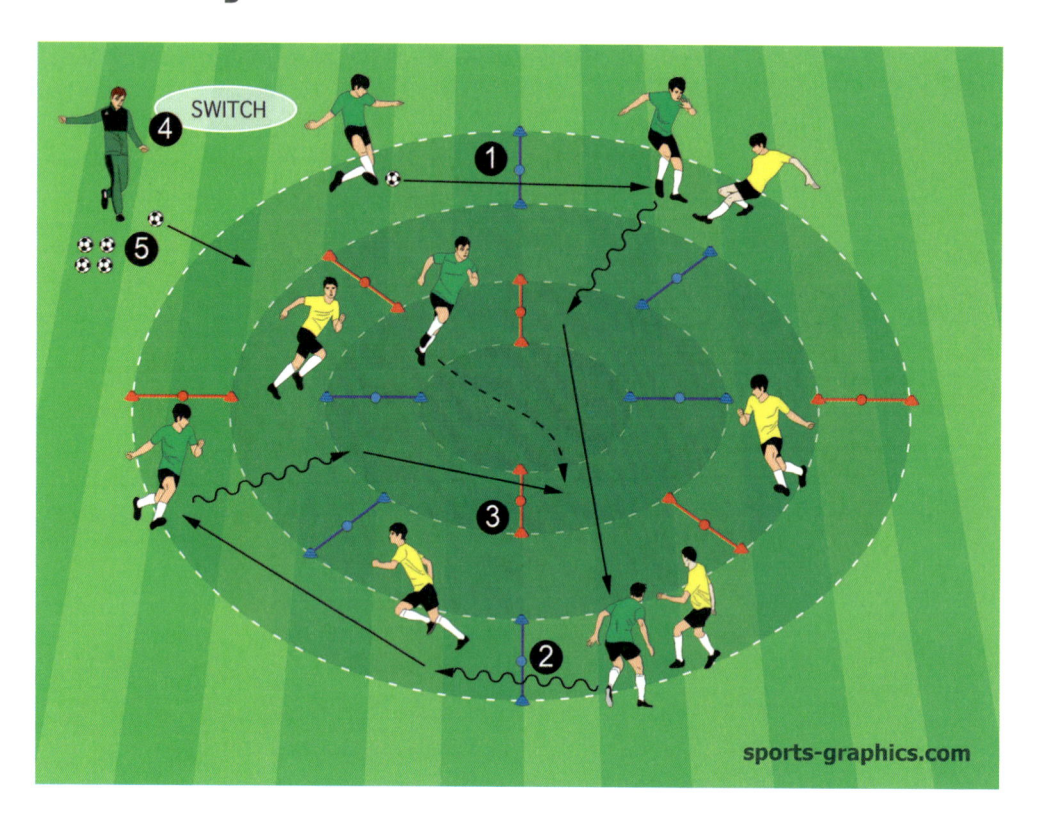

Playing principle

The playing field consists of multiple imaginary rings, although only some cone goals are marked. These marking goals are evenly arranged in the colors RED and BLUE and go outward from the center in a star shape. The underlying objective is to play through the various cone goals with a pass (1) or dribbling (2). A direction of play is specified. For example, the blue cone goals may only be played clockwise (1 and 2) and the red counterclockwise (3). The direction may spontaneously change if the trainer gives the signal (4). A new trainer ball (5) means reorientation and a change of gears for all players.

Provocation rules, point system and variants

This may be made more difficult and specific if the passes may only be made directly through a goal (1) and dribbling only counts with the first ball contact over the line (2). When dribbling, the cone goals may also be used for certain feints or foot changes. Double points are possible for successive combinations of dribbling and passing, so if two cone goals are played in a row (1 and 2).

3.2.19 Labyrinth (Continued)

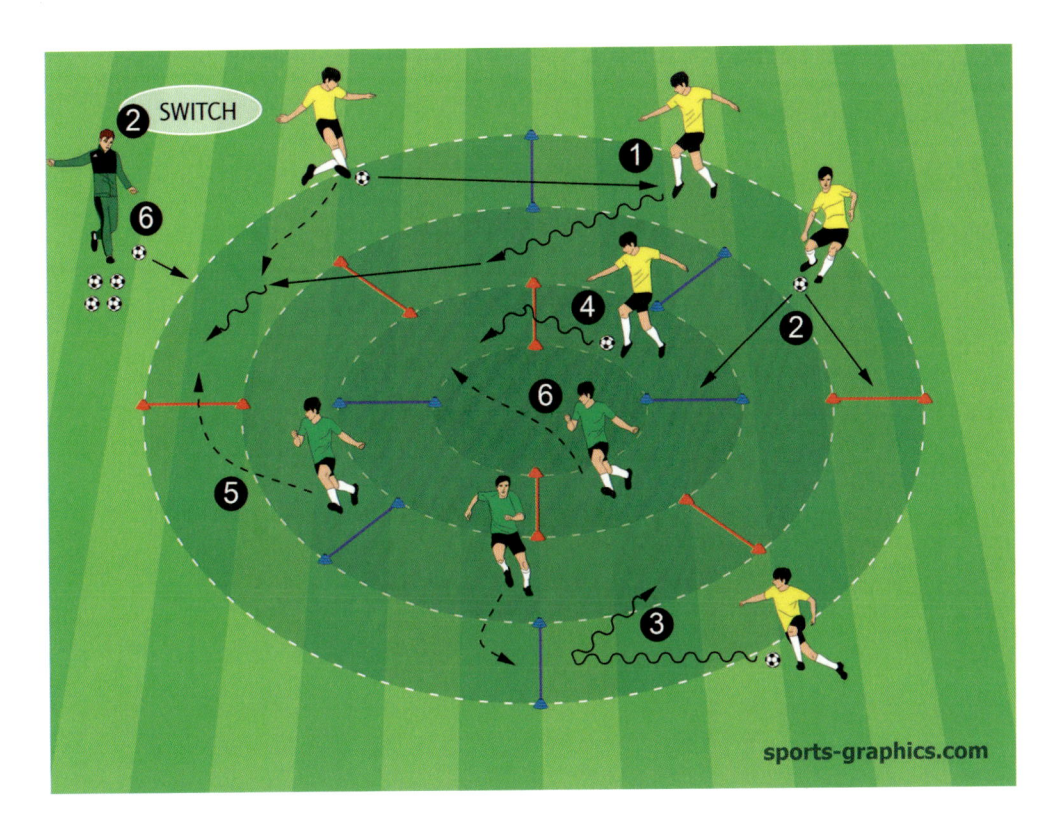

Playing elements and conduct

The offense primarily consists of alternating between the various goals and any changes of direction (1). This requires the players to be able to adapt to the selection of the colored goals currently in play, and gives special significance to the selection and making of decisions that score points. This is especially the case immediately after the trainer gives a signal (2). The player with the ball also has the opportunity to draw and steer any defending players at the various goals only to then perform a fake-out (3) and ultimately have another space or marking goal open. At the individual level, technical actions such as feints or foot changes are required, often under pressure from opponents (4). The defense requires defensive curved runs and approaching critical areas of action (5). Quick alternations for new balls apply equally to both the offense and defense (6).

Coaching points and instructions

- Check your position!
- Prevent points!
- Face the goals!

3.2.20 Cell nucleus

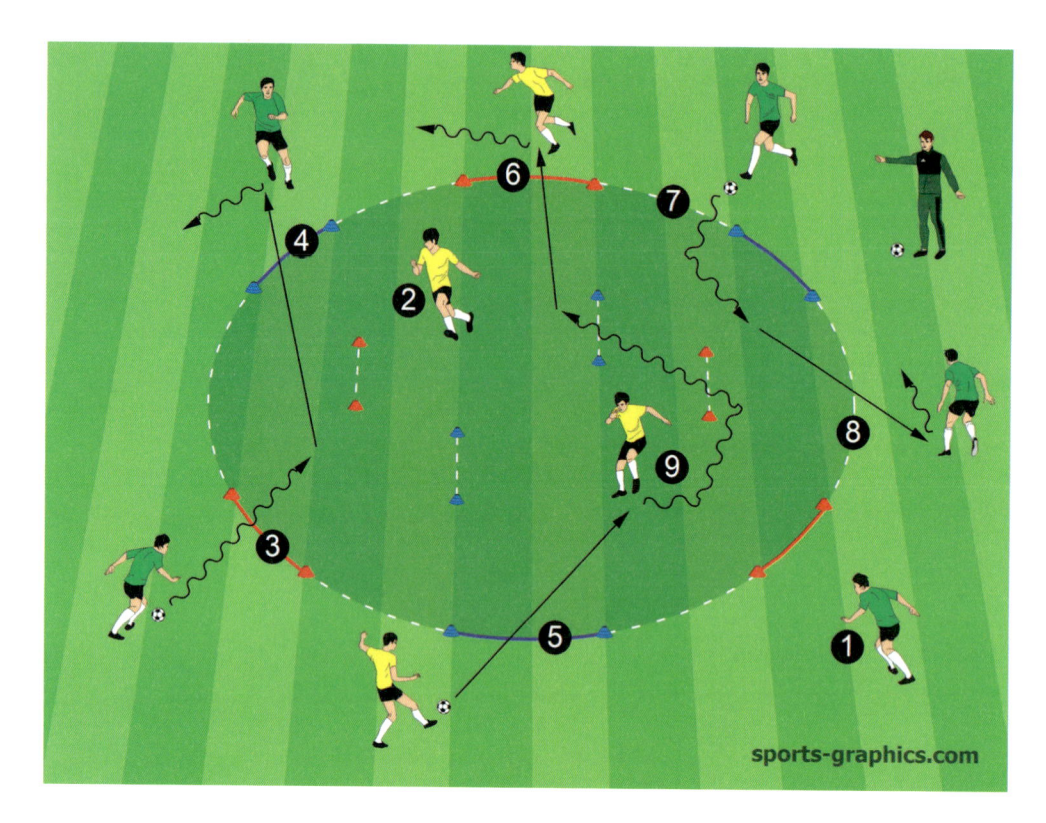

Playing principle

Two teams compete against each other and try to play through the different-colored cone goals on the circle's edge and within the circle. The players may always be outside (1) or inside (2) the circle. The team with the ball scores when they enter the circle (3, 5 or 7) and then leave it (4, 6 and 8). A point is scored when, after entering through a red goal (3) the player exits through a blue goal (4), after entering through a blue goal (5) the player exits through a red goal (6), or they enter and exit through the neutral/non-colored goals (7 and 8). Triple points are awarded if the player is able to dribble through both cone goals in the center in succession (9).

Provocation rules, point system and variants

As a variant, the colors may have different rules. For example, points may be adjusted accordingly and the entrances/exits must be performed through a like-colored cone goal (3 and 6). Passing and dribbling rules may also be set. For example, the player may have to dribble when entering and pass when leaving (3 and 6).

3.2.20 Cell nucleus (Continued)

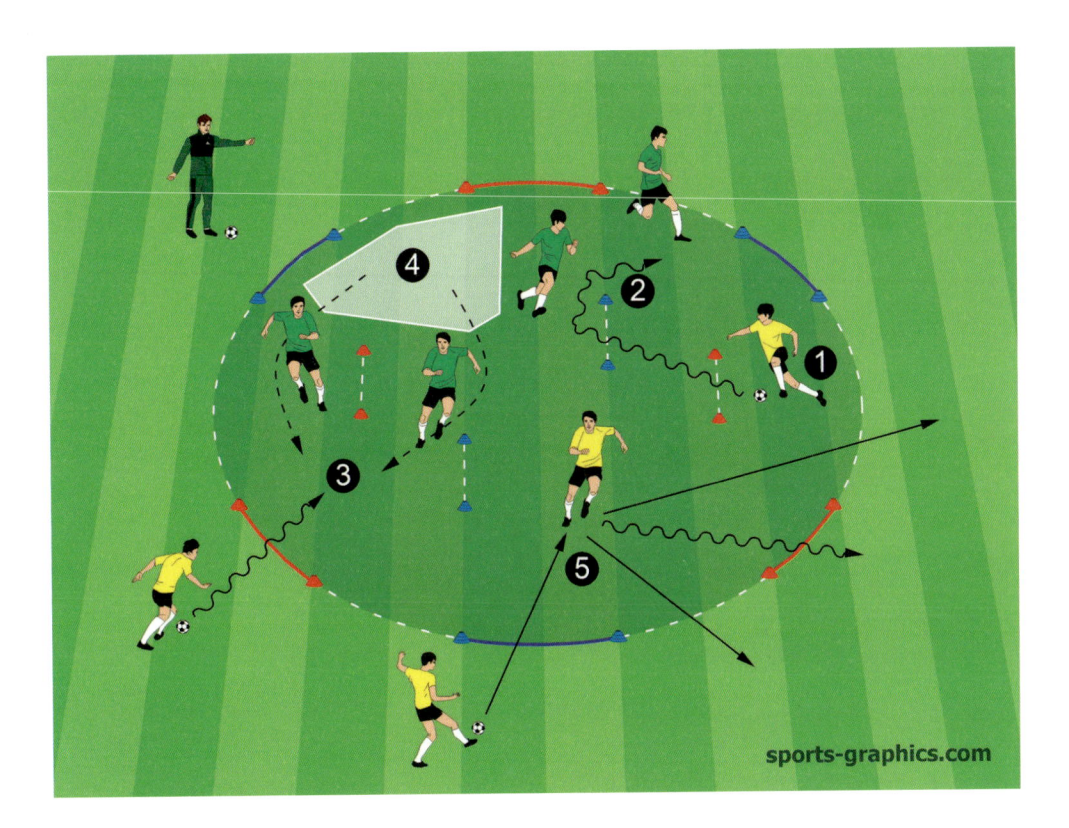

Playing elements and conduct

The target spaces and zones should be constantly threatened and targeted with running and passing. The recurring dribbling and passing to the critical zones, coupled with the frequent one-on-one situations should serve as an introduction for targeted playing in the final third. Bold dribbling is especially required in the center under high opponent pressure (1), and the players are also forced to implement and complete their runs against resistance in a beneficial manner (2). The dribbling entrances toward the center (3) bind or lure defensive players, opening up spaces (4) that are recognized and used when possible. The center serves as a pivot and fulcrum (5) in which decisions must be made for the most sensible direction or continuation of play under high pressure from time and opponents.

Coaching points and instructions

★ Complete your run!
★ Root for points!
★ Bold actions!

3.2.21 Carousel

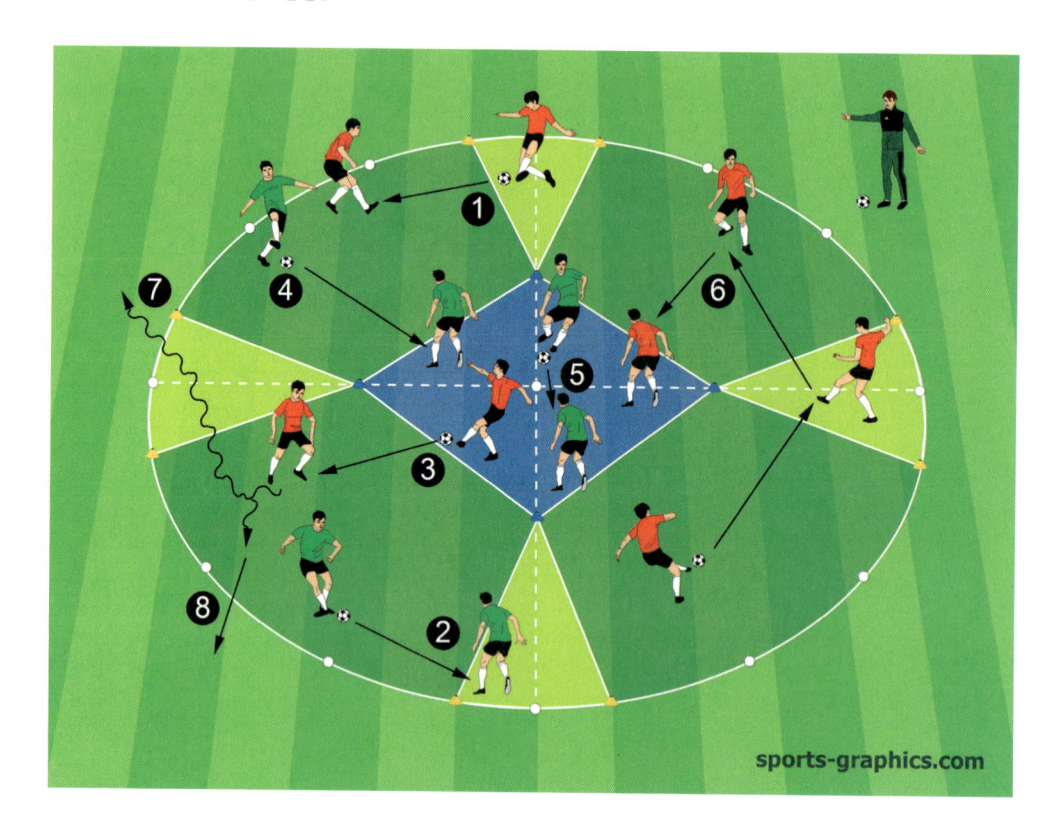

Playing principle

The team with the ball tries to keep the ball for as long as possible while playing through the various circle segments and fields (blue diamond, yellow triangles and green interim spaces) in a certain way in order to earn points. A pass from a triangle (1), a pass into a triangle (2), a pass from the central diamond (3), and a pass into the central diamond (4) are each worth one point. A pass within the central diamond (5) is worth two points, and a combination of triangle, interim space and diamond (6) is worth three points. The players are required to complete four rotating circuits, and to regularly change fields, especially after ball actions.

Provocation rules, point system and variants

The playing form may be organized in various ratios, from three-on-three to six-on-six, or with neutral players. Four teams can also play against each other within one circle at the same time, resulting in constant obstacles. Ball contact limits for the players in possession or certain rules for passing may make technical aspects more difficult and emphasized. In order to straighten out the playing form and to break free from the center, breakaway actions toward the outside may also be required. After the central field (BLUE) has been played through via dribbling or a pass, double points can be awarded if the circle is then exited by dribbling (7) through a yellow field or passing through a green field (8). After successfully breaking away (7 or 8), follow-ups for points can be directed at the mini- or large goals.

3.2.21 Carousel (Continued)

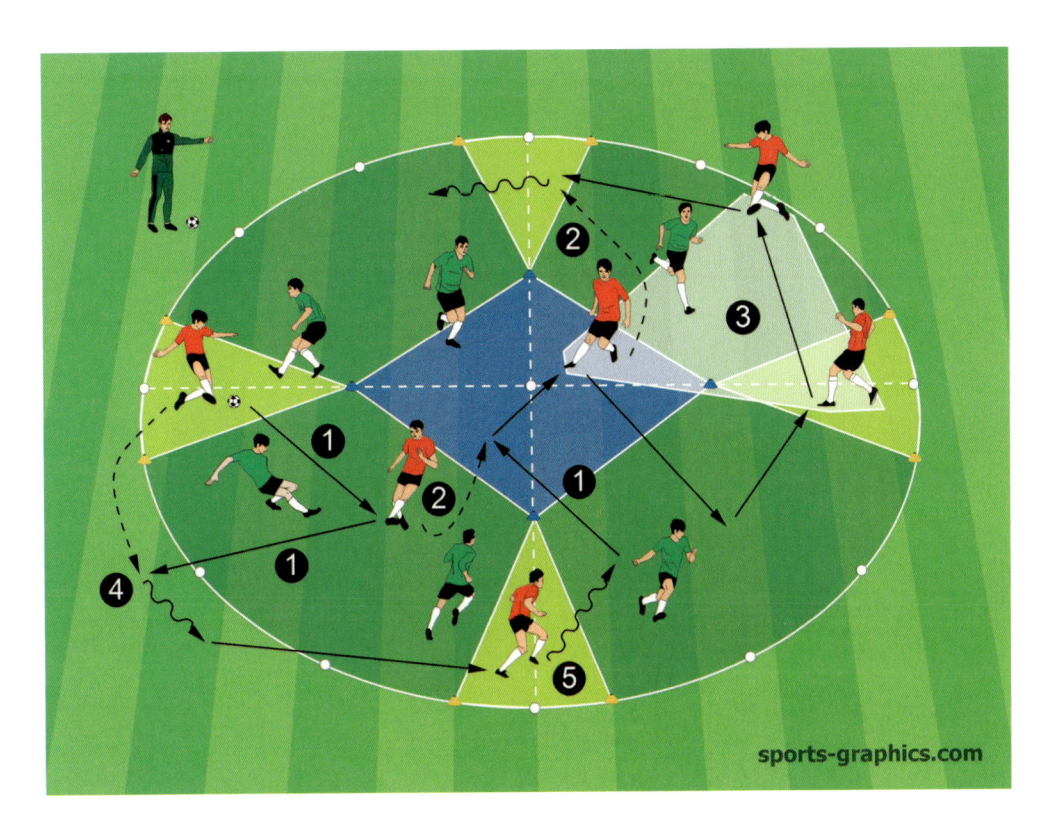

Playing elements and conduct

The organization of this playing form gets rid of the less promising straight pass along the line. Rather, the players are required to make diagonal and slanted passes by the round shape of the field. The playing form also intends for many repetitions, and for pass security in playing forms to be built up and acquired. Other requirements are good offering and free-running (2), expressed in the many recurring triangular formations (3). The playing situations are also continued outside of the circle (4), but the point system lets the players act toward the center and pulls the game toward the middle.

Coaching points and instructions

★ Orient yourself by the shapes!
★ Round has to get into the angular!
★ Find shapes! Find fields!

3.2.22 Molecule

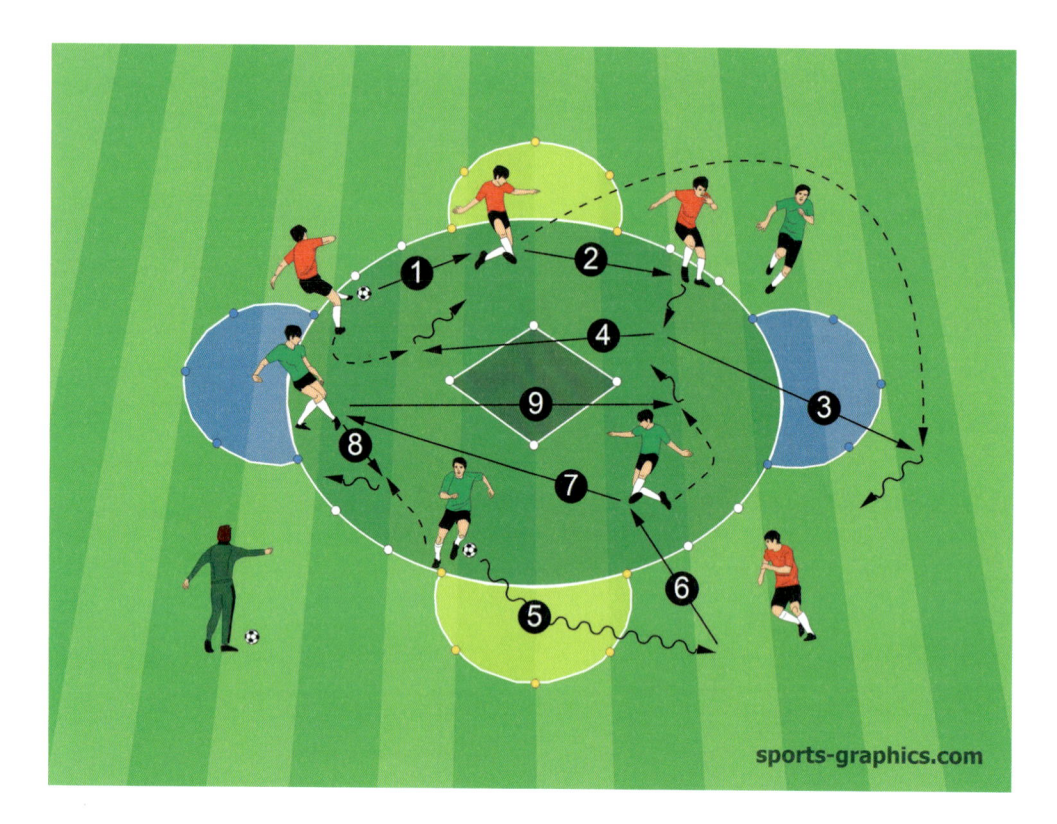

Playing principle

The team with the ball has the choice between two introductory options for achieving a point during a follow-up action. The point may be started either by two passes within the circle (1 and 2) or by dribbling out of the circle via a half-circle (5). In order to earn the point, two complete passes (1 and 2) must be followed by another pass out of the circle via a half-circle (3) or through the central diamond (4). The follow-up pass through the half-circle is awarded one point, and the pass through the diamond gets double. The introductory dribbling out of the half-circle (5) must be followed by a return pass into the circle plus two additional passes within the circle in order for the point to count. The two subsequent passes can both be performed within the circle (7 and 8) or in the circle and through the diamond (7 and 9) for a single point. Both passes in the circle receive one point, a combination through the diamond gets double.

Provocation rules, point system and variants

The focus can lie on technical requirements, with the players being required to use their non-dominant leg for critical passes (3, 4, 6 and 9) or to perform a certain feint (foot change, stepover, fake shot, etc.) when exiting a half-circle (5).

3.2.22 Molecule (Continued)

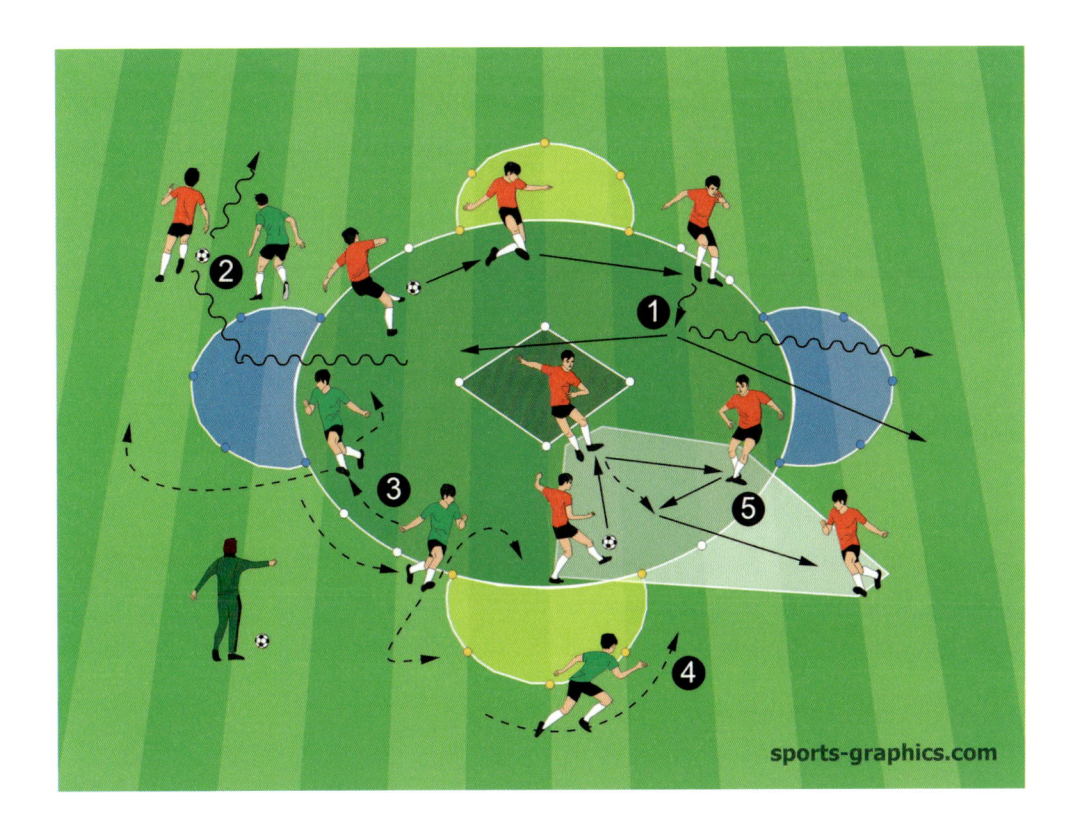

Playing elements and conduct

The unusual shape of the individual zones and fields allows for new learning methods in multifaceted playing situations with multidimensional decision-making possibilities (1). Some objectives require recurring continuations and thus actions back toward the opposing wall. These actions are often associated with opponent pressure, and ideally involve glances over the shoulder and pre-orientation (2). Steering toward the half-circles is desirable while free-running (3 and 4). The offering and free-running behavior is motorically demanding around the curves (3) and aims for open positions (4) and strategic positioning. Within one's own team there are triangle formations, diamond formations, the creation of majority situations near the ball, and (when possible) secure combinations and tactically smart and coordinated positioning (5).

Coaching points and instructions

★ Optimal pass strength! Passes with a message!
★ Pay attention to first ball contact!
★ Paced control!

3.2.23 Soap bubble

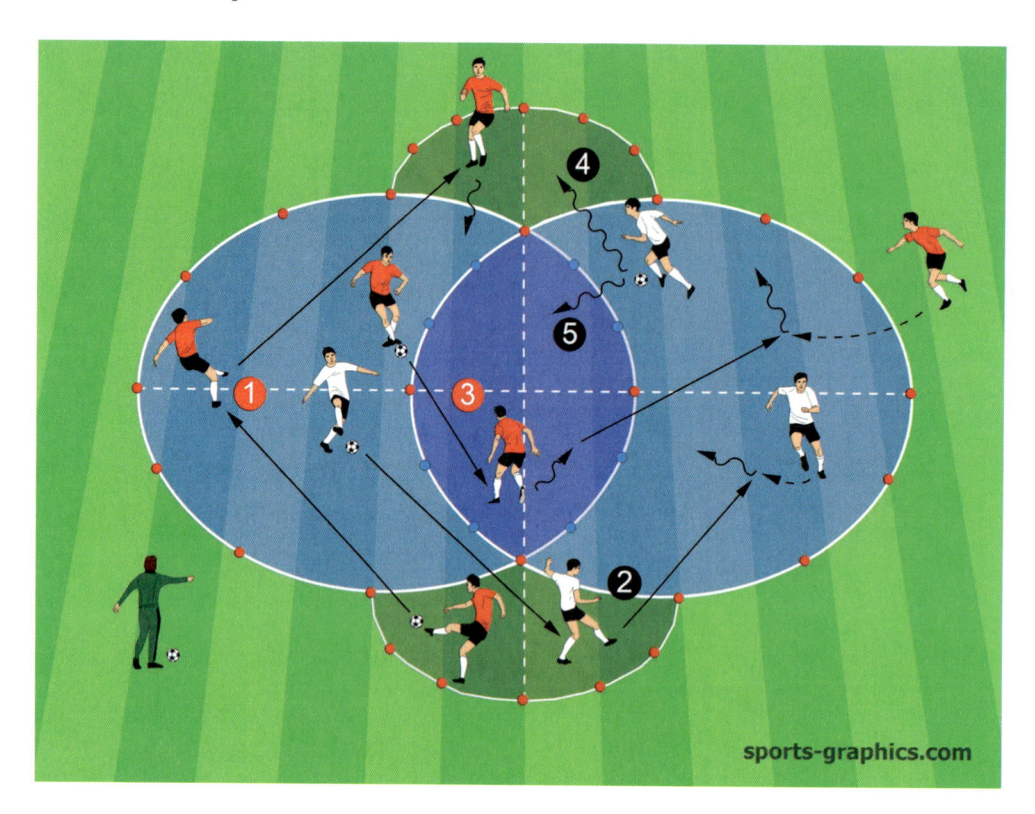

Playing principle

The playing field consists of multiple circles. These circles may be played through according to a variety of rules. The team with the ball can score a point by playing a combination through three circles (1, 2 and 3). It is possible for a small field to be played through via a large field toward a small field (1), the combination to cover one large field via a small field into a large field (2), or for the passes to be made from one circle to another via the center (3). A point at the individual level is possible when a player dribbles from one circle to another (4), and double points when the center is used for it (5).

Provocation rules, point system and variants

The many objectives may be set by the trainer with a signal. Depending on the current trainer signal, there is only one objective and this simplifies the situation for the defense and offense. The trainer would also be able to specify certain sequences for the circles (e.g. large/small/large or large/center/small). The form becomes more intensely focused on the center when the center must be played through after dribbling into a circle from outside.

3.2.23 Soap bubble (Continued)

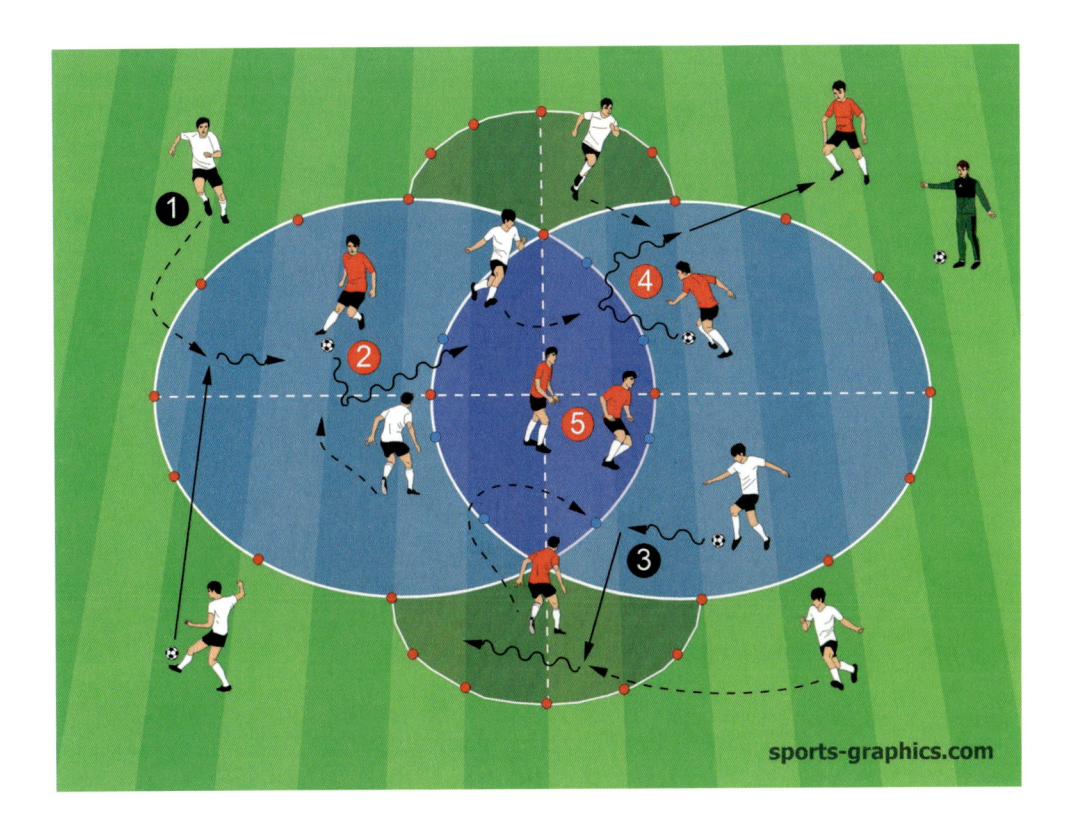

Playing elements and conduct

In the offense, free-running with open positions toward the circles and for optimal continuation of the game is the objective (1). This free-running is coupled with constant views of the center when possible. The basic attitude is constant danger and targeting of the center (2). The tactical decisions are mainly choosing between dribbling or short passes (3). The possibilities to turn and break away (4) should be considered for avoiding simple ball losses. In the defense, the primary concern is that the wall remains compact and the center is jointly tightened and heavily occupied (5).

Coaching points and instructions

- Run through the center! Run free in every circle!
- Dribbling or short pass? Choose quickly!
- Protect the ball!

3.2.24 Orbit

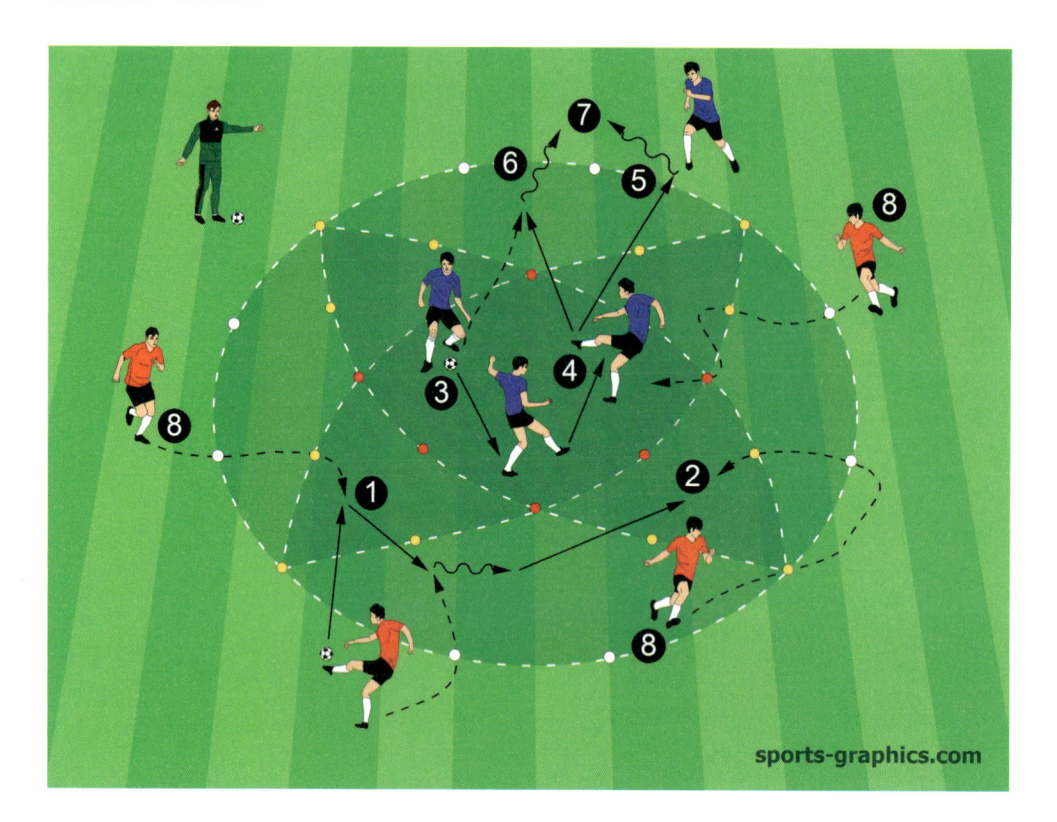

Playing principle

The playing field consists of an outer area and a central circle, which is divided into nine zones. The chief focus lies on passing. It is thus important for the team in possession to play through the various zones with combinations of passes.

Provocation rules, point system and variants

The team with the ball can score when two of the pointed peripheral fields are played through (1 and 2). One point is scored when, after two passes in the central zone (3 and 4), the circle is left through passing (5) or dribbling (6). This may be followed by a play for the large or mini-goals (7). The opportunity to take shots may also be opened after achieving the aforementioned objective (2). The different-colored pads or cones with which the zones are marked may be used for constant free-running with coordinative aspects. The players may be required to run over individual markings in succession (8), or even to complete certain color sequences while doing so.

3.2.24 Orbit (Continued)

Playing elements and conduct

The center is occupied by many offensive and defensive players (1). The offense has to endure pressure situations, claim balls, secure balls, and be able to end a play in order to avoid ball loss. The defensive players should always keep the central space occupied, face strategically important passing routes, and act in a compact wall from the center outward. Offensive objectives must be achieved with well-timed free-running actions (2), the recognition of open spaces with a view of an objective (3), and early offering of options for follow-ups by the players with the ball (4). The positioning in the outer areas should always facilitate deep passing points to make it possible for players in the center with the ball to achieve longer balls (5) and achieve objectives or resolve pressure situations. The free-running behavior in conjunction with the colored markings also trains cognitive and coordinative aspects with or without the ball (6).

Coaching points and instructions

- ★ Offer deep passing points!
- ★ Run freely toward the objective!
- ★ Tighten up or fan out?

3.2.25 Water lily

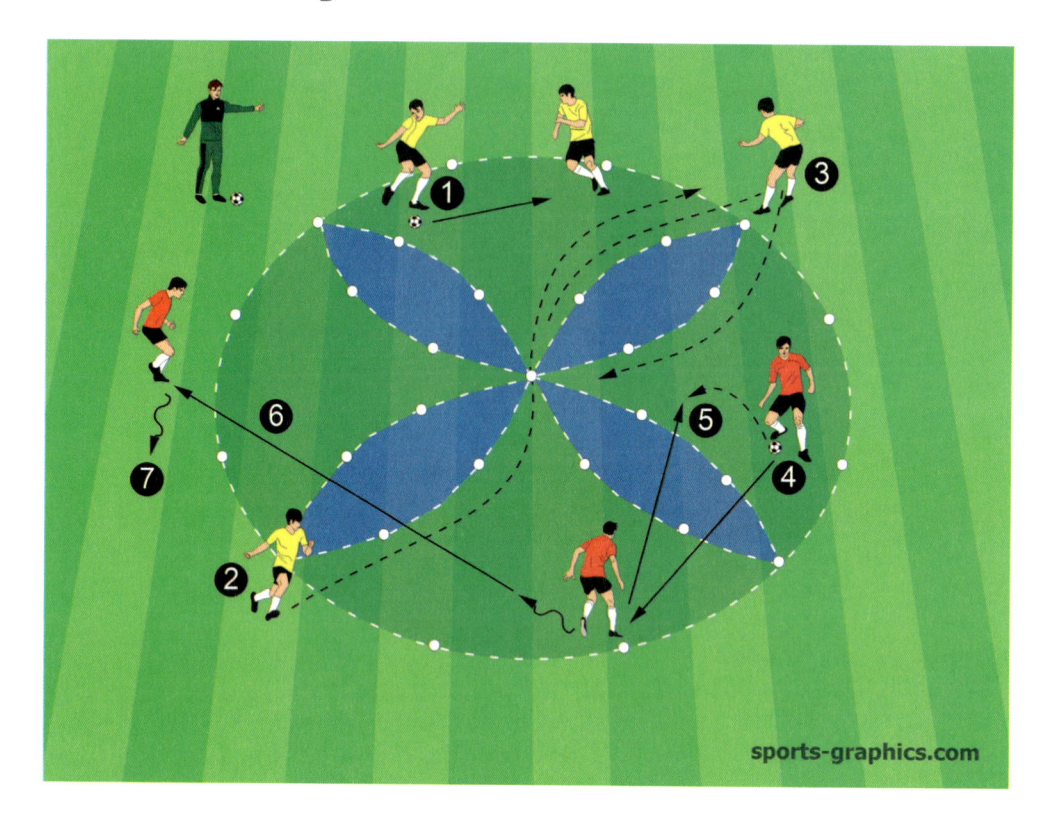

Playing principle

The central circle field is divided by four oval-shaped fields. The green interim spaces are ideal for objectives with multiple players with regard to passes and combinations, and the long, blue fields can be used for running paths, short passes, or individual technical actions. The players may run through all areas of the playing field at any time, regardless of possession.

Provocation rules, point system and variants

The team with the ball can score in the green fields when a specified number of passes has been completed (1). During phases of possession a team may also score through the running path of a player positioned far away. A point is awarded here when a player runs around two blue fields in a curve (2) or, starting from the middle, runs forward and backward around a blue field back to the center (3). The blue fields can be played through with rather short passes (4). One point can be scored with a new return pass though the same blue field (5) or a follow-up pass through another field (6). After completing the objectives, shots can be taken at the large or mini-goals.

3.2.25 Water lily (Continued)

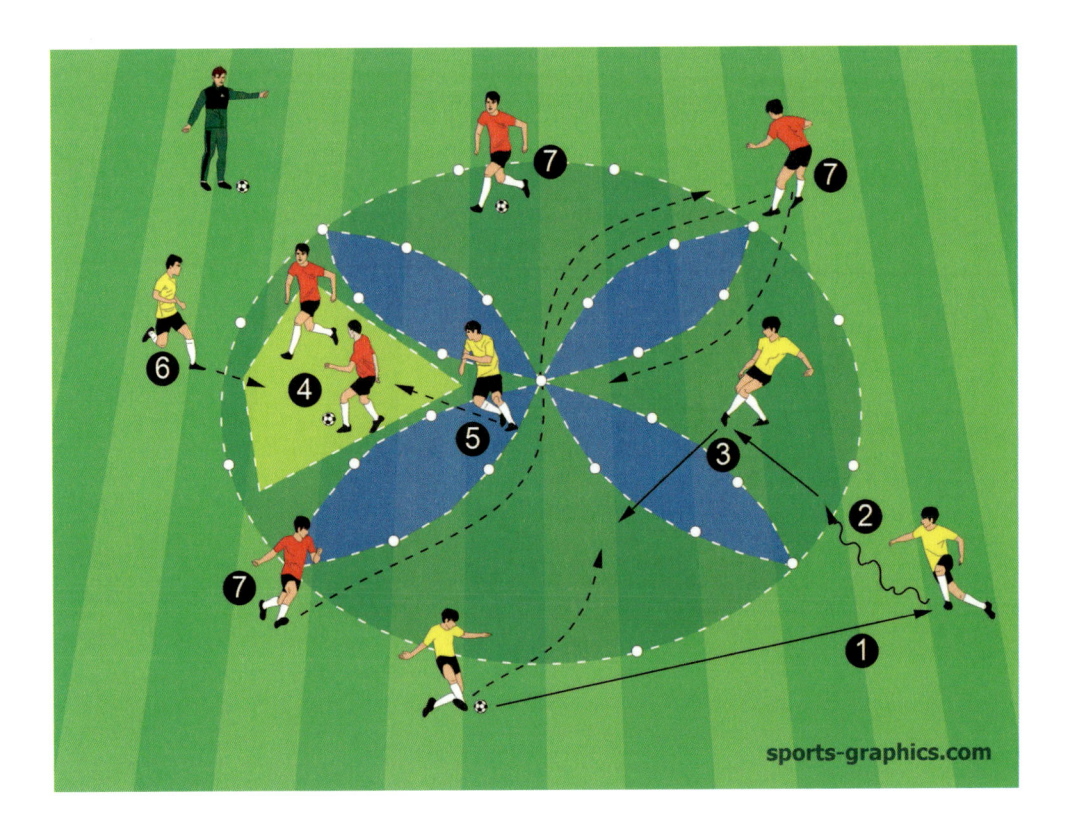

Playing elements and conduct

The preparation of passes into the center is ideally done through long passes (1) and threatening dribbling (2). The objectives involve the alternation between long passes (1), targeted ball control with short, feint-filled dribbling (2), and short passes (3). In certain zones it is important to tighten up or create majority situations (4). The defensive positioning starts from a strengthened center out into the currently critical zone (5) when possible. The defensive players are required to avoid positions far from the center and quickly reduce the distance from the center and close the defensive wall near the center (6), especially after changes in the form of ball loss. The objectives and points for the running paths far from the ball force the players to coach each other. It is ideal if players in a secure position with the ball issue commands to their teammates for runs that will bring points (7).

Coaching points and instructions

★ Run for the points!
★ Form a defensive wall!
★ Switch up passing distance!

3.2.26 Shamrock

Playing principle

The teams play through the central square and the four adjacent half-circles by following different rules and with various points. The objectives result in intense playing situations, especially in the central area. Each team has one player who may only move on the lines of the central square (Players A and B). These players may not threaten or disrupt each other. Once a team loses the ball, the game continues without interruption with the other team in possession. If this ball loss occurs in the central square, one player must enter the penalty position in a half-circle (Player C) and may not leave it.

Provocation rules, point system and variants

The team in possession can score a point when a player enters into a half-circle from outside, changes feet in the half-circle, and leaves it without losing the ball (1). Double points are awarded to the team that makes two passes in a row in the central square (2). The points increase with the number of passes in the center. The penalty for ball loss in the center (Player C) can expire after a specified time (e.g. 20 seconds), after a pass to the penalized player, or after the next loss of the ball in the center.

3.2.26 Shamrock (Continued)

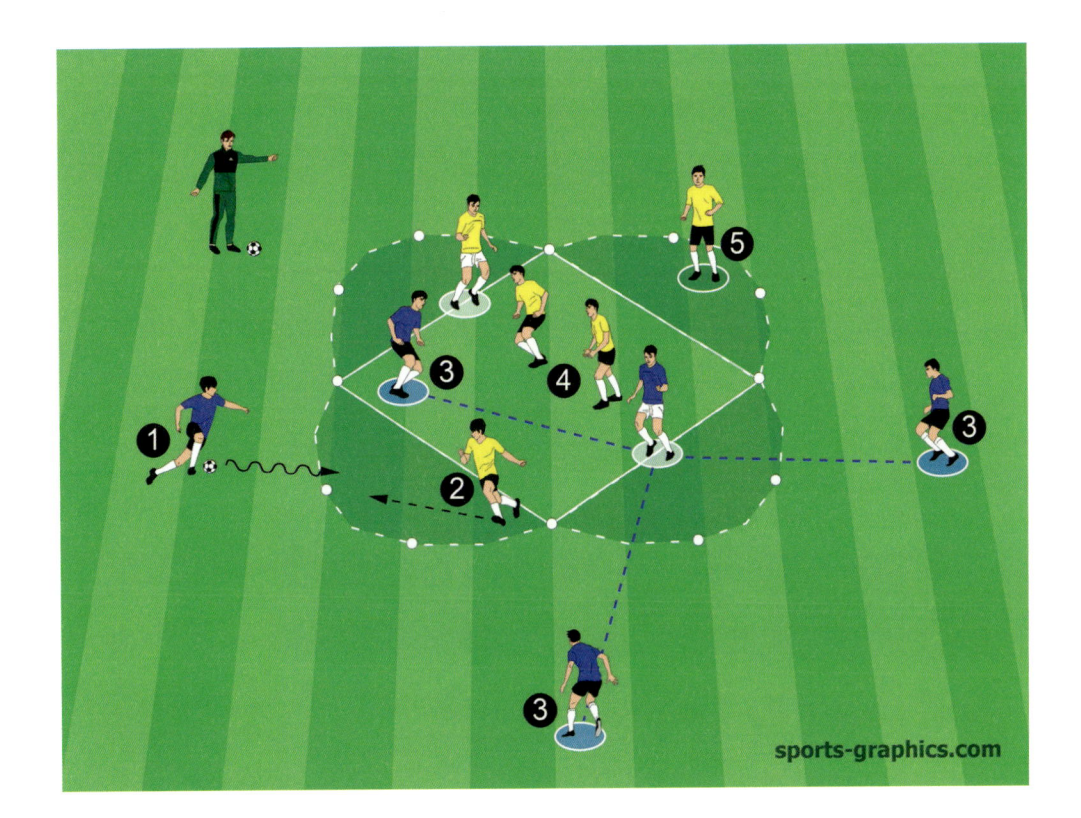

Playing elements and conduct

Each player is required to implement the specified objectives, to boldly use any available opportunities while in possession (1), and be responsible and committed in preventing points for the opponents while defending (2). One player from each team moves on the line in the central field. This player is severely limited in their positioning. Their teammates are thus always required to assess their own relative position (3). To this end the players keep smart and equal distances from each other and do not occupy any double positions when possible. In the defensive wall, the center should be heavily occupied above all else (4). The intensity in the center is especially high, as loss of the ball is a particular disadvantage according to the provocation rules (5). The offensive players are required to prevent ball loss in the central area and defend their own possession.

Coaching points and instructions

- ★ Protect the ball!
- ★ Keep distances!
- ★ Break up the center!

3.2.27 Fortress

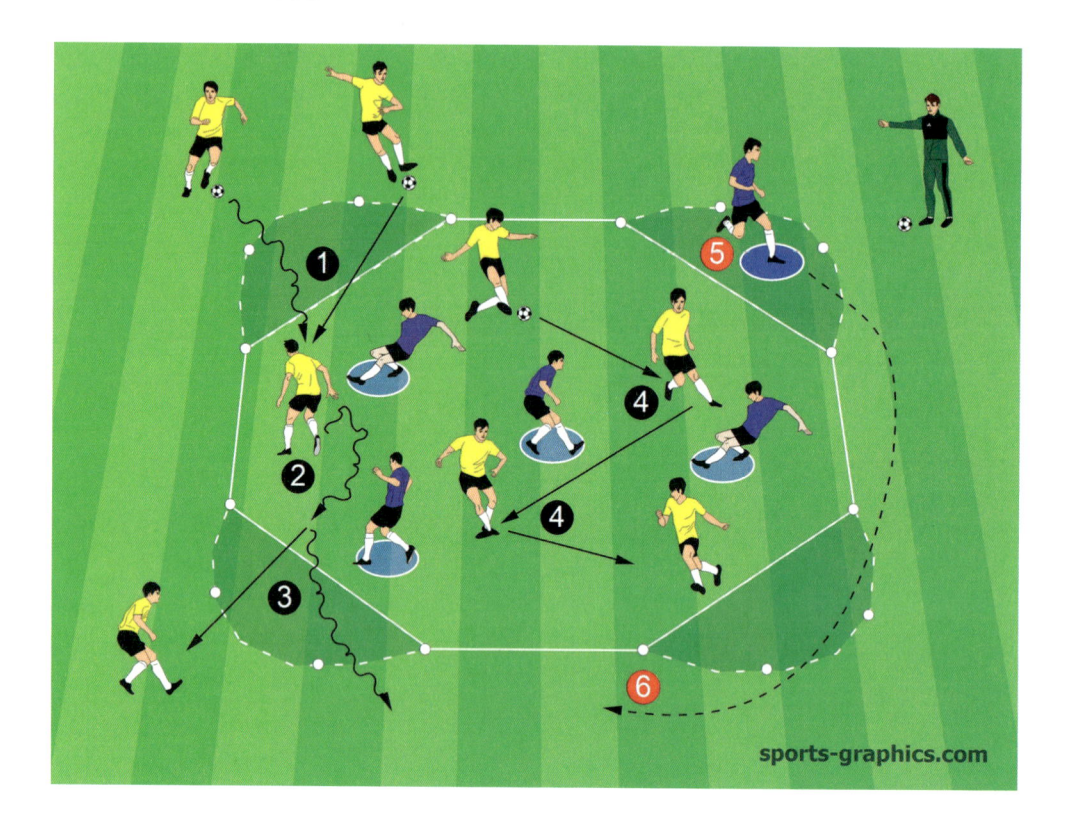

Playing principle

The playing field with one central and four outer fields is interpreted as a fortress (central hexagon) with four towers (outer half-circles). All players may be in and run through all areas and zones of the playing field at any time. The team with the ball tries to storm the fortress while the defending team protects it. The interlopers try to dribble or pass their way in through a tower (1) and leave via another tower (3) by passing and dribbling inside (2). The offensive team also tries to perform a specified number of passes inside the fortress (4). The defending team tries to prevent the offending team from achieving its objectives and take the ball in order to then score a point with their own possession. Once a team in possession completes an objective, a defending player must perform a penalty task.

Provocation rules, point system and variants

The objectives can be made more difficult if group-tactical offensive resources, such as doubling back or playing through a third player. The penalty may also vary. It is possible for a player to be banished to one of the towers for a specified amount of time (e.g. 10 seconds), for which they are unable to participate (5), or only resume after running around all four towers (6).

3.2.27 Fortress (Continued)

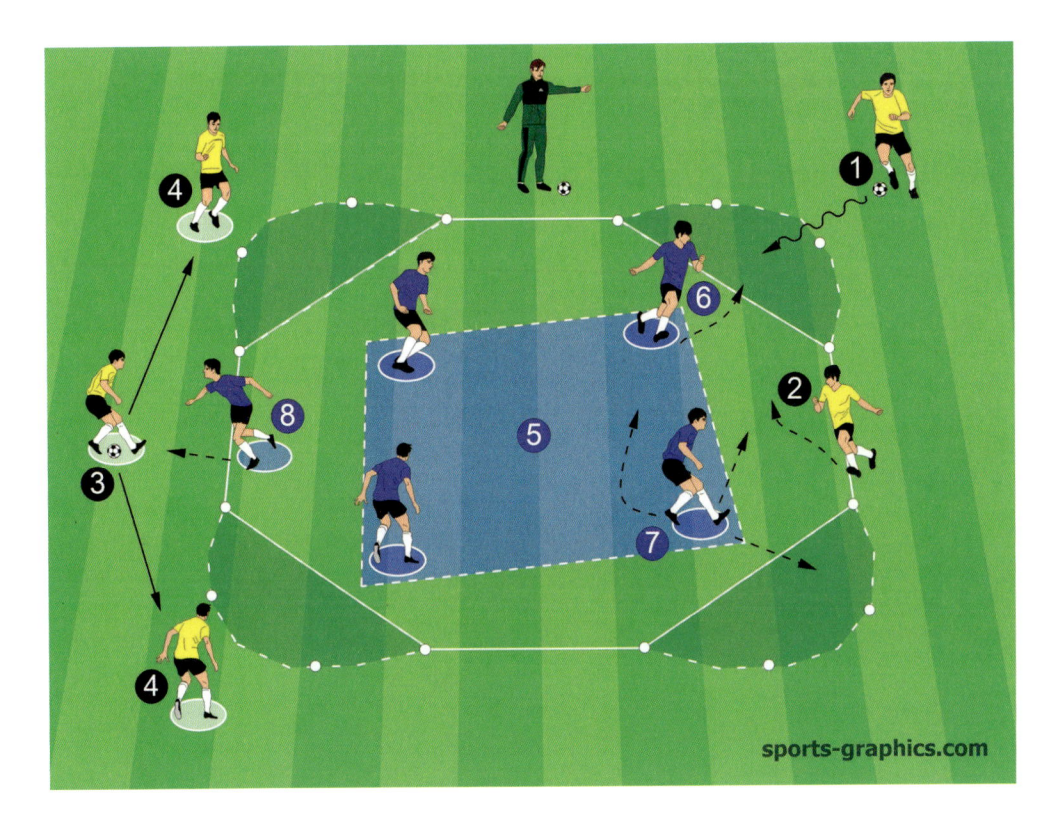

Playing elements and conduct

The offensive players are required to keep an eye on the objectives, to take strategically valuable positions, and act in synchronicity. This applies to the individual entrance through the towers (1), the creation of promising passing points (2), positioning with the most passing options possible (3), and the taking of positions near the critical zones for optimal continuation of play after receipt of the ball (4). The defending players act in a wall when possible, with optimal distances (5) between them in order to strengthen the center and react to the situation from there. Individual players may start and advance from this wall to face opposing players and face dangerous spaces (6) or face passing routes and cover teammates (7). The defense should essentially put constant pressure on the opponents in possession (8).

Coaching points and instructions

- ★ Occupy the fortress! Defend the towers!
- ★ Storm the tower! Storm the fortress!
- ★ Seize the fortress!

3.2.28 Colosseum

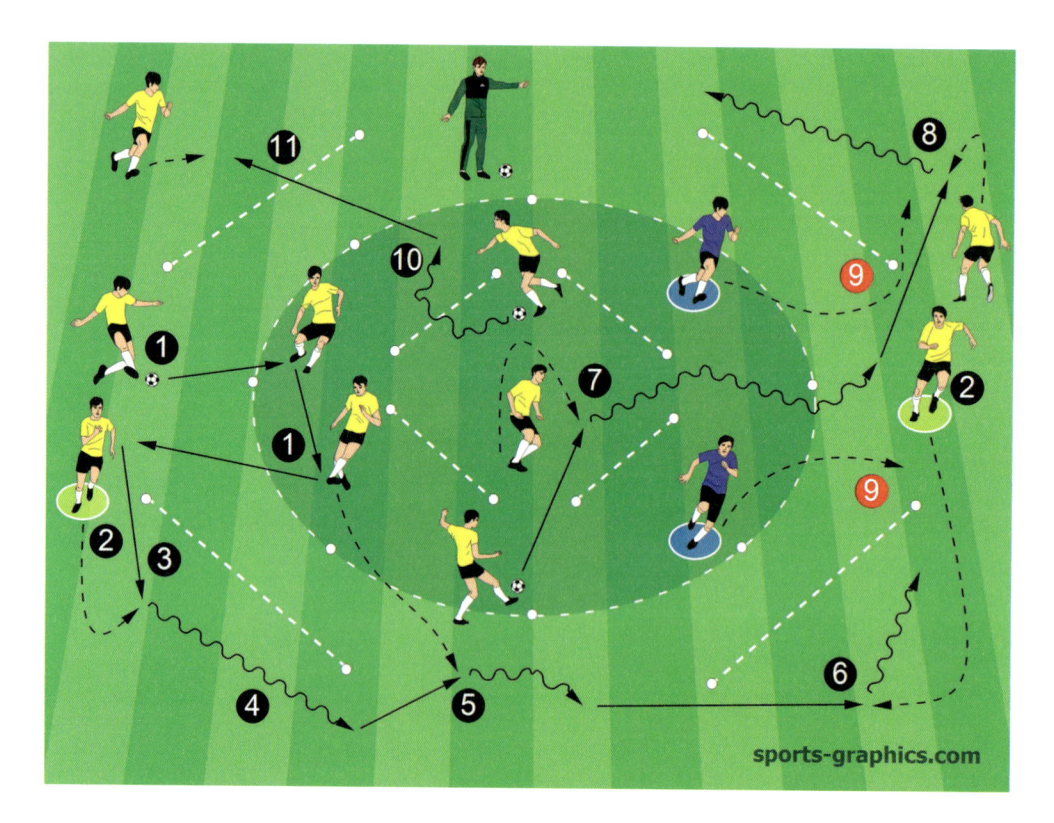

Playing principle

The playing form directs the players' attention to the game at the opponents' backs, and strives for ball control behind one of the dotted lines. Passes may be made within and outside of the circle for preparation (1) and individual players take tactically critical positions at the corners of the lines (2). A point is scored when ball control behind one of the lines (4) and continuation (5) are realized after a pass (3). The primary goal is to control the inner space with both feet. Indirect learning objectives come about through constantly observing centrally positioned players, open gaps, and tactical zones on the lines, or assessing one's own positioning in a tight space.

Provocation rules, point system and variants

The points can be made more difficult when the team with the ball realize two freely selectable lines (4 and 6) in a row or a combination of one line in the circle and one line outside of the circle (7 and 8). For simplicity's sake, the defense can be prohibited from running over a line (9) or the offense may only be allowed to pass next to the lines (3). Furthermore, playing through the lines through ball control can be combined with passing rules in or through the circle. This can result in points when a line is played through after two passes in the circle, a pass is made through the circle or an interim space after a line is played through. It is also possible that the lines may be played through in individual dribbling (10) and with simple passes (11). After achieving the sub-objectives, follow-up actions can be directed toward the large and mini-goals.

3.2.28 Colosseum (Continued)

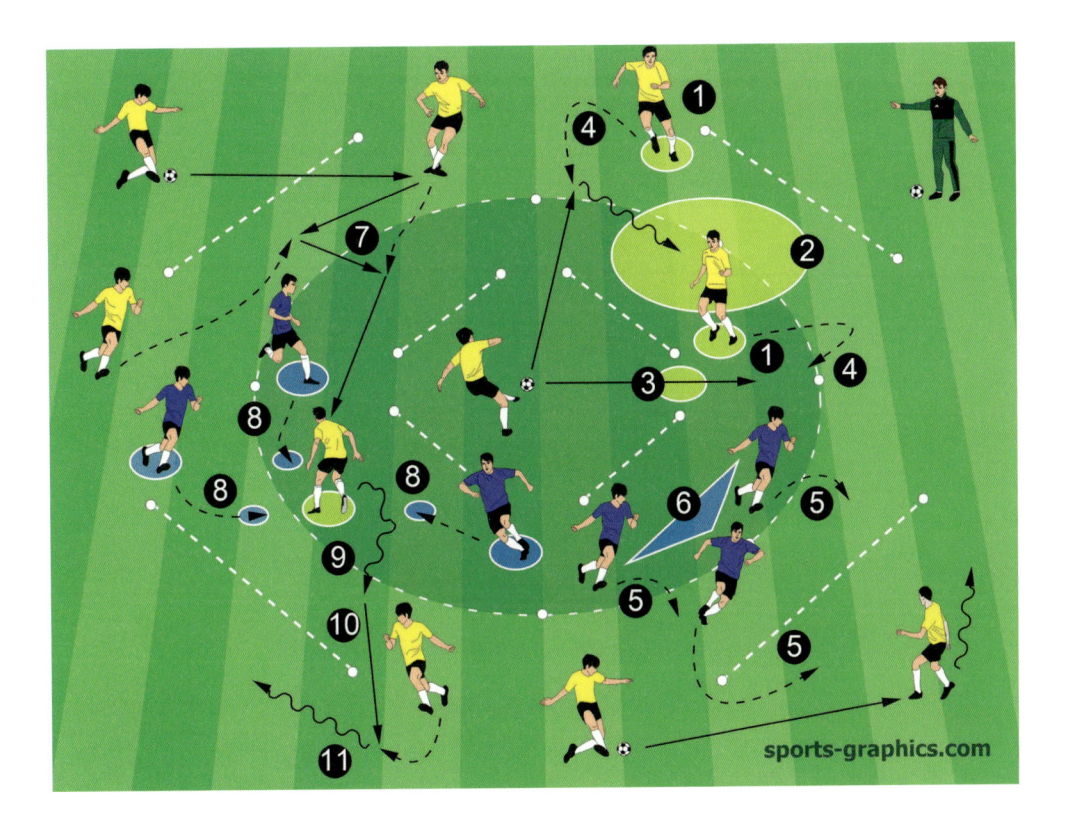

Playing elements and conduct

With this form, the team in possession must combine the taking of tactically appropriate positions alone the corners of the lines (1), recognition of the interim spaces (2), and deliberate playing toward gaps (3) with timed free-running behavior (4). The defense has to actively defend toward the ball (5) and simultaneously block off the center as a group (6). The players are essentially required to use high agility to set the foundation for intensity and action. In order to achieve playing dominance through effective possession, the players are required to make a variety of high-quality passes. In order to improve the quality of usage of both inner sides in tight spaces, various passing distances and a wide variety of technical forms like diagonal passes, vertical passes, or covered passes are required (7). Special attention is paid to recognizing and acknowledging certain situations where there is a lot of opponent pressure (8). For these situations it is necessary to find ways away from this pressure (9) and secure the ball during pressing situations while steering it toward the play and point objectives (10). The first ball contact is thus a good way to effectively score a point behind the lines (11). It thus functions as a litmus test for assessing the performance of individual players and teams, and has a significant impact on actions later on such as quick ball handling, various body feints, and breakaway dribbling.

Coaching points and instructions

- Look to the center! Find the middle! Threaten the interim space!
- Dribble up! Form a grid! Get away from opponent pressure!

3.2.29 Roundabout

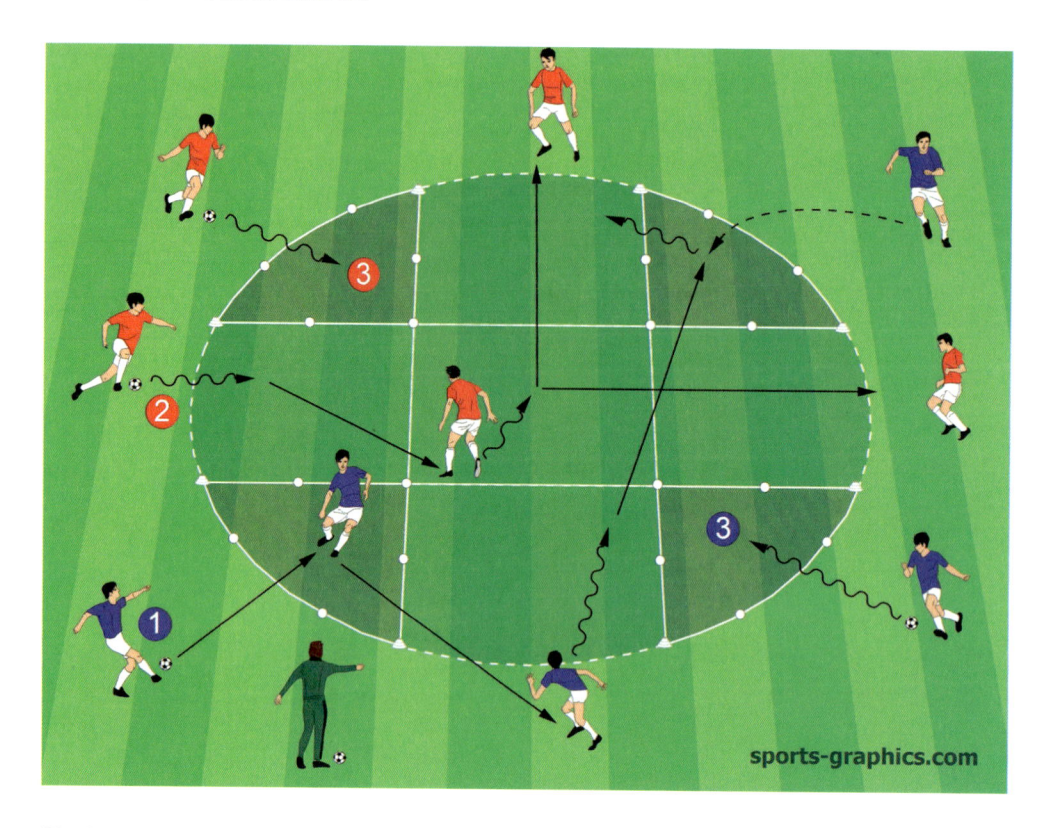

Playing principle

The playing field consists of a circular field with nine inner fields. The inner fields include one central field, four side fields, and four corner fields. The entire circle, individual fields, or combinations of different fields allow for numerous ways to specify objectives worth points. The team with the ball can score when it dribbles or passes through two corner fields in a row (1). It is important that the ball is in the field. A point can also be scored if the central cross is played through, and after entering the player exits through another line of demarcation (2) or a player with the ball dribbles into a triangle from outside and reaches another triangle through the center (3).

Provocation rules, point system and variants

The objectives may vary widely. It may be required to play through two adjacent corner fields, two diagonally located corner fields, the central cross at a 90-degree angle, straight through the central cross, or two triangles while dribbling. An introductory portion is also possible, in which each team plays all fields with their own ball. This can help train speed and possession techniques for the playing form later on.

3.2.29 Roundabout (Continued)

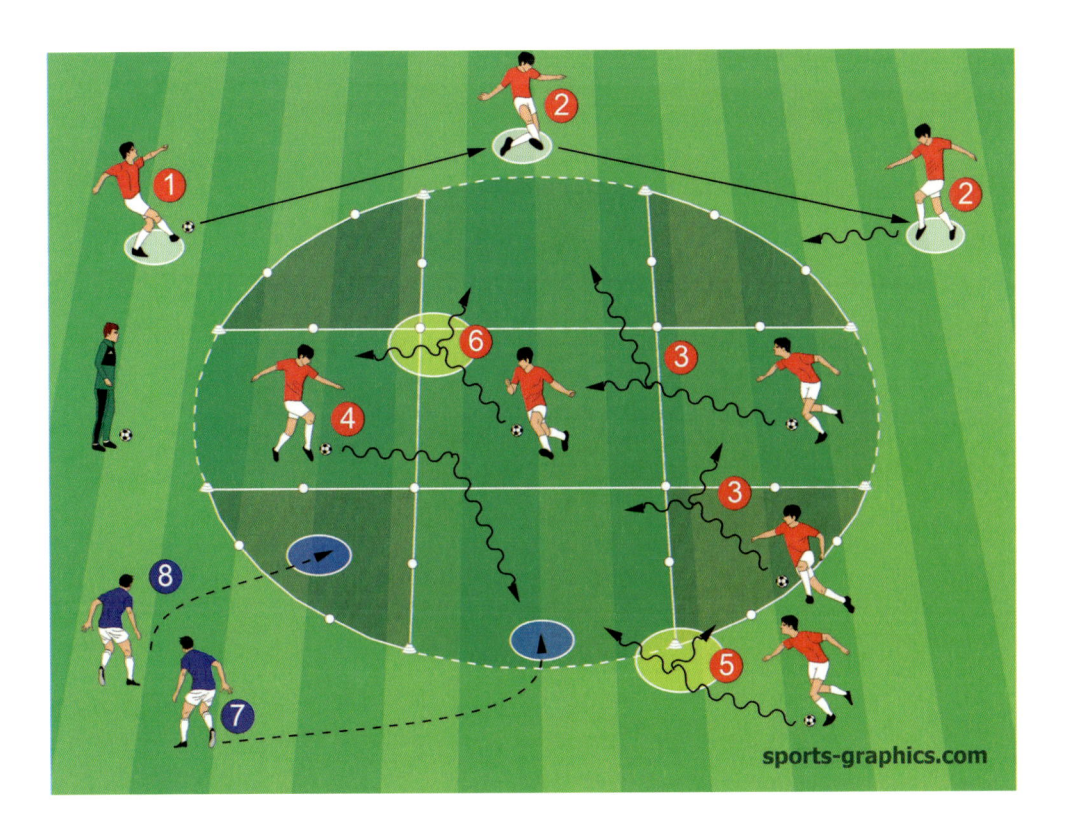

Playing elements and conduct

In the offensive phases of possession, it is beneficial when individual players fan out to prepare for the game in the center (1). Individual positioning in critical zones (2) should also entail appropriate, purposeful and situationally adequate decisions. Quick decisions for promising, and thus correct continuations (3) are just as important as individual and long-range dribbling into open areas (4). The field offers strategically important points and zones (5 and 6) where opponents can be bound and lured in order to be able to realize optimal entry points (5) or continuations (6). The interruption of a current play to secure the ball for reorientation can immediately lead to a new entry with better opportunities. The defensive players should appropriately coordinate their actions in order to face or run to strategically important points, zones and fields (7 and 8).

Coaching points and instructions

- ★ Defend strategically!
- ★ Complete the play!
- ★ Focus on the center!

3.2.30 Chessboard

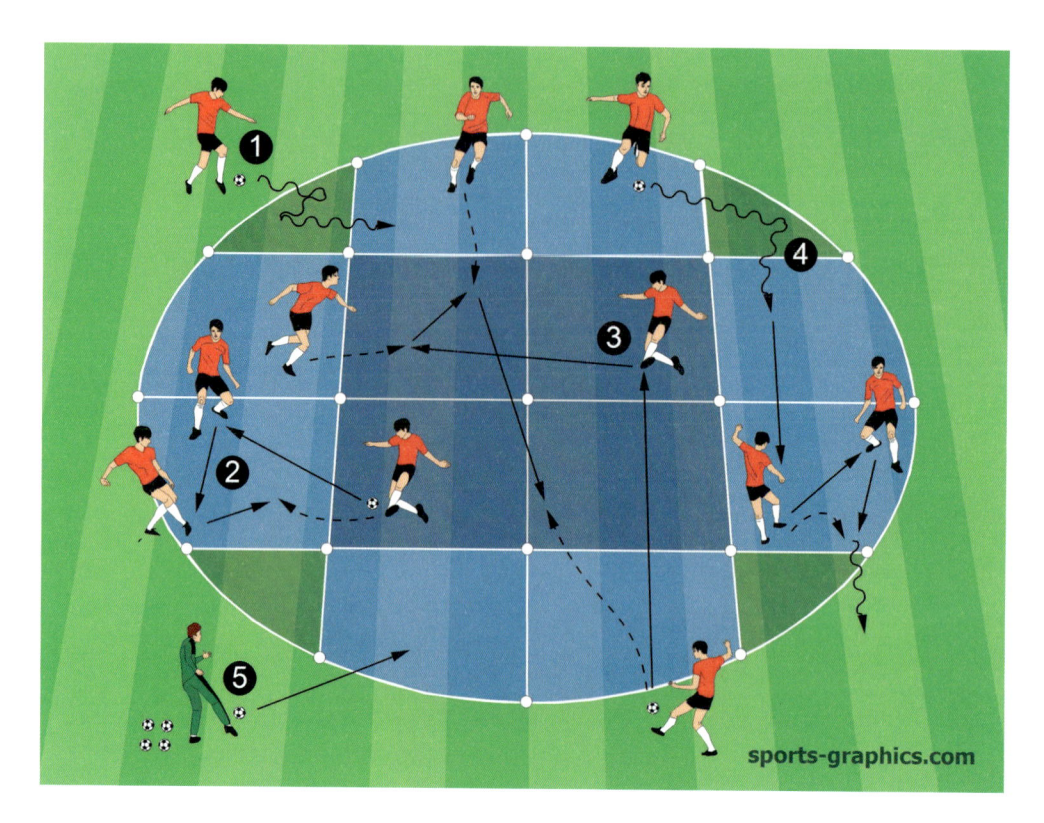

Playing principle

The playing field consists of a circle with four square fields in the center, eight fields on the sides, and four corner fields. The fields may be played through with different rules for each. Multiple fields (the four fields in the center) may also be consolidated to mark one large field. This variety of possibilities results in numerous objectives. The small corner fields are optimal for individual technical actions, like foot changes or feints (1). Two passes may be required in an outer field (2), and three passes in the four consolidated center fields may lead to a point (3). The objectives may also be linked together so that in order to score a point, a feint in a corner field must be followed by two passes in an outer field (4). Each trainer ball may provoke a change of gears and change of possession (5).

Provocation rules, point system and variants

A wide variety of variants and combinations of objectives is possible. The rules for playing the corner fields may involve possession and simultaneous occupation of the field with two players, or the completion of two passes within the field. In the outer field two direct passes, two passes with three different players, or dribbling out of the field toward the center may be required. The four central fields can be used to make three direct passes or dribble into an adjacent field. The connection of the corner field with the center is just as conceivable as the combination of the outer field and center.

3.2.30 Chessboard (Continued)

Playing elements and conduct

During the offensive possession phase, individual players can practice refined actions with the ball under opponent pressure (1). In order to release individual players or create some room for movement, players can strategically prepare the central game via the outside in order to achieve single points on the inside (2). Because of space and opponent pressure, it is critical that the offense is coordinated and allows for timed majority situations (3). Individual fee-running should also provide exit opportunities as freeing passes for the player with the ball, if there is too much pressure from opponents (4). The various objectives and many fields have complex rules and multidimensional decision-making opportunities (5). Mutual coaching, helpful commands, and constant offering and free-running (6) help the players with the ball and those receiving it. The defensive players are required to act jointly, tighten up critical spaces, and put the possessing players under pressure in order to attack them (7).

Coaching points and instructions

★ Attack the possessing player!
★ Check the objective!
★ Prepare for the central play!

160   CIRCLE SOCCER TRAINING

3.2.31 Planetarium

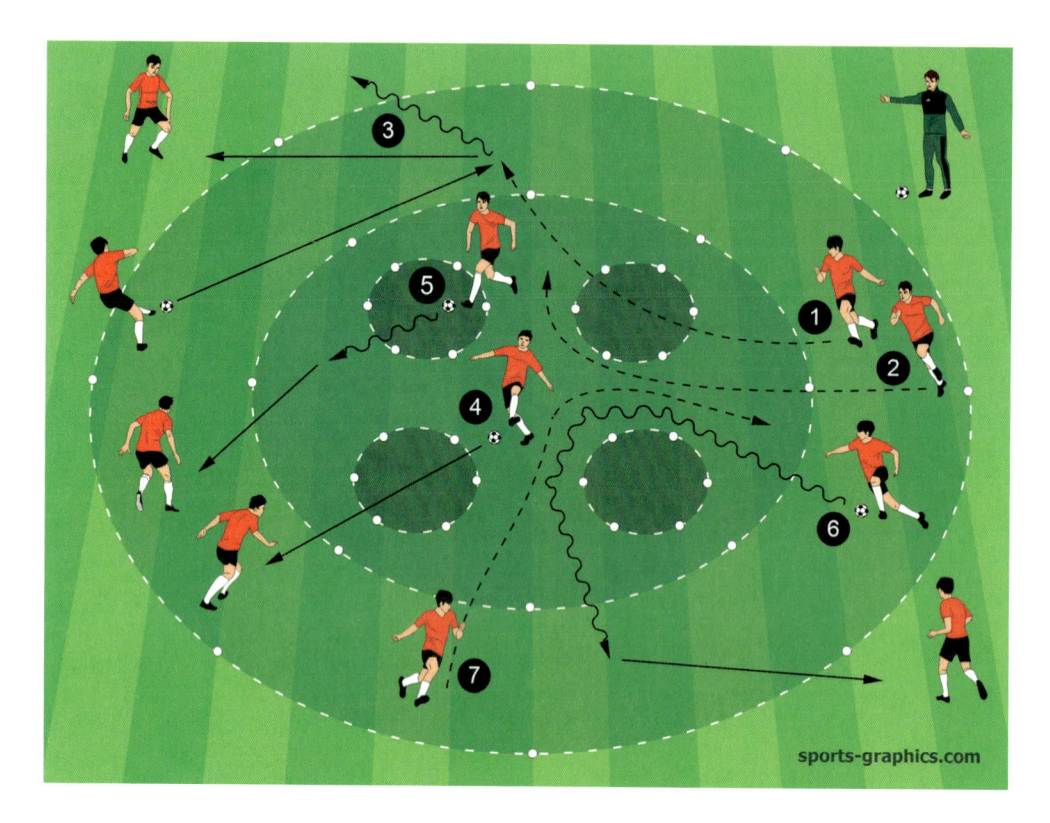

Playing principle

The playing field consists of the outer field without a border, a circle, and an inner area with four small circles. These various shapes create many objectives for the team in possession.

Provocation rules, point system and variants

Receipt of a pass in the ring after running through (1) or around (2) a circle may be rewarded with a point. These actions may be combined with a follow-up action out of the circle in the form of dribbling or a pass (3). The inner circles can also be used to generate passes through a circle into the ring (4) or passes into the ring after dribbling through a circle (5). Individual dribbling, starting from the ring around a circle and back into the ring, without losing the ball, can be rewarded with a point (6). Running out of the ring through the center without the ball, and returning with the ball in the respective team's possession (7) can also be rewarded with a point.

3.2.31 Planetarium (Continued)

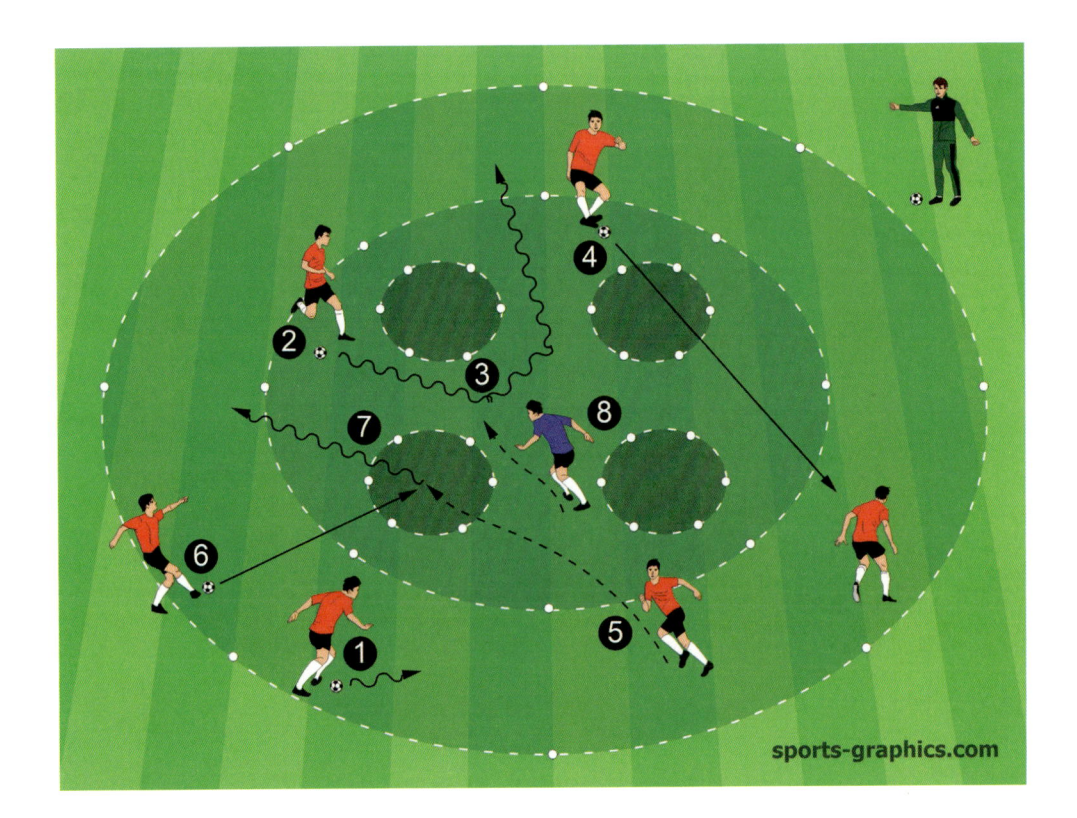

Playing elements and conduct

The objectives to be reached via the center require players to focus on the center. The view of the ball toward the middle is lifted so as to see the player's respective teammates (1). Bold dribbling and threatening actions toward the middle of the field are promising (2). The decisions in the relevant playing situations must usually be made under high opponent pressure (3). Forceful diagonal passes through the center to close distances are also promising (4). Timing while passing and running to escape opponents, and running up to certain areas are especially important (5). Precision and timing are required with all passes to the center (6), ball processing under opponent pressure (7), and corresponding follow-up actions. The defense should configure its game so that tactically critical spaces are recognized and approached in order to face opponents early on and prevent points (8).

Coaching points and instructions

★ Find the gap!
★ Start into the gap!
★ Run through the center!

3.2.32 Pulsar

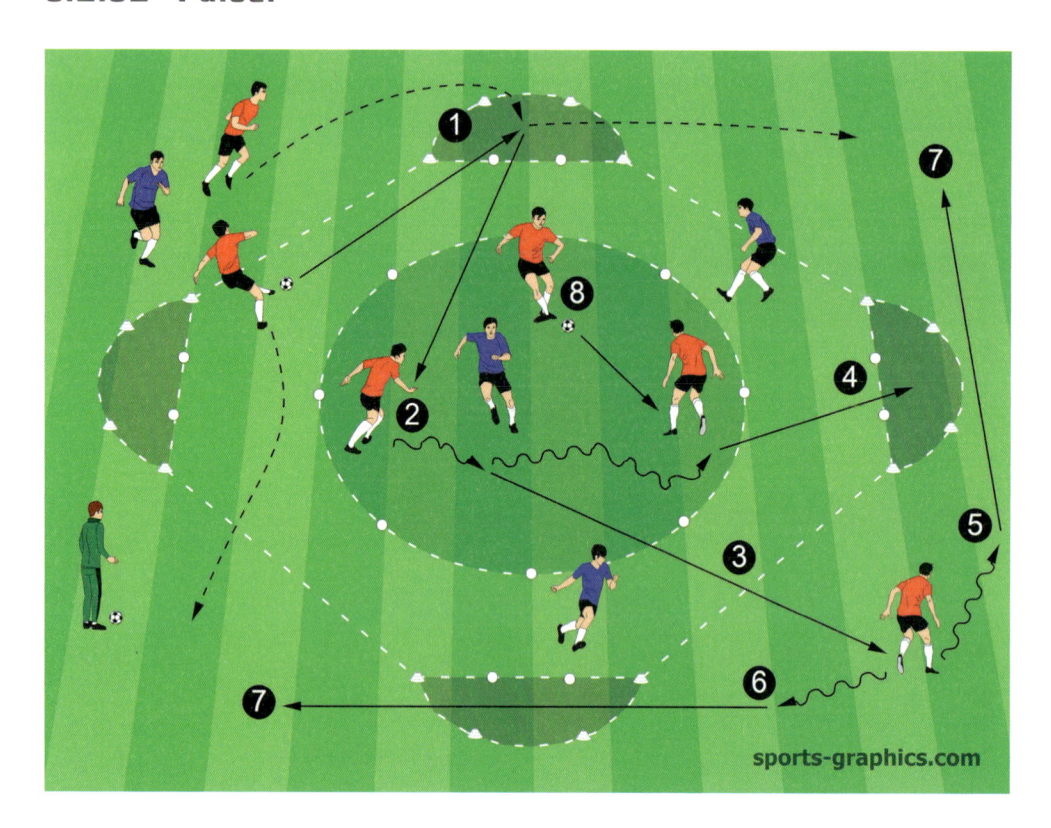

Playing principle

The playing field consists of an inner circle with a ring and four half-circles in the outer area. This playing form strives to create a quick, objective-based, bridging game through the center with entries and exits through certain zones. The team in possession scores with a combination of sub-objectives. An outer circle must be passed or dribbled through (1), whereupon the central circle is played through under high opponent pressure and requirements (2), followed by a deep pass to score a point. The deep pass may be made between two half-circles (3) for one point and through one half-circle (4) for double points. The continuations (3 and 4) should be fluid.

Provocation rules, point system and variants

After the play through the center, additional follow-up actions may be required, so that distance passes behind (5) or through (6) half-circles are required to play through levels. This can be followed by shots at the large or mini-goals (7). The center may also be used to score a point in that a certain number of passes must be completed within the inner circle (8). Contact limits, feints in the center, or a limit on the number of attackers or defenders in the center may also be specified.

MAIN COMPONENT **163**

3.2.32 Pulsar (Continued)

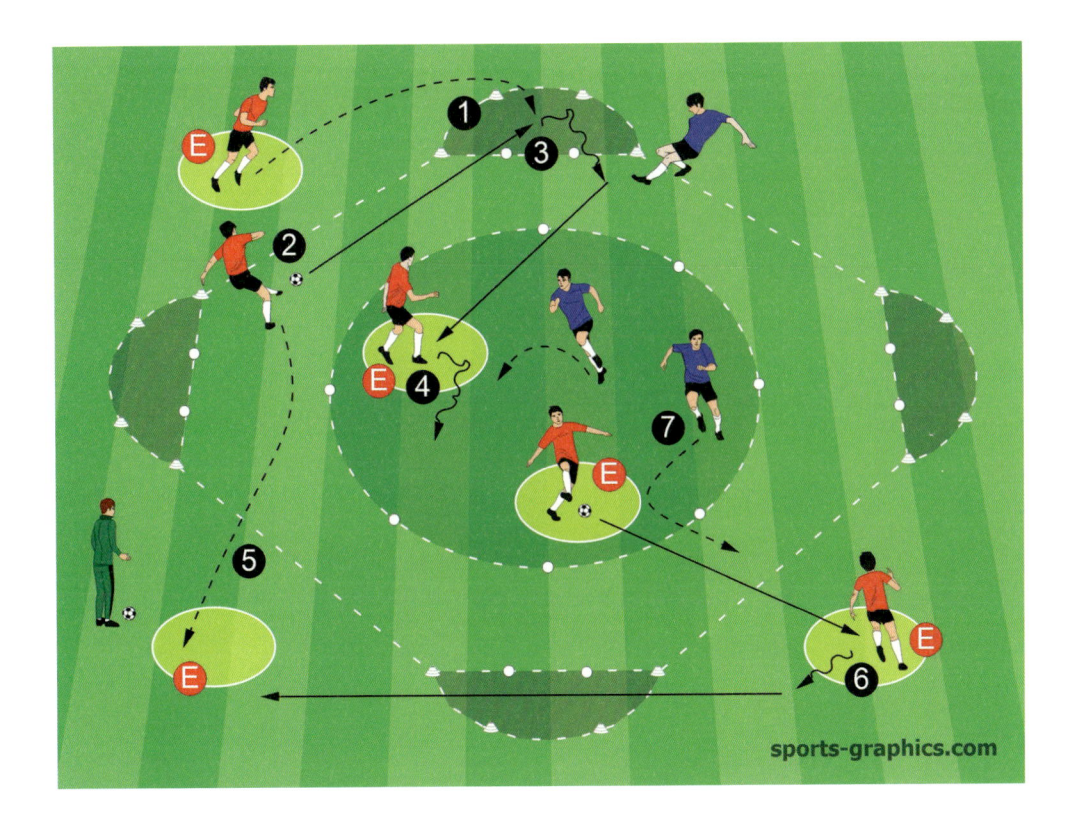

Playing elements and conduct

Along with combining via a heavily occupied center, the players train their conduct and positioning in various levels (E). These levels must be occupied and run toward to achieve the objectives. The offense develops good timing in running to the half-circles and critical spaces, and is required to make decisions for fields that can be played through (1). Precise and well-timed passes (2) are promising. The game in the half-circles involves individual technical actions in the tightest spaces with opponent and precision pressure, as well as targeted follow-up actions to the center (3). Individual technical actions with high opponent, time and precision pressure (4) are also required in the central area. The players are constantly required to create passing opportunities to the target fields for points (5). The playing form involves many alternations and constant follow-up actions. The making of decisions for achieving the objectives is elementary and necessary for completing plays and scoring points (6). In the defense, alternating the focus between the outer areas and center is required (7).

Coaching points and instructions
- Traverse the center!
- Deep passes! Deep runs!
- Occupy the levels!

3.2.33 Stonehenge

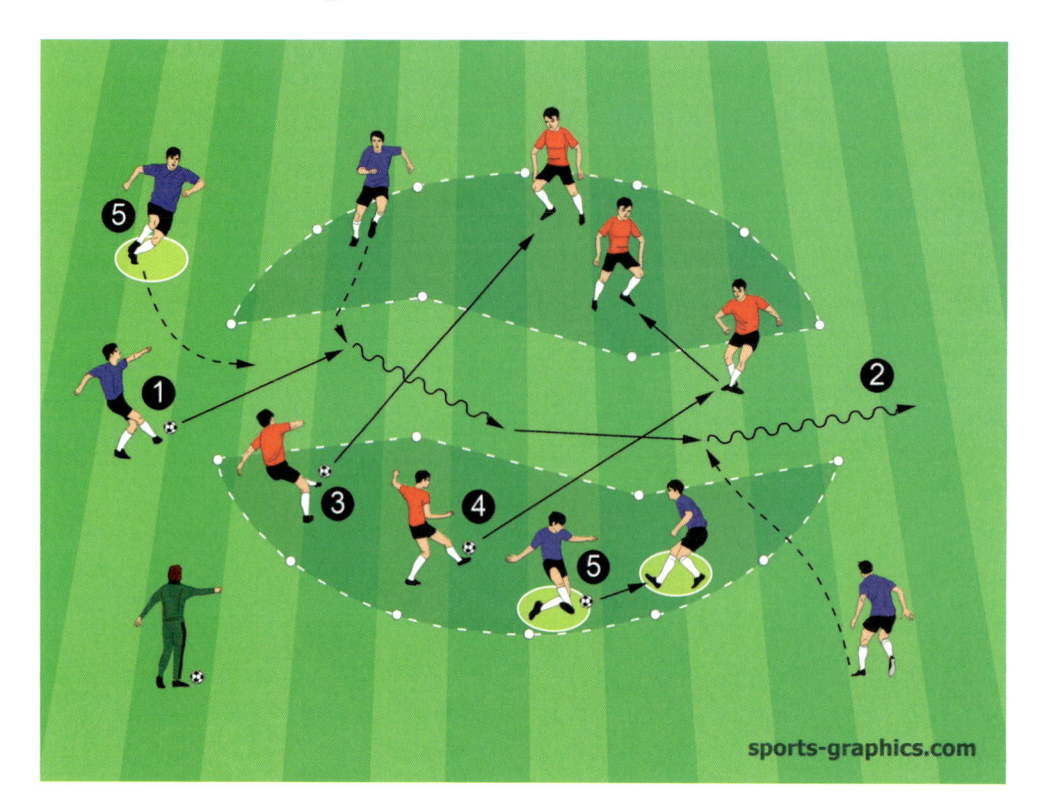

Playing principle

The playing field consists of the outer area and a circle, split by a jagged tunnel. The play in the center is shaped by possession in the circle, and the shape of the tunnel which must also be played through allows for diagonal positioning.

Provocation rules, point system and variants

The team with the ball scores by playing through the tunnel without losing the ball (1 and 2). Passes (1) and dribbling (2) can be used for this. The half-circles offer exit opportunities for securing the ball without scoring a point. Playing from half-circle to half-circle is also rewarded with a point. A long pass through the central corridor gets one point (3) and a combination with contact in the central tunnel gets two (4). A point can also be scored when a player runs through the entire tunnel while their own team claims possession in one of the half-circles (5).

3.2.33 Stonehenge (Continued)

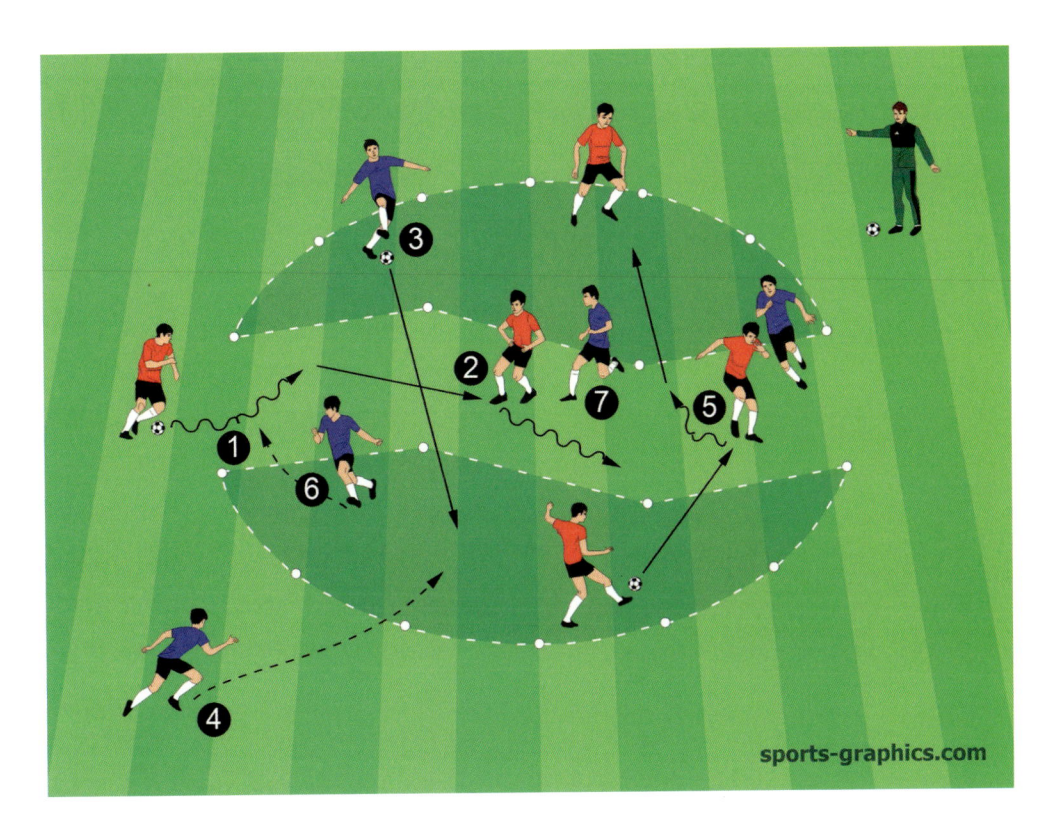

Playing elements and conduct

Bold dribbling as an entrance is desired from the offense, including under immediate opponent pressure (1). The focus lies on the willingness to take risks for one-on-one situations. The confident completion of a play through the center (2) is also required. Here the priority is to claim balls, shake off opponents, and overcome them in a one-on-one situation. The eyes must always be directed toward open spaces and gaps during the required passing (3). For the recipient it is important that the gaps and spaces are occupied with appropriate and timed offering and free-running behavior (4). While plays are performed through the center, pre-orientation with glances over the shoulder is imperative (5). When defending, tactical decisions must constantly be made so that entrance and exit areas can always be faced and run toward (6). In essence, the defense is required to prevent single points by the opponent and suppress plays and combinations (7).

Coaching points and instructions

★ Search for the gap! Find the gap!
★ Complete the play!
★ Be open to the gap!

3.2.34 Pyramid

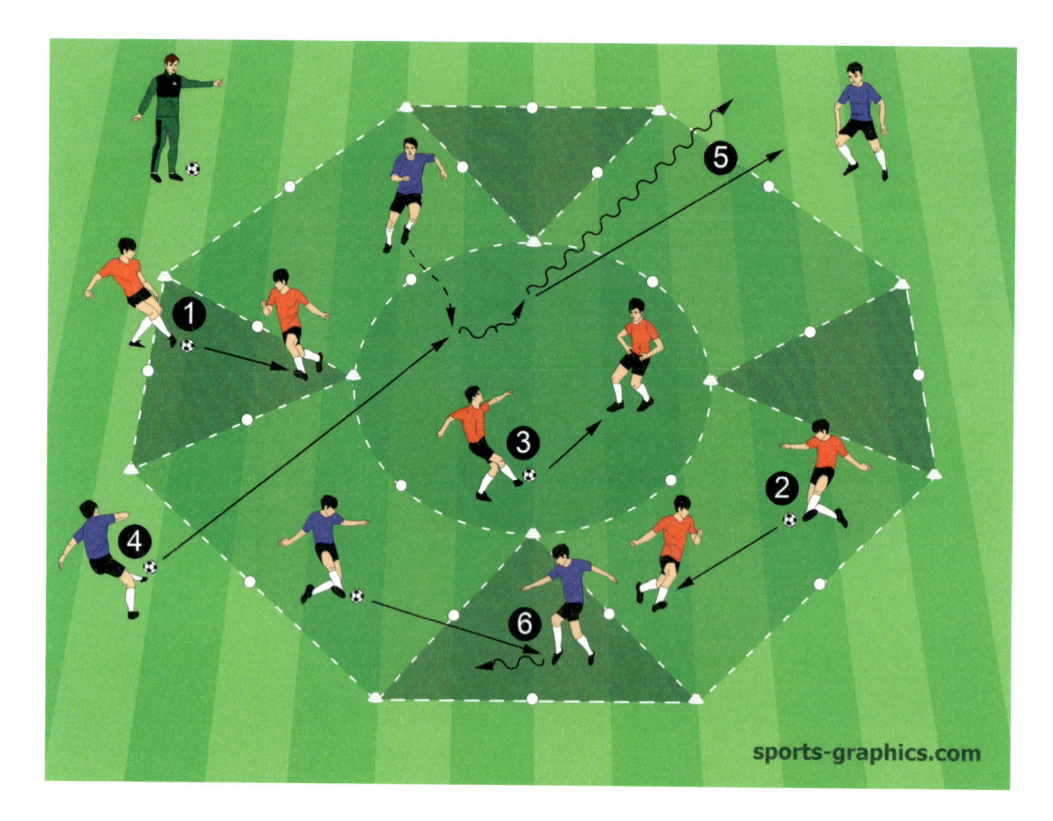

Playing principle

The playing field consists of an inner circle, four adjacent triangles, four long fields adjacent to the central circle, and the outer area. With regard to the objectives, the goal is to play over the center in a certain direction, or create short-term majority situations in certain zones in order to achieve a specified number of passes.

Provocation rules, point system and variants

The team in possession scores when three passes are completed in a triangle (1), a rectangle (2), or the inner circle (3). It is also possible to score a point with a combination through the center. To this end, a pass must be played into the circle from the outer area (4) and then, without changing direction, the field must be left on the opposite side with a pass or through dribbling (5). A point is scored when a player processes a pass in one of the triangles (6) and dribbles out of the triangle. To make it more difficult, the preparatory play outside can be restricted by a maximum pass limit so that the game in and through the center is accelerated.

3.2.34 Pyramid (Continued)

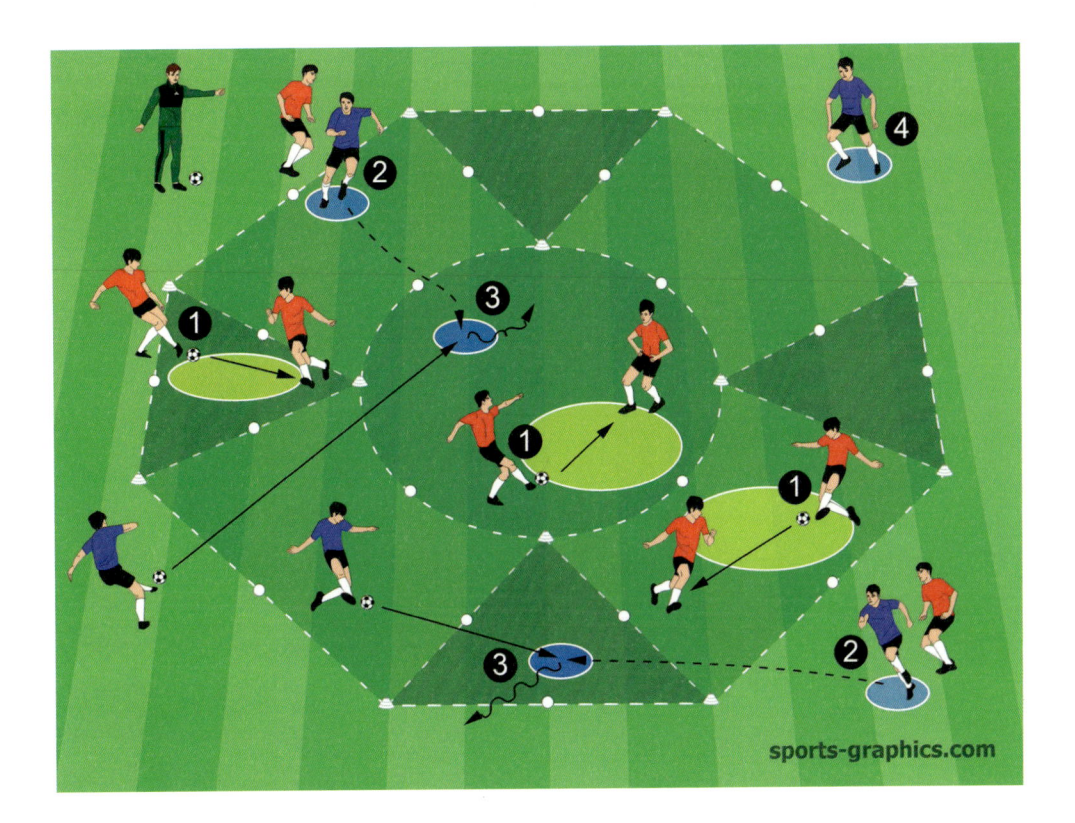

Playing elements and conduct

The offensive actions are shaped by the creation of a situational majority situation and well-timed offering and free-running. In various zones, points can be scored with short passes. It is thus critical that a temporary majority situation is created in these spaces (1). Playing through the triangles and center should be well coordinated. Timing is paramount for the approaching players (2) in order to gain distance from the opposing player and be able to implement an objective-oriented continuation of play (3). Offering deep passing points (4) is important for being able to resolve playing situations, escape increasing opponent pressure in the center, or achieve objectives with a subsequent pass. The defense is constantly required to recognize the offense's objectives and face corresponding zones and fields in order to at least prevent single points with well-timed defensive behavior.

Coaching points and instructions

- Timed running!
- Support the player in possession!
- Where are the zones?

3.2.35 Lotus flower

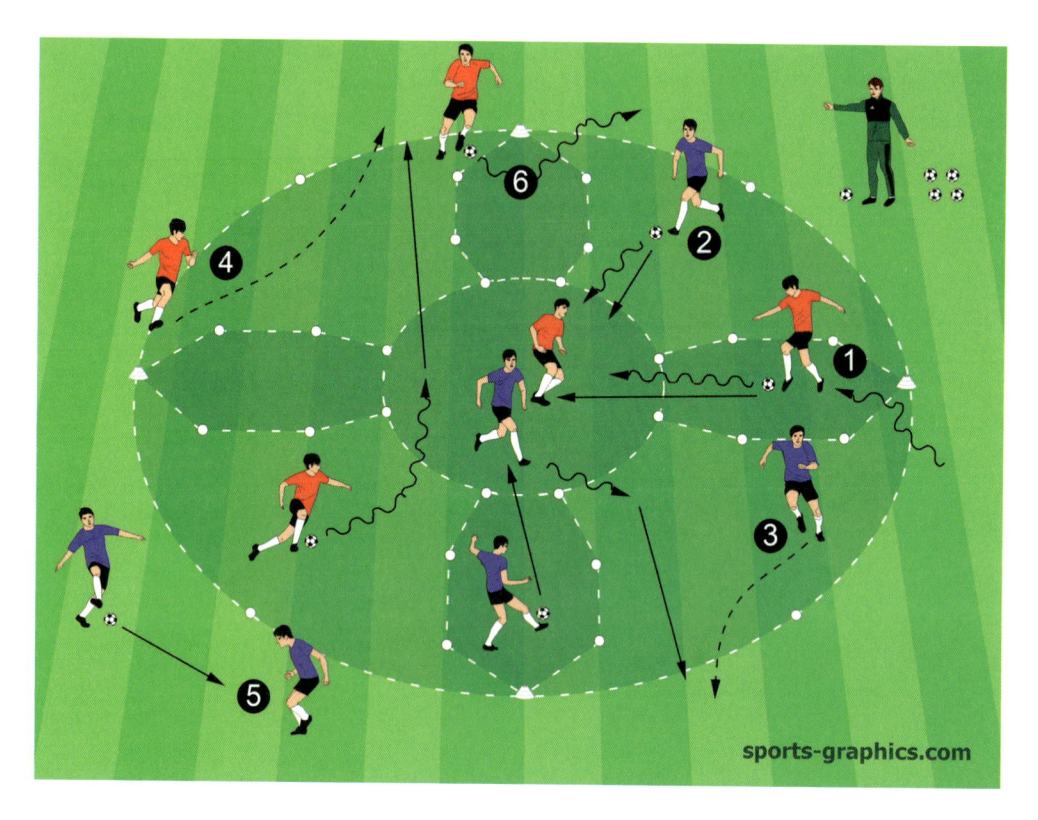

Playing principle

The playing field consists of a small circle in the center, four smaller oval-shaped fields, four larger interim spaces, and the outer area. The fields are used for individual dribbling toward the center as well as various passing combinations.

Provocation rules, point system and variants

The team with the ball scores double points when a player in possession dribbles into an oval field (1) and then immediately plays through the center by dribbling or passing. One point is scored when the team in possession plays through the center directly out of one of the interim spaces (2). The objectives may be supplemented with follow-up actions, such as a subsequent pass out of the circle (3 and 4). The playing form is made more difficult when a maximum of five passes may be played in the outer area (5). This accelerates the game in the center. If this limit is exceeded, the ball immediately changes possession. An individual variant for a point may also be set for the oval fields, in that a player dribbles into such a field and leaves through the other side (6). Feints may be required in the field to make it more difficult.

3.2.35 Lotus flower (Continued)

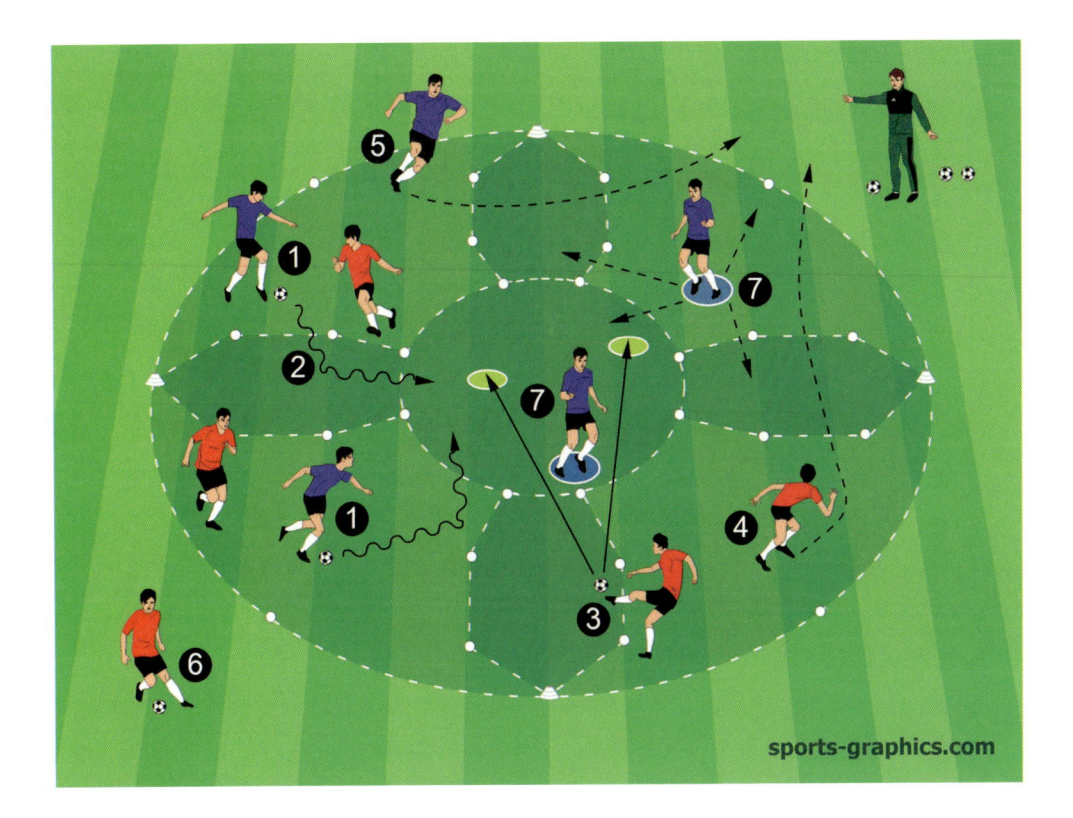

Playing elements and conduct

The offense is forced to perform precise actions for an entry through the oval fields (1). There is increased opponent pressure in the oval fields (2), which must be endured and answered with feint-filled dribbling. The passes into the center must be forceful and precise (3). Gaps and free spaces should be quickly and boldly passed to and taken advantage of. The objectives result in many fast runs deep in the interior (4) and the edge (5). The preparation of the plays and entrances toward the center can begin in the outer areas, with less opponent pressure (6). The defense is required to take tactically smart positions (7) in order to react to the offense's actions as quickly as possible and be able to prevent them from achieving their objectives.

Coaching points and instructions

★ Use the gap! Play into the gap!
★ Be bold when dribbling!
★ Check your position!

170   CIRCLE SOCCER TRAINING

3.2.36 Atlas

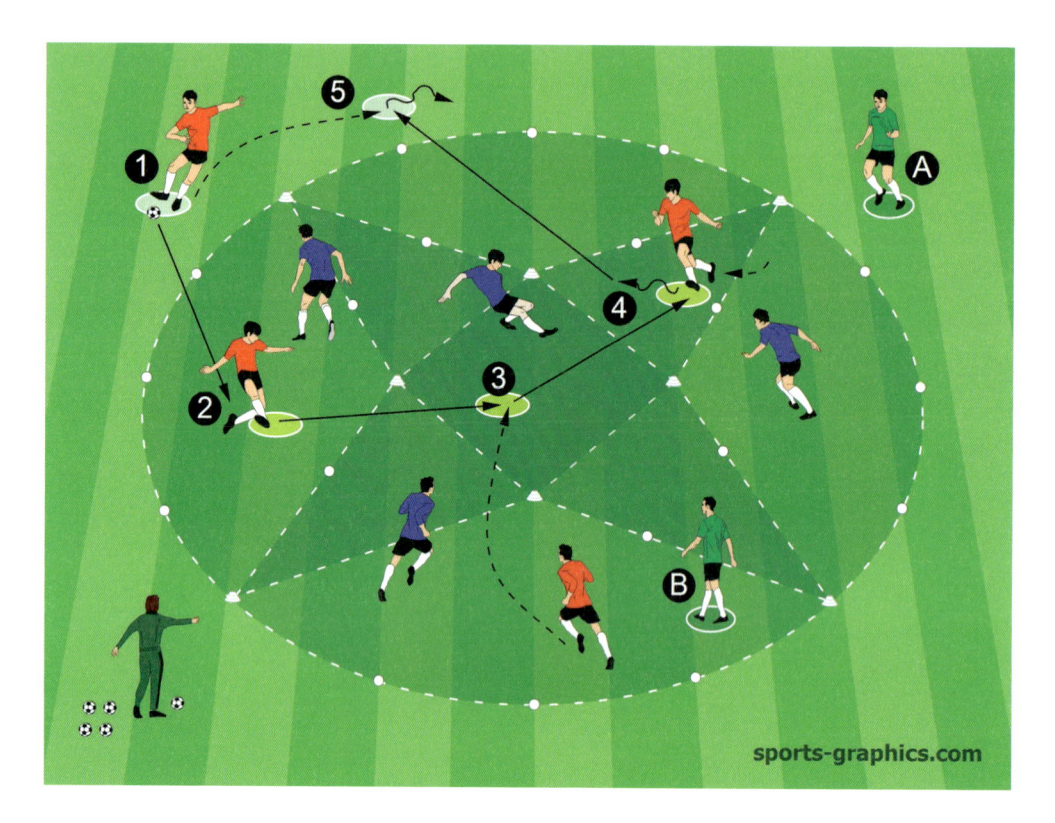

Playing principle

The playing field consists of the outer area, and a central circle with a total of nine fields. The team in possession can score a point by playing the ball into the circle from outside (1), then playing through the fields inside the circle and passing it back to a teammate outside of the circle (5). Every played field is worth one point (2, 3 and 4). A field has been played through when any player from the respective team was in possession in the field. The points only count when the pass out of the circle has been completed (5). When the ball is lost, so are the points that were not completed by the pass (5).

Provocation rules, point system and variants

The entry (1) may be performed through dribbling or passing, or be limited to just one possibility. The same may also apply to the exit (5). The direct return pass after an incoming pass can be prohibited, or at least not be included in the score. Specific rules for playing through the fields (2, 3 and 4) may be set. For example, it is possible for two different fields, at least three different fields, or at least two adjacent fields to have to be played through. Other players may be brought in as neutral players for constant majority situations and simplification (Player A and B). These players may move around freely, or be limited to the outer area (Player A) or the inside of the circle (Player B).

3.2.36 Atlas (Continued)

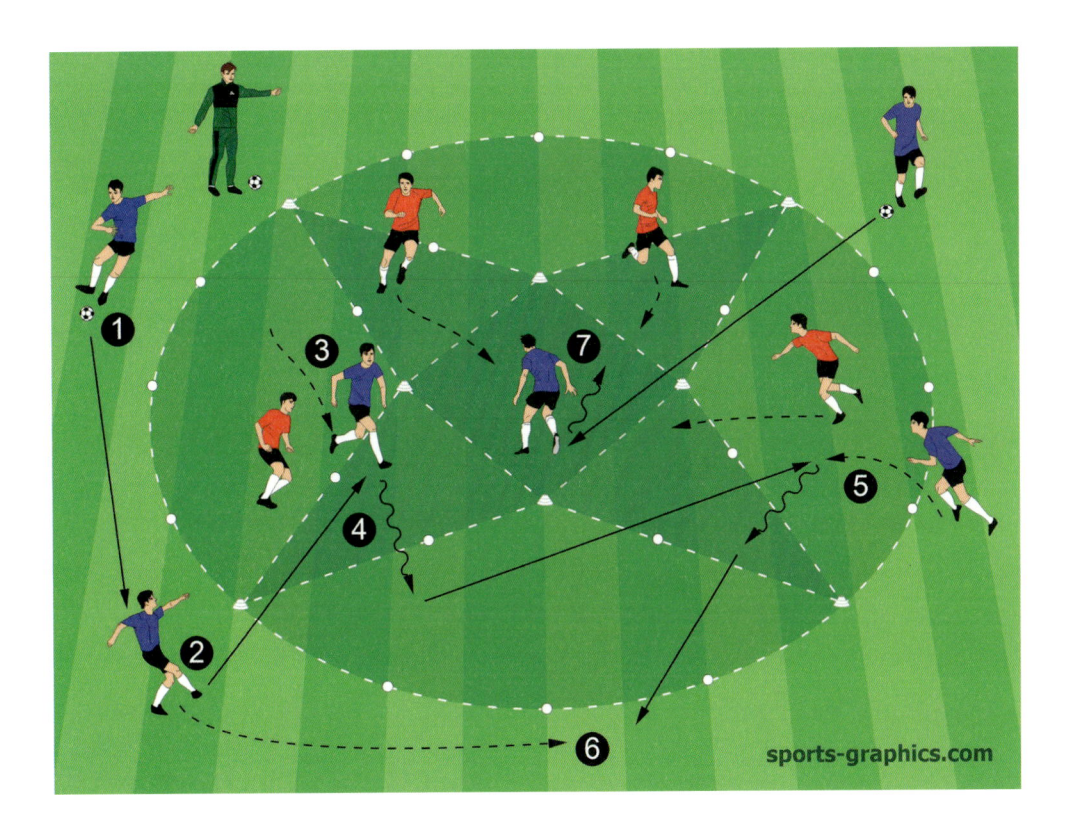

Playing elements and conduct

The offense can prepare the central play from the outside with long and secure passes (1). The starting pass into the center should be deliberately selected and timed with regard to potential continuations for the recipient (2). In order to have good options for continuing the play in the center, optimal timing in free-running for an open position that frees the player from the opponent is promising (3). The decision for continuing the play should be based on the objectives and made with foresight (4). The recipients are required to run toward the objectives (5) in order to achieve them while playing through the various fields. There should be a constant passing opportunity deep in the outside so that points can be scored and the players can make passes to release them from opponents. The playing form entails the introductory pass (2) and a critical pressing moment for all defensive players. The fields inside the circle must be defended, and the opponents must be prevented from scoring therein and instead be provoked to lose the ball.

Coaching points and instructions

★ Collect points! Secure the points!
★ Complete your play!
★ Pressing in the center!

172 CIRCLE SOCCER TRAINING

3.2.37 Revolver

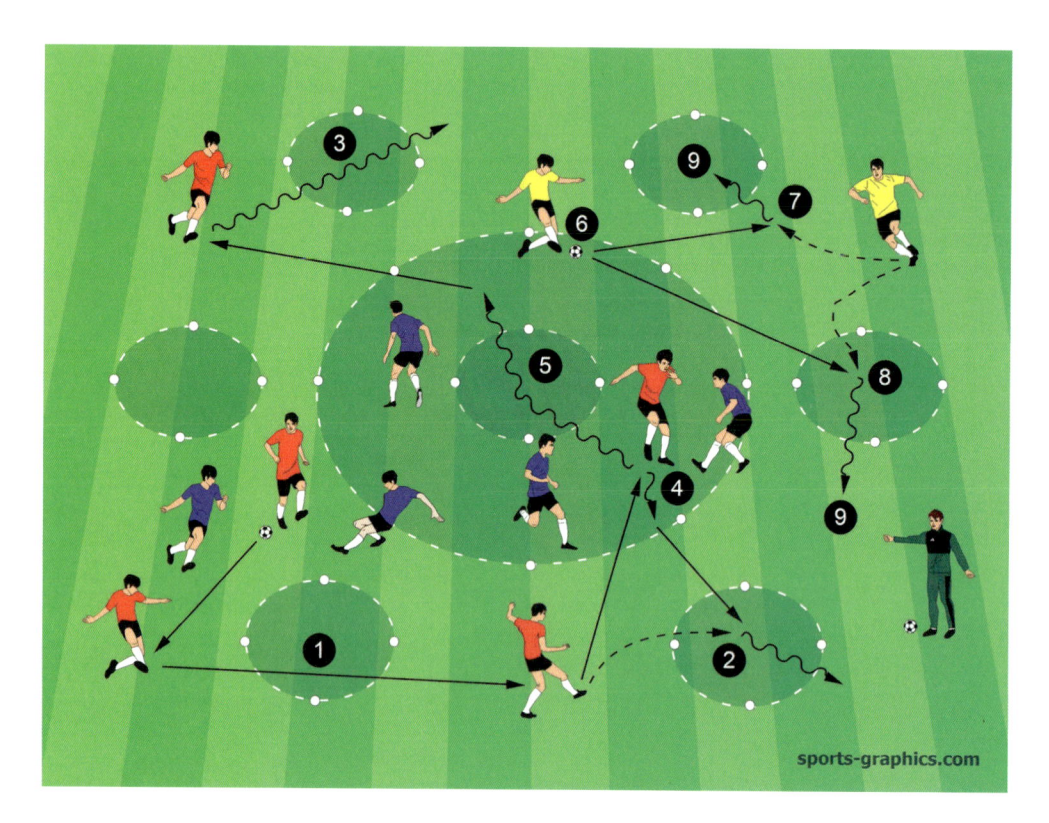

Playing principle

The playing field consists of one large circle, six outer small fields, and one inner small field. Two teams play against each other. They try to achieve certain objectives while in possession, thereby scoring points. Essentially the goal is to place target players in target fields, and bring them into possession.

Provocation rules, point system and variants

The team in possession scores a point when an outer circle is passed through (1), a player in the outer circle is passed to (2), or a player dribbles through an outer circle (3). Furthermore, a player earns a point when they are able to make ball contact four times in the center of the large circle (4). Double points can be earned when a player dribbles through the small circle in the center (5). The field structure can be used for technical exercises or coordinative running warm-ups. Volleys can also be precisely directed to the circle fields during free passes, or curved runs around the individual circles may be required after a ball action. One very precise objective may lie in playing a pass from the central circle (6) to a teammate located outside, who either takes the ball into an outer circle with their first contact (7) or processes the pass in the circle (8). Both cases may be followed by shots at the large or mini-goals (9).

MAIN COMPONENT   **173**

3.2.37 Revolver (Continued)

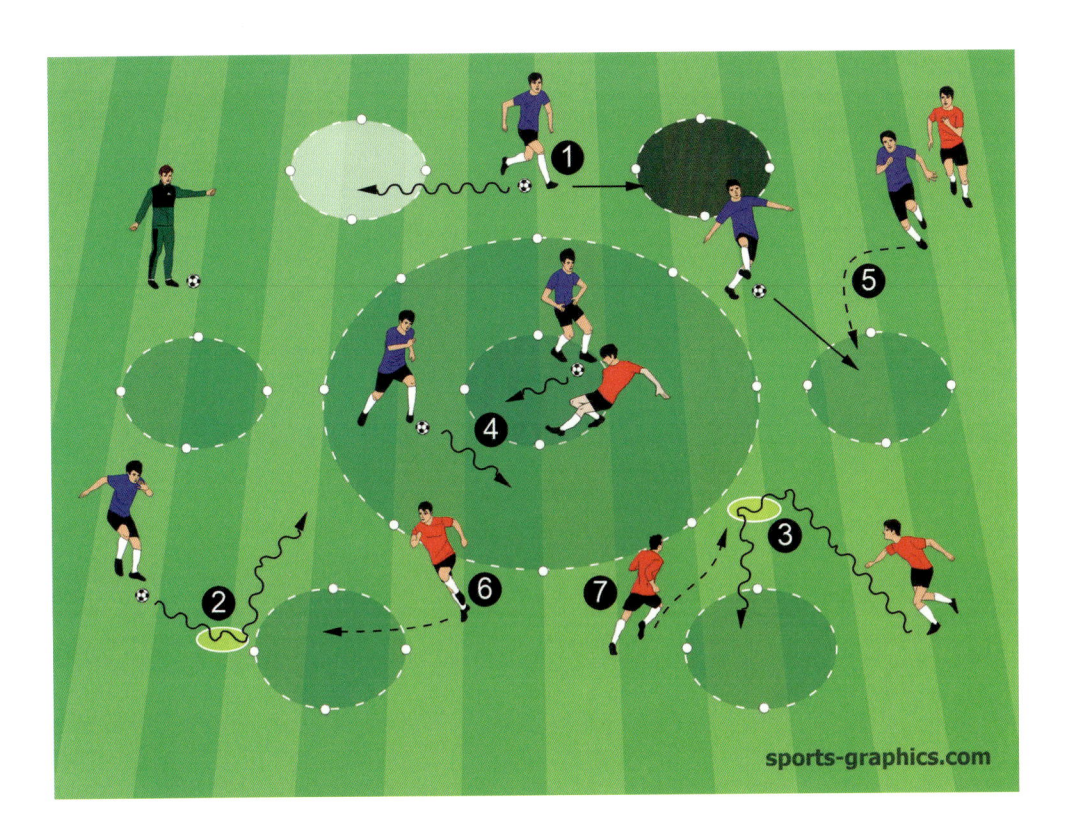

Playing elements and conduct

In possession, the offense is always required to select the best passing or dribbling technique given the situation (1) so as to achieve the objective and scoring. At the individual level, it is ideal when players in possession use a variety of feints to interact with the playing zones, threaten circles from the outside to deceive opponents and head toward the center (2), or threaten the center to create open spaces outside (3). The individual technical actions in the central action must be completed under high opponent and time pressure and with precision (4). In order to create distance from the defending opponent while offering and free-running, timing is required and running feints are helpful (5). For the defense, it is critical that dangerous areas are faced and run toward. This trains anticipation skills (6 and 7) so as to predict the opponent's intent and undermine it.

Coaching points and instructions

- Lure opponents! Trick opponents!
- Always be precise!
- Face spaces!

3.2.38 Tornado

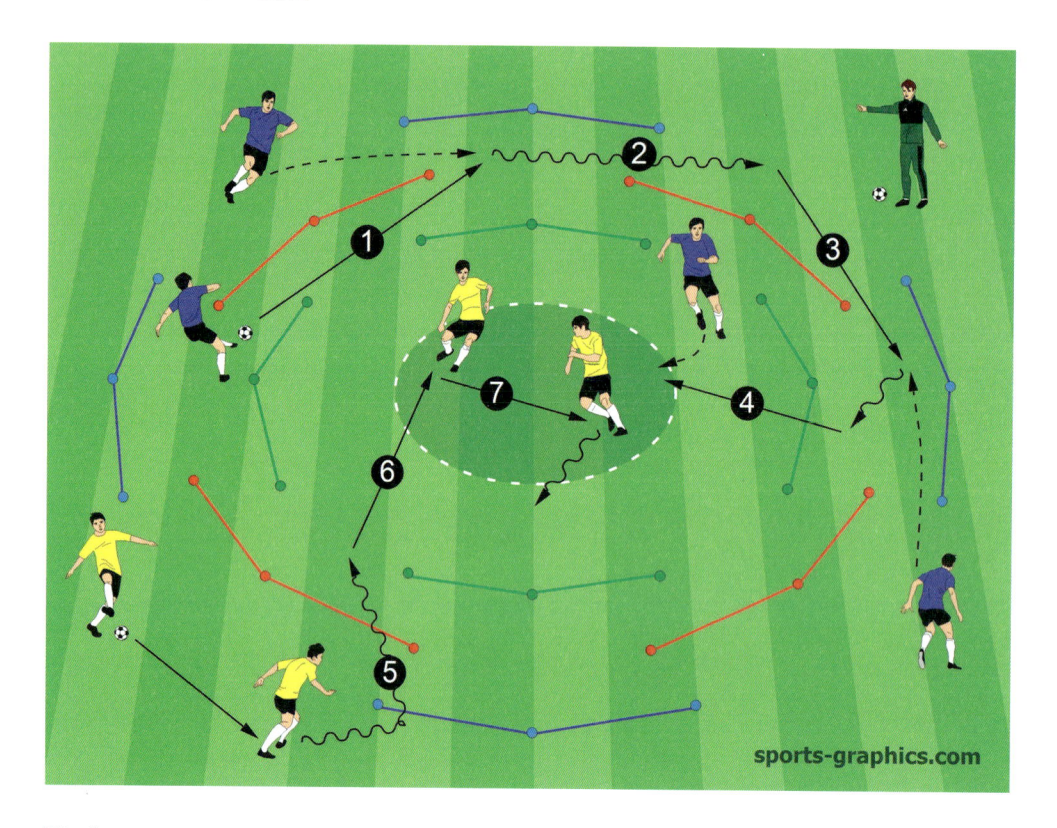

Playing principle

The playing field consists of an inner circle and multiple arch-like and different-colored marking lines, arranged on different levels and rings. Two teams play against each other. No player may run over the lines. The only exception is dribbling (5).

Provocation rules, point system and variants

The team with the ball receives a point when a pass is made between two lines to the running path of a teammate (1), upon dribbling through a space between two lines (2), a pass is made between two lines to an incoming teammate (3), a pass is made over a line into the inner circle to a teammate (4), upon dribbling over two lines from inside to the outside or vice versa (5), a pass is made into the circle to a teammate (6), or a pass is completed between two players within the circle (7). The objectives can be coupled with various trainer signals. There is always one objective in play which may change depending on the situation. For more movement without the ball, the players may be required to change their position to another level after each ball action.

3.2.38 Tornado (Continued)

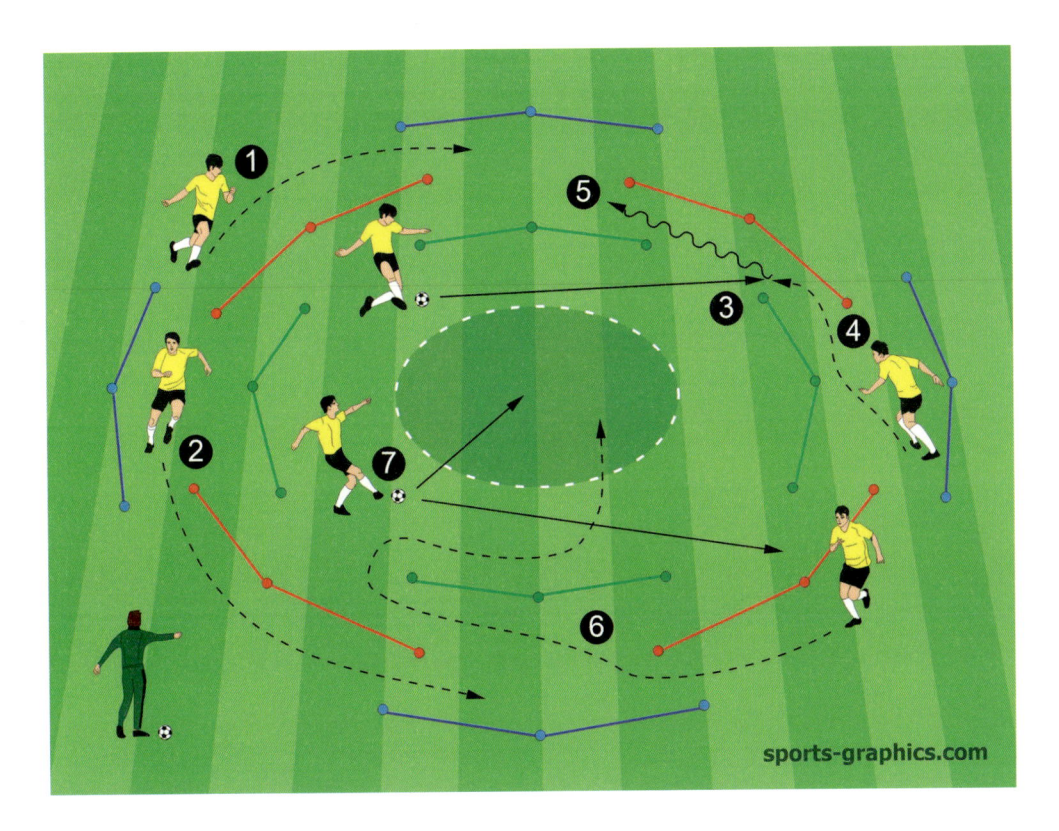

Playing elements and conduct

The objectives emphasize offering and free-running on the basis of position changes, timing and coordinated behavior, thereby illustrating the unique characteristics of the game structure. The field arrangement generates free-running behavior in and on the curve (1), deep runs in interim spaces (2), and precision and timing, especially when passing (3), free-running (4), and during ball processing or dribbling (5). The players are required to always be in motion, not to linger in one position but rather to constantly change their position in order to open up spaces (6). When passing, there is an alternation between diagonal passes and deep passes, especially in the center (7). Qualitative decision-making is the priority here.

Coaching points and instructions

- Open yourself up while running! Vary your positions!
- Control force of passes!
- Run in a curve!

3.2.39 Elevator

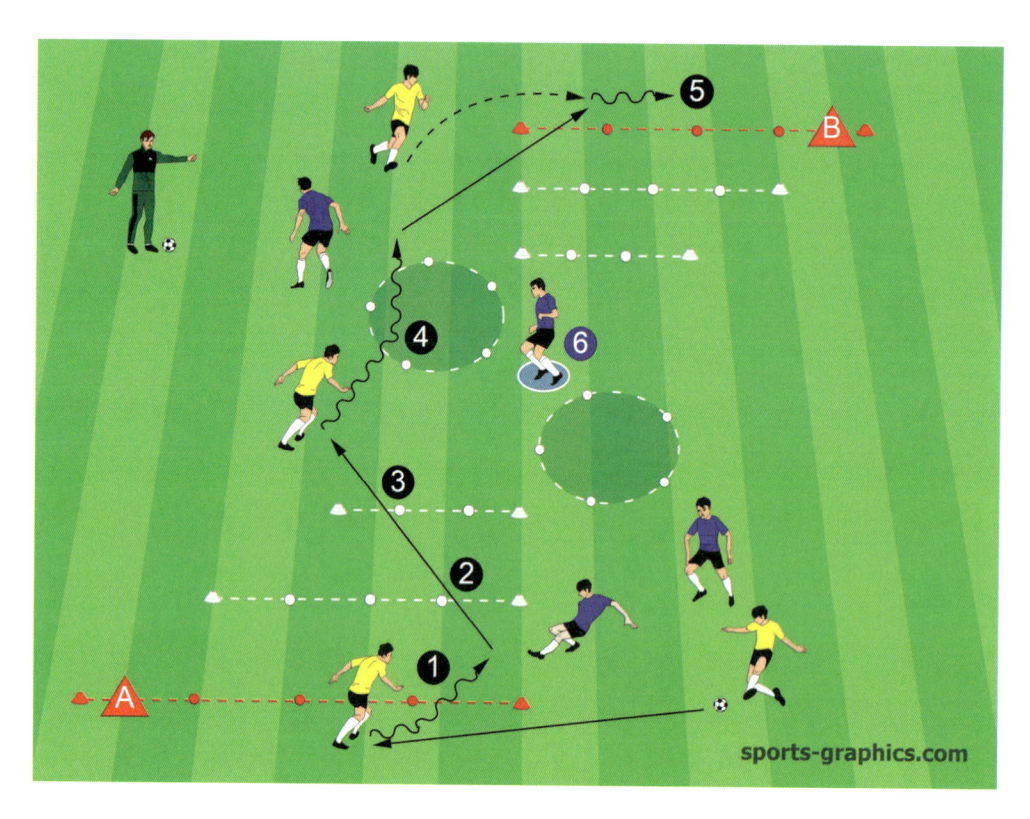

Playing principle

The playing field is framed by critical lines A and B, and the center consists of two circles and more lines. The team in possession may enter over Lines A or B (here Line A) toward the center by dribbling or with a pass from the outside (1). The center is then played through to score points with passing and dribbling actions. The points scored through the center are only valid if the player correctly exits from the opposite side (5) without letting the opposing team take the ball. In order to prevent the defense from only facing the target line, the offense may exit over the entry line once more and secure points. This is possible when both circles in the center have been played through (4).

Provocation rules, point system and variants

Points can be scored when playing through the center by dribbling or passing over a line or a circle (2, 3 and 4). Every line or circle that has been played is worth one point. A maximum of six points is thus possible. The entry and exit lines (Line A and B) do not count. The passing sequence shown here is worth three points. A special point could be awarded if, within the pass combination, one pass has been made between both circles without touching or going over a circle (6).

MAIN COMPONENT **177**

3.2.39 Elevator (Continued)

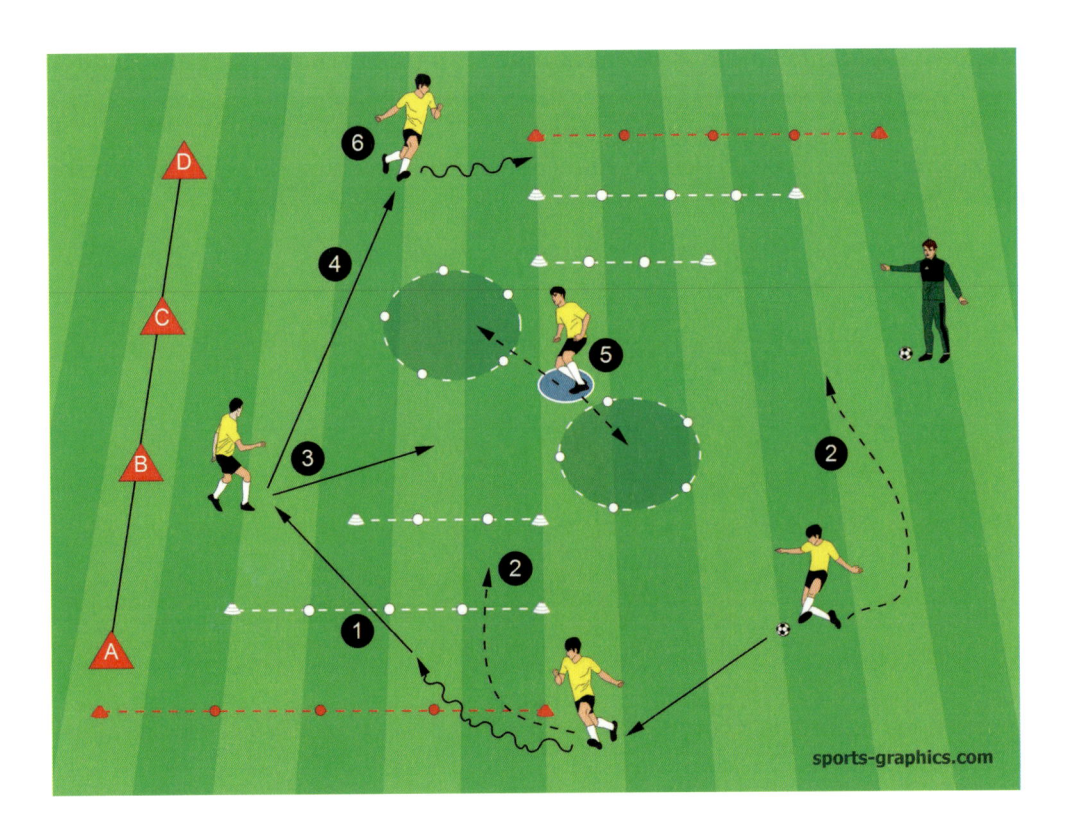

Playing elements and conduct

The playing principle causes all players to pay attention to the different levels and occupy them in coordination. The playing conduct illustrates situations from the playing structure and the game in the final third. In order to play over levels and lines, forceful diagonal passes are ideal (1). The occupation of the various levels (Levels A, B, C and D) and corresponding pursuit, pushback, tightening and covering (2) apply to the offense and defense. In particular, situationally appropriate decisions for promising solutions (3), playing over levels (4), and tactically smart positions are required (5 and 6), especially during plays. The central positions are particularly significant.

Coaching points and instructions

★ Occupy the levels! Play through the levels!
★ Use spaces behind the opponent!
★ Score points!

3.2.40 Quattro

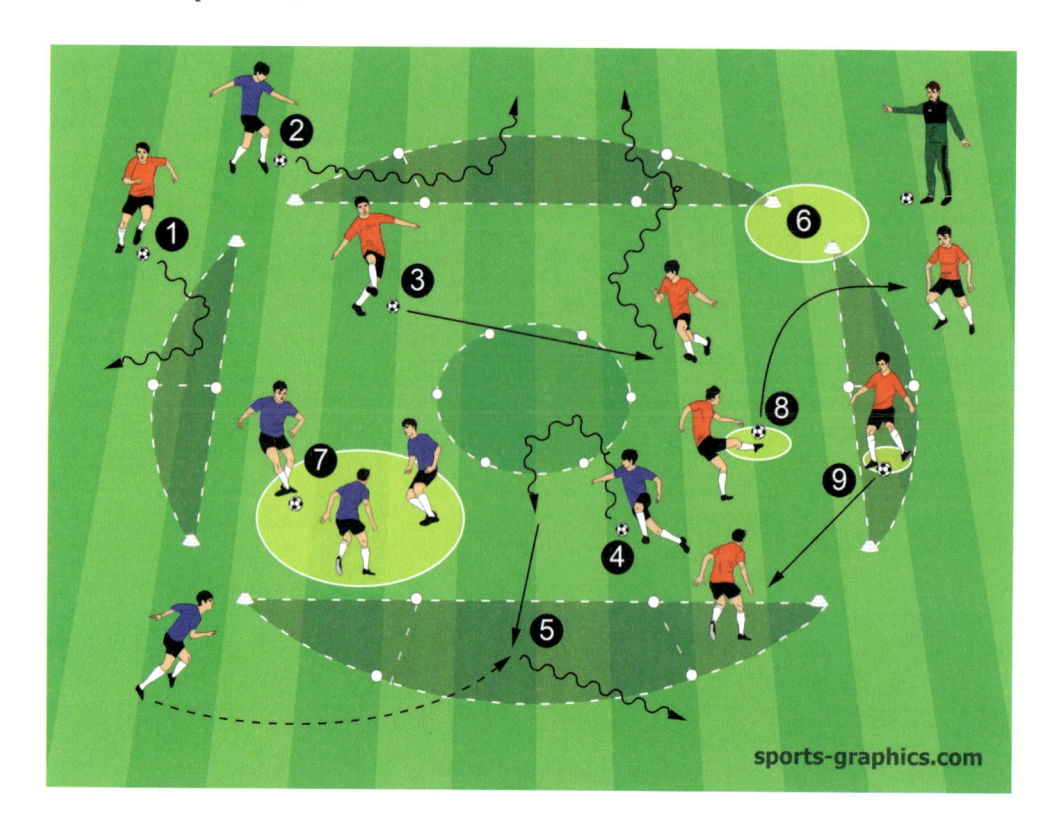

Playing principle

Two teams play against each other. A circle is marked in the center. Multiple fields adjoin one another on the outside. The teams can score points when the fields are played through according to certain rules. A team scores one point when a player in possession changes feet or performs a feint in an outer field, and then leaves this field while dribbling (1), when a player in possession changes feet or performs a feint in two fields in succession (2), when a team makes a pass through the central circle (3), or when a team completes a combination and is able to pass to a teammate in one of the fields after dribbling into the circle (4 and 5).

Provocation rules, point system and variants

The rules for playing through the fields and scoring may vary. They may be made more precise, for example pass combinations must be combined with an individual technique or a pass sequence is specified, e.g. as a fluid receipt of the ball in a field followed by immediate redirection (5). The four interim spaces may be used to define target lines for necessary follow-up passes for scoring (6). Furthermore, more complex objectives may be formulated, e.g. three players must complete three passes in the interim space (7), a peripheral field must be played over with a lob (8), or a pass must be played from one peripheral field to another peripheral field (9).

3.2.40 Quattro (Continued)

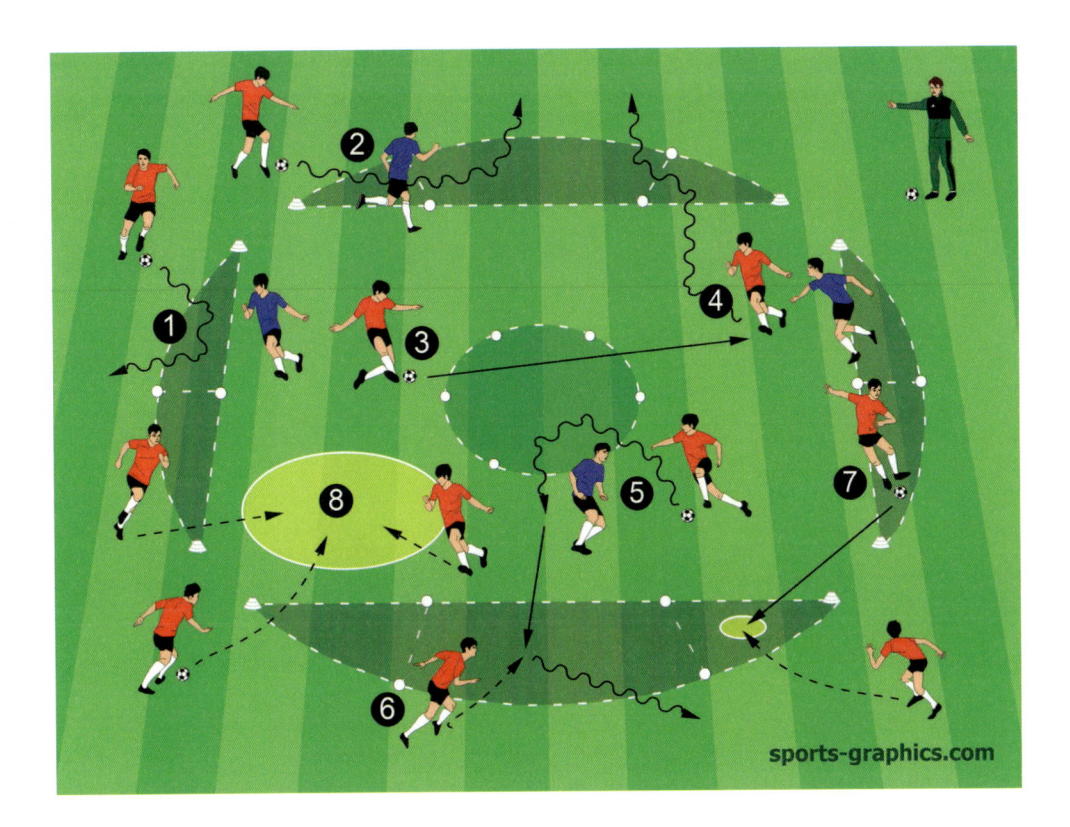

Playing elements and conduct

The playing form provokes quick decision-making with regard to dribbling routes, free spaces, and assessments of opponent pressure (1 and 2). The technical aspects like foot changes, directional changes and feints are performed in tight spaces and under high opponent pressure (1). In a one-on-one situation the player in possession has to escape, shake off opponents, and claim the ball (2) and perform a targeted follow-up if possible. The passing players are required to make forceful passes and give the recipient an advantage by passing to their dominant leg (3). When the recipients are under pressure from opponents, they can be helped by a glance over the shoulder (4) and boldness, as well as a willingness to take risks in offensive one-on-ones (5). The timing when free-running (6) is just as critical as precise and targeted forceful passes (7). Furthermore, the objectives involve spaces that need to be enclosed and the creation of majority situations in critical zones (8).

Coaching points and instructions

* Use both feet! Control forcefulness of passes!
* Take over the zones! Find the spaces!
* Bold dribbling! Take risks and dart around!

3.2.41 Bull's-eye

Playing principle

Two teams play against each other. Marked in the center is a circle. On the outside are four fields surrounding the circle, creating a ring between the center and outer fields. The teams can score points by playing through the fields while completing certain tasks. Objectives for various subjects are possible.

Provocation rules, point system and variants

The team with the ball can score when a player dribbles into the ring from outside via one of the small interim spaces and makes a pass out of the half-space through a second interim space (1), when a player dribbles around at least one marking cone (2), when a pass is played through the middle circle (3), when a pass is played through an outer circle (4), or when a combination of successive plays over multiple fields is realized (5). There may also be rules by which the corner fields must be played around (6) and by which technical actions must be required in the corner fields (7). The scoring may be configured in various ways, so that technical-tactical processes are the main priority. The combination of individual and group-tactical actions may be used as a tool to make the game more difficult. The usage of neutral players to create a constant state of being outnumbered, and to make it easier is also possible.

3.2.41 Bull's-eye (Continued)

Playing elements and conduct

The objectives ensure challenging actions at the individual level. For example, precision in certain target areas under high opponent pressure is required when dribbling (1). Well-timed and coordinated free-running is also required in order to facilitate follow-up actions and achieve the objectives (2). The fields to be played over induce forceful passes from a distance (3), while feint-filled dribbling, topping and changes of direction are promising for one-on-one situations led by the offense (4). Optimal staggering, suitable space distribution, and the occupation of the various levels are required depending on the distances selected between the fields (5).

Coaching points and instructions

★ Always be bold! Always create passing options!
★ Stagger! Form a grid!
★ Use the smallest spaces!

182   CIRCLE SOCCER TRAINING

3.2.42 Triangle

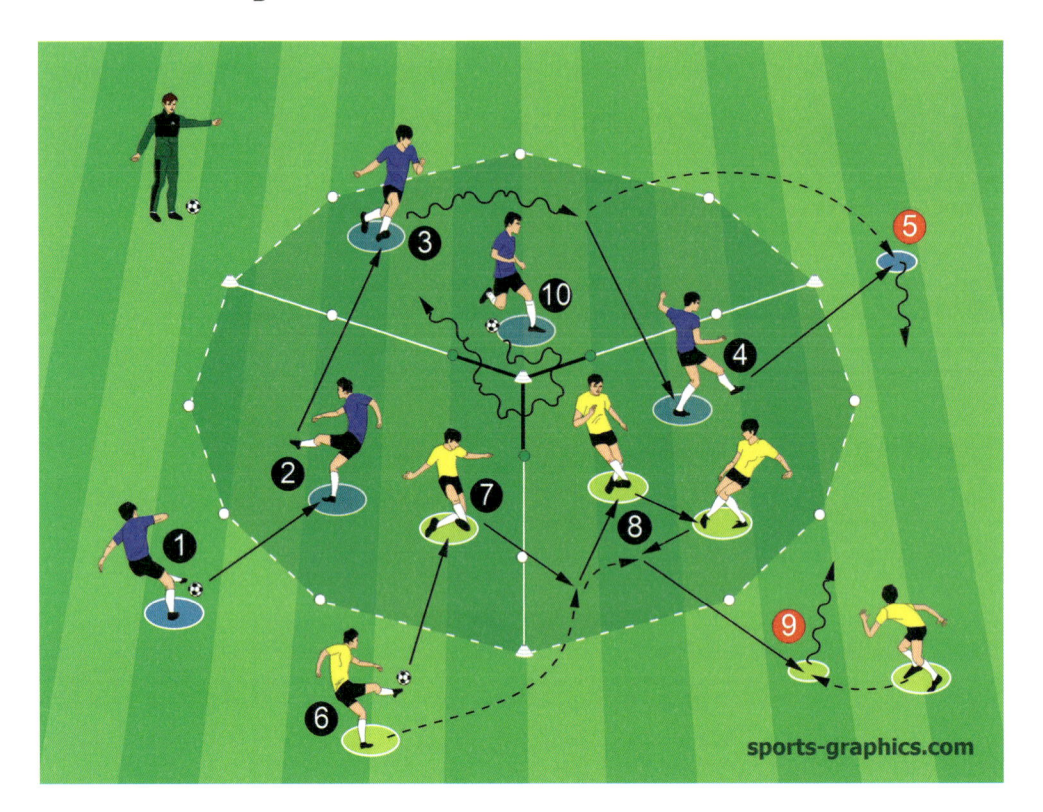

Playing principle

The playing field consists of a circle divided into three zones and the outer playing area. The team in possession must start with a pass into the circle from outside (1 and 6), achieve stipulated objectives, score points that way, and then make a specified exit (5 and 9). In the event of ball loss during the play, the points scored so far will be lost.

Provocation rules, point system and variants

The team in possession has three ways to score a point. For one, the team may enter with a pass into any of the circle sections (1), play through the other fields clockwise or counterclockwise (2, 3 and 4), and score the points with a final pass out of the circle (5). Secondly, a point is scored when another field is passed to (7) after exiting (6), where three complete passes are executed (8) and the exit is successful (9). Thirdly, it is possible for an individual player to dribble near the center over the three connecting lines (10).

3.2.42 Triangle (Continued)

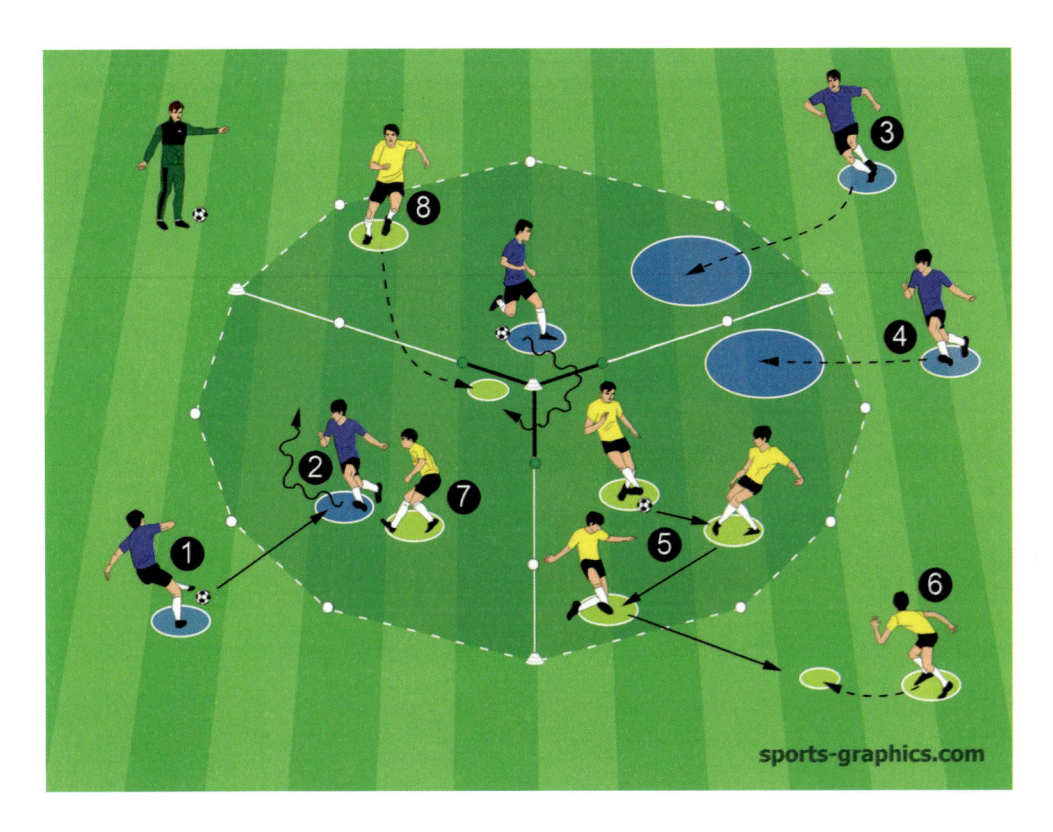

Playing elements and conduct

The entrance into the circle must be prepared, well-timed and coordinated (1). The player awaiting the ball must expect pressure from opponents and may select the optimal direction for continuing the play with good orientation and glances over the shoulder (2). As per the objectives, it is crucial that follow-up actions are facilitated so that the player in possession has passing options (3). The target areas to be passed to may not be run up to early, but rather must be timed (4). Certain zones must be over-occupied depending on the situation in order to create a majority (5). Deep passing points are critical for scoring and exiting out of the circle if there are too many opponents (6). The defense must base their behavior on critical actions by the offense (7 and 8).

Coaching points and instructions

- Keep looking over your shoulders!
- Be open to deep passes!
- Run up! Cut in!

184 CIRCLE SOCCER TRAINING

3.2.43 Diamond

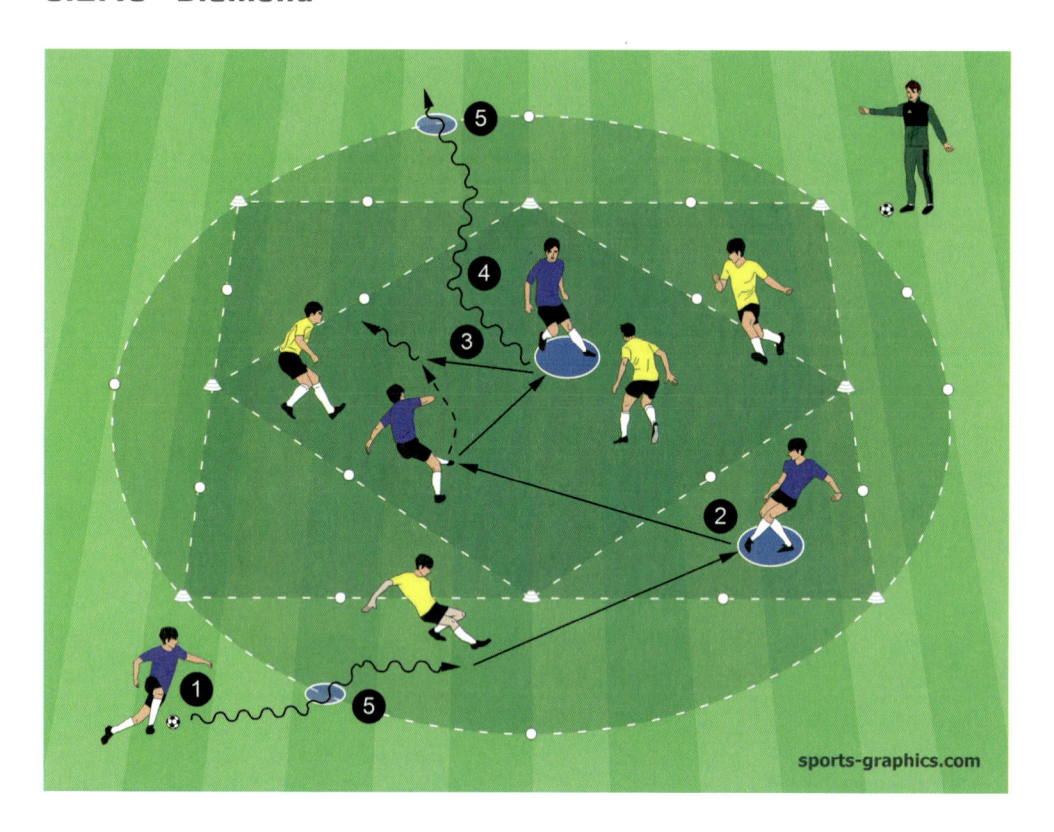

Playing principle

The playing field consists of the outer field and a large circle, which is divided into nine sections by four squares. The team in possession has the opportunity to score a point within the circle by completing three objectives.

Provocation rules, point system and variants

The team in possession must first dribble into the circle (1). This game may be prepared outside of the circle, toward the center. A point can then be scored when a recipient performs a direct pass in a triangle (2). This pass must go into the central square. Another point can be scored in the central square. This also requires a direct pass (3). The third way to score a point is for a recipient in the central square to receive a pass, turn around (4), and dribble out of the playing field on the opposite side from the entry point (5) without losing the ball. The objectives may vary and be made more difficult, e.g. the passes (2 and 3) must be played directly or with two ball contacts, the pass in the center must also be processed in the center (3), the incoming player in the center must be included in the pass sequence (1), or an exit (5) must occur after the passes (2 and 3).

3.2.43 Diamond (Continued)

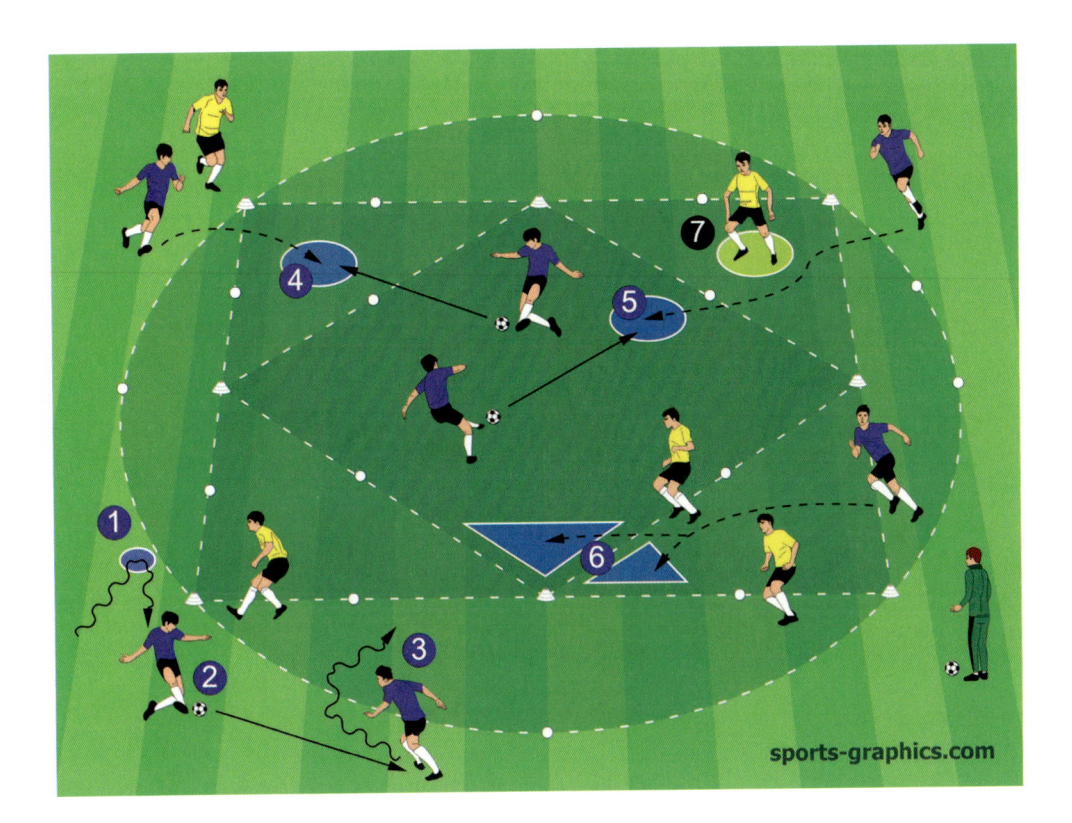

Playing elements and conduct

The entry actions should be shaped by deceiving and binding dribbling (1), long forceful passes (2), and bold dribbling (3). In order to facilitate the best possible continuations and follow-up actions, offering and free-running are critical. It is important that approaches to the critical zones are well-timed (4) in order to minimize opponent pressure as much as possible. Opponents can be bound to certain areas by the running path. Free zones and possible points must be quickly recognized and approached (5). The free-running should also be bold, including under increased opponent presence in the center (6). Precision for the smallest spaces is also necessary. The defense's behavior depends on the critical zones in the center (7). These should be collectively faced and approached at all times.

Coaching points and instructions

★ Precise free-running! Precise offering!
★ Purposeful passes to the center!
★ Use the zones!

3.2.44 Pantheon

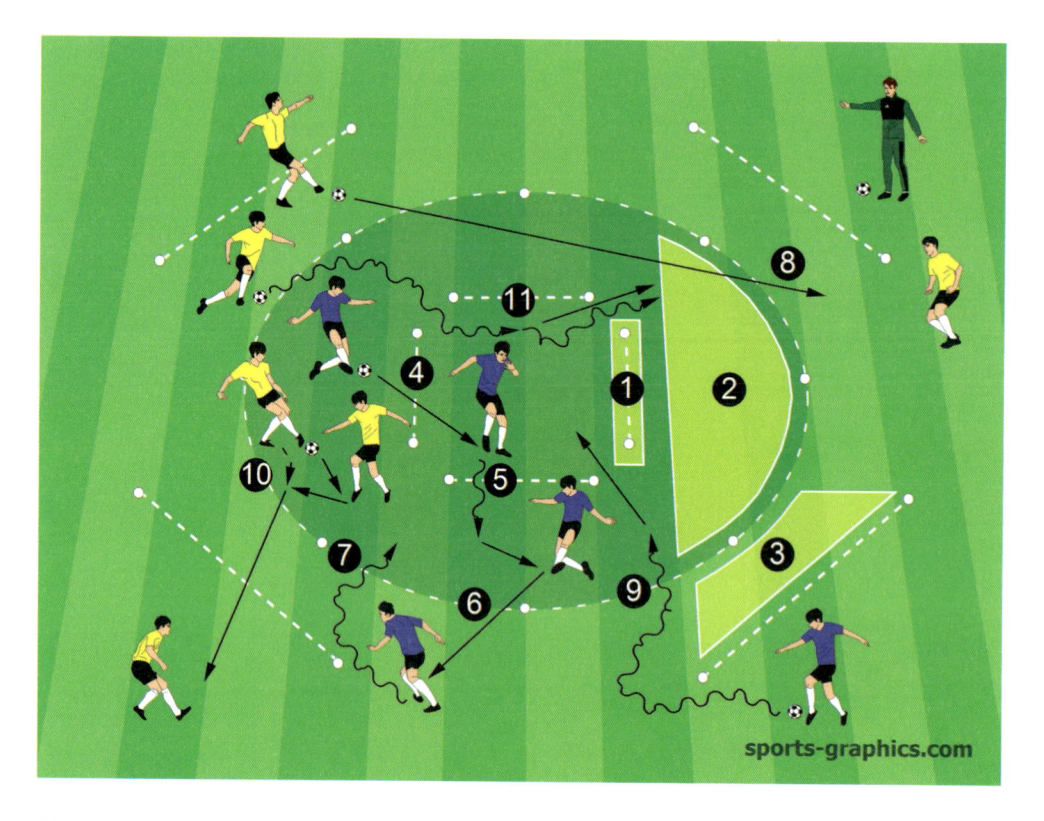

Playing principle

The principle involves playing through lines (1), interim spaces (2), and zones around the central circle (3). Players must perform combinations in certain zones, play through levels, or combine dribbling and passing tasks in order to play toward specified objectives and score points. The objectives involve the preparation of the attacks through the central space of the circle. Instead of wide passes far from the center, the task is to quickly pass to the center of the circle when possible. The principle also involves linking the various provocation rules together and always allowing new rules to be made. The level of variability can increase and be differentiated so as to allow for a quicker adjustment of the players, and thus a positive impact on the capacity for flexibility.

Provocation rules, point system and variants

One point is scored when a pass is played over a line (4), when a player dribbles over a line (5), a pass is played over a circle line (6), a player dribbles over a circle line (7), or a long-distance pass is played through the circle (8). Double points are awarded when a player combines dribbling into the circle with a pass through an interim space (9), when two passes in a half-circle are combined with a pass through an over line (10), or when a player is able to dribble into the center over a line and then exit through an interim pass by dribbling or passing (11). Triple points are awarded when dribbling into the center is combined with two passes over two different lines, when dribbling into the center is combined with two passes over the circle lines, or the player is able to play through three different interim spaces such as the center, half-field, or outer area.

3.2.44 Pantheon (Continued)

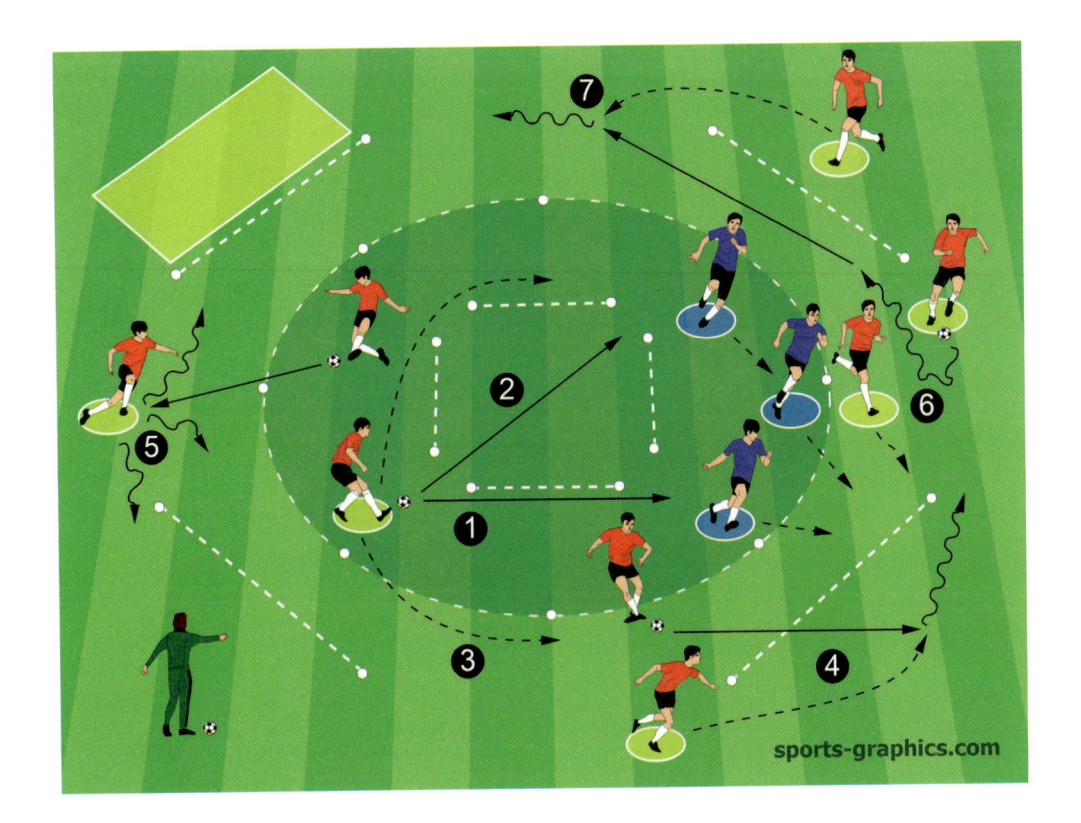

Playing elements and conduct

Playing toward the various objectives and passing to tight spaces and swiftness require a variety of passing and dribbling actions from the players. The lines of the structure of the field, starting from all conceivable positions, create a complex perception task for each player with regard to the straight (1), diagonal (2) or curved lines (3) and the resulting zones. The rules require situationally appropriate offering and free-running (4) as well as quick sideways movements on the lines and the circle, bold threatening of the different objectives, especially with regard to precise initial ball contact (5), as well as constant variation, mixing and metering of acceleration with and without the ball in order to score or prevent points while saving energy. The conservation of energy becomes more important with increasing proximity to the circle, and should also be regulated by the trainer through breaks when necessary. Furthermore, the team in possession can even deliberately provoke the opponent to engage in exaggerated prevention measures (6) in order to then strategically, and with forethought, play toward an objective at other locations (7). In essence, because of the many possible solutions, the observation and assessment of individual players with regard to the quality of their decision-making and playing strategy are worthwhile.

Coaching points and instructions

- Wall off the center! Let no one into the circle!
- Start again! Push back! Pursue!
- Run! Rescue! Complete the run!

3.2.45 Triad

Playing principle

The playing field consists of an outer area and a circle, which holds two triangles. This creates five fields inside the circle. The teams can score points through individual actions or group combinations.

Provocation rules, point system and variants

At the individual level, a player in possession can score by entering into the circle from outside, dribbling around a marking cone on the edge, and exiting the circle again (1). A player receives double points when they dribble around a cone on the edge of the large triangle (2) and then exit the field, or when a player dribbles through the small triangle in the center (3). The team in possession can also score through passing, and receive one point when three passes are played in a peripheral area (4), when three passes are played in the large triangle (5), or when a pass is played through the central small triangle (6). The points may also be secured by a final pass into the outer field (7).

3.2.45 Triad (Continued)

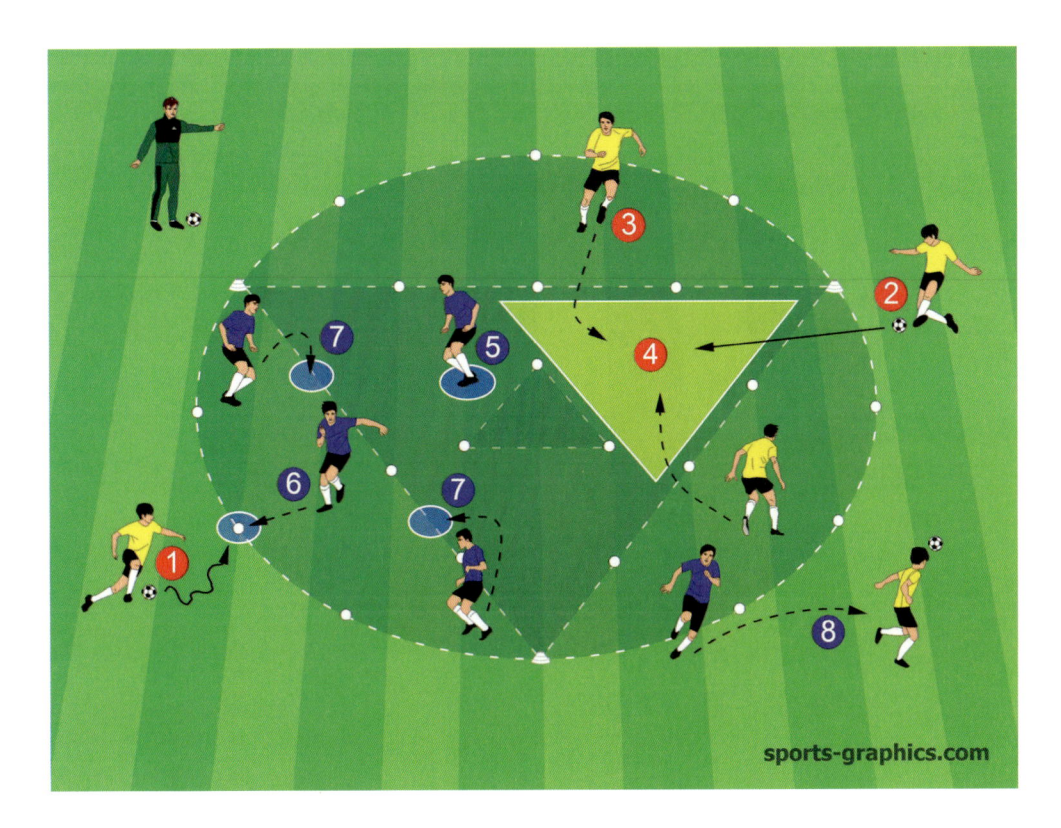

Playing elements and conduct

The offense is constantly required to threaten the center and head toward tactically critical zones (1). The passing players can introduce plays with bold passes into the center and draw recipients to the critical zones (2). The timing of offering and free-running (3) is just as critical as the short-term coverage of relatively small zones to create majority situations (4). The defense is defined by the constant search for tactically sensible positioning in order to be able to react quickly in all directions (5). The center should be protected first. The players in possession must still be run toward and put under pressure (6). Defensive players advancing from the chain or the wall should be covered with deep staggering and the creation of defensive triangles (7).

Coaching points and instructions

★ Cover target areas! Dribble to target points!
★ Keep acting toward the center!
★ Always check your position!

190 CIRCLE SOCCER TRAINING

3.2.46 Hexagon

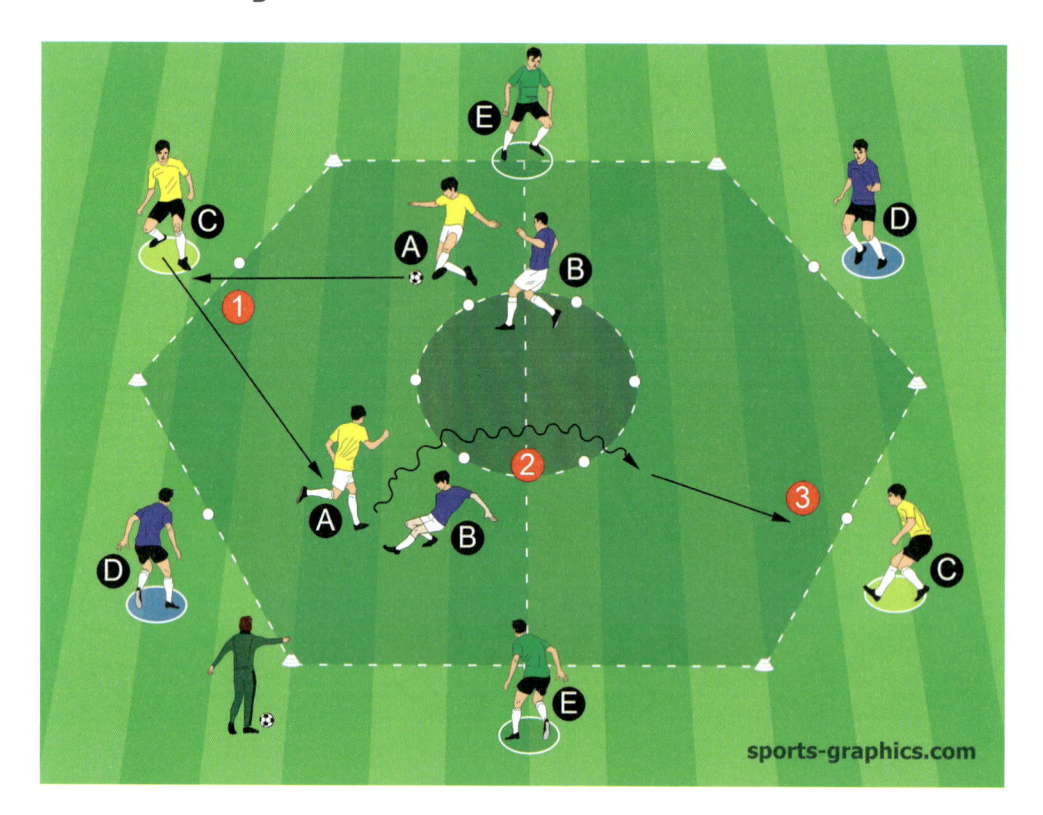

Playing principle

The playing field consists of a hexagon with a central circle and an outer area. A two-on-two situation is played out in the field (Players A and B). Each team has two diagonally positioned outer players (Players C and D), resulting in a constant two-on-two-plus-two (1). The team in possession scores when the central circle is included (2) followed by another pass (3).

Provocation rules, point system and variants

A point is scored when the central circle is dribbled (2) or passed through, followed by another pass (3). Double points can be scored for dribbling or passing from one half of the field into another. There are variants for the number of ball contacts per player, e.g. the outer players must always play directly or may not pass to another outer player. For simplification, it is possible to include two more players as neutral passers. It would also make the game simpler for the team in possession if the two defenders in the center may not enter the inner circle.

3.2.46 Hexagon (Continued)

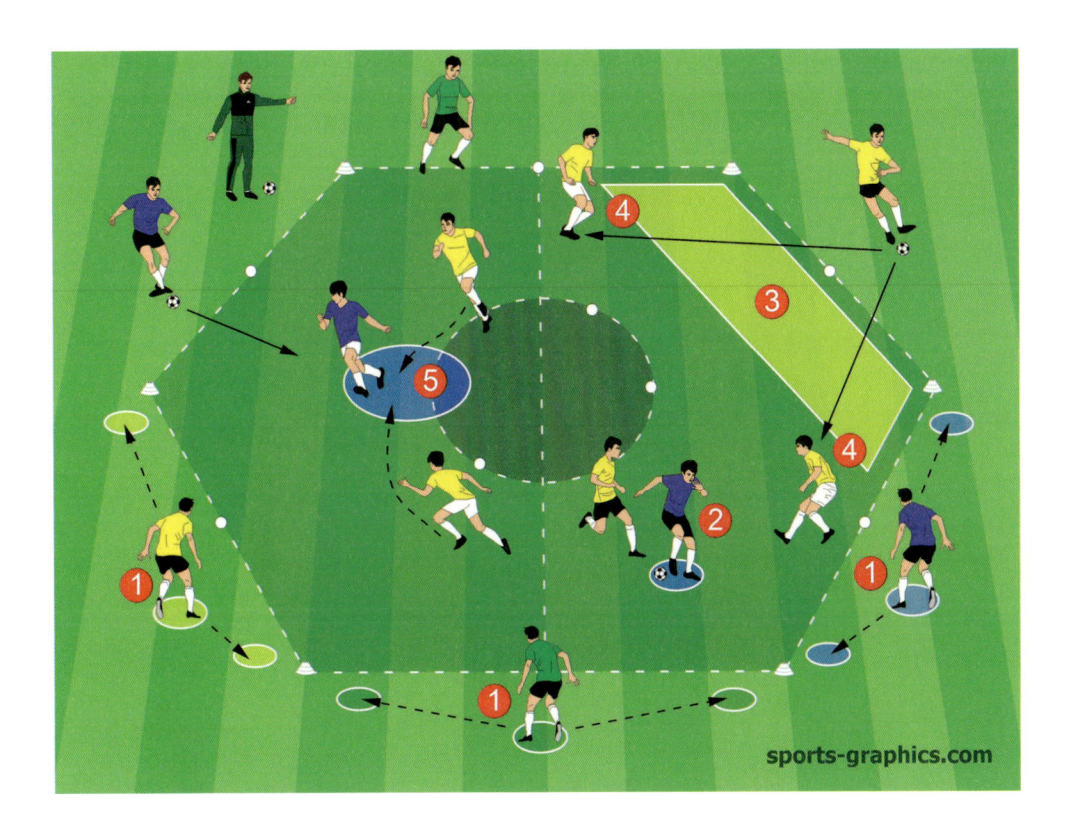

Playing elements and conduct

The playing form necessitates the outer players being smart and tactically sensible in their actions in order to help their teammates in the center with the constant two-on-two situation. The outer players can and must completely use their sideline and move in accordance with the ball (1). The players in the center are subjected to high requirements with regard to swiftness, decision-making, and opponent/space/time pressure (2). The space in front of the outer players should be left open and playable when possible (3) so that there is room to make passes and as many passing options as possible (4). The defense is required to recognize critical and tactically valuable zones, and run up and defend them as quickly as possible.

Coaching points and instructions

★ Position yourself in accordance with the ball!
★ Always look over your shoulder!
★ Take bold actions toward the middle!

3.2.47 Perspective

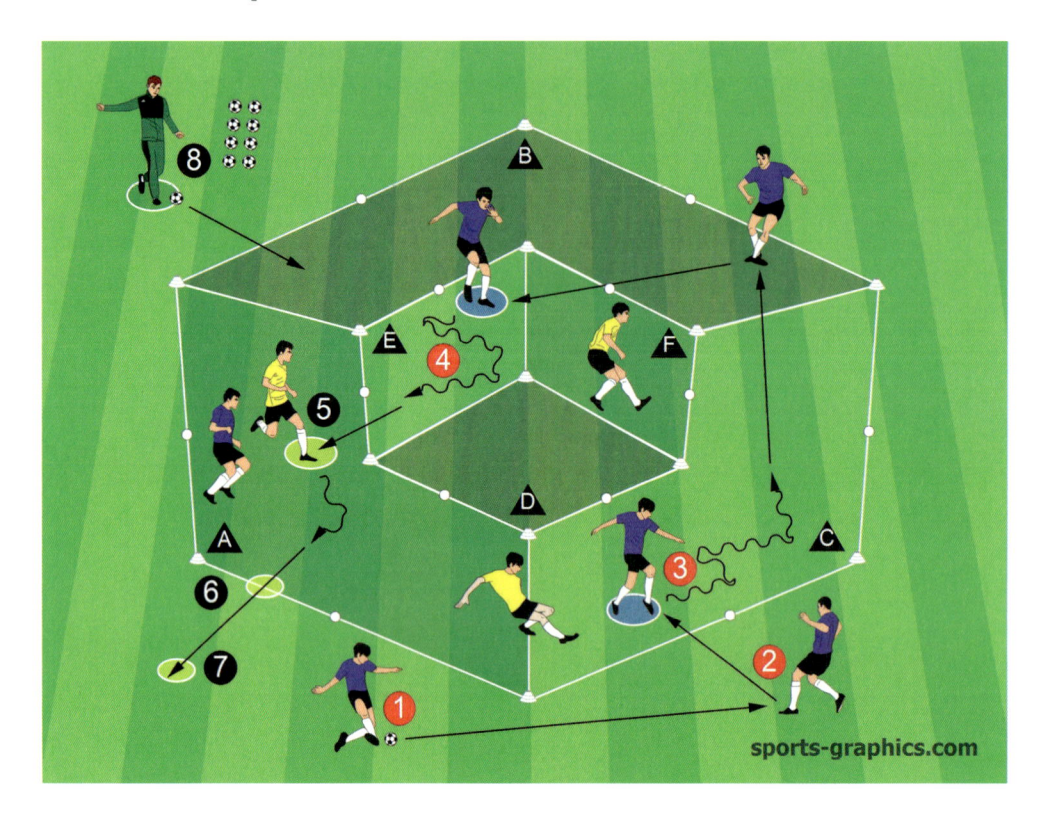

Playing principle

The playing field consists of three large fields (Fields A, B and C), three smaller fields in the center (Fields D, E and F), and the outer area. The team in possession plays with six players against the defensive, which is outnumbered with only three players. The trainer plays 10 balls in a row. The majority team can score during this 10-ball phase. After the 10 balls, the three defensive players are switched.

Provocation rules, point system and variants

The team in possession can combine freely in the outer area (1) and take a moment of their choosing to play into the center (2) and score there. The team in possession can only score in the center through individual actions. They earn one point when a player makes ball contact five times in the Fields A, B or C (3), or four times in Fields D, E or F (4). The outnumbered team tries to take the ball (5) and play out of the field (6). If they are successful, the trainer immediately brings the next ball into play (8). Otherwise, shots may be taken at the mini-goals after each taking of the ball (7). The various fields may also have specific tasks associated with them: Field A (5 left ball contacts), Field B (5 right ball contacts), Field C (2 feints), Field D (3 left contacts), Field E (3 right contacts) and Field F (one feint).

3.2.47 Perspective (Continued)

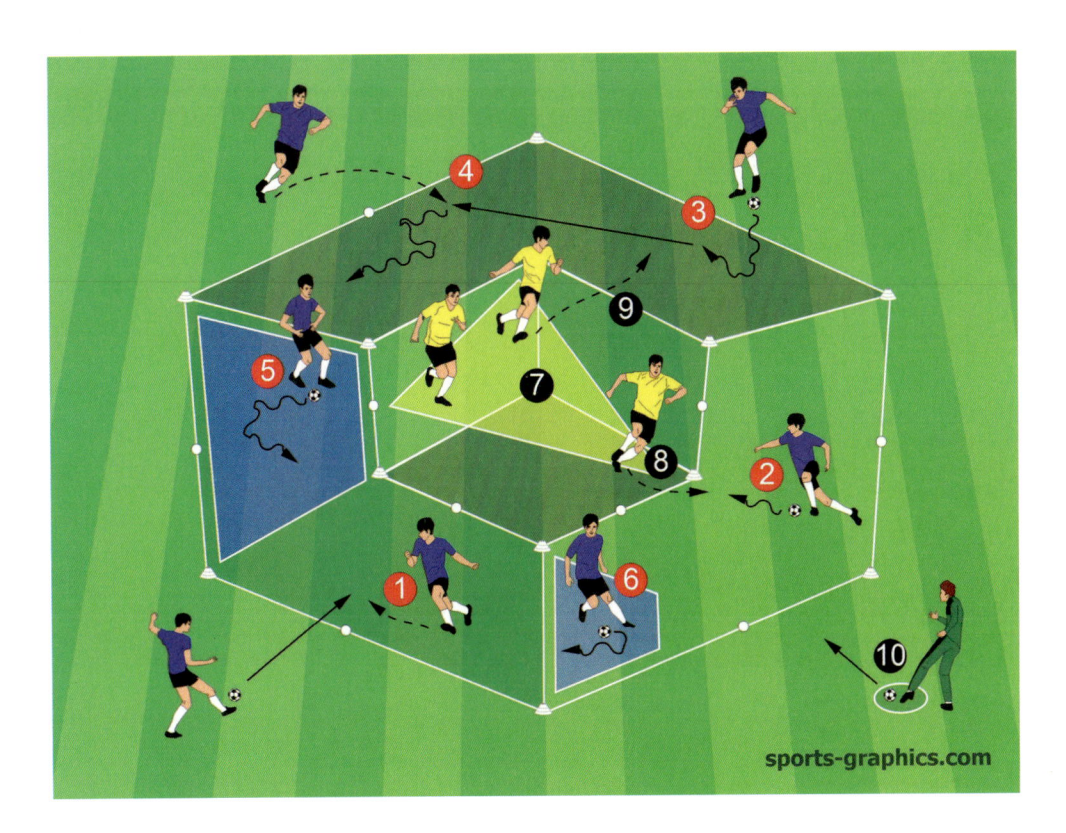

Playing elements and conduct

Well-timed free-running, pre-orientation through glances over the shoulder, and offering to gaps are necessary in the offense (1). The center should frequently be threatened with the ball (2). Defensive players should be lured and bound (3) in order to be able to pass to teammates and create room for ball contacts or feints (4). The individual ball contacts or feinting should be used with the highest speed (5) and in small spaces (6). The defense ideally operates from a closed and mutually securing wall (7). The outer areas, and especially players in possession, must be run toward (8) without individual players being lured too strongly or the wall being lost, resulting in overly large gaps or distances (9).

Coaching points and instructions

★ Defend together!
★ Show your technique!
★ Use all spaces!

3.2.48 Sky disk

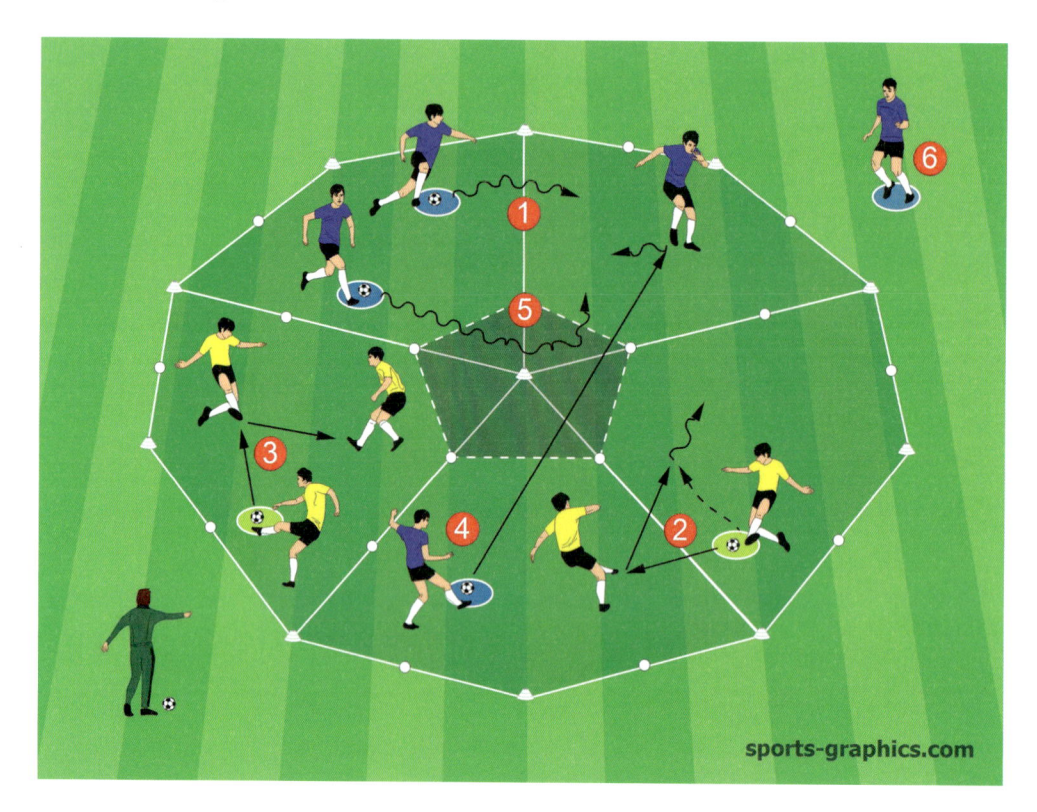

Playing principle

The playing field consists of the outer area and 10 fields. The five outer fields are relatively large and the five central fields near the middle small. The team in possession can score points by completing specific objectives.

Provocation rules, point system and variants

One point is scored when one player dribbles over one of the five field lines (1), a double pass is played over one of the field lines (2), a play is made with a third person in one of the five large fields (3), a pass is made through the central small fields (4), or a player is able to dribble through the central small fields (5). It may be required that each objective must be completed with a pass to the outside (6). It is also possible that the points vary and objectives through the small center can be awarded double points. Different variations of the objectives at the individual level or within the team and small groups are also possible.

3.2.48 Sky disk (Continued)

Playing elements and conduct

The specification of the objectives creates a focus on the center and bold dribbling toward the middle (1). In order to achieve the objectives that must be completed in the center, it is important for the potential recipients in the middle that they leave the defenders' zone of coverage (2), position themselves in an open and optimal position with regard to the objective, and open themselves up to gaps between two defenders (3). It is also important for the offense that they make timed approaches to specific zones and specified areas and briefly cover them so that they can outnumber the defense while achieving their objectives (4). For the defense, it is elementary and critical that players with the ball are approached and faced (5), and that passing routes are run toward (6).

Coaching points and instructions

★ Face the opponents! Put pressure on the player with the ball!
★ Use gaps! Leave the coverage zone!
★ Block the passing routes! Prevent dribbling!

3.2.49 Sundial

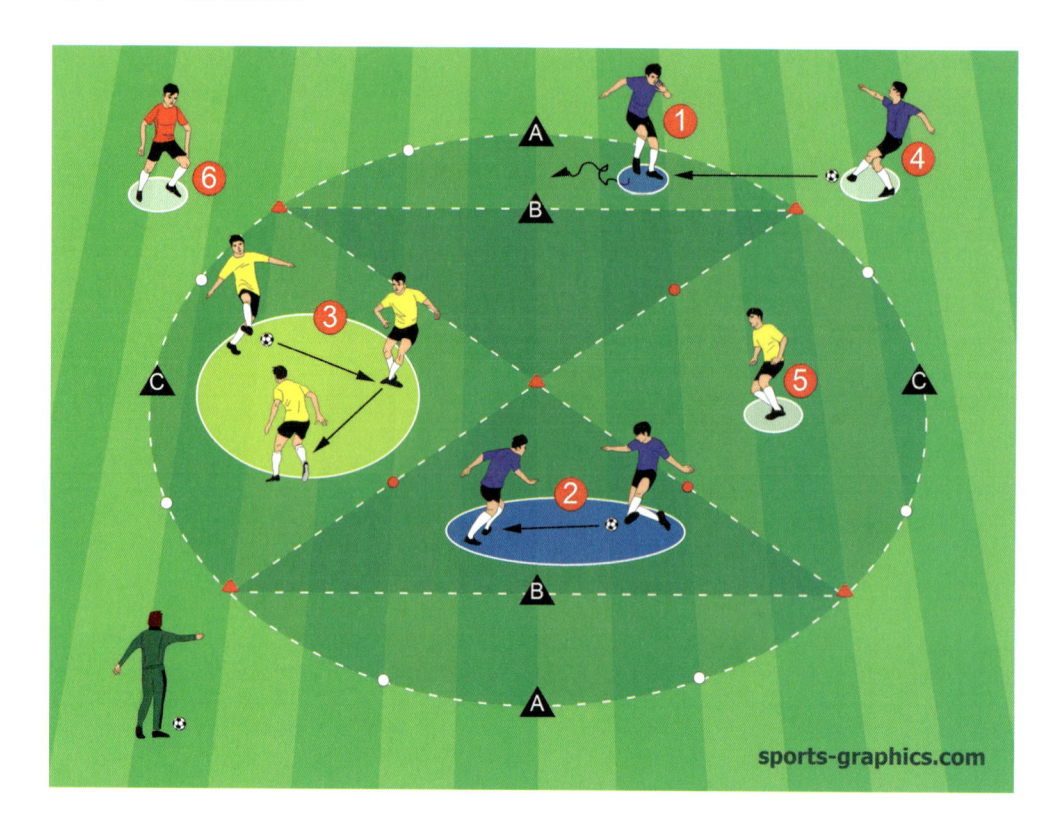

Playing principle

The playing field consists of the outer field and a circle that is divided into six fields. There are two small fields (A), two mid-sized fields (B), and two large fields (C). The team in possession may only score in Fields A with an individual action (1), in Fields B with an action that involves exactly two players (2), and in Fields C with an action that involves exactly three players (3).

Provocation rules, point system and variants

Ball contact numbers, certain feints, or specific technical tasks may be required for the individual actions (1). The actions to be performed by the players (2) may be specified by a simple direct pass, a double pass, or a simple pass with the non-dominant leg. The actions in which three players must be involved (3) may be specified as a play with a third person, a combination with back-running or as a zig-zag combination. It is also possible that certain players may only be in the outer area (4), the central circle (5), or as neutral players constantly in possession (6) for a playing form in the majority or minority.

3.2.49 Sundial (Continued)

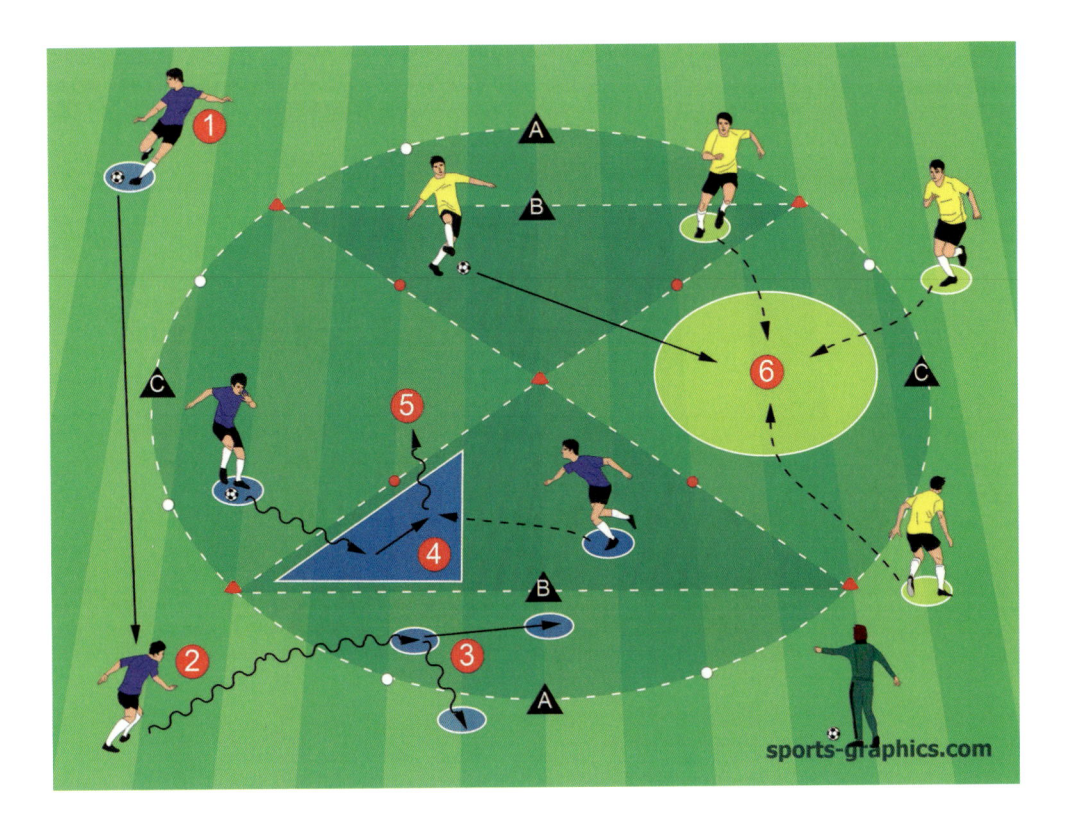

Playing elements and conduct

In the outer area, long-distance passes over multiple levels are sensible when preparing for the central play (1). The actions toward the center should be bold and purposeful (2). The highest possible tempo, precise execution even under space and opponent pressure, and the execution of follow-up actions are required for all actions in the center (3), either as dribbling or passes for securing the ball or steering toward the next objective. The actions in which multiple players are involved can also be performed in tight spaces (4). Immediately following this, the space that was previously played should be left in order to escape the pressure from opponents (5). The tightening of the critical spaces to create majority situations and the achieving of individual objectives must be coordinated and well-timed (6).

Coaching points and instructions

- Look to the center!
- Open up spaces!
- Play through spaces!

3.2.50 Rhombus

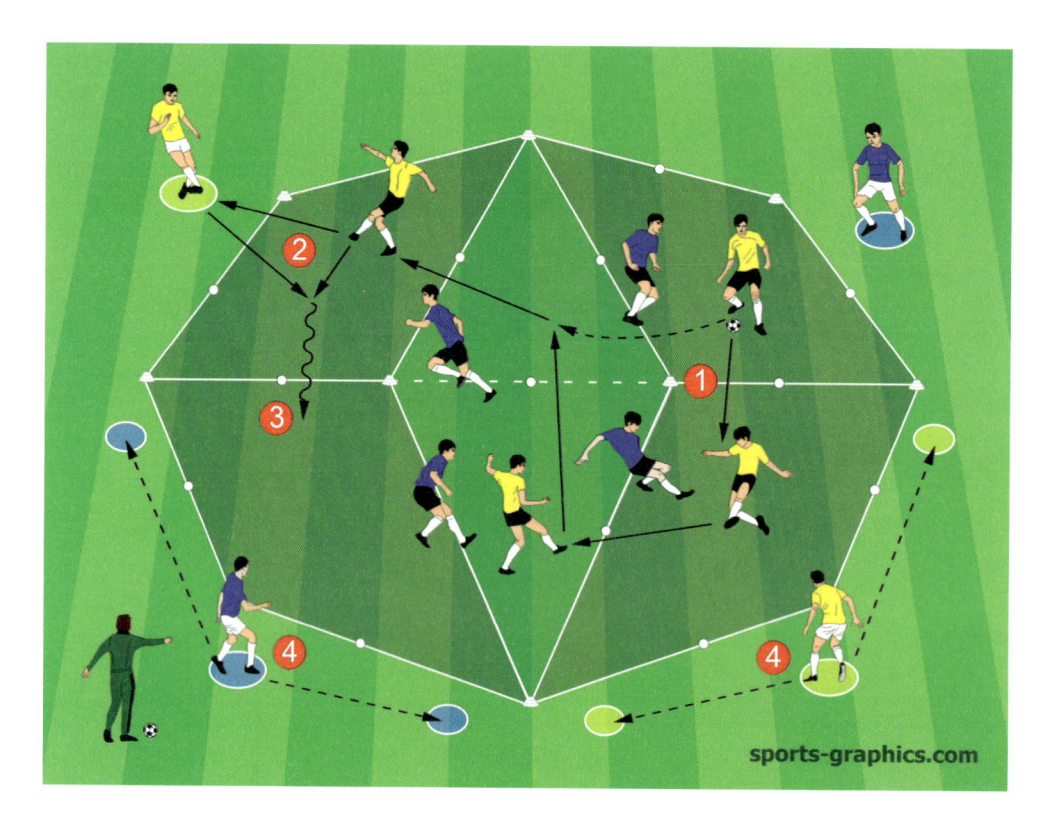

Playing principle

The playing field consists of six adjoining fields. Neutral players are in the outer area. The playing form is organized as four-plus-two-versus-four-plus-two. Each team has two diagonally positioned outer players. The team in possession tries to keep the ball to themselves for as long as possible and may include the two outer players. The rule that a pass may only be played into a neighboring field and only over one field line must be observed (1). The outer players may only return the pass into the field from which they received it (2).

Provocation rules, point system and variants

For simplicity's sake it is possible that the players are also allowed to change feet when dribbling (3). The outer players may, and must, open themselves up according to the situation, thereby using the entire breadth of their own field (4). A point may be scored for every field line that is played over (1 and 3).

3.2.50 Rhombus (Continued)

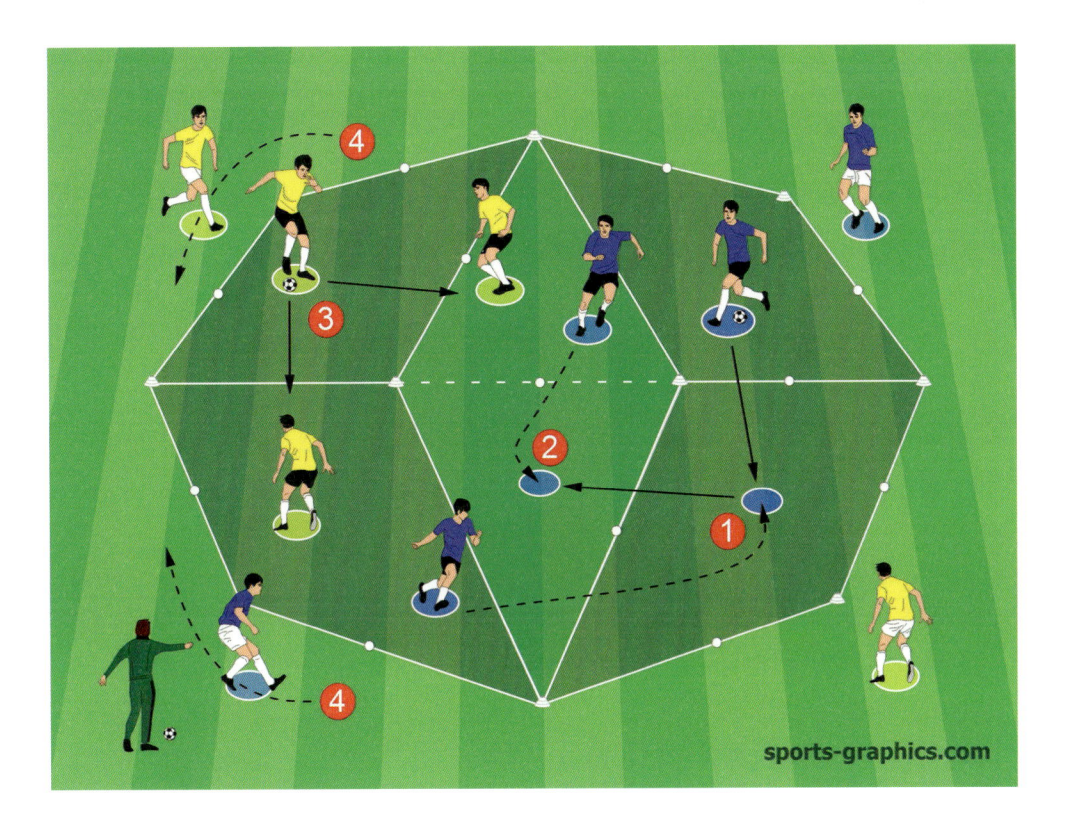

Playing elements and conduct

The player currently in possession must be given passing options in the adjoining fields. That is why it is critical that the teammates orient their offering and free-running by the fields and create opportunities for follow-up actions (1). This necessitates anticipation and reactions so that there are opportunities for further action (2). It is desired, and automatically arises, that the players in possession position themselves in triangles and the player currently in possession has at least two passing points. The outer players are required to move and keep themselves open while running according to the situation.

Coaching points and instructions

- Always keep yourself open!
- Create passing options!
- Form triangles!

4 CONTINUATION

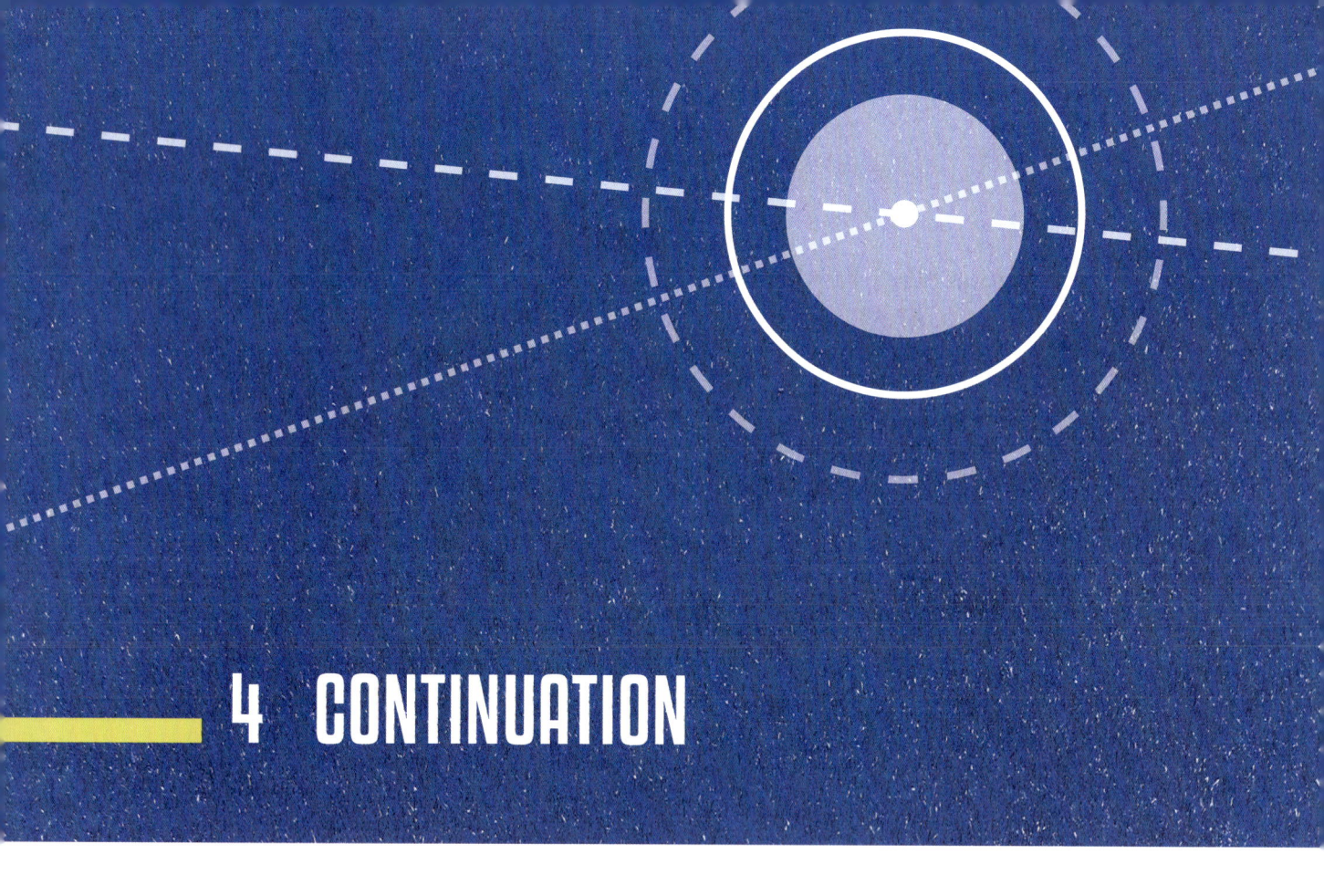

4.1 CONCEPTUAL CONTINUATION

This continuation immediately follows the 50 central circle playing forms and develops more immersive playing ideas for the concept. This continuation expands the core circle playing forms with mini-goals, small goals, and large goals, combines the fields with the same or different circle formations, or opens up additional possible solutions through the usage of colored marking cones. The continuing concepts include the usage of the structure for group-based or individual techniques to the effect that the fields are played with technical stipulations, without pressure from opponents (training form 4.1.1).

Furthermore, it presents the possibility that the preparation, familiarization, and acclimation to the field structure and rules can be done through simplified handball (training form 4.1.2). The generation of finishing opportunities after reaching individual game objectives is a major component of the playing concept, and is realized through the combination of the circular field and mini-goals, small goals or large goals (training form 4.1.3).

The combination and manifold arrangement of the circle fields expands the possible actions as well as choices (training form 4.1.4) and may influence specific entrances and exits depending on the orientation (training form 4.1.5). The connection of multiple fields and additional gates (training form 4.1.6) may create more directions of play and more complex actions, similar to the usage of color markings (training form 4.1.7).

An asymmetrical field structure creates an alternation that affects playability (training form 4.1.8) and mindset (4.1.9). Ultimately, this underlines the idea that an innovative field structure with creative formations can help generate interest, enthusiasm, imagination, creativity, and most importantly be fun (training form 4.1.10).

DESIGN
PREPARATION
FOLLOW-UP ACTION
COLOR MARKINGS
DIRECTION COMPLETE OPTION
GAME COMPREHENSION ASYMMETRY ADAPT
TECHNICAL FORMS SIMPLIFICATION
ACTION OPTIONS HANDBALL
FORMATION INSPIRATION ACTION VARIETY
CREATIVE FORMS COMPLEXITY
PLAYABILITY

4.1.1 Rolling a five – adaptation (technique forms)

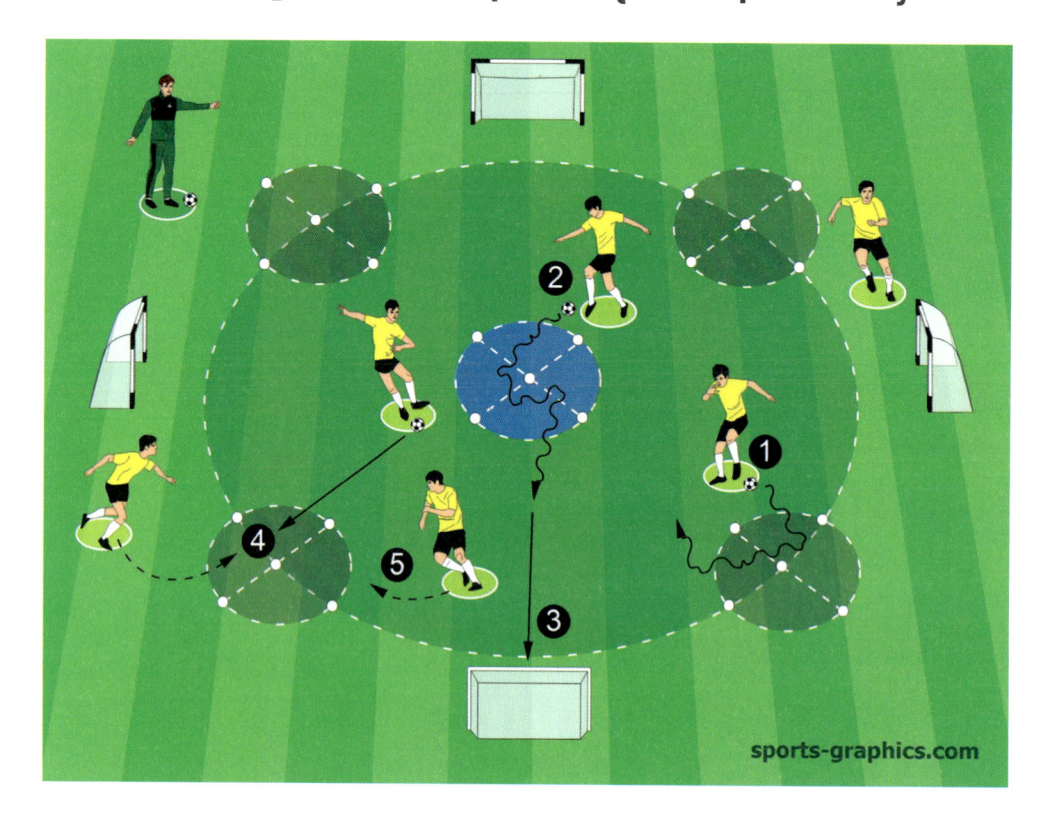

Execution, principles and elements

The central idea of this training form lies in emphasizing on honing technical processes through the field concept. To this end, multiple circular fields are arranged, each marked and divided with a separating line. The players must perform technical tasks in precisely these relatively small circles. The players form a small group to circulate the ball and take it to the individual target fields through free passes in order to perform specified movements and implement techniques. A kick to the mini-goals is one possible conclusion (3). In the circular fields and segments, the players may be ordered to perform feints, changes of direction, or clipping (1). Because of the high pressure from opponents, the circle in the center has special significance (2). This is where the actions with the highest tempo should be performed.

Provocation rules, point system and variants

Depending on the desired emphasis, the circular fields can also be used for precise first-touch control (4). In order to be able to hit the mini-goals, the first-touch control must happen within the circle. It may also be required that the circles can only be entered while dribbling the ball. The separating lines can be used to define even more detailed feint sequences or multiple changes of direction.

4.1.2 Home port – preparation (handball play)

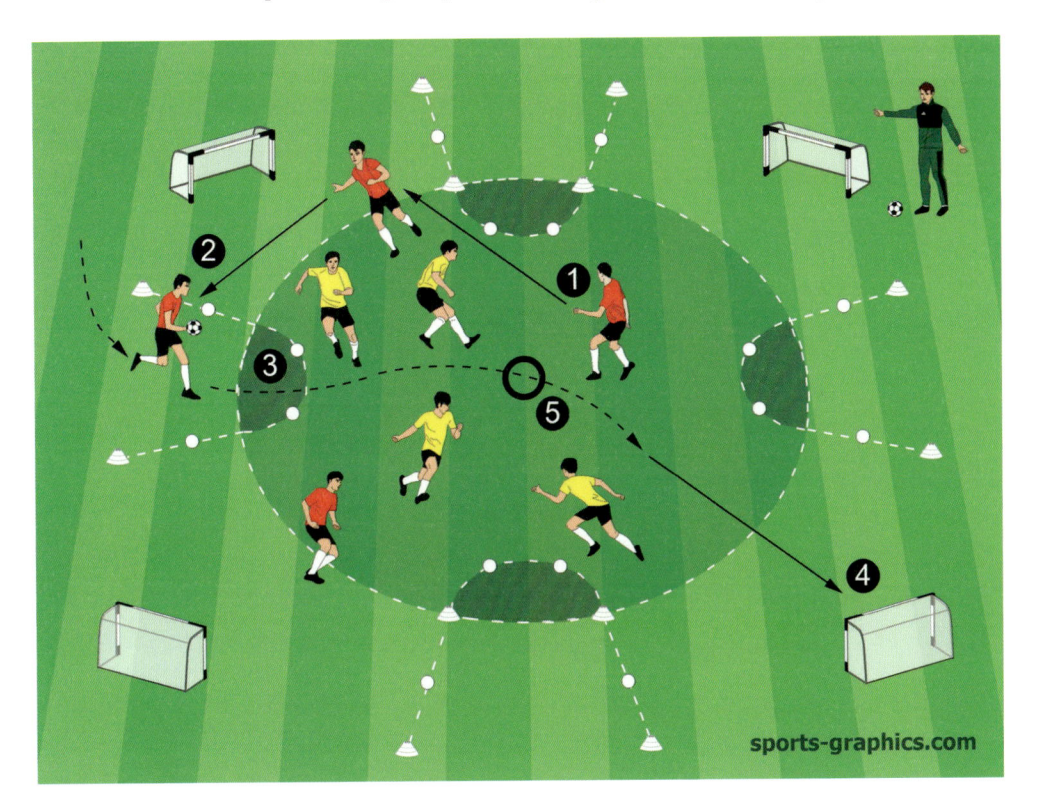

Execution, principles and elements

The training form presented here entails preparation of a soccer playing form involving the hand, and aims to illustrate that all circle playing forms can be prepared with handball. This makes it easier for players to familiarize themselves with unknown field forms. Through the simplification of playing with their hands, the players have better chances of recognizing and observing the field forms. The game can then be played with the feet. The players circulate the ball among their team (1). Once the ball touches the ground, an opposing player catches a pass, or an opposing player tags a player who has the ball, the ball possession instantly changes. The goal is to receive a pass in one of the outer marked zones in front of the inside arcs (2) in order to then run through the arc into the circle (3). Playing toward the mini-goals is then possible.

Provocation rules, point system and variants

The coordination tire placed in the center can also be in play with a run through the tire (5). A goal after playing the central coordination tire can be awarded double points because of the presumably high pressure from opponents in the center.

4.1.3 Ying and Yang – subsequent handling (goal)

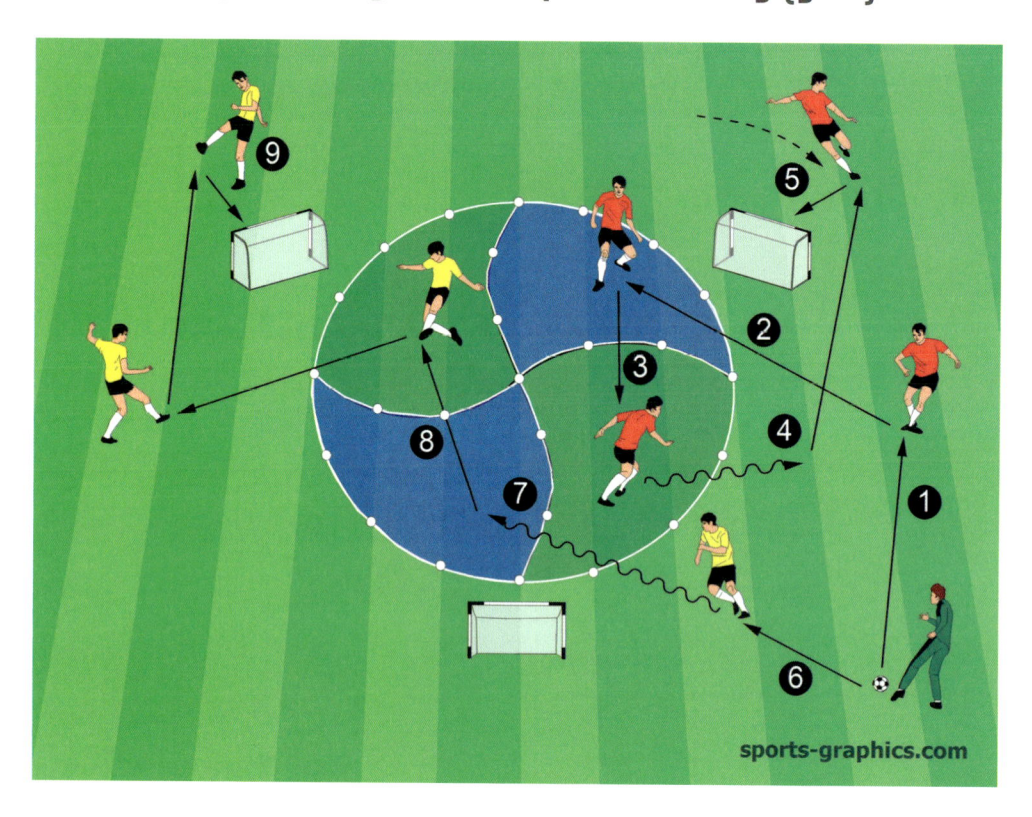

Execution, principles and elements

This training form focuses on follow-up actions toward the goal, and is supposed to illustrate that all circle playing forms with mini or large goals and matching possibilities to score can be combined. Two teams play against each other and try to open up the mini-goals and scoring by playing in the central circle. The trainer brings each new ball outward, away from the circle (1). The first objective of the team with the ball is to pass the ball into the circle (2). The game can now focus on the mini-goals. By passing from one of the four sections into an adjacent section (3), the ball can be directed toward the mini-goals (4). The team with the ball now tries to score a goal (5). After each goal, the trainer brings a new ball into the game (6). The mini-goals can also be played toward (9) by dribbling over an internal line (7) with subsequent pass over a second internal line (8). The learning effect via the geometric shapes aims to facilitate free running and the occupation of promising positions along the lines. The narrow playing room in the center shall be played as precisely and quickly as possible despite pressure from opponents. The trainer's ball induces preparation of the deep actions toward the center.

Provocation rules, point system and variants

Playing the four sections can be configured and expanded in numerous ways. The goal scoring technique (volley, instep kick or inside kick) can also be specified (5 and 9), and the game for the mini-goals set to a time limit.

4.1.4 Crop circles – continued play (alternative actions)

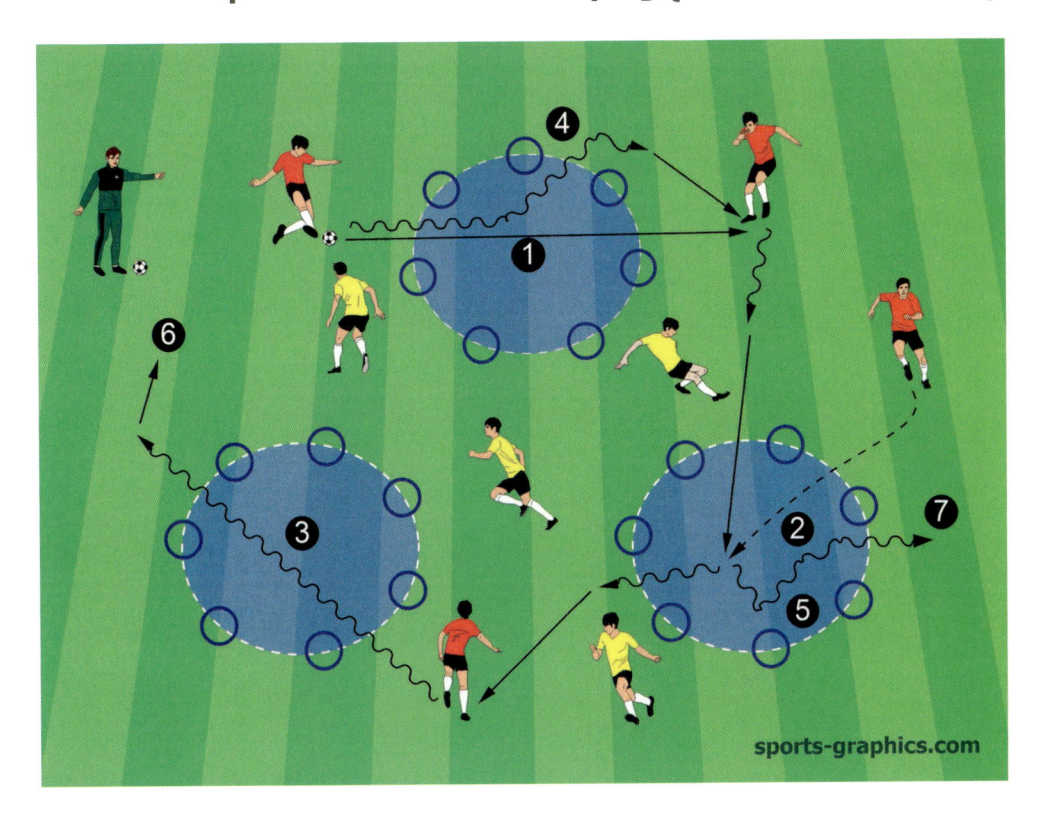

Execution, principles and elements

This training form is characterized by multiple circles, and is supposed to illustrate that individual circles can frequently be arranged next to one another, thus allowing for more playing objectives for combinations. The team with the ball can only score if two or more circles are played as per the objectives. One objective could be for one pass to be played through a circle (1), one pass is played to a player running into a circle (2), dribbling through the circle (3) is complete, or first-touch control must be performed backward in a circle (5). Proper playing of multiple circles in order equals one point. The game then continues fluidly after a point has been scored. This playing form uses principles of space recognition and playing, and focuses on penetrating and breaking out of these spaces. The players are required to remain constantly vigilant. Through the concept of the game, they learn to deliberately move along field edges. The game induces quick and deep runs, and addresses elements of timed offering and free running.

Provocation rules, point system and variants

The rules for passing from the circles to an incoming teammate (2) can be intensified in that the player with the ball can only control the ball from behind, and must dribble it after turning backward out of the circle (5). All rules can also require a follow-up action in the form of a pass (6) or shooting toward the goals (7).

4.1.5 Mandarin – continued play (aiming)

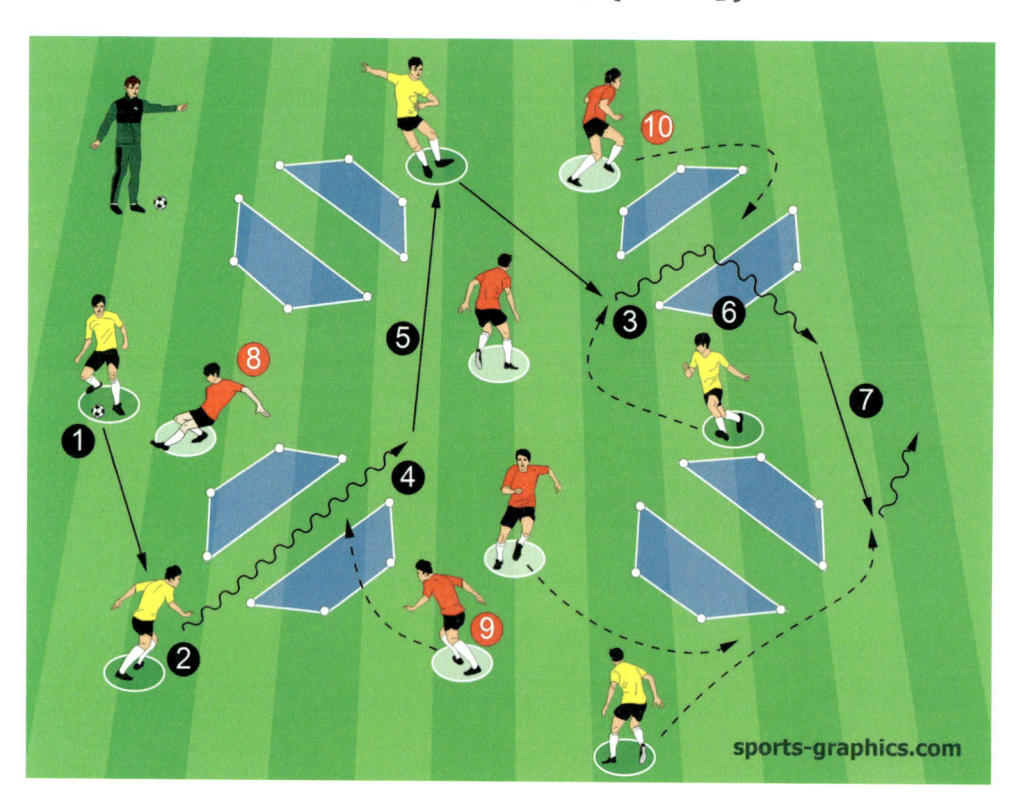

Execution, principles and elements

This training form is characterized by multiple circles, and is supposed to illustrate that the players can have even more possible solutions and alternative actions. Because of the increased complexity, the players are required to quickly recognize the various shapes and aim for them while running. In the form presented here, the team with the ball tries to prepare to play the half-circles with targeted passing (1) and quickly implement it (3). A tunnel or corridor is played when a player completely dribbles through it (2) or moves out sideways from the blue zone by alternating their feet after entering (6). The play is only valid and counts for a point when a follow-up pass has been completed (5 or 7). The opposing team tries to take the ball (8) and can interfere and prevent the play through the circles (9 and 10). The manifold arrangement of the shapes creates eight entry and exit possibilities, with many options to match. The innovative design and complex arrangement inspire the players to make unexpected, creative, and bold decisions.

Provocation rules, point system and variants

The rules for the defending players may vary and require that the circle formations can only be entered from the side (9) or from the front via the entry/exit (10). For the awarding of points, complete dribbling through the entire corridor (2 and 4) can count for double, and the exit (6) for one. The follow-up pass (5 and 7) may not be absolutely required, for simplicity's sake.

4.1.6 Cheeseburger – sphere of action (multidimensionality)

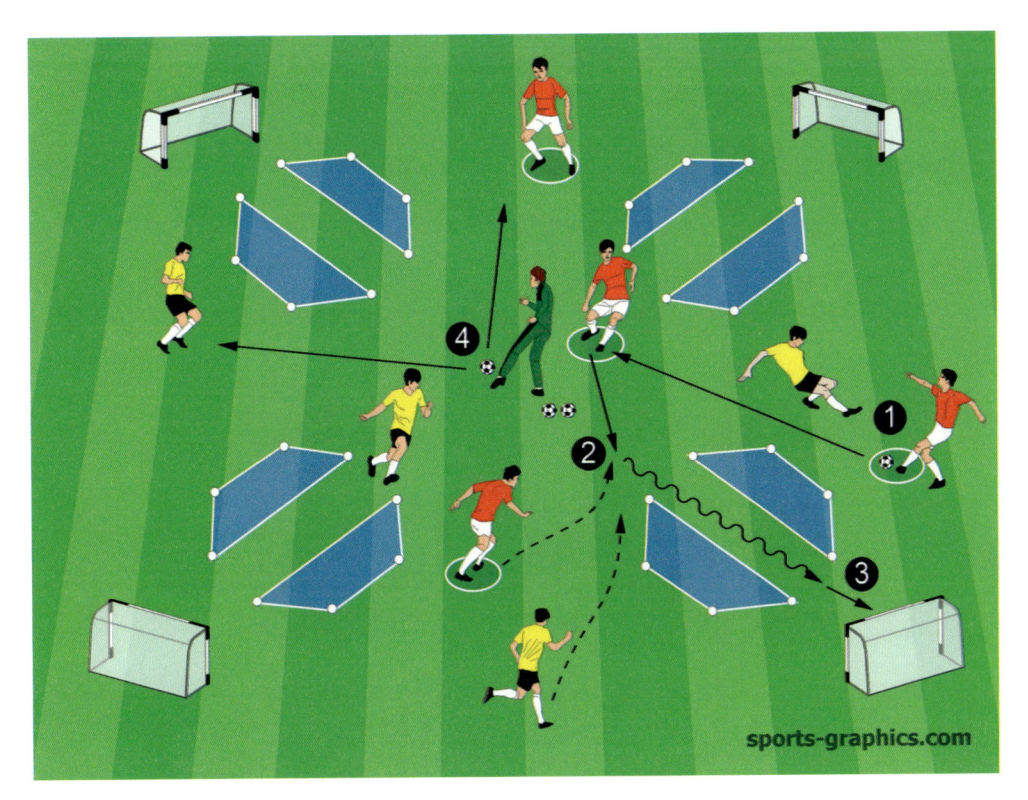

Execution, principles and elements

The training form presented here is characterized by the manifold arrangement of circles in combination with goals, and is supposed to illustrate that the alignment of fields and goals can open up a variety of playing objectives and alternative actions. The team in possession of the ball attempts to keep the ball to themselves and prepare to play through the circles with targeted passing (1). A circle is played when a player enters into the middle corridor and completely dribbles through it, or moves out sideways from the blue zone by alternating their feet after entering. After successfully playing through a circle (2), it is possible to then play toward the mini-goals (3). After a change in ball possession, a circle must again be played in order to earn a point by scoring in one of the mini-goals. After every completion, the trainer brings a new ball into play and can then decide which team receives the pass (4). The connection of the field shapes with the mini-goals creates game-like situations that must then be mastered, and which are rewarded with a goal and a point. Having the combination of four circles and four mini-goals to freely choose from helps to multiply the possibilities and optional actions.

Provocation rules, point system and variants

The playing form may vary depending on ball contact requirements per player, pass technique requirements, team sizes, the addition of neutral players, and the stipulation of scoring techniques.

4.1.7 Hamburger – sphere of action (complexity)

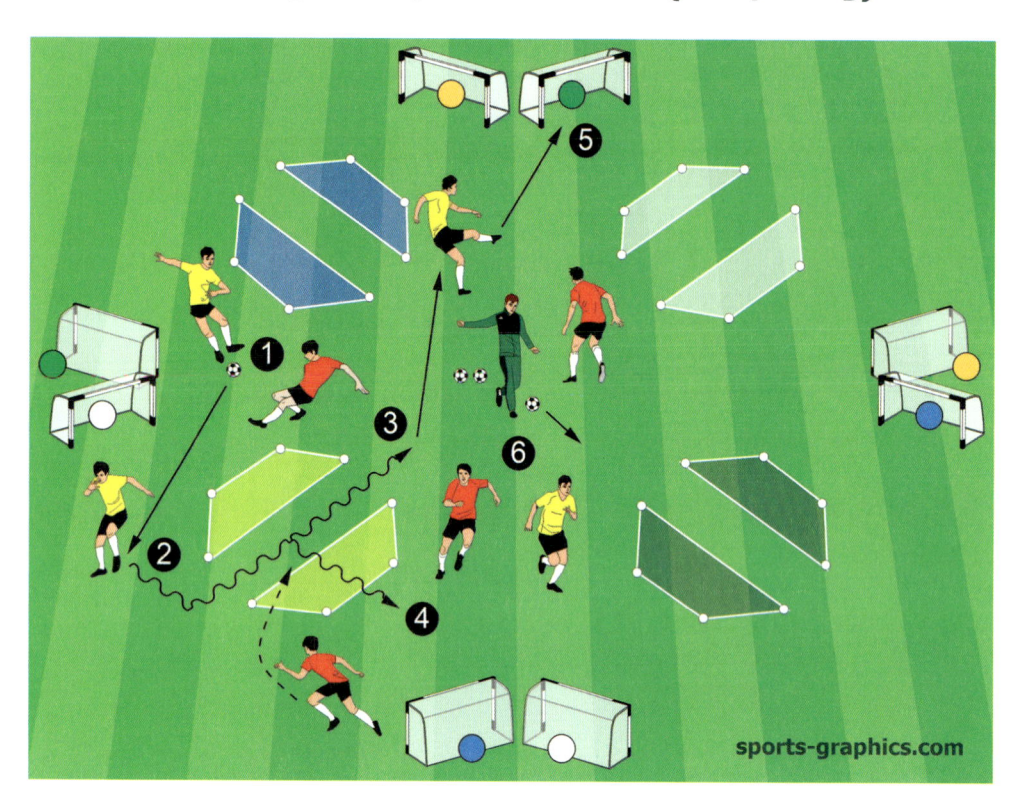

Execution, principles and elements

This playing form is characterized by the manifold arrangement of the circles and variably located mini-goals. It is supposed to illustrate that the circles and goals can be color coded, and playing objectives can thus be differentiated. In the training form presented, the color markings are associated with the sections. The team with the ball tries to keep the ball to themselves (1) and prepare to play through the circles (2). A circle is played through when a player enters into the middle corridor and dribbles through it completely, or exits from the side after entering. After successfully playing through a circle (3 or 4), the goals can be brought into play. The color-coded sections with matching color-coded mini-goals can be connected, with rules applying accordingly. After a change of ball possession, a circle must be played through again in order to earn a point by scoring in one of the mini-goals (5). After every completion, the trainer brings a new ball into play and can then decide which team receives the pass (6). The color-coded association with the mini-goals poses more complex challenges to the players at the cognitive level, namely quickness to act.

Provocation rules, point system and variants

The combination of circle and mini-goal is variable, so for example the complete play-through of the circle (3) can facilitate playing toward the mini-goals of different colors (5), and the lateral exit (4) can only open the two mini-goals of the same color (yellow here). The mini-goals can be color-coded with a marking cone or jersey.

4.1.8 Constellations – asymmetry (playability)

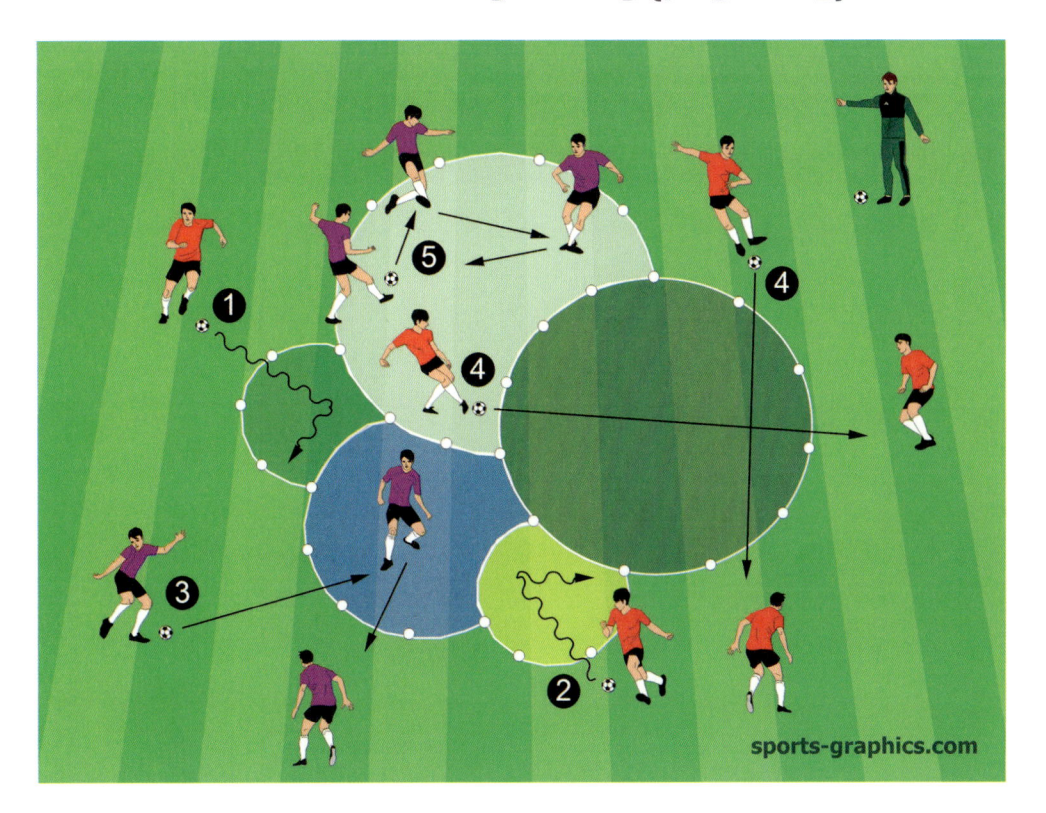

Execution, principles and elements

The central idea of this field concept lies in the asymmetrical arrangement of the areas to be played. The individual areas have their own playing objectives, and must be played through by the two teams in accordance to the requirements of various situations. The team with the ball can score points in the different sections by following certain rules. A team scores through the green circle when a player performs a feint within it (1). A team scores through the yellow circle when a player makes contact with the ball four times within it (2). A team scores through the blue circle when a player within it makes a direct pass to a third player (3). A team scores through the dark circle when a pass is made through it (4). A team scores through the white circle when three passes are made within it (5).

Provocation rules, point system and variants

The point rules can be configured in a number of ways. Furthermore, additional points can be awarded when two circles are played through in succession.

4.1.9 Butterfly – asymmetry (play comprehension)

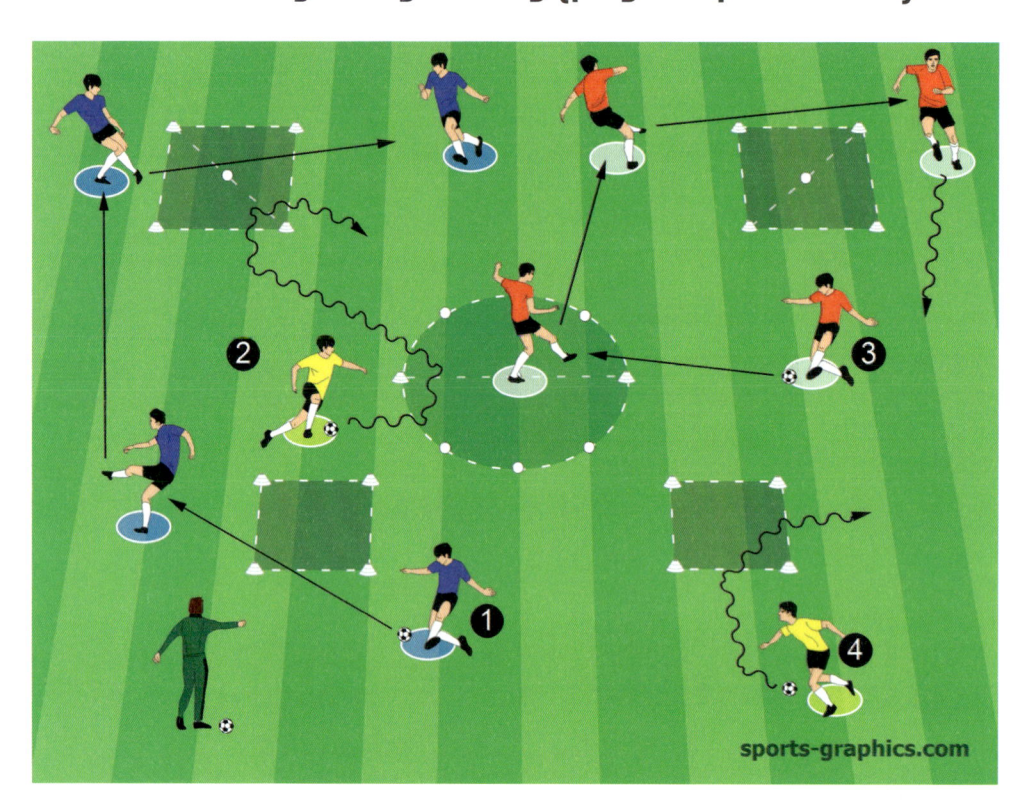

Execution, principles and elements

The central concept of this game lies in the asymmetrical arrangement of geometrically different field shapes. Two teams play against each other. The fields arranged at different distances from the center must be played through in different manners and in succession. The team with the ball may score through the various fields while following certain rules. One point can be earned when a player plays through one square close to the circle and one square far from the circle (1), when a player from the possessing team dribbles across two lines (circle and squares far from the circle) in succession (2), when a team plays through the central circle and then plays around a square far from the circle (3), or when a player has dribbled over two lines of a square close to the circle (4).

Provocation rules, point system and variants

The individual and tactical group rules for scoring points can be simplified or intensified. Numerous possible combinations are also conceivable depending on the desired area of emphasis. The arrangement of the fields may also vary depending on the size of the spaces in between.

4.1.10 Pac-Man© – shaping (creativity)

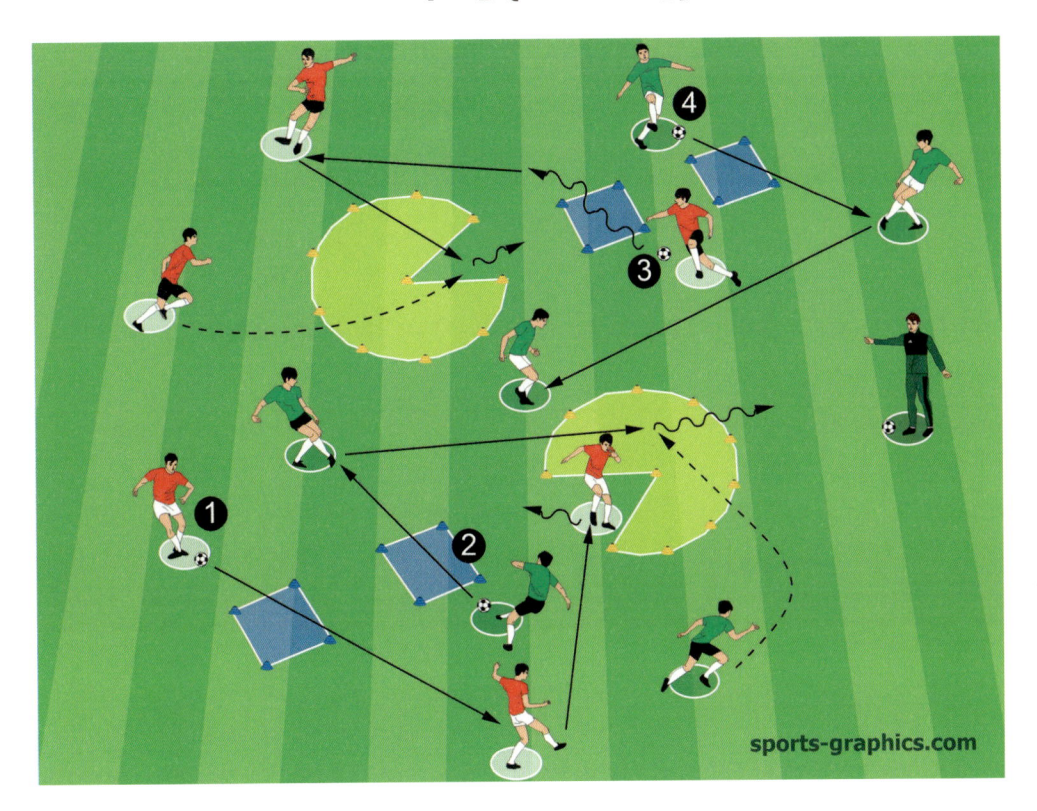

Execution, principles and elements

The central idea of the game lies in the innovative, creative, and (for the players) new field structure. These shapes offer room for original actions. The players' imaginations are stirred by the creative field structure, and this evokes some unexpected scenes and actions. The team with the ball tries to play through the yellow Pac-Man shapes and the blue squares in combination. Points are earned when, after successfully playing through a blue square, a pass is completed into the mouth (1), head (2), or through the head into the mouth (3) of Pac-Man, or between the two figures (4). The squares can be played through with a pass (1, 2 and 4) or dribbling (3). A wide field structure offers room for long passes, long kicks, and the taking of interim positions or rotational players.

Provocation rules, point system and variants

Scoring points becomes more difficult when the passes through the square or toward the figure can only be direct. In order to get the players acclimated to the new type of field environment, the ball position may be simplified through the addition of neutral players, e.g. to make it a 4-4-2 situation.

5 OUTLOOK

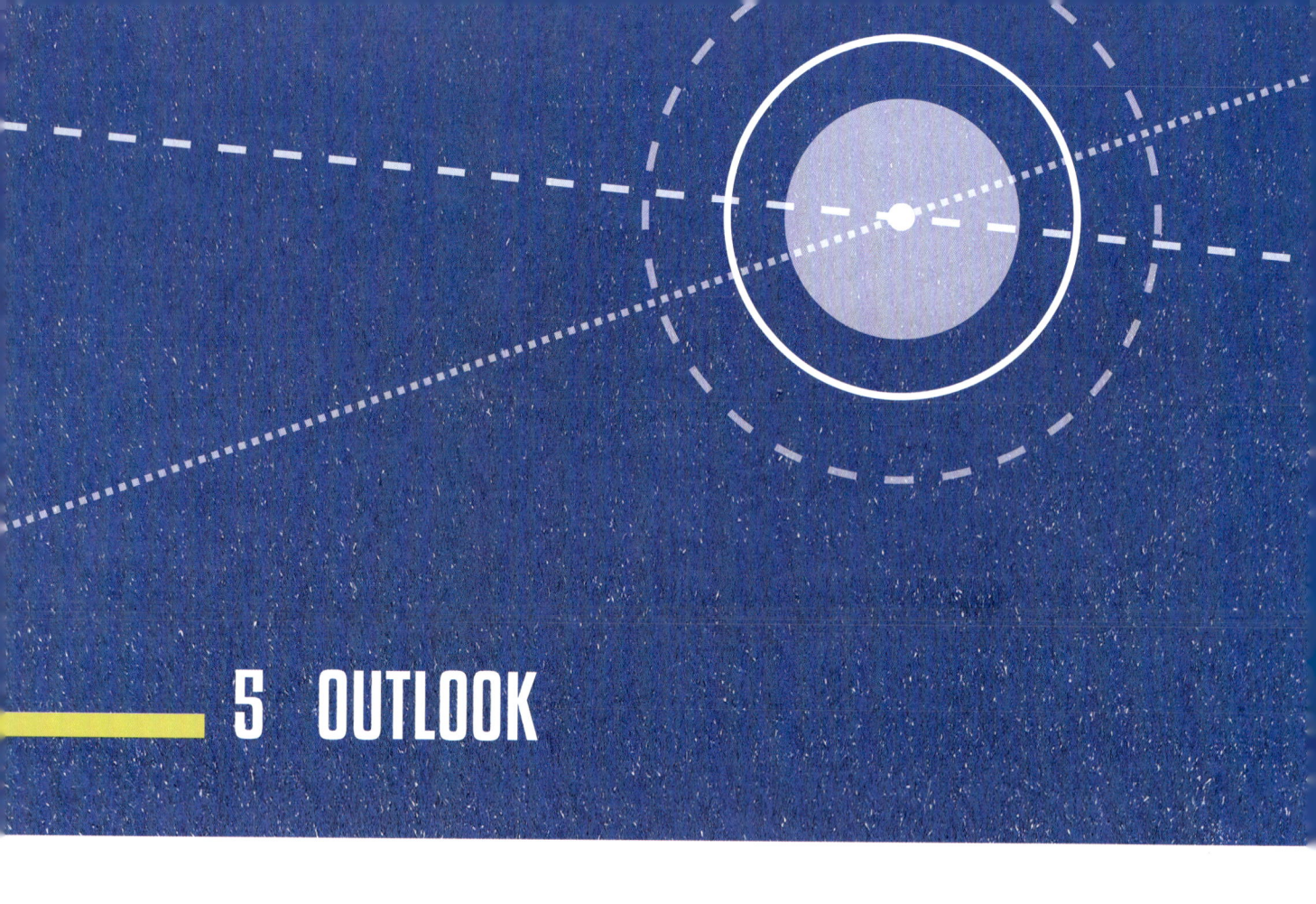

The central circle playing forms can be differentiated and implemented in a variety of ways as described, as per the conceptual continuation. The orientation of the circle playing forms based on the orientation of play can also align itself within the framework of the positioning during actual competition on the pitch (Fig. 55). This illustrates the offensive and defensive scopes of action in game-like situations. Objective on-site training on the playing grounds makes it easier for the players to transfer their training to a playing context, therefore accentuating the desired competitive behavior.

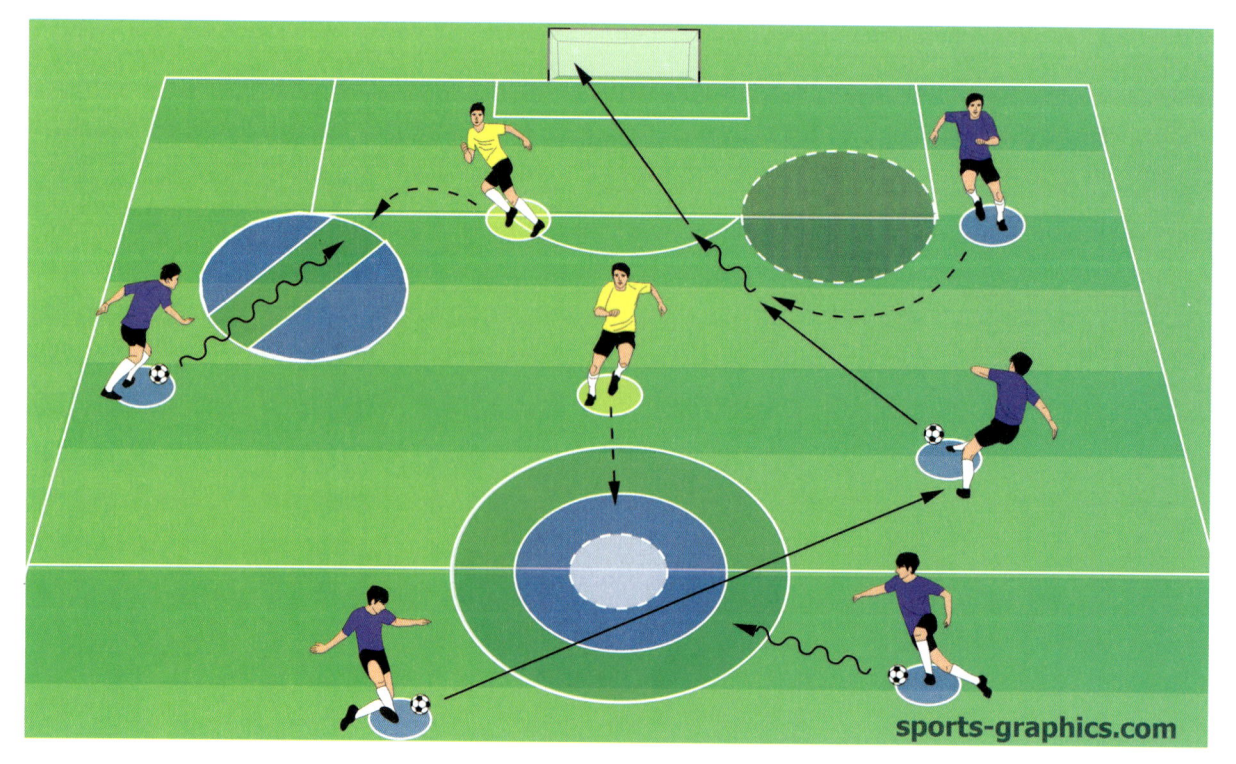

Fig. 55: Competitive circle formation

CONTINUATION **213**

Fig. 56: Circle orientation

The numerous playing objectives of the various circle playing forms can be transferred to the big eleven-on-eleven game (Fig. 56). Connections can be drawn between the circle forms and the basic regulations and playing systems. Individual aspects of the playing concept are thus visualized, and the tactical group behaviors honed through training can be carried over to the tactical team level.

> If you are interested in learning more about the authors' concepts and content, trainers and clubs can contact them via the Meyer & Meyer Sport (thesportspublisher.com). Pending capacity and conditions, there may be a customized method for implementing the contents into clubs' training programs. The playing forms with highly diverse rules and principles may apply to individual training units, and implementation into training cycles is recommended.

APPENDIX

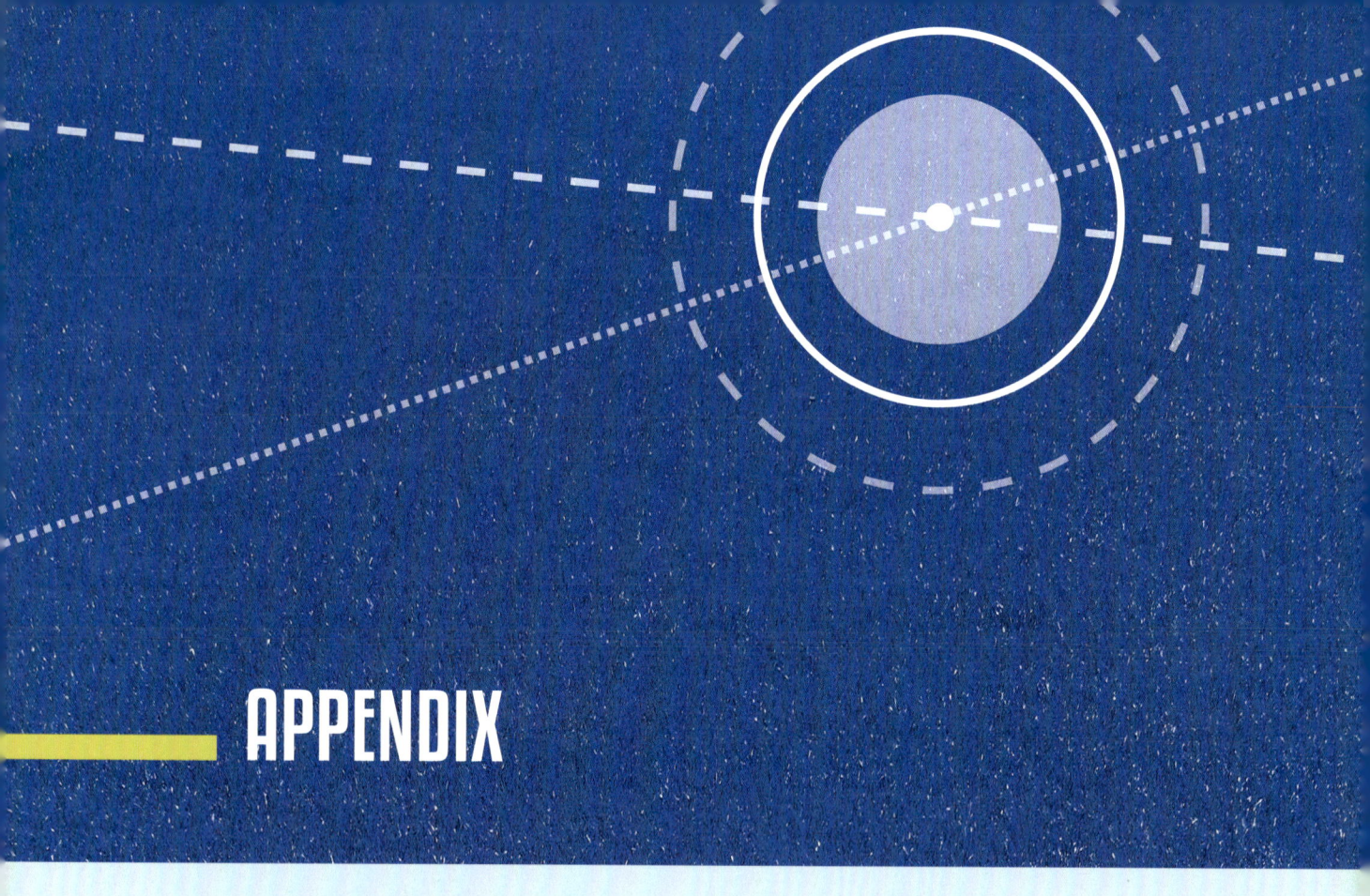

1 Bibliography

Seeger, F. (2016). *Spielnahes Fußballtraining. 350 Trainingsformen für alle Leistungsstufen.* Aachen: Meyer & Meyer.

Seeger, F. & Favé, L. (2017). *Kreatives Fußballtraining. 350 Trainingsformen für ambitionierte Leistungsstufen.* Aachen: Meyer & Meyer.

2 Credits

Cover design:	Annika Naas
Cover image:	Fabian Seeger
Interior design:	Annika Naas
Interior photos:	Norbert Gettschat (www.foto-gettschat.de)
Graphics:	All training pattern graphics were created with easy Sports-Graphics (www.easy-sport-software.com).
Typesetting:	www.satzstudio-hilger.de
Managing editor:	Elizabeth Evans
Copyeditor:	Qurratulain Zaheer

Software for Coaches, Teachers and Authors

easy to handle - professional results

- Organizing Software for ALL SPORTS

- Animation Software for Soccer, Handball, Basketball, Volleyball, Hockey and Ice Hockey

- Drawing Software for Soccer, Handball, Volleyball, Hockey and Ball Sports for Teachers

EASY SPORTS-SOFTWARE

www.easy-sports-software.com
Get your free DEMO an see how easy this software works